CENSORED

"Project Censored is one of the organizations that we should listen to, to be assured that our newspapers and our broadcasting outlets are practicing thorough and ethical journalism."—Walter Cronkite

"[*Censored*] should be affixed to the bulletin boards in every newsroom in America. And, perhaps read aloud to a few publishers and television executives."—Ralph Nader

"[*Censored*] offers devastating evidence of the dumbing-down of mainstream news in America.... Required reading for broadcasters, journalists and well-informed citizens."—*Los Angeles Times*

"A distant early warning system for society's problems."
—*American Journalism Review*

"One of the most significant media research projects in the country."
—I. F. Stone

"A terrific resource, especially for its directory of alternative media and organizations.... Recommended for media collections."—*Library Journal*

"Project Censored shines a spotlight on news that an informed public must have...a vital contribution to our democratic process."
—Rhoda H. Karpatkin, President, Consumer's Union

"Buy it, read it, act on it. Our future depends on the knowledge this collection of suppressed stories allows us."—*San Diego Review*

"This volume chronicles 25 news stories about events that could affect all of us, but which we most likely did not hear or read about in the popular news media."—*Bloomsbury Review*

"*Censored* serves as a reminder that there is certainly more to the news than is easily available or willingly disclosed. To those of us who work in the newsrooms, it's an inspiration, an indictment, and an admonition to look deeper, ask more questions, then search for the truth in the answers we get."—*Creative Loafings*

"This invaluable resource deserves to be more widely known."
—*Wilson Library Bulletin*

CENSORED 2005

2005

The Top 25 Censored Stories

PETER PHILLIPS & PROJECT CENSORED

INTRODUCTION BY GREG PALAST
CARTOONS BY TOM TOMORROW

SEVEN STORIES PRESS
New York / London / Melbourne / Toronto

Seven Stories Press
140 Watts Street
New York, NY 10013
www.sevenstories.com

In Canada: Publishers Group Canada, 250A Carlton Street, Toronto, ON M5A-2L1

In the U.K.: Turnaround Publisher Services Ltd., Unit 3, Olympia Trading Estate, "
Coburg Road, Wood Green, London N22 6TZ

In Australia: Palgrave Macmillan, 627 Chapel Street, South Yarra VIC 3141

College professors may order examination copies of Seven Stories Press titles for a free six-
month trial period. To order, visit www.sevenstories.com/textbook/ or fax on school letter-
head to 212.226.1411.

ISSN 1074-5998

9 8 7 6 5 4 3 2

Book design by Cindy LaBreacht

Printed in the U.S.A.

Contents

Another "Hysteric" Librarian for Freedom[1]

BY NANCY KRANICH

Hours after the terrorist attacks on September 11, 2001, people rushed to libraries to read about the Taliban, Islam, Afghanistan, and terrorism. Americans sought background materials to foster understanding and cope with this horrific event. While the public turned to libraries for answers, the Bush Administration turned to the intelligence community for techniques to secure U.S. borders and reduce the possibility of more terrorism. The result was new legislation, most notably the "Uniting and Strengthening America by Providing Appropriate Tools Required to Intercept and Obstruct Terrorism Act" (USA Patriot Act), passed almost unanimously just six weeks after the events of September 11. The act grants unprecedented powers of federal law enforcement agencies to gather intelligence and investigate anyone they suspect of terrorism. Among the most troubling provisions is one that grants unprecedented authority to law enforcement agencies to obtain search warrants for business records, including those retained by libraries and bookstores, merely by claiming that the desired records may be related to an ongoing terrorism investigation or intelligence activities. Through a "gag order," the Act also prohibits any person or institution served with a search warrant from disclosing what has taken place.

Officially, librarians may not comment on FBI visits to examine library users' Internet surfing and book-borrowing habits, but that has not stopped them from speaking out about the chilling effects of the USA Patriot Act on their users and communities. Responding with their usual swiftness, they began cautioning public officials against eroding freedoms immediately following the terrorist attacks when the American Library Association (ALA) joined forces with other civil liberties groups "In Defense of Freedom." In January 2002, ALA passed a resolution reaffirming the principles of intellectual freedom in the aftermath of the terrorist attacks. That same year, ALA updated its guidelines for coping with law enforcement inquiries and hosted a series of programs to educate librarians about the law and its impact.

While ALA spoke out to defend the public's privacy rights, several members believed that the association was not doing enough to oppose the USA Patriot Act and related measures. Washington insiders warned that policymakers were unreceptive to criticism of the 342-page law, even after the 2002 mid-term elections. Nevertheless, a group of determined ALA activists began drafting resolution language calling for change. In January 2003, the ALA Committee on Legislation and the Intellectual Freedom Committee heard briefings from staff of the Senate Judiciary Committee and then crafted a strong resolution passed by the ALA Council calling on librarians to educate their communities about the problems with the law and Congress to "amend or change the sections of these laws and the guidelines that threaten or abridge the rights of inquiry and free expression." After the conference, many state library associations passed similar resolutions.[2]

One state library association taking action was Vermont. They visited their Representative Bernie Sanders (D–VT) who recalls, "I knew… it wasn't a good piece of legislation. But the people who really educated me were the librarians of Vermont. I received an extraordinarily well-written letter that articulated librarians' concerns and informed me of a number of aspects, especially Section 215, which I had not been familiar with." Growing public concern about the impact of the Patriot Act prompted Sanders to introduce legislation in March 2003 to counter some of the most egregious provisions of the law. Pundits never expected him to add more than a few additional names to the first 24 co-sponsors. By May 2004, however, Sanders had garnered more than 140 sponsors—Democrats and Republicans, liberals and conservatives alike—in support of his "Freedom to Read Protection Act," H.R. 1157, a bill that would exempt libraries and bookstores from Section 215 and would require a higher standard of proof than mere suspicion for search warrants presented at libraries and bookstores. "I think librarians all over this country are unsung heroes and heroines who are doing a tremendous job, against very difficult odds," added Sanders. "I've been impressed by the willingness of librarians to go above and beyond the letter of their jobs… You'd expect them to fight for good budgets and jobs, but the librarians did not have to get on board this issue and say that, as librarians, we believe that all Americans should not have the government looking over their shoulder." [3]

By the spring of 2003, both the media and Congress began examining the USA Patriot Act more closely. Hundreds of stories ran in newspapers, pointing out flaws, focusing on the impact of surveillance on civil liberties in general, and pointing specifically to the impact on local libraries—a tangible example that resonated loud and clear with the public and policymakers. Nevertheless, Attorney General John Ashcroft and his Justice Department staff refuse to acknowledge problems with the legislation, particularly as it affects innocent Americans. Mark Corallo, a Justice Department spokesman, claims, "We're not going after the average American… If you're not a terrorist or a spy, you have nothing to worry about."[4]

Ashcroft launched a late-summer, 16-city "Victory" tour promoting expanded surveillance authority. When he addressed the National Restaurant Association on September 15, 2003, he ridiculed librarians' concerns about the privacy of library users as "baseless hysteria," and claimed that ALA was "duped by the ACLU." The association fired off an immediate, unyielding response to the attack. ALA President Carla Hayden stated, "We are deeply concerned that the Attorney General should be so openly contemptuous of those who seek to defend our Constitution. That's a very unfortunate choice of words, and it does not accurately portray the concerns of librarians," She added, "Rather than ask the nations' librarians and Americans nationwide to 'just trust him,' Ashcroft could allay concerns by releasing aggregate information about the number of libraries visited using the expanded powers created by the USA Patriot Act." She pointed out that librarians have a history of combatting FBI surveillance dating back to the McCarthy era and reminded Ashcroft that under the FBI's Library Awareness Program, agents snooped in libraries up until the 1980s.

The following day, Ashcroft telephoned Hayden and told her that people have misunderstood his commitment to civil liberties and promised to declassify the Justice Department's report on the use of Section 215. After the call, Hayden responded, "I am glad the Attorney General finally agreed to declassify this report after almost two years of seeking an open and full accounting of activity by federal agents in libraries."

Next, Ashcroft wrote in a memo to FBI Director Robert S. Mueller III that "the number of times Section 215 has been used to date is zero." He added that he had decided to declassify the previously secret information "to counter the troubling amount of public distortion and misinformation in connection with Section 215."[5] Hayden immediately expressed ALA's surprise at learning that agents had never utilized Section 215, citing earlier Justice Department statements in March that libraries had become a logical target of surveillance, and in May that federal agents had visited about 50 libraries. But instead of backing off after releasing the memo, Ashcroft stepped up his attacks on his critics. "The fact is, with just 11,000 FBI agents and over a billion visitors to America's libraries each year, the Department of Justice has neither the staffing, the time, nor the inclination to monitor the reading habits of Americans." He continued, "No offense to the American Library Association, but we just don't care."[6]

In a week of escalating controversy and heightened rhetoric, librarians emerged as victors, with a score of Librarians 1, Ashcroft 0.[7] Ashcroft gave the ALA a stunning public relations victory in its ongoing struggle to protect the civil liberties of library users against the excesses of the USA Patriot Act. As of June 2004, citizens and organizations in more than 300 communities have stood up and passed resolutions opposing the USA Patriot Act and related measures,[8] urging local officials contacted by federal investigators to refuse requests that they believe violate civil liberties. In addition, several senators and representatives now lead legislative efforts to counter some of the more egregious provisions of the law. Librarians and booksellers are counting on these efforts, along with public outcry, to stem federal actions that threaten Americans' most valued freedoms without necessarily improving national security. Together, they have launched the "*Freedom*" petition campaign, hoping to deliver 1 million signatures to Congress in 2004, calling for the restoration of reader privacy.[9]

The millions of Americans who sought information from their libraries in the wake of September 11 reaffirm an enduring truth: a free and open society needs libraries and librarians more than ever. Americans depend on libraries to promote the free flow of information for individuals, institutions, and communities. And Americans depend on "hysteric" librarians to ensure their freedoms, especially in uncertain times.

Nancy Kranich is former chair, ALA Intellectual Freedom Committee (2002–2004), past president of the American Library Association (2000–2001), and a Project Censored National Judge.

NOTES:

1. "Another Hysteric Librarian for Freedom" buttons are available from the American Library Association, Office for Intellectual Freedom, <https://www.ala.org/ala/oif/basics/basicre latedlinks/hystericlibrarian.pdf>.

2. American Library Association, "Resolution on the USA Patriot Act and Related Measures That Infringe on the Rights of Library Users" (Chicago, IL: American Library Association, January 23, 2003), <www.ala.org/Template.cfm?Section=ifresolutions&Template=/Content Management/ContentDisplay.cfm&ContentID=11891>; and USA Patriot Act Resolutions of State Library Associations, <www.ala.org/Content/NavigationMenu/Our_Association/Offices/ Intellectual_Freedom3/IF_Groups_and_Committees/State_IFC_Chairs/State_IFC_in_Actio n/USA_Patriot_Act_Resolutions.htm>.

3. Norman Oder, "Politician of the Year 2003: Bernie Sanders," *Library Journal*, September 15, 2003, <www.libraryjournal.com/index.asp?layout=articleArchive&articleid=CA320 875>.

4. Rene Sanchez, "Librarians Make Some Noise Over Patriot Act: Concerns About Privacy Prompt Some to Warn Patrons, Destroy Records of Book and Computer Use," *Washington Post*, April 10, 2003, A20, <www.washingtonpost.com/wp-dyn/articles/A1481-2003Apr9. html>.

5. Dan Eggen, "Ashcroft: Patriot Act Provision Unused," *Washington Post*, September 18, 2003, A13.

6. "Ashcroft Says FBI Hasn't Used Patriot Act Library Provision, Mocks ALA for 'Hysteria,'" *American Libraries*, September 2, 2003, <www.ala.org/al_onlineTemplate.cfm?Section =American_Libraries&template=/ContentManagement/ContentDisplay.cfm&Content ID=44344>.

7. Democratic National Committee Blog, *Kicking Ass*, September 18, 2003, <www.demo crats.org/blog/display/00010020.html>.

8. For a list of communities passing resolutions or assistance in drafting one for your town, see: The Bill of Rights Defense Committee, *Make Your City or Town a Civil Liberties Safe Zone*, <www.bordc.org/index.html>.

9. American Library Association, *The USA Patriot Act vs. Your Freadom: Tell Congress to Restore Reader Privacy Today!* Petition Drive, <www.ala.org/Template.cfm?Section=issues relatedlinks&Template=/ContentManagement/ContentDisplay.cfm&Content ID=56742>.

THIS MODERN WORLD

by TOM TOMORROW

RIPPED FROM THE FRONT PAGES OF TODAY'S NEWSPAPERS--

THE HOMO-SEXUAL MENACE

SURE, POP CULTURE PRESENTS THEM AS *HARMLESS* AND *ADORABLE*... THOSE GAY GUYS ON THAT TV SHOW ARE *HILARIOUS!*

IF ONLY THERE WERE *MORE* HOMOSEXUALS IN THE ENTERTAIN-MENT INDUSTRY!

AND SINCE MANY AMERICANS PRIDE THEMSELVES ON THEIR *TOLERANCE,* GAY *MARRIAGE* SEEMS INCREAS-INGLY *PLAUSIBLE*...

WE JUST WANT THE RIGHT TO AFFIRM OUR COMMITMENT TO EACH OTHER-- LIKE ANY *STRAIGHT* COUPLE!

WELL, I DON'T *LIKE* IT--BUT I GUESS I CAN *TOLERATE* IT...

BUT *DON'T BE FOOLED!* THE HOMOSEXUALS HAVE A *SINISTER AGENDA*--AND THEY'LL DO *ANY-THING* TO ACHIEVE IT!

PSSST! OPERATION *SUBVERT HETEROSEXUALITY* IS PROCEED-ING ACCORDING TO PLAN!

I'LL INFORM H.Q. *IMMEDIATELY!*

BUS STOP

IF THEY'RE ALLOWED TO UNDER-MINE THE SACRED INSTITUTION OF *MARRIAGE*--THERE'S NO *TELLING* WHAT COULD HAPPEN *NEXT!*

THE *HECK* WITH MY TRADITIONAL HETEROSEXUAL LIFESTYLE! *I'M* MARRYING A *GOAT!*

I'M HAVING NON-PROCREATIVE SEX WITH THE ENTIRE CITY OF *TOPEKA, KAN-SAS!*

SO STAY *VIGILANT,* CITIZENS--AND *BEWARE* THE *HOMOSEXUAL MENACE!*

YOU KNOW, I'M NOT *REALLY* SURE GAY MARRIAGE WOULD LEAD IN-EVITABLY TO WIDESPREAD SEX WITH ANIMALS...

WELL, YOU'RE NOT EXACTLY AN IMPARTIAL OBSERVER HERE, ARE YOU?

TOM TOMORROW©2003 ... www.thismodernworld.com

Preface

BY PETER PHILLIPS

In 2003 and 2004, the rich got richer and the rest of us got dumbed down. Danny Schechter, founder of <MediaChannel.org>, says, "The more you watch, the less you know." The Americans who tune in to 24-hour TV news view the top-down stories the power elites of the world want them to hear. Consolidated media are increasingly more deeply embedded in the global corporate power structure and have become the lapdog press to agendas of inequality, globalization, militarism and empire. Weapons of mass destruction combined with weapons of mass deception (John Stauber's book title) create a baffled, afraid, and ignorant citizenry among those who depend on corporate news for understanding the world.

I wish there were a more polite way to address this issue. It is not the journalists inside the corporate media who are at fault. They believe in the First Amendment and the public's right to know. Most journalists want to tell the Watergate stories about the powerful. They want to build an informed electorate with high levels of citizen participation and grassroots democracy. However, huge, often overwhelming, forces of power, greed, and spin challenge journalists inside their own media systems resulting in corporate cultures of self-censorship and fear. This, of course, is not true in every case; nothing is absolute or without exceptions. Still, the fact that, for 28 years, Project Censored has been able to develop an annual list of the most important undercovered "censored" news stories belies the fullness of the belief in a totally free and unhindered media in the United States.

We are proud to dedicate *Censored 2005* to the American Library Association (ALA) and public libraries everywhere. Former ALA President Nancy

Kranich gives us a update on the importance of public libraries and their role as freedom of information centers in the U.S.

Censored 2005's Chapter 6, "Challenging the New American Censorship," addresses the structural specifics of media censorship in the U.S., and Chapter 1, "The Top *Censored* Stories of 2003 and 2004," addresses the substance of the issues by exposing the missing news corporate media has failed to report.

Eventually, the corporate media does cover about one-third of the stories selected by Project Censored each year. Chapter 2, "*Censored* Déjà Vu," is a review and update on important censored stories from prior years.

In contrast to the most important censored news stories is our annual list Junk Food News (Chapter 3, "Junk Food News and News Abuse"), in which a review of the frivolous and serious but overdone stories are ranked and analyzed.

Media ownership charts are presented in Chapter 4, "The Big Media Giants," by NYU's Mark Crispen Miller, with updates researched by Project Censored intern Emilio Licea. Assistant professor Stephanie Dyer from Sonoma State University rounds out Chapter 4 with a qualitative analysis of race and gender on the board of directors of the biggest media corporations.

Now a permanent fixture of the *Censored* yearbook, Fairness and Accuracy in Reporting, *PR Watch,* and the *Index on Censorship* provide a comprehensive review of the state of media news in Chapters 7, 8, and 9 ("The Best of *PR Watch*: Spins of the Year," "FAIR's Fourth Annual 'Fear and Favor' Report—2003," and "*Index on Censorship:* Annual Report," respectively). We much appreciate the research and involvement of Peter Hart and Julie Hollar from FAIR, Laura Miller with *PR Watch,* and Sigrun Rottman form the London-based *Index on Censorship.* Additionally, Project Censored student interns write about the successes of media democracy in Chapter 5 with reviews of San Francisco's Media Alliance, Pacific News Service, We Interrupt This Message, Whispered Media, Youth Media Council, News Without Borders, Indymedia, and Media Channel.org.

Each year Project Censored publishes original research work and media commentary from a broad selection of journalists and authors. *Censored 2005* offers chapter-length investigative reports, including the untold story of the Haiti coup by Lyn Duff and Dennis Bernstein (Chapter 10, "Haiti: The Untold Story"), the U.S. media's biased coverage of Israel and Palestine by Allison Weir (Chapter 11, "U.S. Media Coverage of Israel and Palestine: Choosing Sides"), immigrant bashing and overt racism on AM talk radio by Jose Padin and Shelley Smith (Chapter 12, "Death of a Nation: Conservative Talk Radio's Immigration and Race 'Curriculum'"), a Project Censored special report on Hearst's newspaper monopoly tactics by Geoff Davidian and Project Censored student interns (Chapter 13, "Newspaper Fraud Victims are Diverse"), and the untold stories of antiglobalization movements worldwide by Deepa Fernandes (Chapter 14, "Corporate Media Neglects Antiglobalization Movement"). Rounding out *Censored 2005* is an update on the media reform movement in the U.S. by Project Censored student interns Chris Cox and Josh Sisco (Chapter 15, "The Media Reform Movement and Global Media Concentration").

On behalf of the over 200 students, faculty, and national judges who work on this annual book, welcome to *Censored 2005*.

The Project Censored crew (SSU Faculty, students, and PC staff)

Acknowledgments

Project Censored is managed through the Department of Sociology in the School of Social Sciences at Sonoma State University. We are an investigative sociology and media analysis project dedicated to the freedom of information throughout the United States.

Over 200 people were directly involved in the production of *Censored 2005*. University and program staff, students, faculty, community experts, research interns, guest writers, and our distinguished national judges all contributed time, energy, and money to make this year's book an important resource for the promotion of freedom of information in the United States.

I want to personally thank those close friends and intimates who have counseled and supported me through another year of Project Censored. Most important, my wife Mary Lia-Phillips, who as my lover, friend, and partner provides daily consultative supportive to Project Censored. The men in the Green Oaks breakfast group, Noel Byrne, Bob Butler, Rick Williams, Colin Godwin, and Bill Simon, are personal advisors and confidants who help with difficult decisions. A special thanks also to Carl Jensen, founder of Project Censored, and director for 20 years. His continued advice and support are very important to the Project. Trish Boreta, Project Censored coordinator, is an important daily associate administrator of the project; her dedication and enthusiasm are greatly appreciated. Katie Sims, our story coordinator and student advisor, deserves a special thank-you; she supervised the processing of over 700 story nominations for this year's book and advises the Project Censored TV news team.

A big thanks goes to the people at Seven Stories Press. They are more than a publishing house; rather they have become close friends who help edit our annual book in record time and serve as advisors in the annual release process of the most *Censored* stories. Publisher Dan Simon is just a great progressive human being dedicated to freedom of information through knowledge and literature. He deserves full credit for assembling an excellent support crew, including production director Jon Gilbert; managing editor India Amos; editors Mikola De Roo, Ria Julien, and Greg Ruggiero; academic market director Tara Parmiter; publicists Lars Reilly, Phoebe Hwang, and Ruth Weiner; and book designer Cindy LaBreacht.

Thanks also to Bill Mockler and the sales staff at Consortium Book Sales and Distribution, who will see to it that every independent bookstore, chain store, and wholesaler in the U.S. is aware of *Censored 2005*. Thanks to Hushion House, our distributors in Canada, as well as Turnaround Publishers Services Ltd. in Great Britain and Tower Books in Australia.

Thank you to Greg Palast who wrote the introduction to the *Censored 2005* edition. Greg Palast's work as an investigative journalist is an inspiration for First Amendment supporters everywhere.

Thanks also to the authors of the most *Censored* stories for 2005, for without their often unsupported efforts as investigative news reporters and writers, the stories presented in *Censored* would not be possible.

Our guest writers this year are Jose Padin, Shelley Smith, Norman Solomon, Deepa Fernandes, Mark Crispin Miller, Alison Weir, Peter Hart, Julie Hollar, Stephanie Dyer, Geoff Davidian, Lyn Duff, Dennis Bernstein, Nancy Kranich, Laura Miller, Christopher Robin Cox, Josh Sisco, Sigrun Rottman, and Rohan Jayasekera. They represent a unique combination of scholars, journalists, and activists dedicated to media democracy through a diversity of news and opinion. Thank you to each and all for your unique contribution to *Censored 2005*.

This year's book again features the cartoons of Tom Tomorrow. "This Modern World" appears in more than 90 newspapers across the country. We are extremely pleased to use Tom Tomorrow's wit and humor throughout the book.

Our national judges, some of whom have been involved with the project for 28 years, are among the top experts in the country concerned with First Amendment freedoms and media. We are honored to have them as the final voice in ranking the top 25 most *Censored* stories.

An important thanks goes to our financial donors, including Sonoma State University Instructionally Related Activity Fund, the School of Social Sciences at Sonoma State University, and especially the over 4,000 individuals who purchase books and send us financial gifts each year. You are our financial base who continue to give year after year to this important student-run media research project.

This year we had 111 faculty/community evaluators assisting with our story assessment process. These expert volunteers read and rated the nominated stories for national importance, accuracy, and credibility. In April, they participated with over 100 students in selecting the final top 25 stories for 2005.

Most of all, we need to recognize the Sonoma State University students in the Spring 2004 Media Censorship class and the Fall 2003 Sociology of Media class, who worked long hours nominating and researching some 700 underpublished news stories. Students are the principle writers of the *Censored* news synopses in the book each year. Over 80 students served as interns for the project, working on various teams including: public relations, Web design, news story research, office support, events/fund raising, and TV news production. Student education is the most important aspect of Project Censored, and we could not do this work without the dedication and effort of our student interns.

Daryl Khoo is our Webmaster. The Project Censored Web site, <www.projectcensored.org>, has expanded under his supervision. We are pleased to announce that over 18,000,000 people logged on to Project Censored in 2003.

Finally, I want to thank our readers and supporters from all over the United States and the world. Hundreds of you nominated stories for consideration as the most *Censored* news story of the year. Thank you very much!

In Remembrance

Karen Talbot
1943-2003
Activist, Investigative Reporter and
Project Censored Award Winner 2003 and 2001

PROJECT CENSORED STAFF

Peter Phillips, Ph. D.	Director
Carl Jensen, Ph.D.	Director Emeritus and Project Advisor
Tricia Boreta	Coordinator/Editor
Katie Sims	Research Management/Bookkeeping
Sandy Brown	Office Support
Daryl Khoo	Webmaster

Lisa Badenfort	Teaching Assistant
Lindsey Brage	Teaching Assistant
Suze Cribs	Teaching Assistant
Melissa Jones	Teaching Assistant
Tara Spreng	Teaching Assistant

Spring & Fall 2003 & 2004 Interns and Community Volunteers

Mette Adams, Serena Ahlgren, Sarah Altman, Nikki Amaro, Ramsey Anderson, Laura Aramendia, Yesica Arredondo, Shannon Arthur, Lisa Badenfort, Tina Balderrama, Dana Balicki, Andrea Blake, John Blomquist, Dan Bluthardt, Jocelyn Boreta, Tricia Boreta, Lindsey Brage, Sandy Brown, Alycia Cahill, Patrick Carlson, Jose Castellanos, William Corey Clapp, Eric Common, Christopher Cox, Suze Cribbs, Christina Cutaia, Stephen Dietrich, Ian Elrick, Grace Farasey, Jamie Fearn, Brooke Finley, Tony Flannery, Bill Gibbons, Greg Goethals, Sharone Goldman, Matthew Hagan, Danielle Hallstein, Margaux Hardy, Rose Jager, Cody Jennings, Evan Johnson, Melissa Jones, Sean Kelson, Lauren Kettner, Sita Khalsa, Daryl Khoo, Maria Kyriakos, Megan Larsen, Emilio Licea, Melody Lindsey, Ron Liskey, Ed Longnecker, Melissa Lopez, Lawren Lutrin, Omar Malik, Sylvia Martinez, Julie Mayeda, Anna Megley, Sadie Melgar, Anna Miranda, Kagiso Molefhe, Shaina Murphy, Travis Murray, Michael Oroszi, Odilia Pablo, Ambrosia Pardue, Brian Pederson, Jason Pennetta, Annette Powell, Merisa Rasmussen, Christina Reski, Doug Reynolds, Brittny Roeland, Sean Roney, Chris Salvano, Sara Sass, Chad Seinke, Ben Sheppee, Marcia Simmons, Katie Sims, Josh Sisco, David Sonnenberg, Jason Spencer, Tara Spreng, Adam Stutz, Elise Symonds, Angelica Tercero, Laura Tollafield, Joshua Travers, Naomi Vaede, Mitzie Valdez, Joni Wallent, Mike Ward, Josh Wittman, Jennifer Woodliff, Leah Zabel, and Sarah Zisman.

Student Researchers in Sociology of Media Class, Fall 2003

Nichole Lee Amaro, Danielle Blevins, Sara Brunner, Kelly Marie Bullock, Evelyn Catellanos, Jose Castellanos, Lacy Coker, Ashley Cook, Jessica Cortez, Erin Cossen, Kenneth Crosbie, Brooke Finley, John Hernandez, Janelle Huff, Jessica Koop, Maria Kyriakos, Kelley McGlone, Beth Amber Reiken, Rebekah Spencer, Christine Storbo, Adam Stutz, Marian Terese Williams, and Tanya Wulff.

Student Researchers in Sociology of Media Class, Spring 2004

Shannon Bree Arthur, Sara Brunner, Christopher Cao Bui, Kenneth Crosbie, Cassandra Cyphers, Kate Drewieske, Gina Marie Dunch, Brian Ferguson, Brooke Finley, Jenifer Green, Larissa Heeren, John Hernandez, Hilton Mcewen Jones, Sita Khalsa, Cristin Leeming, Andrea Martini, Julie Mayeda, Elizabeth Medley, Anna Miranda, Caitlyn Pardue, Brian Pederson, Karina Pinon, Philip Rynning, Victoria Silberman, David Sonnenberg, Amelia Strommen, Adam Stutz, Mariah Webener-Vernagallo, and Timothy Zolezzi.

Students in Stephanie Dyer's LIBS 320A.1, Spring 2004
(who worked on Chapter 4)

Kate Bates, Ian Elrick, Jamie Husary, Heidi Jobe, Cathy Keeble, Celeste King, Annie Lapinski, Jessica Liparini, Tiffany Perkins, Nicole Stauffacher, Jane Sublett, Michelle Swift, Stephanie Thompson, and Meredith Wilson.

PROJECT CENSORED 2005 NATIONAL JUDGES

ROBIN ANDERSEN, associate professor and chair, Department of Communication and Media Studies, Fordham University

RICHARD BARNET, author of 15 books and numerous articles for *The New York Times Magazine, The Nation,* and *The Progressive.*

LIANE CLORFENE-CASTEN, cofounder and president of Chicago Media Watch, a volunteer watchdog group that monitors the media for bias, distortions, and omissions. She is an award-winning journalist with credits in national periodicals such as *E Magazine, The Nation, Mother Jones, Ms., Environmental Health Perspectives, In These Times,* and *Business Ethics.* She is the author of *Breast Cancer: Poisons, Profits, and Prevention.*

LENORE FOERSTEL, Women for Mutual Security, facilitator of the Progressive International Media Exchange (PRIME)

DR. GEORGE GERBNER, dean emeritus, Annenberg School of Communications, University of Pennsylvania; founder of the Cultural Environment Movement; author of *Invisible Crises: What Conglomerate Media Control Means for America and the World* and *Triumph and the Image: The Media's War in the Persian Gulf*

ROBERT HACKETT, professor, School of Communications, Simon Fraser University; codirector of NewsWatch Canada 1993–2003, coauthor of *News and Dissent: The Press and the Politics of Canada* (Ablex, 1991), *Sustaining Democracy?: Journalism and the Politics of Objectivity* (Garamond, 1998), and *The Missing News: Filters and Blind Spots in Canada's Press* (Garamond, 2000).

DR. CARL JENSEN, founder and former director of Project Censored; author of *Censored: The News That Didn't Make the News and Why* (1990–1996) and *20 Years of Censored News* (1997)

SUT JHALLY, professor of communications and executive director of the Media Education Foundation, University of Massachusetts

NICHOLAS JOHNSON,* professor, College of Law, University of Iowa; former FCC commissioner (1966–1973); author of *How to Talk Back to Your Television Set*

RHODA H. KARPATKIN, president of Consumers Union, non-profit publisher of *Consumer Reports*

CHARLES L. KLOTZER, editor and publisher emeritus, *St. Louis Journalism Review*

NANCY KRANICH, past president of the American Library Association (ALA)

JUDITH KRUG, director of the Office for Intellectual Freedom, American Library Association (ALA); editor of *Newsletter on Intellectual Freedom; Freedom to Read Foundation News;* and *Intellectual Freedom Action News*

MARTIN LEE, investigative journalist, media critic, and author; an original founder of Fairness and Accuracy in Reporting (FAIR) in New York; and former editor of *Extra Magazine*

WILLIAM LUTZ, professor of English, Rutgers University; former editor of *The Quarterly Review of Doublespeak;* author of *The New Doublespeak: Why No One Knows What Anyone's Saying Anymore* (1966)

JULIANNE MALVEAUX, PH.D., economist and columnist, King Features and Pacifica radio talk show host

ROBERT W. McCHESNEY, research associate professor in the Institute of Communications Research and the Graduate School of Library and Information Science at the University of Illinois, Urbana-Champaign; author of *Rich Media, Poor Democracy; Telecommunications, Mass Media, and Democracy: The Battle for the Control of U.S. Broadcasting 1928–35; The Problem of the Media;* and other books on media

CYNTHIA McKINNEY, the first African–American woman from Georgia to serve in the United States House of Representatives, 1992–2002.

MARK CRISPIN MILLER, professor of media ecology, New York University; director of the Project on Media Ownership

JACK L. NELSON,* professor, Graduate School of Education, Rutgers University; author of 16 books, including *Critical Issues in Education* (1996), and more than 150 articles

MICHAEL PARENTI, political analyst, a lecturer, and author of several books, including *Inventing Reality, The Politics of News Media, Make Believe Media, The Politics of Entertainment,* and numerous other works

DAN PERKINS, political cartoonist, pen name Tom Tomorrow, and creator of "This Modern World"

BARBARA SEAMAN, lecturer; author of *The Greatest Experiment Ever Performed on Women: Exploding the Estrogen Myth* (Hyperion, 2003), *The Doctor's Case Against the Pill, Free and Female, Women and the Crisis in Sex Hormones,* and other books; and cofounder of the National Women's Health Network

ERNA SMITH, professor of journalism, San Francisco State University; author of several studies on mainstream news coverage on people of color

NORMON SOLOMON, syndicated columnist on media and politics; coauthor of *Target Iraq: What the News Media Didn't Tell You* (Context Books, 2003); executive director of the Institute for Public Accuracy

SHEILA RABB WEIDENFELD,* president of D.C. Productions, Ltd.; former press secretary to Betty Ford

* indicates having been a Project Censored judge since its founding in 1976

PROJECT CENSORED 2003 & 2004 FACULTY, STAFF, AND COMMUNITY EVALUATORS

Julia Allen, Ph.D.	English
Melinda Barnard, Ph.D.	Communications
Philip Beard, Ph.D.	Modern Languages
Jim Berkland, Ph.D.	Geology
Barbara Bloom, Ph.D.	Criminal Justice Administration
Andrew Botterell, Ph.D.	Philosophy

Maureen Buckley, Ph.D.	Counseling
Elizabeth Burch, Ph.D.	Communications
Bob Butler, M.S.W.	
Noel Byrne, Ph.D.	Sociology
James R. Carr, Ph.D.	Geology
Yvonne Clark, M.A.	English Literature
Ray Castro, Ph.D.	Chicano & Latino Studies
Liz Close, Ph.D.	Nursing (Chair)
G. Dennis Cooke, Ph.D.	Zoology
Lynn Cominsky, Ph.D.	Physics/Astronomy
Bill Crowley, Ph.D.	Geography
Victor Daniels, Ph.D.	Psychology
Laurie Dawson, Ph.D.	Labor Education
Randall Dodgen, Ph.D.	History
Stephanie Dyer, Ph.D.	Cultural History
Carolyn Epple, Ph.D.	Anthropology
Gary Evans, M.D.	
Michael Ezra, Ph.D.	Chemistry
Tamara Falicov, M.A.	Communication Studies
Fred Fletcher	Community Expert, Labor
Dorothy (Dolly) Friedel, Ph.D.	Geography
Susan Garfin, Ph.D.	Sociology
Patricia Leigh Gibbs, Ph.D.	Sociology
Robert Girling, Ph.D.	Business/Economics
Mary Gomes, Ph.D.	Psychology
Myrna Goodman, Ph.D.	Sociology
Scott Gordon, Ph.D.	Computer Science
Diana Grant, Ph.D.	Criminal Justice Administration
Velma Guillory-Taylor, Ed.D.	American Multicultural Studies
Chad Harris, M.A.	Communication Studies
Daniel Haytin, Ph.D.	Sociology
Laurel Holmstrom, M.A.	Academic Programs
Jeffrey Holtzman, Ph.D.	Environmental Sciences
Sally Hurtado, Ph.D.	Education
Pat Jackson, Ph.D.	Criminal Justice Administration
Tom Jacobson, J.D.	Environmental Studies & Planning
Sherril Jaffe, Ph.D.	English
Paul Jess	Community Expert, Environmental Law
Cheri Ketchum, Ph.D.	Communications

Patricia Kim-Rajal, Ph.D.	American Culture
Mary King, M.D.	Health
Paul Kingsley, M.D.	
Jeanette Koshar	Nursing
John Kramer, Ph.D.	Political Science
Heidi LaMoreaux, Ph.D.	Liberal Studies
Virginia Lea, Ph.D.	Education
Benet Leigh, M.A.	Communications Studies
Wingham Liddell, Ph.D.	Business Administration
Jennifer Lillig, Ph.D.	Chemistry
Tom Lough, Ph.D.	Sociology
John Lund	Business and Political Issues
Rick Luttmann, Ph.D.	Math
Robert Manning	Peace Issues
Regina Marchi, M.A.	Communication Studies
Ken Marcus, Ph.D.	Criminal Justice Administration
Perry Marker, Ph.D.	Education
Daniel Markwyn, Ph.D.	History
Doug Martin, Ph.D.	Chemistry
Elizabeth Martinez, Ph.D.	Modern Languages
David McCuan, Ph.D.	Political Science
Phil McGough, Ph.D.	Business Administration
Eric McGuckin, Ph.D.	Liberal Studies
Robert McNamara, Ph.D.	Political Science
Andy Merrifield, Ph.D.	Political Science
Jack Munsee, Ph.D.	Political Science
Ann Neel, Ph.D.	Sociology
Catherine Nelson, Ph.D.	Political Science
Leilani Nishime, Ph.D.	American Multicultural Studies
Linda Nowak, Ph.D.	Business
Tim Ogburn	International Business
Tom Ormond, Ph.D.	Kinesiology
Wendy Ostroff, Ph.D.	Liberal Studies
Ervand M. Peterson, Ph.D.	Environmental Sciences
Keith Pike, M.A.	Native American Studies
Jorge E. Porras, Ph.D.	Modern Languages
Arturo Ramirez, Ph.D.	American Multicultural Studies
Jeffrey T. Reeder, Ph.D.	Modern Languages
Michael Robinson, Rabbi	Religion

R. Thomas Rosin, Ph.D.	Anthropology
Richard Senghas, Ph.D.	Anthropology/Linguistics
Rashmi Singh, Ph.D.	American Multicultural Studies
Bill Simon, Ph.D.	Mental Health Administration
Cindy Stearns, Ph.D.	Women's Gender Studies
John Steiner, Ph.D.	Sociology
Greg Storino	American Airlines Pilot
Meri Storino, Ph.D.	Counseling
Elaine Sundberg, M.A.	Academic Programs
Scott Suneson, M.A.	Sociology/Political Science
Bob Tellander, Ph.D.	Sociology
Laxmi G. Tewari, Ph.D.	Music
Karen Thompson, Ph.D.	Business
Suzanne Toczyski, Ph.D.	Modern Languages
Carol Tremmel, M.A.	Extended Education
Charlene Tung, Ph.D.	Women's Gender Studies
David Van Nuys, Ph.D.	Psychology
Francisco H. Vazquez, Ph.D.	Liberal Studies
Greta Vollmer, Ph.D.	English
Alexandra Von Meier, Ph.D.	Environmental Sciences
Albert Wahrhaftig, Ph.D.	Anthropology
Tim Wandling, Ph.D.	English
Tony White, Ph.D.	History
Rick Williams J.D.	Attorney at Law
John Wingard, Ph.D.	Anthropology
Craig Winston, J.D.	Criminal Justice
Richard Zimmer, Ph.D.	Liberal Studies

Sonoma State University Supporting Staff and Offices

Eduardo Ochoa: Chief Academic Officer and staff

Elaine Leeder: Dean of School of Sciences and staff

William Babula: Dean of School of Arts and Humanities

Barbara Butler and the SSU Library Staff

Paula Hammett: Social Sciences Library Resources

Jonah Raskin and Faculty in Communications Studies

Susan Kashack and staff in SSU Public Relations Office

Colleagues in the Sociology Department: Noel Byrne, Kathy Charmaz, Susan Garfin, Dan Haytin, Robert Tellander, Myrna Goodman, Melinda Milligan, Tom Lough, Elaine Wellin, and department secretaries Bev Krystosek and Lisa Kelley-Roche

Introduction

ALL THE NEWS THAT DOESN'T FIT THEIR PRINT
BY GREG PALAST

Psst! Come here, buddy. Want to see some real, hot news? Nothing covered up? Just take a look at this: 25 stories the Powers That Be thought you shouldn't see.

2004 was the year that will live in journalism infamy, when America's news media lost all shame, when reporting on the invasion of Iraq was replaced by war-nography. When our journalists weren't embedded in tanks, they were in bed in the State Department, announcing plans for the liberation of Mesopotamia the way Goebbels announced the liberation of Poland. Or, they were in bed in the Justice Department telling us the Fear Color of the day: orange, red, Barney purple, whatever.

This was the year U.S. newspapers and television networks were handed photos of American mercenaries brutalizing Iraqis—and immediately buried the bad news until one magazine reporter, Seymour Hersh, banished years earlier from *The New York Times*, broke the omerta of the military-media complex. Forced to print the story, the U.S. media changed "mercenaries" to "contractors."

In this volume, Peter Phillips and his gutsy gang at Sonoma State University have brought two dozen stories in from the cold, crucial reports shunted off by the so-called "mainstream" into the rivulets of tiny weeklies, Web sites, or foreign outlets. It's good stuff. Of course, I'm prejudiced: I've written one of these reports, the one about Arnold Schwarzenegger's dalliance with power company executives.

I've received several Project Censored awards over the years, and I can't say I'm happy about it. It's like writing a worst-selling book. It tells you your story's unread, and worse: blocked, ignored, crushed, buried while the Fox in the news henhouse lingers on the investigative revelations in the latest *Sports Illustrated* swimwear issue.

Want to know what you're not supposed to know? Here's one, from *Censored* #12, the real story behind last year's coup d'etat in Haiti. Michel Chossudovsky writes in *Global Research* newsletter that the gangsters that grabbed that sad state were backed by...surprise!... the CIA. Here's what you didn't see on Fox Snews:

> The armed insurrection which contributed to unseating President Aristide on February 29, 2004, was the result of a carefully staged military-intelligence operation. The rebel paramilitary army crossed the border from the Dominican Republic in early February. It constitutes a well armed, trained, and equipped paramilitary unit integrated by former members of FRAPH, the "plain clothes" death squadrons, involved in mass killings of civilians and political assassinations during the CIA-sponsored 1991 military coup, which led to the overthrow of the democratically elected government of Aristide. During the military government (1991–1994), FRAPH was (unofficially) under the jurisdiction of the Armed Forces. According to a 1996 U.N. Human Rights Commission report, FRAPH had been supported by the CIA.

Instead what you got in the U.S. media was some contrived cockamamie story about how the elected president was a drug runner who didn't like George Bush. Actually, he was a *priest* who didn't like George Bush, but the canard moved effortlessly from White House lips to news anchor idiot cards.

But worse than the misinformation is the *missed* information. Haiti flashed by on our news screens...those unexplained photos and films of trouble somewhere "down there" in some hot, black country...with nothing to explain the history and horror of America's economic plantation. But the Project Censored book won't leave it alone, violating the U.S. news rule that stories about black nations must get off the air in a week. Here you'll find a real live intelligent follow-up to the story—and the story of the story—by journalists Lyn Duff and Dennis Bernstein. (See Chapter 10, "Haiti: The Untold Story.")

Another story close to my heart is *Censored* #8, "Secrets of Cheney's Energy Task Force Come to Light":

> Documents turned over in the summer of 2003 by the Commerce Department concerning the activities of the Cheney Energy Task Force—as a result of the Sierra Club's and Judicial Watch's Freedom

of Information Act (FOIA) lawsuit—contain a map of Iraqi oilfields, pipelines, refineries, and terminals, as well as two charts detailing Iraqi oil and gas projects and "Foreign Suitors for Iraqi Oilfield Contracts." The documents, dated March 2001, also feature maps of Saudi Arabian and United Arab Emirates oilfields, pipelines, refineries, and tanker terminals. There are supporting charts with details of the major oil and gas development projects in each country that provide information on the project's costs, capacity, oil company, and status or completion date.

Documented plans of occupation and exploitation predating September 11 confirm heightened suspicion that U.S. policy is driven by the dictates of the energy industry.

Think about that a minute. Just a few weeks into office, our vice president and his oil industry buddies are coveting our Mideast neighbors' oil. Well, golly, might this have something to do with why our kids are bleeding in Humvees in Baghdad? Shouldn't, like, some U.S. news guys *investigate*? Well, don't hold your breath for U.S. reporters hunting the big story—that only happens in reruns of *Murphy Brown*.

Now, I have to say the Cheney map story did hit U.S. TV...but only long after the Judicial Watch report of their discovery of the maps, when former Treasury Secretary Paul O'Neill flashed them on CBS. In other words, as long as an established white millionaire from inside is willing to tattle on other members of the club, well, you just won't get the news. Even then, there was no follow-up. (Well, actually, there was: BBC TV Britain assigned me to it, and our team has discovered that there was at the time a *second* secret committee of oil men working for the White House on plans for post-conquest Iraq's oil booty. As it's quite unlikely you'll get that report in the USA, I suspect you'll have to look for it in *Censored 2006*.)

Beyond the 25 samizdat stories, you'll also get Peter Phillips, Peter Hart, Norman Solomon, and other news detectives on the trail of Media Mafia.

One terrific chapter is meant for guys like me who bitch bitch bitch about the U.S. media. Chapter 5 tells you how to get rid of the news blues by taking you to reliable sources of real, hot and heavy information, from Pacific News Service to <MediaChannel.org>.

Let me tell you why you need this book and why you have to buy one for your jerk brother-in-law in Jersey who thinks *The New York Times* is hugely informative and that Dan Rather wouldn't lie to you.

Right after the 2000 election, I discovered, in my 9-to-5 job doing investigative reports for BBC TV London, that politicos in the office of Governor

Jeb Bush of Florida had ordered elections supervisors to block the registration of about 50,000 legal voters, almost every one a Democrat. The order came down six weeks before Jeb's brother won Florida officially by just 537 votes. So this was it, the smoking gun, the damning evidence in black and white that the Family Bush had put in the fix. *CBS Nightly News* got real excited when I gave them the story. But they didn't run it. No, sir.

And why not? "Your story didn't stand up, Greg." Okay, I could live with that. But how did CBS find out the letter was bogus? "Well," said the producer, "We called Jeb Bush's office..." and, believe it or not, Jeb's office said the letter didn't exist. Welcome to American investigative reporting. (I published a copy of the nonexistent letter when I got my hands on a copy in England.)

And that's why I write in exile—to see stories important to my homeland (I'm an L.A. boy) in the Project Censored annual roll call of illicit news.

Dan himself is apologetic. Mr. Rather once confessed the following regarding reports on Bush's wars:

> It's an obscene comparison, but there was a time in South Africa when people would put flaming tires around people's necks if they dissented. In some ways, the fear is that you will be necklaced here, you will have a flaming tire of lack of patriotism put around your neck. It's that fear that keeps journalists from asking the toughest of the tough questions and to continue to bore in on the tough questions so often. Again, I'm humbled to say I do not except myself from this criticism.

He said that on BBC Television to a European audience. In the USA, he said, "George Bush is the president. He makes the decisions and...wherever he wants me to line up, just tell me where."

Now, if you'd rather hear from the journalists who step out of line, here's your book: hot news, cold truths, utterly uncensored.

Greg Palast is the author of the *New York Times* bestseller *The Best Democracy Money Can Buy.* An award-winning investigate journalist, his writings have appeared in the *Washington Post, Harper's, The Nation, The Guardian* (London), and numerous other publication. A California native, he divides his time between New York and London.

How Project Censored Stories Are Selected

Sonoma State University Project Censored students and staff screened several thousand stories each year. About 800 of these are selected for evaluation by faculty and community evaluators. Our 111 faculty/community evaluators are experts in their individual fields, and they rate the stories for credibility and national importance. Often more than one of our evaluators will examine and rate the same story. The top ranked 200 stories are then researched for national mainstream coverage by our upper division students in the annual Media Censorship class. The class examines the corporate media's coverage of the story and takes a second look at the credibility and accuracy of the story in relationship to other news articles on the topic. About 125 stories each year make the final voting level. A collective vote of all students, staff and faculty narrows the stories down to 60 in early March. A second vote is taken a week later, after a short 300-word summary of each of the top 60 stories is prepared and sent out with a voting sheet to all community/faculty evaluators, students, staff, and self-selected national judges. This project-wide voting of some 200+ people establishes which 25 of the stories will be listed in our annual book. The final ranking of stories are made by our national judges, who receive a synopsis and full text copy of the top 25 stories.

While selection of these stories each year is a long subjective judgmental process, we have grown to trust this collective effort as the best possible means of fairly selecting these important news stories. This process, we believe gives us an annual summary list of the most important undercovered news stories in the United States.

PROJECT CENSORED MISSION STATEMENT Project Censored, founded in 1976, is a non-profit project within the Sonoma State University Foundation, a 501(c)3 organization. Our principle objective is the advocacy for and protection of First Amendment rights and freedom of information in the United States. Through a faculty, student, and community partnership, Project Censored serves as a national media ombudsman by identifying and researching important news stories that are underreported, ignored, misrepresented, or censored in the United States. We also encourage and support journalists, faculty, and student investigations into First Amendment and freedom of information issues. We are actively encouraging the development of a national interconnected community-based media news service that will offer a diversity of news and information sources via print, radio, television, and Internet to local mainstream audiences.

HOW TO INVEST IN FREEDOM OF INFORMATION Project Censored is a non-profit tax-exempt organization. Funds for the project are derived from sales of this book and donations from hundreds of individuals. You can send a support gift to us thought our Web site at <www.projectcensored.org> or by mail to:

Project Censored
Sonoma State University
1810 East Cotati Avenue
Rohnert Park, CA 94931

CHAPTER 1

The Top Censored Stories of 2003 and 2004

By Kate Sims, Peter Phillips, Tricia Boreta, Anna Miranda,
Josh Sisco, Adam Stutz, Doug Reynolds, and the students
of the spring 2004 Sociology of Censorship class

People often ask us why we cover so many stories about the American government and American corporations. "There's other stuff going on, you know!" The obvious answer is: because our stories are chosen through a process of voting, and evidently, the large numbers of people involved in the project consider these stories to be important.

But perhaps the more subtle answer is: the people involved with the project consider these stories important because they *are* important. We highlight these stories for the same reason that we write about "Junk Food News": to remind people that journalism has a very specific and valuable role in a free society—and that role is not to entertain (in the Hollywood sense of the word). It is to *inform*.

So if you're going to have a country in which people have a say in the directions their government takes, what do they need to be informed about? Basically, they need information about their country's leaders, people with the power to make decisions that impact everyone else's lives. We need to know who our leaders are and what they are doing. What are their backgrounds, their motivations? What policies and laws are they enacting? What actions are they undertaking with, or against, our consent? We don't need to like them, but we do need to know about them.

We need to remember that governments, businesses, and institutions are all made up of people—with varying degrees of decision-making power. If you do not find news about your leaders entertaining (although some of us do) you should at least find it somewhat interesting. If you don't even find it interesting, my advice to you is—*get interested!* A participatory democracy (or republic) needs people to participate. And the only way you can participate effectively is to know what the heck is going on.

People say, "But it's so overwhelming." Yeah, well, we've got 300 million people here—vying for attention and wanting to set priorities. It's an exciting, frustrating, beautiful, horrible, and complicated world we live in. I don't see it getting any less overwhelming any time soon. And if you don't like the way things are, you can bet that they won't get any better on their own. The only way to *not* live in a completely totalitarian society is to participate in the one you have.

A free society is like a good set of teeth. Ignore it, and it will go away. If you want shiny, healthy teeth, take care of them. If you want a shiny, healthy democracy—*pay attention!*

—Kate Sims, Research Coordinator, Project Censored

Another election year is upon us and the decisions made by Project Censored's 200+ voters reflect those interests. Once again, the mainstream media have managed to ignore the meatier issues. Issues we would like to have seen covered involve our health (*Censored* #19 and #21) and environment (*Censored* #5, #10, and #20), the economy (*Censored* #1, #23, and #25), and energy policy (*Censored* #8, #13, #18). We are interested in the actions taken by the current leaders in Washington (*Censored* #3, #7, and #12). And we want to know what's going on with the war in Iraq (*Censored* #17 and #22) and on terrorism (*Censored* #9, #15, and #24). Perhaps the most important election issue this year has to do with the election itself (*Censored* #6). And, as always, we are interested in policy changes that have the potential to impact our rights (*Censored* #2 and #11) and freedoms (*Censored* #14, #16, and #24).

Here are the stories by category:

POLITICS

#2 Ashcroft vs. the Human Rights Law that Holds Corporations Accountable

#6 The Sale of Electoral Politics

Wealth Inequality in Twenty-First Century Threatens Economy and Democracy

Sources:
Multinational Monitor, May 2003, Vol. 24, No. 5
Title: "The Wealth Divide" (an interview with Edward Wolff)
Author: Robert Weissman

Buzz Flash, March 26 and 29, 2004
Title: "A Buzz Flash Interview, Part I and II" with David Cay Johnston
Author: *Buzz Flash* staff

The Guardian (London), October 4, 2003
Title: "Every Third Person Will Be a Slum Dweller Within 30 Years,
    U.N. Agency Warns"
Author: John Vidal

Multinational Monitor, July/August 2003
Title: "Grotesque Inequality"
Author: Robert Weissman

Faculty Evaluators: Greg Storino and Phil Beard, Ph.D.
Student Researchers: Caitlyn Pardue, David Sonnenberg, and Sita Khalsa

THE DOMESTIC TREND

In the late 1700s, issues of fairness and equality were topics of great debate—equality under the law, equality of opportunity, etc. Considered by the framers of the Constitution to be one of the most important aspects of a democratic system, the word "equality" is featured prominently throughout the document. In the 200+ years since, most industrialized nations have succeeded in decreasing the gap between rich and poor.

However, since the late 1970s, wealth inequality, while stabilizing or increasing slightly in other industrialized nations, has increased sharply and dramatically in the United States. While it is no secret that such a trend is taking place, it is rare to see a TV news program announce that the top 1 percent of the U.S. population now owns about a third of the wealth in the country. Discussion of this trend takes place, for the most part, behind closed doors.

During the short boom of the late 1990s, conservative analysts asserted that, yes, the gap between rich and poor was growing, but that incomes for the poor were still increasing over previous levels. Today most economists, regardless of their political persuasion, agree that the data over the last 25 to 30 years is unequivocal. The top 5 percent is capturing an increasingly greater portion of the pie while the bottom 95 percent is clearly losing ground, and the highly touted American middle class is fast disappearing.

According to economic journalist David Cay Johnston, author of *Perfectly Legal*, this trend is not the result of some naturally occurring, social Darwinist "survival of the fittest." It is the product of legislative policies carefully crafted and lobbied for by corporations and the super-rich over the past 25 years.

New tax shelters in the 1980s shifted the tax burden off capital and onto labor. As tax shelters rose, the amount of federal revenue coming from corporations fell (from 35 percent during the Eisenhower years to 10 percent in 2002). During the deregulation wave of the 1980s and the 1990s, members of Congress passed legislation (often without reading it) that deregulated much of the financial industry. These laws took away, for example, the powerful incentives for accountants to behave with integrity or for companies to put away a reasonable amount in pension plans for their employees—resulting in the scandals involving Enron, Global Crossing, and others, which were well-publicized, but gained visibility too late to prevent them.

THE GLOBAL IMPACT

As always, America's economic trends have a global footprint—and this time, it is a crater. Today, the top 400 income earners in the U.S. make as much in a year as the entire population of the 20 poorest countries in Africa (over 300 million people). But in America, national leaders and mainstream media tell us that the only way out of our own economic hole is through increasing and endless growth—fueled by the resources of other countries.

A series of reports released in 2003 by the U.N. and other global economy analysis groups warn that further increases in the imbalance in wealth throughout the world will have catastrophic effects if left unchecked. United Nations Human Settlement

Program (U.N.-HABITAT), the U.N. agency for human settlement whose goal is to provide viable shelter for all, reports that unless governments work to control the current unprecedented spread in urban growth, a third of the world's population will be slum dwellers within 30 years. Currently, almost one-sixth of the world's population lives in slum-like conditions. The U.N. warns that unplanned, unsanitary settlements threaten both political and fiscal stability within Third World countries, where urban slums are growing faster than expected. The balance of poverty is shifting quickly from rural to urban areas as the world's population moves from the countryside to the city.

As rich countries strip poorer countries of their natural resources in an attempt to restabilize their own, the people of poor countries become increasingly desperate. This deteriorating situation, besides pressuring rich countries to allow increased immigration, further exacerbates already stretched political tensions and threatens global political and economic security.

U.N. economists blame "free-trade" practices and the neoliberal policies of international lending institutions like the International Monetary Fund (IMF) and World Trade Organization (WTO) and the industrialized countries that lead them for much of the damage caused to Third World countries over the past 20 years. Many of these policies are now being implemented in the U.S., allowing for an acceleration of wealth consolidation. And even the IMF has issued a report warning the U.S. about the consequences for its appetite for excess and overspending.

In developing countries, the concentration of key industries profitable to foreign investors requires that people move to cities while forced privatization of public services strip them of the ability to become stable or move up financially once they arrive. Meanwhile, the strict repayment schedules mandated by the global institutions make it virtually impossible for poor countries to move out from under their burden of debt. "In a form of colonialization that is probably more stringent than the original, many developing countries have become suppliers of raw commodities to the world, and fall further and further behind," says one U.N. analyst. World economists conclude that if enough of the world's nations reach a point of economic failure, such a situation could collapse the entire global economy.

For further information on this story, please check out the following excellent Web sites: <www.inequality.org>; *Dollars and Sense,* <www.dollarsandsense.org/>; PBS, <www.pbs.org/now/politics/income.html>; and *The Guardian* (London), <www.guardian.co.uk/usa/story/0,12271,1118425,00.html>. Also found on <Democracynow.org> May 18, 2004.

2 Ashcroft vs. the Human Rights Law that Holds Corporations Accountable

Source:
<OneWorld.Net> and *Asheville Global Report* (*AGR*), May 19, 2003
Title: "Ashcroft Goes After 200-Year-Old Human Rights Law"
Author: Jim Lobe

Faculty Evaluator: Meri Storino, Ph.D.
Student Researchers: Brian Ferguson and Lawren Lutrin

U.S. Attorney General John Ashcroft is seeking to strike down one of the world's oldest human rights laws, the Alien Tort Claims Act (ATCA), which holds government leaders, corporations, and senior military officials liable for human rights abuses taking place in foreign countries. Organizations such as Human Rights Watch (HRW) vehemently oppose the removal of this law, as it is one of the few legal defenses victims of human rights violations can claim against powerful organizations such as governments or multinational corporations. The attempt to dismiss the law comes less than a year after the Ninth Circuit Court of Appeals ruled that Unocal Corporation could be held liable for human rights abuses committed against Burmese peasants near a pipeline the company was building. By attempting to throw out this law, the Bush Administration is effectively opening the door for human rights abuses to continue under the veil of foreign relations.

The ATCA dates back to 1789 when George Washington signed legislation for an antipiracy bill. An obscure segment of the bill gave foreign citizens the right to sue in United States courts over violations of international law. After being used only twice in its first 200 years of existence, the law has been the basis of some 100 lawsuits since 1980. A landmark ruling in that same year awarded a Paraguayan woman $10 million for the torture and murder of her brother committed by a Paraguayan police official, who was living in the U.S. illegally. That ruling effectively opened the door for foreign citizens to seek justice through litigation in U.S. courts.

Business groups argue that human rights lawyers and courts that interpret the ATCA too broadly have wrongly exploited the law. The Bush Administration agrees stating the law interferes with foreign policy. Noncitizens would be allowed to file lawsuits that could potentially embarrass foreign governments from which the U.S. needs cooperation in the war on terrorism. Critics of recent ATCA suits also argue that the original statute provides no actual authority to file suit and only paves the way for Congress to do so (should Congress adopt a separate act defining which violations can be addressed in court).

According to a *Wall Street Journal* article, upholding the law could jeopardize aspects of the war on terrorism. "A U.S. government employee or contractor working in a high-risk law enforcement, intelligence of military operation could be sued for their participation," says Mark Rosen, a retired U.S. Navy captain and specialist in defense and homeland security issues.

UPDATE BY JIM LOBE: The Alien Tort Claims Act has been used as an important tool for human rights activists to keep raising the issue of impunity for severe abuses committed abroad, ordinarily by repressive governments, but increasingly by the U.S. and other corporations that are, at the very least, condoning abusive practices by local governments and their security forces. At the end of March, for example, a federal judge in San Francisco refused to throw out claims that the Chevron-Texaco Corporation might be liable for abuses at a Nigerian oil platform operated by a subsidiary of the company. Of course, Unocal and Exxon Mobil face similar suits.

ATCA—or more accurately the campaign against ATCA—has drawn increasing attention over the past two years. In fact, I've seen some recent ads on *The New York Times* op-ed page attacking ATCA on behalf of a coalition of multinational corporations.

A number of lawsuits are continuing to make it through the federal judicial system, but only one has reached the Supreme Court. It involves a lawsuit brought under ATCA by a Mexican national who was kidnapped by bounty hunters and taken to the U.S. where he was held—wrongly—in connection with the murder of a DEA agent in Mexico. He sued the U.S. government and the bounty hunter under ATCA. A jury awarded him $25,000 in damages. For more on this case, which could be very important to ATCA's fate, I refer you to a *New York Times* piece written on March 31, 2004, by Linda Greenhouse, which summarizes the oral argument and background. At the same time, Dolly Filartiga, the plaintiff in the first ATCA case from 1980, had an op-ed in *The New York Times* on March 30, 2004, entitled "American Courts, Global Justice."

Some background is also included in an editorial in the *Washington Post* published a week later (April 6, 2004) called "Human Rights in Court."

Unocal's case was re-argued to appeals judges sitting en banc just about one year ago, but a decision has not yet been rendered. It usually takes about a year, but there is speculation. The appeals court also wants to wait until the Supreme Court decides the Mexico case.

There has been some coverage of the Unocal case in the mainstream media but mainly about the state court case, which doesn't rely on ATCA. There has been much more attention paid to what ATCA is and why it is being attacked.

Earth Justice and the Center for Constitutional Rights are extremely involved in the campaign against ATCA. For more information, these organizations, as well as Human Rights Watch, are good sources.

SUBSEQUENT UPDATE BY PROJECT CENSORED: On June 29, 2004, the U.S. Supreme Court ruled to keep federal courts open to lawsuits by foreigners who are victims of human rights violations. However, the court reversed the decision by the Ninth U.S. Circuit Court of Appeals in San Francisco, finding that Dr. Humberto Alvarez-Machian was not within his legal rights to sue for being kidnapped in Mexico by the U.S. Drug Enforcement Administration. Dr. Alvarez-Machian was subsequently found not guilty for the charges against him in a U.S. court. The case did not involve a corporate defendant and leaves unresolved such cases as the Unocal human rights violation in Myanmar. (Sources: *The New York Times*, June 30, 2004; *Christian Science Monitor*, June 30, 2004)

3 Bush Administration Manipulates Science and Censors Scientists

Sources:
The Nation, March 8, 2004
Title: "The Junk Science of George W. Bush"
Author: Robert F. Kennedy Jr.

Censorship News: The National Coalition Against Censorship Newsletter, Fall 2003, No. 91
Title: "Censoring Scientific Information"
Author: None Listed

<OneWorld.net>, February 20, 2004
Title: "Ranking Scientists Warn Bush Science Policy Lacks Integrity"
Author: ENS correspondents

Office of U.S. Representative Henry A. Waxman (D–CA), August 2003
Title: "Politics and Science in the Bush Administration"
Prepared by: Committee on Government Reform—Minority Staff
(Updated November 13, 2003)

Faculty Evaluator: Dolly Friedel, Ph.D.
Student Researchers: Sita Khalsa and Jeni Green

Critics charge that the Bush Administration is purging, censoring, and manipulating scientific information in order to push forward its pro-business, antienvironmental agenda. In Washington, DC, more than 60 of the nation's top scientists, including 20 Nobel laureates, leading medical experts, and former federal agency directors, issued a statement on February 18, 2004, accusing the Bush Administration of deliberately distorting scientific results for political ends and calling for regulatory and legislative action to restore scientific integrity to federal policy making.

Under the current administration, the Environmental Protection Agency (EPA) has blacklisted qualified scientists who pose a threat to its pro-business ideology. When a team of biologists working for the EPA indicated that there had been a violation of the "Endangered Species Act" by the Army Corps of Engineers, the group was replaced with a "corporate-friendly" panel. In addition, a nationally respected biologist, Dr. James Zahn, was ordered by EPA representatives not to publish a study identifying a health endangering bacteria in industrial hog farms.

The Bush Administration is appointing unqualified scientists with close industry ties to the advisory boards. The Office of Human Services appointed several individuals with ties to the lead industry. One of their appointees testified that lead levels, seven times the current limit, are safe for children.

In the case of global warming, the Bush Administration has made efforts to stall actions by Congress designed to control industrial emissions. The EPA altered a report on the environmental damage of a hydraulic fracturing process developed by Halliburton, Dick Cheney's former company. Hydraulic fracturing involves the injection of benzene into the ground, which in turn contaminates ground water supplies over the federal limit.

In December 2002, the EPA weakened a Clean Air Act regulation known as the New Source Review (NSR) to make it easier for coal-fired utilities to generate more

THIS MODERN WORLD
by TOM TOMORROW

power without having to install additional emissions controls. The Bush Administration halted the prosecution of some 50 power plants that were alleged to be in violation of the of the old NSR rule while at the same time drastically reducing funding for the Superfund toxic cleanup program. In October 2003, the General Accounting Office, Congress' investigative arm, reported that the revised NSR rule could "limit assurance of the public's access to data about and input on decisions to modify facilities in ways that affect emissions." Essentially, this makes it more difficult for the public to monitor local emissions, health risks, and NSR compliance.

In June 2003, the Administration published its "comprehensive" report on the environment—that contained no information on climate change and did not address global warming.

The EPA claimed a few days after the 9/11 catastrophe that the air quality was safe in the security zone surrounding the World Trade Center. An Inspector General's report released in August 2003 revealed that press releases were being drafted or doctored by White House officials in order to quickly reopen Wall Street.

A study conducted by the EPA found that high levels of atrazine, a carcinogen, were discovered in drinking water, well over the government standard allotment. When the findings were reported, the Bush Administration did not address the level of atrazine, but instead moved the research to a company in Switzerland, taking environmental control away from local scientists.

In January 2003, President Bush appointed marketing consultant Jerry Thacker to the Presidential Advisory Council on HIV/AIDS. Mr. Thacker has referred to homosexuality derogatorily and has described AIDS as the "gay plague." In May 2003, *The New York Times* reported that Health and Human Services (HHS) may be applying "unusual scrutiny" to grants that used key words such as "men who sleep with men," "gay," and "homosexual."

Princeton University scientist Michael Oppenheimer states, "If you believe in a rational universe, in enlightenment, in knowledge and in a search for the truth, this White House is an absolute disaster."

UPDATE BY ROBERT F. KENNEDY JR.: The story was the first comprehensive compilation of the systematic assault of federal science orchestrated by the White House and affecting all the federal departments that oversee the environment and public health.

During the week it was published, the Union of Concerned Scientists published another report detailing the Bush Administration's assault on government science and its practice of purging and muzzling government science whose pronouncements impede corporate profit taking. Twenty Nobel Prize winners have signed a letter to the president condemning the suppressing and distorting of federal science.

Numerous articles have appeared in nationally prominent publications discussing the issue, many of them citing *The Nation* cover story.

You can contact Natural Resources Defense Council (NRDC) or visit their Web site at <www.nrdc.org/>. I am currently writing a book for HarperCollins titled *Crimes Against Nature* to be published this fall (2004) about the administration's attack on the environment. The book is based on the article of the same title, which was published in the December 8, 2003, *Rolling Stone* issue.

High Uranium Levels Found in Troops and Civilians

Sources:

Uranium Medical Research Center (UMRC), January 2003
Title: "UMRC's Preliminary Findings from Afghanistan and Operation Enduring Freedom" and "Afghan Field Trip #2 Report: Precision Destruction—Indiscriminate Effects"
Author: Tedd Weyman, UMRC Research Team

Awakened Woman, January 2004
Title: "Scientists Uncover Radioactive Trail in Afghanistan"
Author: Stephanie Hiller

Dissident Voice, March 2004
Title: "There Are No Words…Radiation in Iraq Equals 250,000 Nagasaki Bombs"
Author: Bob Nichols

New York *Daily News*, April 5, 2004
Title: "Poisoned?"
Author: Juan Gonzalez

Information Clearing House, March 2004
Title: "International Criminal Tribune for Afghanistan at Tokyo,
   The People vs. George Bush"
Author: Professor Ms. Niloufer Bhagwat J.

Evaluator: Jennifer Lillig, Ph.D.
Student Researcher: Kenny Crosbie

Civilian populations in Afghanistan and Iraq and occupying troops have been contaminated with astounding levels of radioactive depleted and non-depleted uranium as a result of post-9/11 United States' use of tons of uranium munitions. Researchers say surrounding countries are bound to feel the effects as well.

In 2003, scientists from the Uranium Medical Research Center (UMRC) studied urine samples of Afghan civilians and found that 100 percent of the samples taken had levels of non-depleted uranium (NDU) 400 percent to 2,000 percent higher than normal levels. The UMRC research team studied six sites, two in Kabul and others in the Jalalabad area. The civilians were tested four months after the attacks in Afghanistan by the United States and its allies.

NDU is more radioactive than depleted uranium (DU), which itself is charged with causing many cancers and severe birth defects in the Iraqi population—especially children—over the past 10 years. Four million pounds of radioactive uranium was dropped on Iraq in 2003 alone. Uranium dust will be in the bodies of our returning armed forces. Nine soldiers from the 442nd Military Police serving in Iraq were tested for DU contamination in December 2003. Conducted at the request of the *Daily News*, as the U.S. government considers the cost of $1,000 per affected soldier prohibitive, the test found that four of the nine men were contaminated with high levels of DU, likely caused by inhaling dust from depleted uranium shells fired by U.S. troops. Several of the men had traces of another uranium isotope, U-236, which is produced only in a nuclear reaction process.

Most American weapons (missiles, smart bombs, dumb bombs, bullets, tank shells, cruise missiles, etc.) contain high amounts of radioactive uranium. Depleted or non-depleted, these types of weapons, on detonation, release a radioactive dust which, when inhaled, goes into the body and stays there. It has a half-life of 4.5 billion years. Basically, it's a permanently available contaminant, distributed in the environment, where dust storms or any water nearby can disperse it. Once ingested, it releases subatomic particles that slice through DNA.

UMRC's field team found several hundred Afghan civilians with acute symptoms of radiation poisoning along with chronic symptoms of internal uranium contamination, including congenital problems in newborns. Local civilians reported large, dense dust clouds and smoke plumes rising from the point of impact, an acrid smell, followed by burning of the nasal passages, throat, and upper respiratory tract. Subjects in all locations presented identical symptom profiles and chronologies. The victims reported symptoms that included pain in the cervical column, upper shoulders, and basal area of the skull; lower back/kidney pain; joint and muscle weakness; sleeping difficulties; headaches; memory problems; and disorientation.

At the Uranium Weapons Conference held October 2003 in Hamburg, Germany, independent scientists from around the world testified to a huge increase in birth deformities and cancers wherever NDU and DU had been used. Professor Katsuma Yagasaki, a scientist at the Ryukyus University, Okinawa, calculated that the 800 tons of DU used in Afghanistan is the radioactive equivalent of 83,000 Nagasaki bombs. The amount of DU used in Iraq is equivalent to 250,000 Nagasaki bombs.

At the Uranium Weapons Conference, a demonstration by British-trained oncologist Dr. Jawad Al-Ali showed photographs of the kinds of birth deformities and tumors he had observed at the Saddam Teaching Hospital in Basra just before the 2003 war. Cancer rates had increased dramatically over the previous fifteen years. In 1989, there were 11 abnormalities per 100,000 births; in 2001, there were 116 per 100,000—an increase of over 1,000 percent. In 1989, 34 people died of cancer; in 2001, there were 603 cancer deaths. The 2003 war has increased these figures exponentially.

At a meeting of the International Criminal Tribunal for Afghanistan held in December of 2003 in Tokyo, the U.S. was indicted for multiple war crimes in Afghanistan, among them the use of DU. Leuren Moret, president of Scientists for Indigenous People and environmental commissioner for the city of Berkeley, testified that because radioactive contaminants from uranium weapons travel through air, water, and food sources, the effects of U.S. deployment in Afghanistan will be felt in Iran, Pakistan, Turkey, Turkmenistan, Uzbekistan, Russia, Georgia, Azerbaijan, Kazakhstan, China, and India. Countries affected by the use of uranium weapons in Iraq include Saudi Arabia, Syria, Lebanon, Palestine, Israel, Turkey, and Iran.

UPDATE BY BOB NICHOLS: Throughout the world, people are familiar with the "smoking gun" solution so prized by murder mystery writers. Many think that once the smoking gun in any mystery is discovered, it is time for the "bad guys" to give up. I only wish it were so.

The smoking guns here are Sgt. Hector Vega, Sgt. Ray Ramos, Sgt. Agustin Matos, and Cpl. Anthony Yonnone from New York's 442nd Guard Unit; they are the first confirmed cases of inhaled uranium oxide exposure from the current Iraq conflict. Dr. Asaf Durokovic, professor of Nuclear Medicine at the Uranium Medical Research Centre, <www.umrc.net/>, conducted the diagnostic tests. The story was released April 3, 2004, in the New York *Daily News* <www.nydailynews.com/front/story/180333p-156685c.html>. There is no treatment, and there is no cure.

Leuren Moret reports, "In my research on depleted uranium during the past five years, the most disturbing information concerns the impact on the unborn children and future generations both for soldiers serving in the depleted uranium wars and for the civilians who must live in the permanently radioactive contaminated regions. Today, more than 240,000 Gulf War veterans are on permanent medical disability and more than 11,000 are dead. They have been denied testing, medical care, and compensation for depleted uranium exposure and related illnesses since 1991."

Moret continues, "Even worse, they brought it home in their bodies. In some families, the children born before the Gulf War are the only healthy members. Wives and female partners of Gulf War veterans have reported a condition known as burning semen syndrome and are now internally contaminated from depleted uranium carried in the semen of exposed veterans. Many are reporting reproductive illnesses such as endometriosis. In a U.S. government study, conducted by the Department of Veterans Affairs on post-Gulf War babies, 67 percent were found to have serious birth defects or serious illnesses. They were born without eyes (anophthalmos), without ears, had missing organs, missing legs and arms, fused fingers, or thyroid or other organ malformations." (See *Life* Photo Essay at: <www.life.com/Life/essay/gulfwar/gulf01.html>.)

Moret concludes, "In Iraq, it is even worse: Babies are born without brains, organs are outside the body, or women give birth to pieces of flesh. In babies born in Iraq in 2002, the incidence of anophthalmos was 250,000 times greater (20 cases in 4,000 births) than the natural occurrence, one in 50 million births. Takashi Morizumi's photos at <www.savewarchildren.org/> record the tragedy in Iraq."

For more information on the American president's continuing campaign of contaminating the land, check the World Uranium Weapons Conference at <www.uraniumweaponsconference.de/>. Check the Uranium Medical Research Center and Dr. Asaf Durakovic at <www.umrc.net>, and for updates on the related Nuclear Power Plants, see Russell Hoffman's Web site at <www.animatedsoftware.com/hotwords/index.htm>. Write Leuren Moret, independent scientist and radiation specialist, city of Berkeley environmental commissioner, and past president of Association for Women Geoscientists at <leurenmoret@yahoo.com>.

See also "Depleted Uranium: The Trojan Horse of Nuclear War" by Leuren Moret, *World Affairs Journal,* July 2004 at <www.mindfully.org/Nucs/2004/DU-Trojan-Horse1jul04.htm>. These YahooGroups host discussions about uranium munitions:

<du-list@yahoogroups.com>; <du-watch@yahoogroups.com>;<pandora-project@ yahoogroups.com>; <nucnews@yahoogroups.com>; <abolition-caucus@yahoogroups. com>; and <earthfirstalert@yahoogroups.com>. Read Bob Nichols at <www.dissident voice.org/>.

UPDATE BY TEDD WEYMAN: UMRC found artificial uranium in bomb craters, surrounding watercourses, and the bodies of civilians exposed to U.S. coalition bombing in Afghanistan. Civilians surveyed presented with the classical symptoms of internal contamination by uranium, which began after exposure to the bombing. The presence of artificial uranium in environmental and biological samples indicates that the bunker buster warheads used in Afghanistan are made of uranium.

Uranium is a chemically and radiologically toxic element, clinically proven to be a cause of various types of cancer and congenital malformations (birth defects). Internal contamination of uranium is responsible for variety of systemic and organ system problems, which has never been considered or studied by the Defense Department or veterans' health programs as possible cause of Gulf War Illness. The symptoms of internal contamination by uranium in Iraq and Afghanistan civilians are identical to the symptoms of U.S. and coalition veterans complaining of Gulf War Syndrome.

The Pentagon and the Department of Defense (DOD) have interfered with UMRC's ability to have its studies published by managing a progressive and persistent misinformation program in the press against UMRC and through the use of its control of science research grants to refute UMRC's scientific findings and destroy the reputation of UMRC's scientific staff, physicians, and laboratories. UMRC is the first independent research organization to find depleted uranium in the bodies of U.S., U.K., and Canadian Gulf War I veterans and has subsequently, following Operation Iraqi Freedom, found depleted uranium in the water, soil, and atmosphere of Iraq as well as in biological samples donated by Iraqi civilians.

The United States and several of its coalition partners and NATO allies have been deploying in battlefield and experimenting with chemically toxic and radioactive heavy metals in various types of bullets, bombs, and warheads since the early 1970s. After it has been mixed with nuclear reactor waste products and spent fuel, uranium powder is taken from the nuclear fuel reprocessing cycle to supply the nonfissile weapons' manufacturing industry.

Uranium is preferred over all other "ballistic" metals (e.g., lead, iron, and tungsten) because it offers a set of unique metallurgical properties: it is extremely dense yet ductile metal (not brittle); it is pyrophoric (uranium dust burns spontaneously at room temperature); and solid metal uranium is autoigniting at 170° F. Uranium metal has a very unusual property not available in any other metal: It is "self-sharpening," meaning that when it hits a target at high velocities (1 km/sec), it erodes and breaks in such a way as to continuously resharpen its point. The leading points of all other warhead metals flatten or mushroom under these conditions. These properties give uranium a superior performance as a penetrating warhead alloy capable of breaching the hardest and thickest armor plating, retaining penetration capabilities at 15 percent greater distances and lower speeds than the most common alternative metal, tungsten. Burning uranium is hard to extinguish, and if doused with water, it will explode. Uranium used in specially designed high velocity liquid metal penetrators can bore through 20 feet of super-reinforced concrete bunkers in classified weapons called "shaped charges" and "explosively formed penetrators." The hard (dense), resilient (ductile), and heavy (momentum-sustaining) characteristics of uranium also make its optimal in the warhead of robust earth-penetrating bombs to carry them into buried targets and caves.

The mainstream press in the U.S. and Canada does not show any general interest in the story, let alone an investigative interest. European mainstream press is more interested and follows key developments. The New York *Daily News* (April 5, 2004) has covered Gulf War II results by UMRC's studies of U.S. veterans. DOD has lied and misled the public and the veterans in an attempt to undermine the significance of the story. There is significant alternative press and internet press coverage. The technique for coverage is to approach the story as a debate between government and independent experts in which public interest is stimulated by polarizing the issues rather than telling the scientific and medical truth. The issues are systematically confused and misinformed by government, U.N. regulatory agencies—World Health Organization (WHO), United Nations Environment Program (UNEP), International Atomic Energy Agency (IAEA), Centers for Disease Control and Prevention (CDC), Department of Energy (DOE), etc.—and defense sector (military and the weapons developers and manufacturers).

UPDATE BY STEPHANIE HILLER: When I learned that the United States used nondepleted uranium weapons in Afghanistan, I was shocked out of my skin. I have friends in Kabul. Under the lofty name of Operation Enduring Freedom— did they mean enduring radiation?—the U.S. has doomed the proud people of this beleaguered nation, survivors of 24 years of war, to incurable illness and generations of genetic deterioration. I soon understood that the use of depleted uranium is a death sentence for the people of the entire region. Even though these nuclear weapons are not atomic bombs, they spread deadly radiation throughout the civilian population. This is a war crime of terrifying proportions.

Continued research shows that we have all been irradiated here in the United States, at an enormous cost to the public health. Cancer rates alone show that genetic mutation has been rapidly increasing since the first bomb was tested in 1945. The effects of low-level radiation have been systematically hidden from public view.

The *Daily News* story about vets from the recent Iraq war got the attention of New York Senator Hillary Clinton (D–NY). She held a teleconference, but Durakovic and Moret were excluded! Media silence on the use of these weapons as well as the contamination here at home is staggering. People will travel to the region without knowing they will be exposed to radiation. Our own soldiers are not informed.

Durakovic has posted a warning to NGOs on his Web site. He was interviewed by Amy Goodman on *Democracy Now!* The BBC and the *Seattle Post-Intelligencer* have covered the story, but otherwise, there has been no mainstream coverage.

To learn more about uranium weapons, start with the world Uranium Weapons Conference held last October in Hamburg at <www.uraniumweapons conference.de>. The PowerPoint by Dr. Ali reveals the excruciating consequences: horribly deformed babies. Women for a Better World (WBW), working with the Alliance for Democracy, has begun an information campaign to educate the public about DU, especially young people who might be called to join the military. Come to our Web site, <www.awakenedwoman.com/wbw.htm>, for more information and flyers; also, please consider signing our petition opposing the draft.

 # The Wholesale Giveaway of Our Natural Resources

Sources:
In These Times, November 23, 2003
Title: "Liquidation of the Commons"
Author: Adam Werbach

High Country News, Vol. 35, No. 11, June 9, 2003
Title: "Giant Sequoias Could Get the Ax"
Author: Matt Weiser

Evaluator: Mary Gomes, Ph.D.
Student Researcher: Gina Dunch

Not since the McKinley era of the late 1800s has there been such a drastic move to scale back preservation of the environment. In 1896, President William McKinley was extremely pro-industry in terms of forests and mining interest giveaways. Mark

Hanna, McKinley's partner against American populist William Jennings Bryan, raised more than $4 million in campaign contributions, stating that only a government that catered first to the needs of corporate interests could serve the needs of the people.

The Bush Administration's environmental policies are destroying much of the environmental progress made over the past 30 years. A prime example is the Bush Administration's Clean Skies Initiative. The Clean Air Act of 1970 has made skies over most cities cleaner by cutting back pollution let out by major power companies. However, the Clean Skies Initiative allows power plants to emit more than five times more mercury, twice as much sulfur dioxide, and over one and a half times more nitrogen oxides than the Clean Air Act.

Another example is in Gillette, Wyoming, where a significant amount of natural gas (coal bed methane) exists. The only way to extract the gas is by draining ground water to the level of the coal in order to release it. The Bureau of Land Management estimates that if all goes ahead as planned, the miners will discard more than 700 million gallons of publicly owned water a year. The mining of coal bed methane is as expensive as it is wasteful, and the industry has received promises from Congress of a $3 billion tax credit to help them on their way. It makes little economic sense to drill for marginal coal bed methane when larger deposits are elsewhere. Meanwhile, the U.S. government agencies normally responsible for protecting the land now serve as customer relations organizations for mining companies.

Bush's Healthy Forests Initiative is funding projects for logging companies to gain access to old growth trees and paying them for brush clearing. The new draft for the Forest Service management plan, which allows logging of up to 10 million board feet of lumber each year, could even include removal of the very trees the monument was established to preserve—the giant sequoias, which are found nowhere else in such abundance.

The administration poses the problem as one of unnecessary regulations that oppose tree thinning. Yet U.S. Forest Service records show that in the four national forests in Southern California that burned in early November 2003, environmentalists had not filed a single appeal to stop Forest Service tree-thinning projects to reduce fire risk since 1997. And when Governor Davis requested money to remove unhealthy trees throughout California's forests, the request for emergency funds went unanswered by the Bush Administration until the end of October—and then, it was denied.

President Bush appointed Vice President Cheney to head a secretive energy task force to craft the administration's energy policy, which constituted the same types of giveaways as McKinley's. Not only are corporate interests put first, but taxpayers are also now paying to clean up the mess left behind. The Bush Administration has cut the Superfund budget, and Congress is shifting the burden of cleanup from polluters to the American taxpayer.

Some administration officials still have active ties to corporate interests. Under-secretary of the Interior J. Steven Griles, a former industrial lobbyist, is still being paid by his former employer, National Environmental Strategies (NES). NES lobbies for coal, oil, gas, and electric companies.

Coal bed methane development, the Clear Skies Initiative, and the Healthy Forests Initiative are just a few examples of the Bush Administration's efforts to undo 30 years of environmental progress. With the Senate approval of Governor Mike Leavitt of Utah, an individual who is acquiescent to the Bush Administration's environmental policies, as the head of the Environmental Protection Agency, the situation can only get worse.

UPDATE BY ADAM WERBACH: The Bush Administration's war on terror has pushed the most rapid destruction of the commons witnessed this century into the back pages of major newspapers. The article "Liquidation of the Commons" published by *In These Times* detailed the Bush Administration's "say one thing, do another" policies, which have symbolized his administration's efforts to allow industry to pollute the skies and cut down our last remaining ancient forests.

While most American news consumers can describe in detail the military hardware deployed in Iraq, the loss of hundreds of billions of dollars worth of America's common assets is absent from political conversation. From the planned sale of trees in the Tongass National Forest in Alaska to the weakening of FCC media ownership caps on the people's airwaves, the Administration's policy has been to sell off, neglect, or destroy the commons—those resources that we own collectively.

It will probably be years until we understand the full cost of what we've lost during the Bush Administration. Thousands of seemingly small regulatory changes, secret out-of-court settlements that have sacrificed endangered species, and lax enforcement of existing laws, are only a few of the symptoms of the administration's liquidation of the commons. In the words of Supreme Court Justice Louis Brandeis, "sunlight is the best disinfectant, electric light the best policeman." Thankfully, Project Censored is helping to bring these stories to light.

For more information about Bush's environmental policies, visit Common Assets at <www.commonassests.org/>, Tomales Bay Institute at <www.tomales.org/>, the Sierra Club at <www.sierraclub.org/>, and Apollo Alliance at <www.apolloalliance.org/>.

6 The Sale of Electoral Politics

Sources:
In These Times, December 2003
Title: "Voting Machines Gone Wild"
Author: Mark Lewellen-Biddle

The Independent (U.K.), October 13, 2003
Title: "All The President's Votes?"
Author: Andrew Gumbel

Democracy Now!, September 4, 2003
Title: "Will Bush Backers Manipulate Votes to Deliver G.W. Another Election?"
Reporter: Amy Goodman and the staff of *Democracy Now!*

Evaluators: Andy Merrifield, Ph.D., Wendy Ostroff, Ph.D., and Scott Gordon, Ph.D.
Student Researcher: Adam Stutz

Conflicts of interest exist between the largest suppliers of electronic voting machines in the United States and key leaders of the Republican Party. While the technical problems with the voting machines themselves have received a certain amount of coverage in the mainstream media, the political conflicts of interest, though well documented, have received almost none. Election analysts on both sides of the fence are charging that while particular industries have traditionally formed alliances with one or another of the parties, political affiliations within the voting machine industry are inappropriate—and have dangerous implications for our democratic process.

Election Systems & Software (ES&S), Diebold, and Sequoia are the companies primarily involved in implementing the new, often faulty, technology at voting stations throughout the country. All three have strong ties to the Bush Administration and other Republican leaders, along with major defense contractors in the United States. ES&S and Diebold, owned by brothers Bob and Todd Urosevich, will be counting about 80 percent of the votes cast in 2004. Each one of the three companies has a past plagued by financial scandal and political controversy:

> ➤ In 1999, the Justice Department filed federal charges against Sequoia alleging that employees paid out more than $8 million in bribes. Shortly thereafter, election officials for Pinellas County, Florida, cancelled a $15-million contract with Sequoia after it was discovered that Phil Foster, a Sequoia executive, faced indictment for money laundering and bribery.

- Michael McCarthy, owner of ES&S (formerly known as American Information Systems), served as Senator Chuck Hagel's campaign manager in both the 1996 and 2002 elections. Senator Hagel (R–NE) owns close to $5 million in stock in the ES&S parent company. In 1996 and 2002, 80 percent of Senator Hagel's votes were counted by ES&S.

- Diebold, the most well-known of these three major groups, is under scrutiny for a memo that Diebold's CEO, Walden O'Dell, sent out promising Ohio's votes to Bush in the 2004 election. Beyond this faux pas, intra-office memos were circulated on the Internet stating that Diebold employees were aware of bugs within their systems and that the network is poorly guarded against hackers.

Diebold has now taken steps to use an outside organization, Scientific Applications International Corporation (SAIC) of San Diego, to take responsibility for security issues within their software. But this presents yet another conflict of interest. A majority of officials on the board are former members of either the Pentagon or the CIA, many of whom are closely allied with Defense Secretary Donald Rumsfeld. Members of the board of directors include:

- Army Gen. Wayne Downing, former chief counterterrorism expert on the National Security Council;

- former CIA Director Bobby Ray Inman;

- retired Adm. William Owens, who served as former vice chairman of the Joint Chiefs of Staff and who now sits on Donald Rumsfeld's Defense Policy Board;

- and Robert Gates, former director of the CIA and veteran of the Iran-Contra scandal.

THIS MODERN WORLD
by TOM TOMORROW

Additionally, SAIC has had a plethora of charges brought against them including indictments by the Justice Department for the mismanagement of a Superfund toxic cleanup and misappropriation of funds in the purchase of F-15 fighter jets.

Some of the most generous contributors to Republican campaigns are also some of the largest investors in ES&S, Sequoia, and Diebold. Most notable of these are government defense contractors Northrup Grumman, Lockheed Martin, Electronic Data Systems (EDS), and Accenture, a member of the U.S. Coalition of Service Industries and a major proponent of privatization and free trade of services provided by the World Trade Organization (WTO) and the General Agreement on Tariffs and Trade (GATT). None of these contractors are politically neutral, and all have high stakes in the construction of electronic voting systems. Accenture was involved in financial scandals and charged with incompetence in both Canada and the U.S. throughout the 1990s and 2000s.

Under the Help America Vote Act (HAVA) passed in October 2002, states have been required to submit plans to make the switch from punch cards to a primarily electronic system in time for the 2004 elections. It should be noted that the voting machine companies continue to hold title to the software—even after implementation. Populex, the company contracted to provide voting systems in Illinois has former Defense Secretary Frank Carlucci on its advisory board.

UPDATE BY MARK LEWELLEN-BIDDLE: I think this story concerns one of the most important issues of our time. From the beginning of the year, articles expressing concerns over the security of electronic voting machines and the lack of a verifiable paper trail have appeared in newspapers around the country as well as in mainstream magazines. Since nearly 50 million Americans will cast votes on electronic voting machines during the coming November elections, security and the verifiability of our

votes is undeniably important. I believe, however, that the ongoing debate, as necessary as it is, remains focused on peripheral issues.

Few, if any, of the authors are pursuing questions raised in the original article: why are IT companies and defense contractors so deeply involved in the movement to foist electronic voting machines onto not only the American electorate, but voters around the world? Why is there so much secrecy surrounding the companies who have designated themselves the certifiers of the security and reliability of electronic voting machines and software? Why is one of those self-designated testing centers, Wyle Labs, who recently admitted to certifying Sequoia software despite known flaws, still being allowed to certify voting software? If electronic voting is as safe and reliable as its proponents claim it to be, why did the Election Systems Task Force (Northrop Grumman, Lockheed Martin, EDS, and Accenture) deem it necessary to hire a high-powered Washington, DC-based lobbying firm (Information Technology Association of America) to convince us? One does not have to be conspiratorially bent to admit that these are intriguing questions.

Another issue that is receiving no public scrutiny is that by taking the control of the electoral process away from local officials and placing it in the hands of a very small number of for-profit corporations, we are effectively privatizing America's most public endeavor. After a recent election here in Lafayette using Diebold voting machines, I called election officials to ask some questions. One of them was, "Where were the votes counted?" The election official responded, "Right here; we count them ourselves." I asked how the votes were counted. Changing her tone to that of one instructing a third-grader, the official patiently explained to me that, "Each machine has a memory card that stores the votes. When the polls close, we bring all the cards back to headquarters and insert them into a machine and count the votes." Understanding full well that the official missed the irony of her words, I thanked her for her time, and hung up.

I first became interested in electronic voting machines when I read Bev Harris's *Black Box Voting*. It is an invaluable book for anyone concerned with the direction in which the American electoral process appears to be headed. Her Web site, <www.blackboxvoting.org/>, contains a wealth of information, as well as numerous links to other organizations working toward the development of open voting solutions.

7 Conservative Organization Drives Judicial Appointments

Source:
The American Prospect, Vol. 14, Issue 3, March 1, 2003
Title: "A Hostile Takeover: How the Federalist Society is Capturing the Federal Courts"
Author: Martin Garbus
Title: "Courts vs. Citizens"
Author: Jamin B. Raskin

Faculty Evaluators: Barbara Bloom, Ph.D. and Tony White, Ph.D.
Student Researcher: Liz Medley

In 2001, George W. Bush eliminated the longstanding role of the American Bar Association (ABA) in the evaluation of prospective federal judges. ABA's judicial ratings had long kept extremists from the right and left off the bench. In its place, Bush has been using The Federalist Society for Law and Public Policy Studies—a national organization whose mission is to advance a conservative agenda by moving the country's legal system to the right.

The Federalist Society was started in 1982 by a small group of radically conservative University of Chicago law students—Steven Calabresi, David McIntosh, and Lee Liberman Otis. Reagan's Attorney General Edwin Meese was an early sponsor of the society. The society today includes over 40,000 lawyers, judges, and law professors. Well-known members include: John Ashcroft, Solicitor General Theodore Olson, Supreme Court Justices Clarence Thomas and Antonin Scalia, Senate Judiciary Committee Chairman Orrin Hatch, and Federal Appellate Judge Frank Easterbrook. Under both Bush Administrations, "judicial appointments have been coordinated by the office of the [legal] counsel to the president." The counsel's staff is comprised mainly of federalists.

Journalist Jamin B. Raskin writes that traditional concerns about conservative judges are that they will fail to "protect the rights of political minorities from an attack by an overzealous majority." Raskin says the concern is now the opposite. These judges are a political minority undermining the "democratic rights of the people."

With the help of The Federalist Society, Bush has the capability to turn the courts over to ultra right-wing ideologues. The Federalists intend to control all federal circuit courts, which will be devoted to fulfilling the radical right's agenda on race, religion, class, money, morality, abortion, and power. Currently, anti-abortion judges control 7 of the 12 federal circuit courts.

Federal judges enjoy lifetime appointments, and approximately 40 percent of Bush appointees are members of The Federalist Society. The federal circuit courts are the spawning ground for Supreme Court nominees, and some of these judges will be given this highest of judicial nominations. In an attempt to ensure a continuation of a conservative agenda, Bush is appointing younger judges. Justice Scalia, who was 50 years old when appointed to the Supreme Court, has already served for 17 years. There has not been a vacancy on the Court for the past 11 years.

The Federalist Society, which heads this conservative judicial movement, has been very aggressive in attacking judges they do not agree with. Former Senator Bob Dole spoke out against 3rd Circuit Judge H. Lee Sarokin, placing him in a judicial "hall of shame" along with some of his colleagues. This hostility forced Sarokin to resign, saying, "I see my life's work and reputation being disparaged on an almost daily basis, and I find myself unable to ignore it."

One of the legal theories The Federalists are now operating under could make many federal regulations unconstitutional. Federalist Society publications, strategy sessions, and panel discussions attack cases that place individual rights above property rights, agencies that regulate business, and judges who seek to expand federal civil-rights laws and gender-equality protections. The Federalist Society sponsors "practice groups" to shape their policy. They have organized groups in areas such as religious liberty, national security, cyberspace, corporate law, and environmental law.

UPDATE BY MARTIN GARBUS: One of the most important issues in the country is the control of one of the three branches of government, the judiciary. While presidents and congressmen get elected every few years, judicial appointments are for life, and some federal court appointments have gone from 40 to 50 years. Our courts deal with nearly every aspect of our lives: work conditions and wages, schools, civil rights, affirmative action, crime and punishment, abortion, and the environment, among others.

Since the publication of my article, Bush tried to force through the most conservative group of nominees ever submitted by a president. He succeeded at times, but other appointments were rejected or stalled. Bush retaliated by making appointments while Congress was not in session. On May 18, 2004, a disastrous agreement was approved: Bush agreed not to make further recess appointments, and the Democrats agreed to let Bush have 25 "free" appointments.

There will, of course, be future books and articles about this subject. My book, *Courting Disaster*, is one of them. It examines the court from 1980 to the present. The best Web sites are those maintained by People for the American Way, <www.pfaw.org/>; the Alliance for Justice, <www.allianceforjustice.org/>; and the American Civil Liberties Union (ACLU), <www.aclu.org/>. The sole focus of the Alliance for Justice is to try and stop extreme conservative judicial nominations.

The article and the book in which it appeared drew a great deal of attention. One of the results was that I had a series of four debates with Ken Starr, the former independent prosecutor, on this and a number of other issues. I also did a good deal of television, radio, and other public speaking on the issue of judicial appointments.

 # Secrets of Cheney's Energy Task Force Come to Light

Sources:
Judicial Watch, July 17, 2003
Title: "Cheney Energy Task Force Documents Feature Map of Iraqi Oilfields"
Author: Judicial Watch staff

Foreign Policy in Focus (FPIF), January 2004
Title: "Bush-Cheney Energy Strategy: Procuring the Rest of the World's Oil"
Author: Michael Klare
Faculty Evaluators: James Carr, Ph.D. and Alexandra Von Meier, Ph.D.
Student Researchers: Cassie Cypher and Shannon Arthur

Documents turned over in the summer of 2003 by the Commerce Department concerning the activities of the Cheney Energy Task Force—as a result of the Sierra Club's and Judicial Watch's Freedom of Information Act (FOIA) lawsuit—contain a map of Iraqi oilfields, pipelines, refineries, and terminals, as well as two charts detailing Iraqi oil and gas projects and "Foreign Suitors for Iraqi Oilfield Contracts." The documents, dated March 2001, also feature maps of Saudi Arabian and United Arab Emirates oilfields, pipelines, refineries, and tanker terminals. There are supporting charts with details of the major oil and gas development projects in each country that provide information on the project's costs, capacity, oil company, and status or completion date.

Documented plans of occupation and exploitation predating September 11 confirm heightened suspicion that U.S. policy is driven by the dictates of the energy industry. According to Judicial Watch President Tom Fitton, "These documents show the importance of the Energy Task Force and why its operations should be open to the public."

When first assuming office in early 2001, President Bush's top foreign policy priority was not to prevent terrorism or to curb the spread of weapons of mass destruction—or any of the other goals he espoused later that year following 9/11. Rather, it was to increase the flow of petroleum from suppliers abroad to U.S. markets. In the months before he became president, the United States had experienced severe oil and natural gas shortages in many parts of the country, along with periodic electrical power blackouts in California. In addition, oil imports rose to more than 50 percent of total consumption for the first time in history, provoking great anxiety about the security of the country's long-term energy supply. Bush asserted that addressing the nation's "energy crisis" was his most important task as president.

The energy turmoil of 2000–2001 prompted Bush to establish a task force charged with developing a long-range plan to meet U.S. energy requirements. With the advice of his close friend and largest campaign contributor, Enron CEO Ken Lay, Bush picked Vice President Dick Cheney, former Halliburton CEO, to head this group. In 2001, the task force formulated the National Energy Policy (NEP), or Cheney Report, bypassing possibilities for energy independence and reduced oil consumption with a declaration of ambitions to establish new sources of oil.

The Bush Administration's struggle to keep secret the workings of Cheney's Energy Task Force has been ongoing since early in the president's tenure. The General Accounting Office, the investigative arm of Congress, requested information in spring of 2001 about which industry executives and lobbyists the task force was meeting with in developing the Bush Administration's energy plan. When Cheney refused disclosure, Congress was pressed to sue for the right to examine Task Force records, but lost. Later, amid political pressure building over improprieties regarding Enron's colossal collapse, Cheney's office released limited information revealing six Task Force meetings with Enron executives.

With multiple lawsuits currently pending, the Bush Administration asserts that its right to secrecy is a matter of executive privilege in regard to White House records. But because the White House staffed the task force with employees from the Department of Energy (DOE) and elsewhere, it cannot pretend that its documents are White House records. A 2001 case, in which the Justice Department has four times appealed federal court rulings that the vice president release task force records, has been brought before the Supreme Court. The case *Richard B. Cheney v. U.S. District Court for the District of Colombia*, No. 03-475, to be heard by Cheney's friend and duck hunting partner, Justice Scalia, is now pending. Cases based on the Federal Advisory Committee Act and Freedom of Information Act, which require the task force to have a balanced membership, open meetings, and public records, are attempting to beat the Bush Administration in its battle to keep its internal workings secret.

UPDATE BY MICHAEL KLARE: The issue of U.S. dependence on imported oil has only become more critical over the past few months as U.S. oil demand has risen and global supplies have contracted, pushing up gasoline prices in the U.S., and thereby threatening the economic recovery now (supposedly) under way. This, in turn, has made oil prices and dependency an issue in the presidential election, with President George W. Bush defending the status quo and Senator John Kerry (D–MA), the presumed Democratic nominee, calling for dramatic action to reduce U.S. dependence on imported petroleum.

The contraction of global supplies is due in large part to political turmoil in the major producing areas—precisely the sort of situation I predicted in my article. In particular, the pace of overseas oil production has been moderated by repeated sabotage of oil infrastructure in Iraq, terrorist strikes on foreign oil firms in Saudi Arabia, ethnic unrest in the Delta region of Nigeria, and continuing political turbulence in Venezuela. Together, these developments have pushed oil prices to their highest levels in decades. At the same time, the Bush Administration has shown no inclination to reduce U.S. military involvement in major overseas producing areas, especially the Persian Gulf, the Caspian Sea basin, and Africa.

All of this has had one effect: The major news media are beginning to pay much closer attention to the links between political turmoil abroad and the economics of oil at home. Most major newspapers, including *The New York Times* and the *Wall Street Journal*, have published articles on various aspects of this problem. Still, the media remains reluctant to explain the close link between the energy policies of the Bush Administration and U.S. military strategy.

A number of new books have come out (or soon will) that bear on this subject. My own book, *Blood and Oil: The Dangers and Consequences of America's Growing Petroleum Dependency*, will be published by Metropolitan Books in August 2004. Also highly recommended are *Out of Gas* by David Goodstein (W.W. Norton); *The End of Oil* by Paul Roberts (Houghton Mifflin); and *The Party's Over* by Richard Heinberg (New Society Publishers).

UPDATE BY PROJECT CENSORED: On June 24, 2004, the Supreme Court ruled by a vote of 7 to 2 not to order the release of Cheney's Energy Task Force records. Although this represents a major victory for the Bush Administration's claim to secrecy, the case, *Richard B. Cheney v. U.S. District Court for the District of Colombia*, No. 03-475, was sent back to the lower courts, setting the stage for further examination and federal litigation. The ruling does, however, assure that these records will remain closed until after the 2004 presidential election.

9 Widow Brings RICO Case Against U.S. Government for 9/11

Sources:
<scoop.co.nz>, November 2003
Title: "9/11 Victim's Wife Files RICO Case Against G.W. Bush"
Author: Philip J. Berg, Esq.

<scoop.co.nz>, December 2003
Title: "Widow's Bush Treason Suit Vanishes"
Author: W. David Kubiak

Faculty Evaluator: Andy Merrifield, Ph.D.
Student Researcher: Amelia Strommen

Ellen Mariani lost her husband, Louis Neil Mariani, on 9/11 and is refusing the government's million-dollar settlement offer. Louis Neil Mariani, a passenger, died when United Air Lines flight 175 was flown into the South Tower of the World Trade Center.

Ellen Mariani has studied the facts of the day for nearly two years and has come to believe that the White House "intentionally allowed 9/11 to happen" in order to launch the "war on terrorism." Her lawyer, Phillip Berg, former Deputy Attorney General of Pennsylvania, who filed a 62-page complaint in federal district court charging that President Bush and officials, including, but not limited to, Cheney, Rumsfeld, Rice, and Ashcroft: (1) had adequate foreknowledge of 9/11, yet failed to warn the country or attempt to prevent it; (2) have since been covering up the truth of that day; (3) have therefore abetted the murder of plaintiff's husband and violated the Constitution and multiple laws of the United States; and (4) are thus being sued under the Civil Racketeer Influenced and Corrupt Organizations (RICO) Act for malfeasant conspiracy, obstruction of justice and wrongful death.

Berg plans to call former federal employees with firsthand knowledge and expertise in military intelligence to provide a foundation for the RICO Act charge. Mariani intends to prove that the defendants have engaged in a "pattern of criminal activity and obstruction of justice" in violation of the public trust and laws of the United States, thrusting our nation into an endless war on terror in order to achieve personal and financial gains.

The suit documents the detailed forewarnings from foreign governments and FBI agents; the unprecedented delinquency of our air defense; the inexplicable half-hour dawdle of our commander in chief at a primary school after hearing the nation was under deadly attack; the incessant invocation of national security and executive privilege to suppress the facts; and the obstruction of all subsequent efforts to investigate the disaster. It concludes that compelling evidence will be presented in this case, through discovery, subpoena power and testimony, that defendants failed to act to prevent 9/11, knowing the attacks would lead to an international war on terror.

Berg believes that defendant Bush is invoking a long standard operating procedure of national security and executive privilege claims to suppress the basis of this lawsuit.

On November 26, 2003, a press conference was set up to discuss the full implications of these charges. Only Fox News attended the conference and taped 40 minutes; however, the film was never aired. Journalist W. David Kubiak asks, "When you present documented charges of official treachery behind the greatest national security disaster in modern history, and the press doesn't show, doesn't listen, and doesn't write, what is being communicated?"

UPDATE BY W. DAVID KUBIAK: Three thousand unresolved deaths, strong evidence of treason, and a horizon of endless war still remain matters of capital concern. To this date, the scenario of complicity alleged in Ellen Mariani's landmark RICO suit remains the most cogent and credible 9/11 narrative ever offered to an America raised on *Court TV*.

Her case lays out the facts and logic so clearly that even ordinary folks can "get it" and start waking up their own. That is this story's unique and mortal danger and the reason big media still shun it to this day.

The 9/11 Commission's maximal presumption of "failure" and "incompetence" spawns wildly more trivial questions than an inquest that does not rule out foreknowledge or complicity. The commission perforce dithers over policy issues, miscommunications, organizational defects, and a tragic litany of regrettable (but blameless!) bureaucratic mistakes.

Examining those same 9/11 facts from a detective's point of view—as an unsolved and as yet quite successful crime—exposes far deeper concerns. The prime questions now become prosecutorial and focus attention on the critical issues of motive, opportunity, and means. Who ultimately gained most from the attacks? Who had the power to commit, permit, or abet them? Who spotted or created the chance for them to occur?

Ellen's case is historic simply because it was the first to apply these obvious questions, especially "cui bono?"—who really profited?—to all the 9/11 news of recent years. Last summer, her reading of the official story's lies and contradictions sparked an unprecedented "racketeering!" shazam, but given her elemental *Law & Order* approach to the facts at hand, any country sheriff might have made the same call.

Today in light of this year's revelations from Paul O'Neill, Richard Clarke, and Sibel Edmonds, Ellen's early attempts at connecting the dots—between the war-hungry neoconservatives' public longing (in September 2000) for "some catastrophic and catalyzing event, like a new Pearl Harbor" and the subsequent ignored warnings, quashed inquiries, and crippled air defenses that finally made their dream come true—all appear pattern perfect thus far.

Since Ellen's charges imply not just criminal conspiracy, but also literal treason, they are fast reviving a long ailing impeachment debate. An April 2004 national Retro Poll showed that 39 percent of the public favored a Bush impeachment if only for his Iraq war lies. This growth of popular outrage was remarkable, but hardly actionable because Impeachment Articles must issue from the same feckless House of Representatives that signed off on the war. However, as Bush's polls and credibility continued to plummet and GOP solons watched his coattails turn to lead, it became more plausible that a survivalist few might recognize that in 9/11 at least, they shared no collective guilt and might be more willing to swap doomed leaders for their own electoral skins.

By May 2004, such intuitions were starting to bubble up in the antiwar zeitgeist, partially inspired by loud 9/11 truth demands from Ed Asner, Howard Zinn, the U.S. Green Party, theologian David Ray Griffin, and Commission-disillusioned victim family groups. These lofty calls were further reinforced by rather amazing facts on the ground. On May 26, the *Toronto* Star reported on a national poll showing that 63 percent of Canadians believed the U.S. government had "prior knowledge of the plans for September 11, and failed to take appropriate action."

To galvanize this awareness into action, movement leaders turned to Ellen's RICO suit as an ideal impeachment template because it could flush the entire puppeteer crew and not just Howdy Dubya from the stage. It also held the promise of a national "teachable moment" as the whole military-petro-industrial backdrop of the crime at last heaved into view. Finally, 9/11 impeachment offered progressives a far more energizing course of Bush-lethal action than half-hearted huzzahs for the stay-the-course mantra and globalization banzais of the Kerry campaign.

All of this ferment will doubtless be peaking as *Censored 2005* hits the stands. If you want to join in and help remake history, first read David Ray Griffin's *The New Pearl Harbor* or Nafeez Mosaddeq Ahmed's *The War on Freedom*. Then check in at <www.911Truth.org/>, and find something patriotic (in the old sense) to do.

UPDATE BY PHILIP J. BERG, ESQ.: The tragedy of 9/11 is the most significant event of our lifetimes. It is a great honor for this story to be selected. It is our firm belief that the RICO lawsuit we filed is one of the most significant cases in our history. To date, the Bush Administration has done more to diminish individual rights than any other administration in 225 years. With the enactment of the Stabilization Act and Patriot Act I, the attempted enactment of Patriot Act II, the photographing and fingerprinting of individuals entering the United States from certain countries and the planned "color coding" of everyone in the United States by the summer of 2004, "1984" is becoming a reality today, 20 years after the date it was projected. 9/11 has provided the pretext for the global military expansion we are seeing today, with its enormous costs in lives, federal funding, and environmental damage.

After speaking around the country, we have found that people are amazed at the lack of media coverage of the RICO lawsuit filed on behalf of Ellen Mariani and all law-abiding citizens of the United States and the world. The mainstream press has ignored our RICO lawsuit as well as most aspects of 9/11 until recently. But Bush's arrogance in placing pictures of 9/11 in his reelection ads, along with the continued stonewalling of and the ineffectiveness of the 9/11 Commission has now brought this story to the forefront.

RICO was created in the 1960s by Congress to go after the mafia, the mob. It is our position that there is a "mob" in the Bush White House. When the events of 9/11 are investigated and when the right questions are posed, there is no way to avoid the conclusion that 9/11 occurred with the complicity of Bush and his administration.

The RICO lawsuit is the best available vehicle for bringing all of the overwhelming, independent research concerning 9/11 to the point where the truth of 9/11 will be revealed.

During the six months since the RICO lawsuit was filed, we have been involved in procedural issues. We have therefore withdrawn the case from Philadelphia and re-filed it in federal court in Washington, DC, so that the events of 9/11 can be in front of the court as soon as possible.

Our updated Web site, <www.911forthetruth.com/>, can be reviewed daily for developments in the RICO lawsuit. Our petition, available on the Web site, is important for two reasons: 1) signing it shows support for the truth of 9/11; and 2) more important, reading the comments from the hearts of individuals around the world serves—like the writings of Anne Frank—to help people realize the actual effects of 9/11. We feel it is essential for the mainstream and independent media to report the truth of 9/11, the most important event of our lifetimes. It must be revealed now, not for 40 years from now, as has occurred with other major events in history.

Other pro-active groups where the RICO lawsuit is referenced, include <www.truth.org>, <www.visibility.org>, <www.septembereleventh.org>, <www.digitalstylecreations.com>, <www.tomflocco.com>, <www.cooperativeresearch.org>, <www.911citizenswatch.org>, <www.911independentcommission.org>, <www.fromthewilderness.com>, <www.unansweredquestions.org>, <www.askquestions.org>, and <www.scoop.co.nz>.

Additional resources include *INSIDE JOB: Unmasking the Conspiracies of 9/11* by Jim Marrs (with a preface by Ellen Mariani and with major excerpts from the

Mariani RICO filing in the appendix); <www.InsideJob-911.com>; *The New Pearl Harbor: Disturbing Questions about the Bush Administration and 9/11* by David Ray Griffin.

 **New Nuke Plants: Taxpayers Support, Industry Profits**

Sources:
Nuclear Information and Resource Service, November 17, 2003
Title: "Nuclear Energy Would Get $7.5 Billion in Tax Subsides, U.S. Taxpayers Would Fund Nuclear Monitor Relapse If Energy Bill Passes"
Authors: Cindy Folkers and Michael Mariotte

WISE/NIRS Nuclear Monitor, August 2003
Title: "U.S. Senate Passes Pro-Nuclear Energy Bill"
Authors: Cindy Folkers and Michael Mariotte

Faculty Evaluators: Lynn Cominsky, Ph.D. and Tamara Falicov, Ph. D.
Student Researchers: Andrea Martini and John Hernandez

Senator Peter Domenici (R–NM), along with the Bush Administration, is looking to give the nuclear power industry a huge boost through the new Energy Policy Act. The Domenici-sponsored bill will give nuclear power plants a production credit for each unit of energy produced. This provision, costing taxpayers an estimated $7.5 billion, will be used to build six new privately owned, for-profit, reactors across the country. This is in addition to the $4 billion already provided for other nuclear energy programs.

Through the Energy Policy Act, Senator Domenici intends to create more incentives for nuclear power. It gives $1.1 billion for the production of hydrogen fuel and $2.7 billion for research and development of new reactors under the Nuclear Power 2010 program. The Nuclear Power 2010 program is a joint government/industry effort to identify sites for new nuclear power plants and develop advanced nuclear technologies. In 2003, Congress approved an amendment to the Senate energy legislation, giving approximately $35 million to the Nuclear Power 2010 program. The program's aim is to advance and expand the nuclear industry's Vision 2020 policy, which has, as its goal, the addition of 50,000 megawatts of atomic power generation (i.e. 50 new reactors) by the year 2020. Toward this effort, the bill provides new regulations and subsidies to promote private sector investment by 2005 in order to get new power plants deployed in the U.S. by 2010.

Total capital investment for a new nuclear reactor could be in excess of $1.6 billion. The bill, which is up for vote in Congress, will establish a "preferred equity investment" provision requiring taxpayers to back private investment in new facilities up to $200 million. The nuclear power bill provides a set volume at which the government will buy power from nuclear companies. Nuclear companies would charge the government 50 percent above the market price, and the government would in turn resell the power to taxpayers at higher than normal rates to make up for the difference.

Domenici's bill will allow leach mining of uranium and push for more uranium enrichment facilities, maintaining that they are necessary for energy production. Although a new revision of the bill addresses some of the environmental concerns of a number of senators, the charge is that this has been done simply to push the nuclear program forward. The new bill still allows depleted uranium to be treated as "low-level" waste and requires the Department of Energy (DOE) to take possession and dispose of waste generated at privately owned facilities (at no cost to the owner). The bill makes it easy to construct enrichment facilities by speeding up the process and easing Environmental Protection Agency regulations.

The Energy Policy Act's promotion of enrichment facilities is likely to benefit Louisiana Energy Services, which is run by a European corporation, Erenco. This corporation has made unsuccessful attempts to build private uranium enrichment plants in Louisiana and Tennessee and is looking to get a license to build an enrichment plant in New Mexico, Domenici's home state.

Finally, the bill will repeal a ban on exporting highly enriched uranium to other countries, ignoring provisions made in the House that protect against terrorist attacks. The chance that nuclear bomb material could fall into terrorist hands would be much increased with an open market for highly enriched uranium. Also, more reactors in the United States provide terrorists with more targets. The current administration supports the expansion of nuclear energy, yet has made no attempt to provide for its safety or oversight under Homeland Security legislation.

UPDATE BY CINDY FOLKERS AND MICHAEL MARIOTTE: The 2003–2004 Bush energy bill has continued to stall in the Senate despite use of several convoluted legislative procedures to pass it. This legislation was born from the secretive Cheney Energy Task Force meetings, which have been the focus of much legal action. The secrecy of this task force is renowned and is yet another attempt by the Bush Administration to cut off the public from government access. The energy industry trade organization, Nuclear Energy Institute, met with the task force more times than any other single energy interest. It is no surprise that the bill is loaded with tax breaks, subsidies and policy initiatives for old energy sources, giving very little to energy efficiency or renewable energy efforts. This is an energy policy more suitable for 1960 and lacks vision and any foundation for our energy independence.

Through the relentless efforts of the Nuclear Information and Resource Service (NIRS) and many other national and local activists and environmental groups, the Energy Bill (H.R. 6) was defeated on November 21, 2003 by a cloture vote of 57-40. Bill proponents could not overcome a filibuster supported by both Republicans and Democrats. The many controversial provisions contained in H.R. 6, including the $6 billion to $15 billion tax production credit for new nuclear reactors, made it unpopular among both parties. In total, there was more to hate about this bill than to like and it couldn't even be brought to the floor for a final vote.

In 2004` Senator Domenici introduced the energy bill again as S. 2095. This bill had changed very little from the original legislation. The notable exception is that the nuclear tax production credits (PTC) were excluded. Nevertheless, the bill still did not have the support to pass the Senate, so Domenici decided to split the bill in two, attempting to pass the policy and tax sections separately. NIRS is now in the process of opposing these two bills. The policy portion of the bill has failed at this point, but the tax portion of S. 2095 could still pass as an amendment to another bill. Again, the nuclear PTC is not part of this energy tax package, but Domenici has threatened to add it separately. This tax credit will amount to at least $6 billion and could reach as much as $15 or even $19 billion, according to estimates by EarthTrack.

Throughout this entire process, the press has covered the overall bill, especially controversial MTBE-related provisions, and numerous newspapers have taken strong editorial stands against it. However, virtually without exception, these stories are/were woefully silent on the bill's nuclear provisions. Since the PTC could be upwards of $15 billion in total cost, it deserves the spotlight as yet another amazing giveaway to the nuclear industry, this time to initiate a nuclear resurgence with taxpayer-supported construction of new reactors.

For more information, contact NIRS, 1424 16th Street, NW, Suite 404, Washington, DC 20036; Tel: (202) 328-0002; Web site: <www.nirs.org>; E-mail: <nirsnet@ nirs.org>. Alternatively, contact Public Citizen's Critical Mass Energy and Environment Program, 215 Pennsylvania Avenue, SE, Washington, DC 20003, Tel: (202) 546-4996; Web site: <www.citizen.org/cmep>.

11 The Media Can Legally Lie

Sources:

CMW Report, Spring 2003
Title: "Court Ruled That Media Can Legally Lie"
Author: Liane Casten

Organic Consumer Association, March 7, 2004
Title: "Florida Appeals Court Orders Akre-Wilson Must Pay Trial Costs
for $24.3 Billion Fox Television; Couple Warns Journalists of Danger
to Free Speech, Whistleblower Protection"
Author: None Listed

Faculty Evaluator: Liz Burch, Ph.D.
Student Researcher: Sara Brunner

In February 2003, a Florida Court of Appeals unanimously agreed with an assertion by Fox News that there is no rule against distorting or falsifying the news in the United States.

Back in December of 1996, Jane Akre and her husband, Steve Wilson, were hired by Fox as a part of the Fox "Investigators" team at WTVT in Tampa Bay, Florida. In 1997, the team began work on a story about bovine growth hormone (BGH), a controversial substance manufactured by Monsanto Corporation. The couple produced a four-part series revealing that there were many health risks related to BGH and that Florida supermarket chains did little to avoid selling milk from cows treated with the hormone, despite assuring customers otherwise.

According to Akre and Wilson, the station was initially very excited about the series. But within a week, Fox executives and their attorneys wanted the reporters to use statements from Monsanto representatives that the reporters knew were false and to make other revisions to the story that were in direct conflict with the facts. Fox editors then tried to force Akre and Wilson to continue to produce the distorted story. When they refused and threatened to report Fox's actions to the FCC, they were both fired (*Censored* #12, 1997).

Akre and Wilson sued the Fox station and on August 18, 2000, a Florida jury unanimously decided that Akre was wrongfully fired by Fox Television when she refused to broadcast (in the jury's words) "a false, distorted, or slanted story" about the widespread use of BGH in dairy cows. They further maintained that she deserved protection under Florida's whistleblower law. Akre was awarded a $425,000 settlement. Inexplicably, however, the court decided that Steve Wilson, her partner in the case, was ruled *not* wronged by the same actions taken by Fox.

Fox appealed the case, and on February 14, 2003 the Florida Second District Court of Appeals unanimously overturned the settlement awarded to Akre. The Court held that Akre's threat to report the station's actions to the FCC did not deserve protection under Florida's whistleblower statute, because Florida's whistleblower law states that an employer must violate an adopted "law, rule, or regulation." In a stunningly narrow interpretation of FCC rules, the Florida Appeals court claimed that the FCC policy against falsification of the news does not rise to the level of a "law, rule, or regulation"; it was simply a "policy." Therefore, it is up to the station whether or not it wants to report honestly.

During their appeal, Fox asserted that there are no written rules against distorting news in the media. They argued that, under the First Amendment, broadcasters have the right to lie or deliberately distort news reports on public airwaves. Fox attorneys did not dispute Akre's claim that they pressured her to broadcast a false story; they simply maintained that it was their right to do so. After the appeal verdict, WTVT general manager Bob Linger commented, "It's vindication for WTVT, and we're very pleased… It's the case we've been making for two years. She never had a legal claim."

UPDATE BY LIANE CASTEN: If we needed any more proof that we now live in an upside down world, the saga of Jane Akre, along with her husband, Steve Wilson, could not be more compelling.

Akre and Wilson won the first legal round, and in the process, they also won the prestigious "Goldman Environmental" prize for their outstanding efforts. However, Fox appealed the verdict and won. In the appeal, the court implied there was no restriction against distorting the truth. Technically, there was no violation of the news distortion because the FCC's policy of news distortion does not have the weight of the law. Thus, said the court, Akre-Wilson never qualified as whistleblowers.

What is more appalling than this stunning reversal is that the five major media outlets filed briefs of Amici Curiae—or friend of Fox—to support Fox's position: Belo Corporation; Cox Television, Inc.; Gannett Co., Inc.; Media General Operations, Inc.; and Post-Newsweek Stations, Inc. Their statement said, "The station argued that it simply wanted to ensure that a news story about a scientific controversy regarding a commercial product was present with *fairness and balance*, and to ensure that it had a sound defense to any potential defamation claim."

"Fairness and balance?" Monsanto hardly demonstrated "fairness and balance" when it threatened a lawsuit and demanded the elimination of important, verifiable information!

The Amici position was that "if upheld by this court, the decision would convert personnel actions arising from disagreements over editorial policy into litigation battles in which state courts would interpret and apply federal policies that raise significant and delicate constitutional and statutory issues." After all, Amici argued, 40 states now have whistleblower laws; imagine what would happen if employees in those 40 states followed the same course of action?

The position implies that First Amendment rights belong to the employers—in this case, the five power media groups. And when convenient, the First Amendment becomes a broad shield to hide behind. Let's not forget, however; *the airwaves belong to the people*. Is there no public interest left while these media giants make their private fortunes using the public airwaves? Can corporations have the power to influence the media reporting, even at the expense of the truth? Apparently so.

In addition, the five "friends" referred to FCC policies. The five admit they are "vitally interested in the outcome of this appeal, which will determine the extent to which state whistleblower laws may incorporate federal policies that touch on sensitive questions of editorial judgment."

Anyone concerned with media must hear the alarm bells. The Bush FCC, under Michael Powell's leadership, has shown repeatedly that greater media consolidation is encouraged, that liars like Rush Limbaugh and Ann Coulter are perfectly acceptable, that to refer to the FCC interpretation of "editorial judgment" is to potentially throw out any pretense at editorial accuracy if the "accuracy" harms a large corporation and its bottom line. This is our "Brave New Media," the corporate media that protects its friends and now lies, unchallenged if need be.

The next assault: The Fox station then filed a series of motions in a Tampa Circuit Court seeking more than $1.7 million in trial fees and costs from both Akre and Wilson. Motions were filed on March 30 and April 16, 2003 by Fox attorney William McDaniels—who bills his client at $525 to $550 an hour. The costs are to cover legal fees and trial costs incurred by Fox in defending itself at the first trial. The issue may be heard by the original trial judge, Ralph Steinberg—a logical step in the whole process. However, Judge Steinberg must come out of retirement if he is to hear this, so the hearing, set for June 1, may go to a new judge, Judge Maye.

Akre and her husband feel the stress. "There is no justification for the five stations not to support us," she said. "Attaching legal fees to whistleblowers is unprecedented, absurd. The 'business' of broadcasting trumps it all. These news organizations must ensure they are worthy of the public trust while they use *our* airwaves, free of charge. Public trust is alarmingly absent here."

Indeed. This is what our corporate media, led by such as Rupert Murdoch, have come to. How low we have fallen.

Jane Akre can be reached at: <jakre@bellsouth.net>.

12 The Destabilization of Haiti

Sources:

Flashpoints, April 1, 2004
Title: "Interview with Aristide's Lawyer, Brian Concannon"
Reporter: Dennis Bernstein

<globalresearch.ca>, February 29, 2004
Title: "The Destabilization of Haiti"
Author: Michel Chossudovsky

Dollars and Sense, September/October 2003
Title: "Still Up Against the Death Plan in Haiti"
Author: Tom Reeves

Democracy Now!, March 17, 2004
Title: "Aristide Talks with *Democracy Now!* About the Leaders of the Coup and U.S. Funding of the Opposition in Haiti"
Reporter: Amy Goodman

Associated Press, March 16, 2004
Title: "Aristide Backers Left Out of Coalition"
Author: Ian James

Faculty Evaluators: Tony White, Ph.D. and Richard Zimmer, Ph.D.
Student Researchers: Brooke Finley and Jocelyn Boreta

On February 29, 2004, President Jean-Bertrand Aristide was forced into exile by American military. While the Bush Administration and the corporate press implied that Aristide left willingly, Aristide was able to give a detailed account of his kidnapping by the American military to a Haitian journalist in the United States via cell phone, who in turn, broadcast his speech on Pacifica Radio's *Flashpoints* on KPFA. While the U.S. was forced to acknowledge the kidnapping allegations, they were quick to discredit them and deny responsibility. The circumstances underlying the current situation in Haiti, as well as the history of U.S. involvement, is being ignored by U.S. officials and mainstream media.

In 1990, after the brutal 15-year rule of dictator "Baby Doc" Duvalier, 70 percent of Haiti's people voted for Aristide in their first democratic election. During his first term, Aristide began to make good on his populist platform, revising the tax code to require import fees and income-based taxation on the rich and pressing for an increase in the minimum wage. He was, however, soon under pressure from International Financial Institutions (IFIs) and the U.S. Agency for International Development (USAID) to reverse these proposals. A few months later, Aristide was overthrown by the rebel paramilitary army known as the Front for the Advancement and Progress of Haiti (FRAPH). FRAPH had been trained and sponsored by the CIA. In fact, several FRAPH leaders were on the CIA payroll.

During the coup period, from 1991–1994, Aristide's 1990 presidential opponent, former World Bank official Marc Bazin, was appointed prime minister by the military junta, and the exploitation and terrorization of the country continued as it had during the Duvalier period. Under Bazin, 4,000 civilians were executed, and more than 60,000 refugees fled. It was in this context of CIA-supported FRAPH killings that Bazin became a poster boy for World Bank, International Monetary Fund (IMF), and Washington Consensus policies.

With the help of the Clinton Administration, Aristide returned to his position as president of Haiti in 1994. His return was conditional, based on his support of IMF and World Bank proposals implemented during his years in exile. During that time, Haiti had racked up huge amounts of external debt and was forced to turn to the IMF and World Bank for loans. In response, the IMF formed the "Economic Recovery Program." Supposedly intended to help Haiti get back on its feet, the program instead imposed a budget reform program that reduced the size of Haiti's civil service and ultimately led to the collapse of Haiti's state system. Aristide served until the end of his presidential term in 1996.

Aristide was reelected in Haiti's 2000 presidential elections, the same year that George W. Bush entered office. Aristide won with 92 percent of the vote in an election declared free and fair by the Organization of American States (OAS), of which the U.S. is a member. However, shortly after Bush's own tainted election, his administration questioned the election of seven senators from Aristide's Fanmi Lavalas party. Despite the resignation of the senators, the Bush Administration used these inflated allegations to justify the withdrawal of $512 million in Inter-American Development Bank loans to Haiti. The Administration pressured the World Bank, the IMF, and the European Union to follow with reduction of other planned assistance.

While obstructing aid and loans, the U.S. spent millions to fund the "Democratic Platform of Civil Society Organizations and Opposition Political Parties." The Democratic Platform, developed by the National Endowment for Democracy (NED) and funded by the International Republican Institute, combines the "Democratic Convergence" (DC) and "The Group of 184 Civil Society Organizations" (G-184) in opposition to the Aristide's government. The DC consists of 200 small political organizations ranging from Maoists to free-market liberals and ultra-right-wing Duvalierists, who refuse participation in electoral processes and who are responsible for violent attacks on the Haitian government. The G-184 is a group of civil society organizations headed by Andre Apaid, U.S. citizen and owner of Alpha Industries, one of Haiti's largest cheap labor exporters producing for a number of U.S. firms including IBM, Sperry/Unisys, Remington, and Honeywell.

Following the forced removal of Aristide, the National Liberation and Reconstruction Front, the new paramilitary group comprised of former FRAPH members, is now collaborating with the Democratic Platform in the form of neoliberal structural adjustment. Their intent is to assist "civilian" political parties and non-governmental organizations (NGOs) with the installation of American style democracy/corporate domination. Incidentally, NED also provided funds to the "Democratic Coordination," another "civil society organization" based in Venezuela, which initiated the attempted coup against President Hugo Chavez.

These opposition groups, funded, trained, and supplied by U.S. forces, are waging a Contra-style war against Haiti. The new government, led by Interim Prime Minister Gerard Latortue, is made up of human rights criminals, drug dealers, and thugs involved in the 1990 and 2004 insurrections. A consistent and systematic campaign of terror and violence is being carried out by the likes of Guy Philippe, Louis Jodel Chamblain, and Jean Tatoune. Philippe, a drug dealer and former police chief, plucked from the Haitian army to be specially trained by U.S. forces in Ecuador, organized the Haitian opposition from the Dominican Republic where he was required to check in with the CIA two to three times a month. Chamblain, former number-two man in FRAPH, sentenced twice for murder and convicted in the 1994 Raboteau massacre and in the 1993 assassination of democracy-activist Antoine Izmery, joins Philippe to lead seminars on "democratic" opposition with machine guns slung over their shoulders. Tatoune, another FRAPH leader also convicted of massacre in Raboteau and identified by victims as having shot several civilians, arrived in an U.S. helicopter to stand next to the de facto prime minister as a "freedom fighter."

While Haiti's economy was bankrupted by IMF reforms, the narcotics transshipment trade still thrives. As the hub of Caribbean drug traffic, important in the transport of cocaine from Colombia to the U.S., Haiti is responsible for an estimated 14 percent of all cocaine entering the U.S. The CIA protected this trade during the Duvalier era as well as during the military dictatorship of 1991–1994. The money from the drug transshipment trade flows out of Haiti to criminal intermediaries in the wholesale and retail trade, to the intelligence agencies, which protect the trade, and to the financial and banking institutions where the proceeds are laundered. Wall

Street and European banks have a vested interest in installing "democracy" in order to protect investment in Haiti's transshipment trade routes.

Since Bush Sr.'s presidency, the U.S. has worked hard to forge an opposition against Aristide and his administration. This opposition has been fueled by Aristide's refusal to privatize Haiti's public enterprises and his increase of the minimum wage. When Aristide returned to Haiti in 1994, U.S. officials expected that many of its public enterprises (the telephone company, electrical company, airport, port, three banks, a cement factory, and a flour mill) would be sold to private corporations, preferably U.S. multinationals working in partnership with the Haitian elite. Aristide refused, prompting the withdrawal of $500 million in promised international aid. In February 2003, Aristide moved, again against strong opposition from the business sector, to double the minimum wage. This increase affected more than 20,000 assembly line workers contracted by corporations such as Disney and Wal-Mart.

Haiti's government worked for alternatives to neoliberal development, corporate domination, and essentially U.S. hegemony, joining with the Caribbean Community (CARICOM) to form a trade bloc against the Free Trade Area of the Americas (FTAA) and other initiatives. They established cooperative projects with Venezuela and Cuba, securing regular shipments of oil from Venezuela at very reduced prices and substantial medical assistance from Cuba. CARICOM has called for an investigation into the abduction of President Aristide, and President Hugo Chavez has offered Aristide asylum in Venezuela. After two weeks exile in the Central African Republic, Aristide has been granted temporary asylum in Jamaica, only about 130 miles from Haiti.

UPDATE BY LYN DUFF AND DENNIS BERNSTEIN: For an update on this story, please see Chapter 10, "Haiti: The Untold Story." Dennis Bernstein is executive producer of Pacifica Radio's *Flashpoints* (KPFA in Berkeley, California). Lyn Duff (E-mail: <lynduff@aol.com>) is a writer currently based in Jerusalem. She traveled to Haiti in 1995 to help establish that country's first children's radio station. She is writing a book on Haiti. This story was written on March 19, 2004.

13 Schwarzenegger Met with Enron's Ken Lay Years Before the California Recall

Sources:
Common Dreams, August 17, 2003
Title: "Ahnuld, Ken Lay, George Bush, Dick Cheney, and Gray Davis"
Author: Jason Leopold

The Observer (London), October 6, 2003
Title: "Arnold Unplugged—It's Hasta la Vista to $9 Billion"
Author: Greg Palast

Additional Sources:
San Francisco Chronicle and *Common Dreams*, October 11, 2003
Title: "Schwarzenegger Electricity Plan Fuels Fears of Another Debacle"
Author: Zachary Coile

San Francisco Chronicle, May 26, 2001
Title: "Enron's Secret Bid to Save Deregulation: Private Meeting With Prominent Californians"
Authors: Christian Berthelsen, Scott Winokur, and *Chronicle* Staff Writers

Faculty Evaluators: Laurie Dawson and John Lund
Student Researchers: Karina Pinon, Chris Bui, and Josh Sisco

Arnold Schwarzenegger's "solutions to California's energy woes" reflect those of former Enron chief Ken Lay. On May 17, 2001, in the midst of California's energy crisis, which was largely caused by Enron's scandalous energy market manipulation, Schwarzenegger met with Lay to discuss "fixing" California's energy crisis. Plans to "get deregulation right this time" called for more rate increases, an end to state and federal investigations, and less regulation. While California Governor Gray Davis and Lieutenant Governor Cruz Bustamante were taking direct action to re-regulate California's energy and get back the $9 billion that was vacuumed out of California by Enron and other energy companies, Schwarzenegger was being groomed to overthrow Davis in the recall, thus canceling plans to re-regulate and recoup the $9 billion.

After the California's energy debacle of 2000, Davis and Bustamante filed suit under California's unique Civil Code provision 17200, the "Unfair Business Practices Act," which would order all power companies, including Enron, to repay the nearly $9 billion they extorted from California citizens. The single biggest opponent of the suit, with the most to lose, was Enron's CEO, Ken Lay. Lay, a very close friend and longtime associate of President Bush and Vice President Cheney and one of their largest campaign contributors, hastily assembled a meeting with prominent Californians (confirmed by the release of 34 pages of internal Enron e-mail) to strategize opposition to the Davis-Bustamante campaign and garner influential support for energy deregulation.

Included in the meeting were Michael Milken, the "junk bond king" convicted of fraud in 1990 who currently runs a think tank in Santa Monica that focuses on global and regional economies; Ray Irani, chief executive of Occidental Petroleum; former Los Angeles Mayor Richard Riordan; and movie star Arnold Schwarzenegger. (Riordan and Schwarzenegger were at that time being courted as GOP gubernatorial candidates.)

Attendees of the meeting received a small four-page packet entitled "Comprehensive Solution for California." The packet called for an end to the federal and state investigations into Enron's role in California's energy crisis and proposed saddling consumers with the $9 billion loss. Discussions further focused on preventing Davis's proposed re-regulation of energy markets.

With Davis in office and Bustamante his natural successor, there would be little chance of dismissing rock-solid charges of fraudulent reporting of sales transactions, fake power delivery scheduling, and blatant conspiracy. The grooming of a governor amenable to a laissez-faire and corrupt energy market was essential. Recalling Davis and replacing him with Schwarzenegger was the solution. With Governor Schwarzenegger in office, Bustamante's case is dead, as few judges will let a case go to trial to protect a state whose governor has allowed the matter to be "settled."

Governor Schwarzenegger is currently preparing a push to deregulate California's electricity markets with an energy strategy driven by some of the same members of former Governor Pete Wilson's team who led the push for energy deregulations in the 1990s. Consumer groups are warning that the governor's proposals would expose electricity users to greater fluctuations in prices while limiting state oversight of power trading—a combination that could allow the type of market manipulation that plagued California during the state's energy crisis of 2000–2001. "Deregulation has already cost the state $50 billion, give or take," said Mike Florio, senior attorney for the Utility Reform Network. "Why on earth anyone would want to do that again is mystifying to us."

UPDATE BY JASON LEOPOLD: There's a certain amount of prejudice the mainstream media has toward investigative news stories that are published by alternative news outlets. News stories appearing in alternative publications are often dismissed or ignored by major news outlets as the work of conspiracy theorists, to cite just one example.

Often times, reporters for major newspapers never bother to follow up on a story printed in an alternative publication because, the way they see it, if it was that important it would have appeared in a bigger publication. Such was the case with the Arnold Schwarzenegger/Enron/George Bush/Dick Cheney story, which I wrote about in August 2001 while Schwarzenegger was campaigning for governor of California.

There were one or two major newspapers that made scant reference to the secret meeting Schwarzenegger attended in May 2001 at the Peninsula Hotel in Beverly Hills with Ken Lay, the disgraced former chairman of Enron, the energy company that exploited California's electricity market for financial gain. Schwarzenegger was tapped by Lay because of his celebrity clout in addition to the fact that he was being courted by Republicans to replace Davis as governor.

But those publications failed to put the timing of the meeting into context. Had they done so, it may have saved Gray Davis's job. If they dug a little deeper, they would have found that while Schwarzenegger listened to Lay's pitch on why California shouldn't abandon deregulation, one energy company was nailed by federal energy regulators for shutting down its power plants to create an artificial shortage and boost wholesale prices in the state. The discovery, however, was kept secret by federal energy regulators so Vice President Dick Cheney could release his National Energy Policy in May 2001. Had federal energy regulators released the evidence of the manipulation that took place in California it would have certainly derailed Cheney's energy policy because it called for deregulating energy markets nationwide.

However, while Schwarzenegger shook hands with Ken Lay, former Governor Gray Davis was lobbying President Bush and Cheney for price controls on soaring electricity prices. Bush and Cheney publicly blamed Davis for the crisis, saying he was too slow to act and dismissed his claims about an energy cartel manipulating the state's power market. That, in part, skewed public opinion and left many in the state thinking that the crisis was Davis's fault.

Two years later, following Enron's bankruptcy, however, evidence emerged proving Davis was right. Energy companies were manipulating the market and were responsible for skyrocketing prices and blackouts. After I connected the dots, showing how Schwarzenegger allowed himself to be courted by Lay, I asked him about the meeting at the Peninsula Hotel. Schwarzenegger said he didn't remember.

But now, three years to the day after he left the Peninsula with the outline Lay handed him for keeping deregulation in place, Schwarzenegger is implementing Lay's vision. In late April, the new governor sent a proposal to the state's Public Utilities Commission urging regulators to reopen California's power market to competition.

Since this story was published, Reliant Energy was indicted by federal prosecutors for manipulating the California electricity market, the first criminal charges ever brought against a corporation related to the 2000–2001 energy crisis.

California's energy woes are of particular importance today because the state's grid operator is forecasting a shortage of electricity in the summer of 2004 if unusually high heat blankets the state, which is exactly what the National Weather Service predicted in early 2004. For consumer groups, hot weather combined with a free market is a recipe for disaster. They fear that a heat wave will force electricity prices through the roof in a competitive market and that there aren't enough safeguards in place to protect consumers from another round of manipulation.

Attorney General Bill Lockyer agrees. In April 2004, Lockyer published a 96-page report saying that California's power market is still ripe for manipulation. Schwarzenegger, meanwhile, won't heed the warnings. He's surrounded himself with a who's who of special interests to advise him on energy policy. But Schwarzenegger's aides won't reveal the identity of the people advising the governor on his energy plan. In a page pulled straight out of President Bush and Dick Cheney's playbook on government secrecy, Schwarzenegger's aides have refused to disclose the names of the individuals who helped write the governor's energy plan, the one that was sent to the state's Public Utilities Commission in April 2004. The aides claim that the governor met with consumer groups before drafting the state's energy policy, but the state's three leading consumer groups, all of which have been at the forefront of the energy debate since 1999, have never spoken with Schwarzenegger or his staff. The governor's aides won't say which consumer groups he met with or how many meetings he had. Not surprisingly, the consumer groups oppose the governor's energy policy because it benefits big business at the expense of consumers and puts the state in a vulnerable position again.

For more information on this topic, the following Web sites are extremely useful. Consumer groups that have been on top of the energy story include: The Foundation for Taxpayer and Consumer Rights, <www.ftcr.org>; The Utility Reform Network, <www.turn.org>; and The Utility Consumers Action Network, <www.ucan.org>. These government agencies publish the most up-to-date news on the state's energy issues: The California Public Utilities Commission, <www.cpuc.ca.gov> and The California Independent System Operator, <www.caiso.com>. To monitor the state's refund issue, see The Federal Energy Regulatory Commission,< www.ferc.fed.us>.

14 New Bill Threatens Intellectual Freedom in Area Studies

Sources:
Yale Daily News, November 6, 2003
Title: "New Bill Threatens Intellectual Freedom in Area Studies"
Author: Benita Singh

Christian Science Monitor, March 11, 2004
Title: "Speaking in 'Approved' Tongues"
Author: Kimberly Chase

Faculty Evaluator: Robert Manning
Student Researchers: David Sonnenberg and Josh Sisco

The International Studies in Higher Education Act of 2003 threatens the freedom of education and classroom curriculum. In 1996, the Solomon Amendment was passed, denying federal funding to any institution of higher learning that refused to allow military recruiters on private and public university campuses. On September 17, 2003, Congress passed House Resolution 3077, the "International Studies in Higher Education Act of 2003."

The bill was first proposed in a June 2003 congressional hearing called "International Programs in Higher Education and Questions about Bias." It was authored by Representative Peter Hoekstra (R–MI), chairman of the House Subcommittee on Select Education and chairman of the House Subcommittee on Technical and Tactical Intelligence. He states, "The changes would let the government keep closer track of how the money is spent."

The bill portrays academic institutions as hotbeds for anti-American sentiment, specifically area studies programs. It proposes an advisory board that would be responsible for evaluating the curricula taught at Title VI institutions, course materials assigned in class, and even the faculty who are hired in institutions that accept Title VI funding. The advisory board would report to the secretary of education and make funding recommendations based on their findings.

Included in the monumental Civil Rights Act of 1964, Title VI prohibits any "discrimination on the basis of race, color, and national origin in programs and activities receiving federal financial assistance."

Both college leaders and lobbyists stated that the complaints of bias were inaccurate and that the new board would be used to interfere with curricular decisions on their campuses. Representative Peter Hoekstra tried to "alleviate those concerns by adding to the bill language that would bar the advisory board from 'mandating, directing, or controlling' the curriculums of such college programs." However, some "Democratic lawmakers feel that even greater protections were needed in the bill to ensure that the advisory board would not be used to intimidate scholars to toe an ideological line" (*The Chronicle of Higher Education*, October 31, 2003). Professors fear not what such a board is supposed to do, but what it would try to do.

Conservative academic Stanley Kurtz testified in support of H.R. 3077 and the advisory board. Kurtz stated that "the ruling intellectual paradigm in academic area studies is 'post-colonial theory.'" His problem with this idea is that "the core premise of post-colonial theory is that it is immoral for a scholar to put his knowledge of foreign languages and culture at the service of American power." According to author Benita Singh, Kurtz argues that "the root of anti-Americanism is not our repeated missteps abroad, unilateral occupation, or the continuing deaths of innocent civilians, but rather post-colonial scholarship." He feels that post-colonial theory is the cause for bias against America, driving his conclusion that Title VI programs are putting national security at risk as they indoctrinate their students with a hatred of America.

With the ratification of H.R. 3077, any academic discipline that includes cultural studies will be under the scrutiny of the advisory board. These include African, European, Latin American and Iberian, Middle Eastern, and East Asian studies departments as well as any language program. To add to this horrific agenda for control, "professors whose ideological principles may not support U.S. practices abroad can have their appointments terminated, any part of a course's curriculum containing criticism of U.S. foreign policy can be censored, and any course deemed entirely anti-American can be barred from ever being taught."

"Proponents of H.R. 3077 insist that no one is forced to agree with government policies unless they want government money" (Michael Bellesiles, *Sunday Gazette*, January 11, 2004). To add to this, the government states that schools with Title VI funding must also push students within the areas of study listed above into government security jobs. If they do not, they could be denied government funding.

According to an editorial written by University of California–Berkeley history professor Beshara Doumani, The driving forces behind the provision of this bill are the same individuals who have been promoting the war on Iraq. Their aim is to defend the foreign policy of the Bush Administration by stifling critical and informed discussions on U.S. college campuses (*Seattle Post-Intelligencer*, April 2, 2004: 7). "All this is doing is placing anyone in international studies under a stricter control of the government" (Michael Bellesiles , *Sunday Gazette*, January 11, 2004).

With the ratification of House Resolution 3077, the bill "would rob our society of the open exchange of ideas on college campuses that is vital to our democracy"

(*Seattle Post-Intelligencer*, April 2, 2004: 7). This bill could allow the government to begin programming and censoring what students are being taught at institutes of higher education that receive Title VI funding.

15 U.S. Develops Lethal New Bioweapon Viruses

Source:
The New Scientist, October 29, 2003
Title: "U.S. Develops Lethal New Viruses"
Author: Debora MacKenzie

Faculty Evaluator: Lynn Cominsky, Ph.D.
Student Researcher: Brian Pederson

Mainstream media coverage: *CBS News*, November 1, 2003, and *CNN News*, October 31, 2003

Scientists funded by the U.S. government have developed a way to make pox viruses incredibly deadly. Ostensibly, this research is being conducted as part of the plan to fight possible bioterror attacks. The new virus kills all mice even if they have been given antiviral drugs along with a vaccine that would normally protect victims from death. Mark Buller of the University of St. Louis has managed to modify mousepox, rabbitpox, and cowpox viruses so that they are deadly to vaccinated mice nearly 100 percent of the time through the introduction of an immunosuppressant protein called Interleukin-4 (IL-4). The modified pox viruses eliminate the immune system's cell-mediated response. They are now immune to the antiviral drug Cidofovir, known to be the last line of defense in treating resistant viruses.

Scientists at the Australian National University in Canberra made the original discovery by accident, though their virus only killed off 60 percent of infected mice. As a side effect of introducing IL-4 into pox viruses, the virus becomes species-specific and noncommunicable, though no one is quite sure why this is the case.

The implications of this discovery and their disclosure are staggering. IL-4 is a protein common in genetic research and as such is available on the Internet for as low as $60 dollars. Furthermore, the procedure is simple, something that a biology graduate student should be able to manage without trouble. The bioterrorist potential for an IL-4 modified pox virus that infects humans is extraordinary. Like anthrax, only those who come into contact with the virus itself would become infected. The virus would not spread and infect the attackers. Neither would it require state of the art scientific facilities to create such a virus. Buller and his team are currently working on a drug to resist the new viruses, but have so far been unsuccessful in making it 100 percent effective.

For more information on this story, please go to *The New Scientist* Web site at <www.newscientist.com/news/news.jsp?id=ns99994318> or the Howard Hughes Medical Institute at <www.hhmi.org/news/karupiah.html>.

16 Law Enforcement Agencies Spy on Innocent Citizens

Sources:
Agenda, July/August 2003
Title: "Big Brother Gets Bigger—Domestic Spying and the Global Intelligence Working Group"
Author: Michelle J. Kinnucan

Community Alliance, April 2003
Title: "Police Infiltrate Local Groups"
Author: Mark Schlosberg

CovertAction Quarterly, Fall 2003
Title: "Denver Police Keeping Files On Peace Groups"
Author: Loring Wirbel

North Bay Progressive, Vol. 2, No. 8, October 2003
Title: "Fresno Peace Group Infiltrated by Government Agent"
Author: Mike Rhodes

World Socialist Web Site, <www.wsws.org>, January 10, 2004
Title: "Bush Administration Expands Police Spying Powers"
Author: Kate Randall

Faculty Evaluator: Andrew Botterell
Student Researcher: Joni Wallent

With virtually no media coverage or public scrutiny, a major reorganization of the U.S. domestic law enforcement intelligence apparatus is well underway and, in fact, is partially completed. The effort to create a new national intelligence collection, analysis, and sharing system has frightening implications for privacy and other civil liberties.

In the aftermath of 9/11, the International Association of Chiefs of Police (IACP) with Department of Justice (DOJ) assistance decided to organize a summit in early 2002; the topic was "Criminal Intelligence Sharing: Overcoming Barriers to Enhance Domestic Security." At the summit, a select group of 100 "criminal intelligence experts" and VIPs from local, state, and federal agencies—including the military—formulated what came to be known as the "National Criminal Intelligence Sharing Plan" (MONEY LAUNDERING).

The IACP summit report calls for the creation of a "Criminal Intelligence Coordinating Council" (CICC). The Global Intelligence Working Group (GIWG) became operational under the umbrella of John Ashcroft's Department of Justice (DOJ) as the first incarnation of the CICC in the fall of 2002.

While they invoke the terror of 9/11, the MONEY LAUNDERING and related documents offer no argument that 9/11 could have been prevented with better intelligence sharing between federal and state/local law enforcement. The IACP summit report simply asserts, "While September 11 highlighted urgency in improving the capacity of law enforcement agencies…to share terrorism-relevant intelligence data…the real need is to share all—not just terrorism-related—criminal intelligence." Information would be shared throughout all channels of enforcement agencies. State and local agencies are to act as partners in the participation of collection, analysis, and dissemination, ultimately resulting in police infiltration collecting criminal intelligence.

Several police departments have increased surveillance and intelligence gathering activity against innocent citizens exercising their constitutional rights to participate in religious assemblies and social protests. The Denver Police were collecting criminal intelligence data on American citizens participating in "political, religious,

THIS MODERN WORLD

by TOM TOMORROW

and social gatherings. The Denver Police Intelligence Bureau has conducted infiltration and observation on groups such as: American Friends Service Committee, Citizens for Peace in Space, and Pikes Peak Justice and Peace Commission. Records on participants of these events were filed and shared between undercover police groups in Denver and national agencies.

The American Civil Liberties Union (ACLU) filed a lawsuit against the city of Denver and the police admitted to maintaining files on 3,200 individuals and 208 organizations.

In Fresno, California, a local peace and justice group discovered that they had been infiltrated by an undercover law enforcement officer. Fresno Sheriff Aaron Kilner, known to the Peace Fresno group as Aaron Stokes, attended several peace meetings and antiwar vigils. Peace Fresno found out about the infiltration when a local obituary reported the death of Officer Kilner in a motorcycle accident. Officer Kilner was listed in the obituary as working for the Joint Terrorism Task Force.

On the same day that Saddam Hussein was captured, President Bush signed into law the Intelligence Authorization Act for 2004. The act essentially expanded the Patriot Act by allowing government to request personal information on individual citizens from stockbrokers, car dealerships, credit card companies, and any other businesses where cash transactions occur. By broadening definitions of financial institutions, the Bush Administration expanded the 2001 USA Patriot Act. The FBI does not have to appear before a judge nor demonstrate "probable cause." Moreover, a national security letter comes attached with a gag order thereby preventing businesses from informing their clients that their records have been surrendered to the FBI.

The intentions of current intelligence gathering activities have little use in the prevention of terrorist attacks and have more to do with the reconstruction of local, state, federal, and private enforcement agencies with unrestricted access to citizen records.

UPDATE BY MICHELLE KINNUCAN: The story of the Global Intelligence Working Group is more important now than when it was first published because its National Criminal Intelligence Sharing Plan (NCISP) has largely been put into service. There was a flurry of mainstream media attention on May 14, 2004, in response to a Department of Justice (DOJ) signing ceremony and press conference. Unfortunately, the coverage had little, if any, analysis, and most articles mainly regurgitated a DOJ press release. Here's an excerpt from the press release:

> Attorney General John Ashcroft today announced the launch of the [NCISP], an initiative designed to link federal, state, and local law enforcement agencies so that they can share intelligence information to prevent terrorism and crime. He was joined in the announcement by Robert Mueller, director of the FBI; Deborah Daniels, assistant attorney general for the Office of Justice Programs; General Frank Libutti, undersecretary for information analysis and infrastructure protection at the Department of Homeland Security; Chief Joe Polisar, president of the International Association of Chiefs of Police; Melvin Carraway, superintendent of the Indiana State Police and chairman of the Global Intelligence Working Group; and Carl Peed, director of the Office of Community Oriented Policing Services. The NCISP is built around three guiding reforms: prioritization, with the emphasis on prevention, mobilization of resources, and coordination of intelligence gathering and integration.
>
> The [NCISP] is the first of its kind in the nation, uniting law enforcement agencies of all sizes and geographic locations in a truly national effort to prevent terrorism and criminal activity," said Attorney General John Ashcroft. "By raising cooperation and communication among local, state, and federal partners to an unprecedented level, this groundbreaking effort will strengthen the abilities of the justice community to detect threats and protect American lives and liberties."

The implementation announced by Ashcroft in May differs from earlier proposals in several ways, but the significant threats to the civil liberties of Americans and resident aliens are undiminished. The protections of a republican form of government and the inadequate safeguards erected during the 1970s and 1980s have been further weakened with little, if any, notice or opposition from politicians or the media. The American Civil Liberties Union sounded the alert last year when the DOJ proposed to change the "Criminal Intelligence Systems Operating Policies." Beyond that, however, they and other civil liberties organizations seem unaware of the threats to civil liberties posed by the changes in federal, state, and local police spying and information sharing. Activists should contact the ACLU, National Lawyers Guild, and other civil liberties groups to alert them.

A slightly more recent version of the original article appears on the Political Research Associates Web site at <www.publiceye.org/liberty/repression/big-broth-kin.html>. The Federation of American Scientists Intelligence Resource Program has posted some of the relevant documents in its news section, <www.fas.org/irp/news/index.html>; their *Secrecy News* is also recommended and can be found at <www.fas.org/sgp/news/secrecy/index.html>). The DOJ's GIWG site at <it.ojp.gov/topic.jsp?topic_id=56> remains an important source of information although they have apparently removed some files from the site.

 # U.S. Government Represses Labor Unions in Iraq in Quest for Business Privatization

Sources:
The Progressive, December 2003
Title: "Saddam's Labor Laws Live On"
Author: David Bacon

Left Turn, March/April 2004, Vol. 12
Title: "Ambitions of Empire: The Radical Reconstruction of Iraq's Economy"
Author: Antonia Juhasz

Faculty Evaluators: Heidi LaMoreaux, Ph.D. and Susan Garfin, Ph.D.
Student Researchers: Katie Drewieske and Adam Stutz

In the *Wall Street Journal* on May 1, 2003, an article leaked the confidential Bush Administration documents outlining "sweeping plans to remake Iraq's economy in the U.S. image. Hoping to establish a free-market economy in Iraq following the fall of Saddam Hussein, the U.S. is calling for the privatization of state-owned industries such as parts of the oil sector." This all-inclusive plan for mass privatization of Iraq is divided into three stages. In the first stage, corporations are not only able to establish their businesses in Iraq, they are also able to own Iraqi resources, including two of the most precious Iraqi resources: oil and water. In the second stage, all Iraqi resources would be turned over to private ownership. The final stage includes the establishment of a free trade area in the Middle East paving the way for U.S. domination of the entire region.

The beginning of the corporate invasion was signaled by the many multimillion dollar contracts that were handed to corporations via the Bush Administration. The

U.S. Agency for International Development (USAID) secretly sent out bids for contracts. Iraqis, humanitarian organizations, the United Nations, and any non-U.S. led business were left out of the contract bids. Although Halliburton and Bechtel are some of the most well-known corporations that have received these contracts, there are a plethora of others that have been included in these secret bids:

- ➤ MCI/WorldCom
- ➤ DynCorp/Computer Sciences Corp
- ➤ Flour Intercontinental
- ➤ Creative Associates International Inc.
- ➤ Research Triangle Institute

With Halliburton now responsible for the extraction and redistribution of oil, Bechtel has now been handed the contract to oversee the management of water systems and waste water management. As the largest private company in the world responsible for water management, with involvement in over 200 water and waste water treatment plants around the world, Bechtel's contract has been extended to include the distribution of water just as Halliburton's was for oil. With this in mind, the private ownership of Iraqi water supplies could have devastating consequences for the Iraqi population.

In addition to the privatization of the Iraqi resources, the U.S.-led Coalition Provisional Authority (CPA) in Iraq has kept in place many of Saddam Hussein's anti-labor practices.

In 1977, Saddam Hussein purged unions and made radical parties illegal. Many labor leaders were executed or fled the country to live in exile. Ten years later, Hussein reclassified the people who worked in large state enterprises as civil servants. That meant that the government employed 70 percent of Iraqi workers, and it was illegal for them to form unions or to bargain for better working conditions.

Since the Hussein regime fell last April 2003, workplace-organizing activity has exploded. Union organizers emerged quickly, spearheading a drive for better wages. A worker strike was held in Basra two days after British troops arrived. Workers demanded the right to organize and protested the appointment of a Baath party official as the new mayor. Similar demonstrations have been going on throughout the country. Four hundred union activists met in Baghdad in June 2003 to form the Workers Democratic Trade Union Federation and planned to reorganize unions in many of Iraq's major industries.

But the CPA, while striking down almost all of Hussein's other laws, has kept the ban on unions, keeping wages low and unemployment high (at about 70 percent). They are privatizing the state enterprises that employed most of the workers. As of December 2003, 138 of the 600 state-owned businesses were being offered for sale.

On September 19, 2003, the CPA published Order No. 37, which suspends income and property taxes for a year and limits future taxes to 15 percent. Later that day, they issued Order No. 39, permitting 100 percent foreign ownership of businesses (except oil) and allowing repatriation of profits. Outright ownership of, access to, and profits from Iraqi oil fields is still under dispute, although it is likely that U.S. interests will prevail.

The CPA has set an emergency pay scale for Iraqi workers' wages, which for most is $60 a month. This is the same wage scale that workers had under the Hussein regime. Benefits under Hussein included frequent bonuses, profit sharing, medical coverage, and food subsidies. There is no overtime pay under the CPA and no benefits, and an increase in the exchange rate has made imports and essential items very expensive. Workers have had a drastic cut in income since April 2003 as a result of CPA decisions.

Low wages aren't the only problems unions hope to combat. Working conditions are exhausting and dangerous. Under the Hussein regime, the workday was seven hours long. Now a day shift is 11 hours, a night shift is 13 hours. Safety glasses and other safety equipment are virtually unknown in most industries. If workers get sick or hurt, they must pay for their own medical care and also lose pay for the time they miss. "Life has gotten much worse," said one worker. "Everything is controlled by the coalition. We don't control anything."

Workers in the businesses to be privatized could face even more problems in the future. If they have no legal union, no right to bargain, and no contracts, they may not be able to oppose the privatization of their plants and potential huge job losses. A plant manager in one industry seems willing to talk to the union in his factory, but because finances and wages are controlled by the CPA, he is not able to sign any kind of contract with the group.

The factory manager pointed out that under the Hussein regime, the 3,000 workers were guaranteed jobs for life. He was not allowed to lay off anyone. But if his business were privatized he would have to fire about 1,500 people in order to make a profit; because there is no unemployment insurance, he will be killing those workers and their families.

Iraqi Labor Undersecretary Nuri Jafer says he would like to start an unemployment insurance program, but so far no country is willing to help fund it. Meanwhile, none of the $87 billion that Congress allotted for Iraq will go to increase wages or implement a large jobs program.

A delegation from U.S. Labor Against War—a group of American union and labor councils—visited Iraq in October to investigate conditions. They asked Jafer repeatedly whether or not the 1987 law banning unions would be repealed, but he would not answer the question. The British CPA representative at the Labor Ministry also refused to answer and complained that the foreign union delegations that visited the ministry were wasting the labor minister's time.

UPDATE BY DAVID BACON: The disaster that is the occupation of Iraq is much more than the war that plays nightly across U.S. television screens. The violence of grinding poverty, exacerbated by economic sanctions after the first Gulf War, has been deepened by the U.S. invasion. Every day the economic policies of the occupying authorities create more hunger among Iraq's working people, transforming them into a pool of low-wage, semi-employed labor, desperate for jobs at almost any price.

The effects of U.S. policy on daily life, especially the economic situation of most Iraqis, go largely ignored in the U.S. media, although anyone walking the streets of Baghdad cannot miss them. Children sleep on the sidewalks. Sewage still pours into the Tigris River, and those who must depend on it for drinking or cooking continue to get sick. The violence of poverty is not held to be a violation of human rights in the United States, just one manifestation of the great division in the world between the wealthy, industrialized north, and the developing south. The U.S. does not recognize that human rights include economic and social rights, in part because they are collective rights of groups, social classes, or even nations.

The story on labor in Iraq detailed these violations of human rights. Most of the specific CPA decrees mentioned in the story, suppressing union rights and setting the stage for privatization, are unarguably violations of international human rights standards.

Conventions 87 and 98 of the International Labor Organization, guaranteeing freedom of association, makes the continued enforcement of the 1987 ban on unions illegal. Convention 135, preventing retaliation against workers for union activity, makes the arrests of union leaders, and their expulsion from their offices, illegal as well.

The story exposed not only the growing poverty of Iraqi workers, but also the conscious effort to use a falling standard of living as an attraction for foreign investment. After the story appeared in *The Progressive*, the situation for workers and unions grew worse. Members of the national executive board of the Iraqi Federation of Trade Unions were arrested in December, along with leaders of the Union of the Unemployed of Iraq. In January and February, a wave of work stoppages and labor confrontations in the south hit Iraq's key industries: oil and electrical generation. Worker resistance grew so heated that the occupation authority was forced to withdraw decrees that would have lowered wages even further.

In an especially Orwellian moment, George Bush even declared in his January State of the Union speech that U.S. intervention in Iraq would promote the formation of free trade unions in the Middle East. Nevertheless, as of April, the occupation authority continued to enforce the Saddam-era ban on union in most workplaces.

Few other media outlets picked up the story of the violation of Iraqi labor rights. A notable exception was the labor press, especially *The Dispatcher* (of the International Longshore and Warehouse Union) and the *Guild Reporter* (of the Newspaper Guild). This labor attention reflects the growing antipathy and opposition to the war and occupation among U.S. unions, a story in itself.

There was some attention on the radio, due in part to the efforts of the Institute for Public Accuracy. None of the major national daily U.S. newspapers, however, and none of the television networks, have run any news stories at all about Iraqi labor and workers. Perhaps this is just an extension of their failure to cover unions and workers in the U.S., but given the need to develop the institutions of civil society in Iraq capable of governing the country, ignoring unions and their allied popular organizations seems a kind of willful blindness typical of the occupation generally.

The best source for continued and up-to-date information about Iraqi workers and unions can be found on the Web site of U.S. Labor Against the War, the national network of unions opposed to the Bush war policy, at <www.uslaboragainstwar.org>.

18 Media and Government Ignore Dwindling Oil Supplies

Sources:
New Internationalist, October 31, 2003
Title: "Running on empty; Oil is Disappearing Fast"
Author: Adam Porter

Guardian Unlimited, December 2, 2003
Title: "Bottom of the Barrel"
Author: George Monbiot

Faculty Evaluator: Rick Luttmann, Ph.D.
Student Researchers: Philip Rynning , Julie Mayeda, and Anna Miranda

If the former industry executives, geologists, and statisticians in the Association for the Study of Peak Oil (ASPO) are correct, oil may have already reached its highest levels of production potential. But U.S. leaders and the mainstream media refuse to acknowledge that we are headed for an inevitable oil crisis with extreme consequences sure to impact every aspect of our lives. As the peak is reached, oil prices will start to rise (as they have every year since 2000). As the oil decline accelerates, prices will rise even faster.

The problem is that our lives have become hard-wired to the oil economy. Oil powers the machinery of modern society and lubricates its engines. Materials need to be transported, and companies need working people to make them. Workers in turn need to run a car, pay for electricity to heat their house, and buy food (that is packaged in plastic). High transportation prices mean high food prices. Oil is the main ingredient in plastics and polyester: the clothes we wear, the carpets we walk on, the frames for our computers, the seats we sit on, the bottles we drink from, and the band-aids that salve our wounds. Who will be able to afford them as the price of oil starts to rise? What will replace them? This story isn't about the end of oil as it is often portrayed; it is the beginning of the end of oil. But this still means a paradigmatic shift at a level not seen since the Industrial Revolution.

Our government has yet to begin diversifying our energy. Head of the energy investment bank Simmons & Co. International, Matthew Simmons said, "I am an advisor to the Bush Administration—although I'm not sure they are listening. What I basically told them is that we had some looming energy problems: that we were barreling into a really nasty energy crisis. We need a new energy." But a viable alternative has yet to be developed. These economic problems will be exacerbated by the direct connection between the price of oil and the rate of unemployment. The last five recessions in the U.S. were all preceded by a rise in the oil price.

Alternative energy, such as hydrogen, which President Bush mentioned in his State of the Union speech in January of 2004, has its own complexities and system requirements. Hydrogen, natural gas, biodiesel, and nuclear energy sources are all considered alternative fuels. Wind and solar power are considered renewable energy resources. The viability of these options depends directly on how we plan to implement them.

The only rational response to both the impending end of the oil age and the menace of global warming is to redesign our cities, our farming, and our lives. But this will not happen without massive political pressure, and our problem is that no one ever rioted for austerity. People tend to take to the streets because they want to consume more, not less.

Author Adam Porter offers these tips: Eliminate non-essential energy use, and encourage others to do the same. Move towards renewable sources. Drive only when necessary. Buy local to defray the strain from transportation consumption. Get involved locally to plan within the community. Write your local paper as well as your representatives. The greater the demand for public discourse, the sooner the U.S. government will supply a solution. In 1976, President Jimmy Carter said, "We must face the prospect of changing our basic ways of living. This change will either be made on our own initiative in a planned way or forced on us with chaos and suffering by the inexorable laws of nature."

UPDATE BY ADAM PORTER: The story that global oil output is peaking, that the demand will continue to outstrip production, is simply the biggest story of the age. Bar none. It connects to everything else. It is a building block for all other stories, be it Iraq, corporate greed, Chinese growth, or basic political power. You want to travel to Mars with no oil? You want to watch the Super Bowl half time with no electricity? You want Michael Jackson to moonwalk on his limo outside court when even he can't afford to drive there anymore? Think again. It's all about oil.

Since publication of the story in *New Internationalist* magazine, the price of oil has risen to $41 a barrel from about $30, oil workers are being killed in Saudi, pipelines and platforms are being destroyed in Iraq, Shell mislaid 23 percent of its reserves (whoops), and of course, oil companies are making record profits.

Mainstream response to my story was zero, nada. Some outlets are now looking at the subject in more detail. But then again they can hardly miss it. It would be a bit like not covering the Iraq war. Most of the coverage is ignorant of basic facts; all quoted reserves are lies and parrot oil company and government policy. At least it's consistent.

If one would like more information on the subject simply go to the Internet and Google for "oil production"; there are enormous amounts. Other than that, go to <www.peakoil.net>; that is a good place to start. In Spanish, go to <www.crisisenergetica.org>.

UPDATE BY GEORGE MONBIOT: Since my story was published, both Shell and BP have been forced to downgrade the size of their reserves. The oil price has continued to climb: At the time of writing, it stands at over $40. The mainstream media is at last waking up to the idea that this nonrenewable resource won't last forever. *The New York Times*, *The Times* (London), and CBS have all followed up on the story I wrote. Perhaps, just perhaps, humanity will, almost for the first time in history, do something before it's too late.

Recommended Web sites include: <www.peakoil.net/>; <www.lifeaftertheoilcrash.net/>; The Oil Depletion Analysis Centre, <www.odac-info.org/>; and <www.hubbertpeak.com/>.

19 Global Food Cartel Fast Becoming the World's Supermarket

Source:
Left Turn, August/September 2003
Title: "Concentration in the Agri-Food System"
Author: Hilary Mertaugh

Evaluator: John Lund
Student Researcher: Anna Miranda

Over the last two decades, agribusiness and food retail mergers, acquisitions, joint ventures, and informal contract agreements have transformed the agri-food system into a powerful network of transnational corporations that have the power to control the world's food supply at every stage of food production—from gene to market shelf. By cooperating with one another rather than competing, transnational corporations escape the scrutiny of federal antitrust regulators and manipulate the market through "non-merger alliances." In April 2002, the world's two largest seed corporations, DuPont and Monsanto announced that they would agree to swap their key patented agricultural technologies and drop all outstanding patent lawsuits.

The flurry of mergers and acquisitions throughout the agri-food system has created highly concentrated markets as agribusinesses expand their dominance by diversifying their commodities. Cargill is among the top five companies in the U.S. market for flour milling, grain and oilseed processing, salt production, corn and soybean exports, turkey production and processing, pork processing, and beer processing.

As fewer corporations control each stage of food production, farming is becoming a kind of serfdom. Consolidation among suppliers and processors leave farmers with few choices of who to buy from and who to sell to. Dominant agribusinesses have the ability to drive up the prices they charge for inputs while watering down the prices they pay for outputs. Furthermore, the rise of patented seed varieties places farmers in an even worse position, as agricultural biotech companies gain ownership of the germplasm itself.

Consolidation in the food system is not limited to the production and processing side. Consolidation activity among food retailers has catalyzed a domino effect of mergers and acquisitions. ConAgra, a company few Americans have heard of, is a major force in food production in the U.S. and has continued to aggressively acquire small rivals while expanding its operation worldwide. It is estimated to be the number-three seller of retail food products in the world. Although consumers might be unfamiliar with the name ConAgra, they will recognize some, if not all, of ConAgra's popular brand names: Armour, Butterball, Chef Boyardee, Healthy Choice, La Choy, Orville Reddenbacher, Parkay, and Hebrew National, just to name a few. ConAgra is also known for a recall of 19 million pounds of tainted beef after 47 people were sickened and one died from *E. coli* poisoning in 2002.

The top five supermarket chains capture one-half of all food sales in the U.S., and it is widely predicted that there will soon be only six major retail supermarkets selling the majority of the world's food. Because it is necessary for each and every one of us to eat and drink, we will pay what it takes to make sure we do not go hungry or thirsty. Although food may appear to be "cheap" with fewer and fewer retailers, lack of competition will ultimately lead to higher prices, lack of choice, and poorly paid employees. Wal-Mart typically sells grocery products at prices 14 percent lower than competing grocers, in part because the company is a non-union employer that hires clerks at below-poverty wages.

Food corporations rely on the consumers' lack of knowledge as to where their food comes from, how it is produced, and who wins the profits. The trend toward consolidation at every stage along the food production chain has dramatically impacted the global economy and distribution of income and wealth. Given the complexities of the domestic policy making and legislative processes, and the numerous mergers, acquisitions, joint ventures, and "non-merger mergers," it is not surprising that few people are aware of the degree to which food companies influence food safety policies and competition, and decide where and how food is produced and how much it will cost.

Prior to committing suicide as an act of political protest on September 10, 2003 against the World Trade Organization in Cancun, Mexico, Lee Kyung Hae, a 56-year-old farmer from South Korea circulated the following statement. "My warning goes to all citizens that human beings are in an endangered situation in which uncontrolled multinational corporations and a small number of big WTO official members are leading undesirable globalization of inhumane, environmentally degrading, farmer-killing, and undemocratic policies. It should be stopped immediately, otherwise the false logic of neoliberalism will perish the diversities of global agriculture with disastrous consequences to all human beings."

20 Extreme Weather Prompts New Warning from U.N.

Source:
The Independent (U.K.), July 3, 2003
Title: "Extreme Weather Prompts Unprecedented Global Warming Alert"
Author: None Listed

Mainstream media coverage: CNN, July 3, 2003; *USA Today*, October 29, 2003; and *The New York Times*, December 17, 2003.

Faculty Evaluator: Ervand Peterson, Ph.D.
Student Researchers: Shannon Arthur, Cassie Cyphers, and Melissa Jones

The U.N.'s World Meteorological Organization (WMO) views the events of 2003 in Europe, America and Asia as so astonishing that the world needs to be made aware of it immediately. The WMO reports extreme weather and climate occurrences all over the world. Reports on record high and low temperatures, record rainfall, and record storms in different parts of the world are consistent with the predictions of global warming. The significance of this particular report is that it comes from the highly respected U.N. organization known for its conservative predictions and statements. Based in Geneva, the WMO collects its information from the weather services of 185 countries.

Supercomputer models show that, as the atmosphere warms, the climate is not only becoming hotter, but very unstable, with the number of extreme events more likely to increase. In southern France, record temperatures were recorded in June 2003. Temperatures rose above 104° F (40° C) in some places, which is 41 to 44° F above average. In Switzerland, it was the hottest June in over 250 years. In Geneva, daytime temperatures made it the hottest June ever recorded.

In the United States, there were 562 tornadoes in the month of May, causing 41 deaths. This year's pre-monsoon heat wave in India brought about temperatures of 113° F (45° C), which is 40° F above normal. This extreme heat was responsible for at least 1,400 deaths. In Sri Lanka, heavy rainfall from tropical Cyclone 01B resulted in floods and landslides, killing at least 300 people. The infrastructure and the economy of southwest Sri Lanka were heavily damaged. England and Wales experienced the warmest June since 1976 with average temperatures of 61° F (16° C).

A WMO representative said, "New record extreme events occur every year somewhere in the globe, but in recent years the number of such extremes has been increasing." Extreme heat waves that scorched Europe in August 2003 were responsible for tens of thousands of deaths. The Earth Policy Institute reports there were 35,118 deaths. Most of the deaths occurred in France with 14,802 fatalities, followed by Germany with 7,000 and Spain and Italy each suffering over 4,000 losses. The United Kingdom, Netherlands, Portugal, and Belgium combined had over 4,000 deaths.

According to recent reports of the joint WMO/United Nations Environmental Panel on Climate Change, the global average surface temperature has increased around 34° since 1861. New analyses of proxy data for the Northern Hemisphere indicate that in the twenty-first century increases are likely to be the largest in any century over the past 1,000 years. Average global land and sea surface temperatures in May 2003 were the second highest since records began in 1880. The 10 hottest years in the 143-year-old global temperature record have all been since 1990, with the three hottest being 1998, 2001, and 2002.

 # Forcing a World Market for GMOs

Sources:
<Globalinfo.org>, December 3, 2003
Title: "Agriculture: Biotech Links to Big Lenders Worry Farm Experts"
Author: Katherine Stapp

Inter Press Service News Agency, May 14, 2003
Title: "U.S. WTO Dispute Could Bend Poor Nations to the GMOs Groups"
Author: Emad Mekay

CMW Report, Summer 2003
Title: "A Rebuttal to the *Tribune*"
Author: Liane Casten

SF Weekly, June 2–8, 2004
Title: "Bioscience Warfare"
Author: Alison Pierce

Faculty Evaluators: Al Wahrhaftig, Ph.D. and Eric McGuckin, Ph.D.
Student Researcher: Larrisa Heeren

The Bush Administration, backed by the biotech industry, intends to force the European Union (EU) to drop trade barriers against genetically modified organisms (GMOs). Their claim is that such a trade barrier is illegal under World Trade Organization (WTO) rules and that the distribution of GMOs is a necessary part of the campaign to end world hunger. However, the reason behind U.S. governmental support for GMOs may have more to do with heavy lobbying, campaign contributions, and the close relationships between government agencies and biotech companies than actual science and the war against hunger. U.S. industry loses some $300 million a year of possible GMO exports to the EU. Biotechnology promoters like Monsanto and agri-business have strenuously lobbied the administration to bring a formal WTO case against the EU while suppressing studies that show GMOs may have adverse effects on health and the environment.

The connections between biotech companies and U.S. regulatory agencies are deep. According to <globalinfo.org>, Ann Veneman, U.S. Department of Agriculture Secretary, used to serve on the board of Calgene, the company that brought us the biotech tomato. She also used to head Agracetus, a subsidiary of Monsanto. In another example of the "revolving door" between biotech companies and regulatory agencies, the person who wrote the GMO regulations for the Food and Drug Administration (FDA) was a lawyer who "previously" represented biotech giant Monsanto. After writing the FDA legislation, the lawyer returned to work for Monsanto.

Another factor that has powerfully influenced the growth of the GMO industry throughout the world is the link between international development organizations (such as the World Bank) and the biotech industry. Under an approved "staff exchange program" the World Bank trades its employees with employees from companies like Dow, ARD, and Aventis. There are also exchanges with academic institutions, governments, and UN development agencies. One startling example involves Eija Pehu, a senior scientist with the World Bank's department of agriculture and rural development. The former president of a Finnish biotech company, Pehu is also listed as a board member for the International Service for the Acquisition of Agri-Biotech Applications (ISAAA), an influential lobbying organization whose funding comes from companies like Monsanto, Syngenta, and Bayer. The ISAAA's objective is "the transfer and delivery of appropriate biotechnology applications to developing countries." They have successfully pursued this program with projects in at least 12 developing nations.

The U.S. has a history of attempting to push GMOs on developing nations through the use of food aid. Yet, despite enormous pressure and Washington PR campaigns, Zambia, Zimbabwe, and Mozambique have turned down shipments of U.S. GMO aid because of health and environmental concerns. Ronnie Cummins, national director of Organic Consumers, says the real aim of the United States is to frighten poor developing nations into complying and opening their markets for controversial products. But while GMO companies continue to open new markets abroad, the jury is still out on whether or not their products are likely to provide any real benefits. Controversy and scandal surround the biotech industry and charges that it manipulates the results of research performed on GMOs. Biotech companies create relationships with universities that conduct research on their products by providing sorely needed funding for university research departments. (Over the last three decades, funding provided to U.S. universities by the industrial sector grew faster than any other source.) Researchers who have come forward with evidence showing that GMOs can be harmful claim they have experienced pressure from university research alliances to alter results. Some assert that the priorities of private sponsors influence what should have been impartial findings. One researcher who found less than desirable results, and discussed them publicly, had the misfortune of being blacklisted and the target of a powerful GMO PR campaign to discredit his work. In 1998, Arpad Pusztai, a scientist at the Rowett Research Institute in Aberdeen, Scotland discovered that genetically modified potatoes caused inflammations and tumors in the lining of stomachs of lab rodents. After publishing his story, his home was burglarized, his research was stolen, he lost his job at Rowett after 30 years of employment, and he was maligned by the Royal Medical Society (after his research was published in the reputable scientific journal *Lancet*). This story was Censored #7 in 2001.

The European Union denies that it has enacted a trade moratorium and says it simply needed more time to develop systems for tracing and labeling GM foods and feed. However, even if the EU were to abide by the WTO's rules, "there is no way in hell they can force the European consumers, supermarkets, or farmers to stock GMO tainted crops," says Ronnie Cummins.

Meanwhile, the anti-GMO movement in the United States is rapidly gaining steam. In March 2004, Mendocino, California became the first county in the U.S. to ban the growing of genetically modified crops and animals.

UPDATE BY KATHERINE STAPP: With public concerns over genetically modified (GM) foods intensifying this year, the agricultural biotechnology industry appears to be focusing even more intently on developing countries, where regulations governing their use are generally more lax.

In April, the European Union announced tougher labeling requirements for genetically modified products. In May, agricultural giant Monsanto said that it was dropping plans to commercialize a variety of GM wheat in the United States and Canada because of consumer and farmer opposition.

By contrast, India's $200-million National Technology Project (NATP), funded in part by the World Bank, has stepped up experimentation with transgenic cotton, rice, sorghum, groundnut, chickpea, and pigeon pea. According to reports from the Pesticide Action Network (PAN), dozens or more World Bank-funded projects in Brazil, Indonesia, India, Peru, Romania, Ethiopia, Mozambique, and Kenya refer explicitly to agricultural biotechnology.

In a related development (because many of the same companies involved in biotech also manufacture pesticides), PAN also gave the World Bank a failing grade on sustainable farming practices. Its review of 100 World Bank projects determined that only 9 percent comply with the World Bank's stated commitment to reduce pesticide use in its agricultural projects.

This growing divide between north and south is illustrated by estimates from industry groups like the International Service for the Acquisition of Agri-Biotech Applications (ISAAA), which tout the spread of GM crops. In January 2004, the ISAAA announced that "7 million farmers in 18 countries—more than 85 percent resource-poor farmers in the developing world—now plant biotech crops, up from 6 million in 16 countries in 2002."

Activists are also focusing on World Bank funding for GM trees through its Prototype Carbon Fund, which facilitates emissions trading to comply with the Kyoto Protocol on greenhouse gases. They fear that pollen drift from these GM "carbon sinks" could contaminate native species and also open the door for widespread planting of GM trees in developing countries.

The World Bank's lack of accountability to governments or civil society is at the heart of many complaints about its activities, underlining the importance of the independent media in exposing abuses. In terms of the mainstream press's response to the IPS story, I'm not aware that there was one.

More information can be found at PAN's Web site at <www.panna.org>, the Global Justice Ecology Project at <www.globaljusticeecology.org>, the World Bank's Staff Exchange site, <www.staffexchange.org>, which lists its "corporate partners," and a new book titled *Gene Traders: Biotechnology, World Trade and the Globalization of Hunger* by Brian Tokar (Toward Freedom Press, 2004).

22 Exporting Censorship to Iraq

Sources:
The American Prospect, Vol. 14, Issue 9, October 1, 2003
Title: "Exporting Censorship to Iraq"
Author: Alex Gourevitch

Asheville Global Report (AGR), May 12, 2003
Title: "U.S Army Major Refuses Order to Seize Iraq TV Station"
Author: Charlie Thomas

Faculty Evaluator: Jeffrey Holtzman, Ph.D.
Student Researchers: Sara Brunner and Doug Reynolds

Soon after coalition forces toppled the Saddam Hussein regime in Iraq, occupying Chief L. Paul Bremer III, reflecting on the new freedom in Iraq, told journalists that they were no longer constrained by the government and were now "free to criticize whoever, or whatever, you want." But he was not telling the truth. Everything changed very quickly when Bremer was the person coming under that very criticism.

When negative critiques of his policies appeared on the Iraqi Media Network (IMN), Bremer placed controls on its content. IMN was an American-run outfit contracted by the Pentagon to put out news after the fall of Saddam. IMN's mission was two-fold: to be both a PBS-style broadcaster and a means for the occupying authorities to communicate with the Iraqis. Bremer issued a nine-point list of "prohibited activity" that included incitement to violence, support for the Baath Party, and publishing material that is patently false and calculated to promote opposition to the occupying authority. He clamped down further on the independent media in Iraq by closing down a number of Iraqi-run newspapers and radio and television stations. The IMN was bound to find a conflict in encouraging democratic values while under pressure to go along with the coalition forces ruling by force.

From the beginning, Pentagon decisions seemed to run counter to its well-publicized intention to create a free Iraqi society. Early last year, rather than hiring a media outlet to run the IMN, the Pentagon chose a defense contractor, Scientific Applications International Corp. (SAIC). With SAIC's orientation leaning more toward information control than information dissemination, it is hard to see how they were going to create a public broadcasting-style multimedia operation in post-war Iraq. The IMN was created in April 2003, and it was not long before journalists hired by the SAIC realized their double role. The occupying authority told them to stop conducting man-on-the-street interviews because some were too critical of the American presence and to stop including readings from the Koran as part of cultural programming. IMN was also forced to run an hour-long program on recently issued occupying authority laws despite objections from Don North, a senior TV advisor to the IMN station.

Additionally, coalition forces were ordered to seize the only TV station in Mosel Iraq because they had televised some programs from the network Al Jazeera in its broadcast. The independent station had lost its cameras to looters so they had turned to a mix of Arabic news channels and NBC to continue broadcasting. The commander of the 101st Airborne Division, Maj. Gen. David Petraeus gave the order to seize the station. But in a surprising show of bravery and professional ethics Maj. Charmaine Means, the head of the Army public affairs office in Mosul, would not agree to the seizure. Maj. Means said that to do so would mean the station would be intimidated into airing only material approved by the U.S. military. She refused twice to follow her superior officers' orders, after which she was relieved of her duties. The station was eventually taken over by coalition forces. IMN has said that it would like to take over the offices in Mosul. IMN's direct control over the facilities would give the American authority a broadcasting foothold in northern Iraq.

The occupying authority is now developing an independent media commission run by journalists rather than the U.S. Army to enforce Bremer's rules more judiciously and to develop a more rational set of media regulations.

UPDATE BY ALEX GOUREVITCH: My main interest in writing the article was to identify the core problems with the idea of "exporting democracy" to other countries. I had heard there were problems with developing an independent and public media in Iraq and thought that looking at how the U.S. tried to manage the development of open media and "free speech" would be an excellent way of showing how external "democratization" doesn't work because democracy has to come from the inside. The people have to define the parameters of their politics, interpret principles like free speech, for themselves.

I thought my article exposed the contradiction between the logic of occupation and the logic of democratic politics, and I think this continues to be a problem. For instance, one of the triggering events of the recent and ongoing Sadrist uprising was the CPA's decision to shut down *al-Hawza al-Natiqa*, a low circulation newspaper supportive of Moqtada al-Sadr. Less radical Iraqis have also responded negatively to heavy-handed treatment of the media. On May 4, the *Washington Post* reported that the editor-in-chief of *Al-Sabah*, the U.S. funded newspaper in Iraq, Ismael Zayer, resigned along with some editors and reporters. Zayer told the *Post* that "We thought that Americans were here to create a free media" but "instead, we were being suffocated."

The CPA justifies its restrictions and censorship on the grounds that there is a trade-off between liberty and security, especially when it comes to potentially incendiary speech. The problem isn't that Iraqis don't appreciate this trade-off; the problem isn't even that the CPA is perceived as uneven and politically motivated in its application of the law. Rather, what upsets Iraqis is that it is the CPA that reserves the authority to decide when security, or some other value, trumps liberty. In fact, it appears that after the June 30 "handover of sovereignty," the CPA will keep its authority to enforce Article 14 (the statute allowing the shutting down of media outlets if they are deemed to threaten law and order). The essential problem here is not just whether the CPA's decisions are fair or proper, but that they get to make the decisions in the first place.

What kind of sovereignty do the Iraqis have if they are not allowed to interpret their own constitution? The contradiction between the logic of occupation and the logic of democracy continues and will persist so long as the CPA or the coalition force remains in Iraq.

There has been some mainstream press coverage of this issue, although my story in particular has not received a great deal of attention. *The New York Times* did publish a short summary and snippets of the article in its September 28–October 4 issue of *The Week in Review Reading Desk: The Reading File* section. Other than that, it has not received a great deal of attention. For further information on these topics, the best places to go are independent media watchdog groups like *Index on Censorship*, <www.index online.org>; Reporters Without Borders <www.rsf.org>; and <www.indymedia.org>.

UPDATE BY CHARLIE THOMAS: After Maj. Charmaine Means was relieved of command, she was reassigned to a stateside post at Fort Bragg. Maj. Gen. David Petraeus was promoted to Lt. General and is back in Iraq in charge of training all Iraqi military and security forces.

Since the seizure of the Mosul TV station, the whole world has become aware of the illegal actions of the U.S. in Iraq. Fresh reports of violations of the Geneva Convention are frequent. Col. David Hogg, in an off-the-cuff remark, noted that U.S. forces routinely take hostages: "...his troops picked up the wife and daughter of an Iraqi lieutenant general. They left a note: 'If you want your family released, turn yourself in.'" (*Washington Post*, July 28, 2003). Article 34 of the Geneva Convention is specific: "The taking of hostages is prohibited."

Many news outlets reported that U.S. forces kept sick and injured civilians away from the hospitals during the siege of Falluja, but none noted that this behavior is a war crime.

And now comes former Staff Sergeant Jimmy Massey, a veteran of the invasion of Iraq, reporting that he and his troops were ordered to, and did, fire on unarmed protestors, killing most of them.

After the World Trade Center attack, the U.S. essentially declared itself exempt from international norms. The military is following the civilian leadership. According to a memorandum to the president by White House Counsel Alberto Gonzales on January 25, 2002, "In my judgment, this new paradigm renders obsolete Geneva's strict limitations on questioning of enemy prisoners and renders quaint some of its provisions."

Brazil Holds Back in FTAA Talks, But Provides Little Comfort for the Poor of South America

Sources:

<Globalinfo.org>, November 15, 2003
Title: "Trade: U.S. Moves to Squeeze FTAA Opponents"
Author: Emad Mekay

Left Turn, March/April, 2004
Title: "Lula's First Year"
Author: Brian M. Campbell

Faculty Evaluators: Robert Girling, Ph.D. and LeiLani Nishime, Ph.D.
Student Researchers: Hilton Jones and Chris Cox

The Free Trade Area of the Americas (FTAA) could become the biggest trading block in history, expanding NAFTA to 34 countries from Canada to the bottom of South America. This deal is unlikely to meet its January 2005 deadline, now that the second largest player in the negotiations, Brazil, is holding back. Brazil played an important part in the November 2003 Cancun WTO meeting. Led by President Lula, a 20-country coalition that opposed the agenda of the northern countries caused the meeting to end abruptly and collapse.

The United States has reacted swiftly by making bilateral agreements with individual Central and South American countries and threatening to restrict their access to U.S. markets if they refuse to cooperate. In many cases, these poorer countries have no choice but to agree to the very strict and unfair agreements that the United States demands. Countries such as Peru, Panama, the Dominican Republic, Colombia, Ecuador, and many other Central American nations involved in the FTAA want access to U.S. markets, even if it means relaxing antitrust laws and workers' rights. This tactic of coercing countries one by one has, so far, been successful in isolating Brazil from building coalitions with neighboring countries. Brazil is the fifth largest nation in the world, both in size and population. Boasting a consumer market of 182 million people, the United States desperately wants in.

Luiz Inacio "Lula" da Silva, the president of Brazil, has taken a very anti-Washington stance in the recent talks on the FTAA. All 34 countries had demands put upon them in a two-tier system. Because the United States and Brazil both sit comfortably in the top tier, they are able to opt out of any negotiations not favorable to them. This has allowed the United States to keep its farm subsidies, which is the only way the U.S. sugar industry can compete with the largest sugar exporter in the world, Brazil. In return, Brazil is not obligated to open up any of its service industry and government contracts to foreign competition.

Because NAFTA did little to stop jobs in Mexico from going overseas, particularly to China, where wages and operating costs are even cheaper than Mexico, Brazilian politicians are very hesitant to sign up for Washington's latest economic plan. A poll by the University of Miami indicated that 76 percent of Latin American business people, journalists, academics, and government officials believe that the FTAA plan would benefit the United States and not Brazil. This is one reason President Lula is staying away from the FTAA and bolstering talks abroad with India and China that focus on technology and natural resources.

UPDATE BY BRIAN M. CAMPBELL: The election of Luis Inacio "Lula" da Silva and the Workers Party in Brazil was heralded as a defeat for neoliberalism and the beginning of a new era in Brazil, where people would be put before the dictates of international capital. The aim of this story was to look at what had happened to that promise during the first year of the Lula Administration.

Latin America has been the guinea pig for neoliberal policies. Free market theories were given the green light immediately after the military coup on September 11, 1973, that murdered the elected president of Chile, Salvador Allende. The result has been 30 years of escalating poverty and economic collapse across the region.

During the period 1980 to 2000, per capita income grew at a mere one-tenth of the rate of the previous decade, leaving the continent scarred by poverty and inequality. In Brazil, out of a population of 175 million, 53 million are poor, 23 million are homeless, and 8 million are unemployed. Meanwhile, 3 percent of the population own two-thirds of the land. Argentina has an unemployment rate of 21.5 percent; a country that used to feed the world can no longer feeds its own people. In Bolivia, 60 percent of the population is defined as poor. These figures are not unique to these countries, but rather sum up the experience of countries from Mexico to Chile: By the end of the 1990s, 11 million more people lived in poverty than at the beginning of the decade.

In 2003, the United Nations Economic Commission for Latin America, the body that coined the phrase "lost decade" to sum up the regions experience during the 1980s, issued another report that asserted: "Half the countries in the region have seen GDP per head fall in the past five years, and the economies that grew rapidly during the 1990s have slowed down." Perhaps the most extreme example of the failure of the neoliberal model was the economic implosion and social uprising in Argentina in December 2001.

The desperation inflicted by the neoliberal economic model has not gone unchallenged by the people of the region. Fights against International Monetary Fund-mandated privatization plans have raged in El Salvador, Colombia, Peru, Ecuador, and Bolivia. Many have been successful, but have at best delayed the neoliberal juggernaut.

It was under these conditions and in this atmosphere that the people of Brazil went to the polling booths. The result was an entire country saying no to the dictates of neoliberalism.

During the election campaign, the mainstream media had spread various scare stories about the impact that a Workers Party Administration would have on the health of the Brazilian economy, meaning the ability of foreign-owned companies to take money out of the country. Such talk caused a crisis in the economy and forced Lula to agree to abide by IMF rules. After Lula was inaugurated, he followed the rules of the international banking institutions and subsequently was lauded by newspapers such as the *Financial Times* and the *Wall Street Journal*. Any failure to follow through on preelection commitments to Brazil's poor has not been covered.

The best source to follow the progress of the Lula Administration can be found on the Brazilian Landless Laborers Web site at <www.mstbrazil.org/>. Another useful resource is the ZNET Web site, especially the pages on Latin America and Brazil, at <www.zmag.org/LAM/index.html>.

 # Reinstating the Draft

Sources:
Salon, November 3, 2003
Title: "Oiling up the Draft Machine?"
Author: Dave Lindorff

<Buzzflash.com>, November 11, 2003
Title: "Would a Second Bush Term Mean a Return to Conscription?"
Author: Maureen Farrell

War Times, October/November, 2003
Title: "Military Targets Latino Youth"
Author: Jorge Mariscal

Evaluator: Robert Manning
Student Researchers: Jenifer Green and Adam Stutz

The Selective Service System (SSS), the Bush Administration, and the Pentagon have been quietly moving to fill draft board vacancies nationwide in order to prepare for a military draft that could start as early as June 15, 2005. In preparation, several million dollars have been added to the 2004 SSS budget. The SSS Administration must report to Bush on March 31, 2005 that the system, which has lain dormant for decades, is ready for activation. The Pentagon has quietly begun a public campaign to fill all 10,350 draft board positions and 11,070 appeals board slots nationwide. An unpopular election year topic, military experts and influential members of Congress are suggesting that if Rumsfeld's prediction of a "long, hard slog" in Iraq and Afghanistan (and a permanent state of war on terrorism) proves accurate, the U.S. may have no choice but to draft.

Congress brought twin bills S. 89 and H.R. 163 forward in 2003, introduced by Representative Charles Rangel (D–NY) and Senator Fritz Hollings (D–SC). Entitled the Universal National Service Act of 2003, their aim is "to provide for the common defense by requiring that all young persons (age 18-26) in the United States, including women, perform a period of military service or a period of civilian service in furtherance of the national defense and homeland security, and for other purposes." These active bills currently sit in the Committee on Armed Services.

Dodging the draft will be more difficult than those from the Vietnam era remember. College and Canada will no longer be options. In December 2001, Canada and the U.S. signed a "Smart Border Declaration," which could be used to contain would-be draft dodgers. The declaration involves a 30-point plan that implements, among other things, a "pre-clearance agreement" of people entering and departing each country. Reforms aimed at making the draft more equitable along gender and class lines also eliminate higher education as a shelter. Underclassmen would only be able to postpone service until the end of their current semester. Seniors would have until the end of the academic year.

In May 2000, Delaware was the first state to enact legislation requiring that driver's license information be sent to the SSS. By August 2003, 32 states, two territories, and the District of Columbia followed suit. Noncompliance with sending information to the SSS has always been punishable by up to five years in prison and a $250,000 fine. Up to now, the government has never acted on these measures, but levied punishment would bar violators from federal employment and student loans. The SSS has altered its Web site at <www.sss.gov> to include a front-page denial of a draft resurrection, but continues to post the twenty-four page Annual Performance Plan, which includes its June 15 deadline still intact.

In addition to the possibility of a draft, the continual recruitment of Latinos into the armed forces has been creating volatile reactions from antirecruitment advocates. The target recruitment of Latinos began during Clinton's tenure in office. Louis

Caldera, then secretary of the army, was able to discern that Latinos were the fastest growing group of military-age individuals in the United States. In May of 2003, the military was involved in a diplomatic dispute when recruiters made their way across the border. The headmaster of a Tijuana high school threw out the recruiter, and the Mexican government was vehemently upset. The Pentagon has preyed on the fact that Latinos and Latinas often enter the military in search of "civilian skills" they can apply in the workforce.

In 2001, Department of Defense (DOD) statistics showed that while 10 percent of military forces are comprised of Latinos, 17.7 percent of this group occupies "front-line positions." This includes "infantry, gun crews, and seamanship." With the army's continual banter about educational subsidies of up to $30,000 for college and completion of GED requirements, the "glitz and glamour" of the military has enhanced misconceptions about the nature of military service for Latinos.

Charles Pena, director of defense studies at the libertarian Cato Institute presents a comparable conflict between the United States and the Middle East and the British and Northern Ireland where the occupying army encountered hostile opposition amongst civilian populations. In that situation, the occupying army needed a ratio of 10 or 20 soldiers per 1,000 civilians; "...If you transfer that to Iraq, it would mean you'd need at least 240,000 troops and maybe as many as 480,000." With no sign of retreat or resolution and every indication of increasing opposition in locations occupied by troops, it will likely be deemed necessary to increase and maintain military presence. Additionally, there is the massive exodus of ally troops and aid from positions of occupation and combat. The U.S. has been unable to draw major assistance from other countries, and high enlistment bonuses have been both ineffective and expensive in light of rapidly growing debt. Add to the growing list of unfavorable realities an unwillingness of soldiers to re-enlist, and the U.S. is unable to meet the soldier quotient needed to continue occupation of Iraq alone. Exacerbating this dilemma is the probability of expanding occupation and the White House promise of war in multiple theaters.

UPDATE BY MAUREEN FARRELL: While the draft became newsworthy in the immediate aftermath of September 11, the mainstream media brushed most concerns aside. "Military Draft Unlikely for 'War' on Terrorism," *ABC News* reported on September 18, 2001, citing military analysts' opinions. The Brookings Institution's Michael O'Hanlon, however, admitted that, should the U.S. military become involved in an extended occupation, then perhaps we'd be looking at "the kinds of man power requirements that would advise in favor of a draft." By May 2004, O'Hanlon updated his prediction, citing mounting casualties and an overreliance on National Guard and reserve troops in Iraq. "The most likely cause [for reinstatement of the draft] would be an even more severe overdeployment of the all-volunteer force... " he wrote in the *Los Angeles Times*.

Although Representative Charles Rangel also addressed conscription concerns, by the time my story appeared on <BuzzFlash.com>, little had been written about changes that would make "draft dodging" more difficult. Few mentioned that draft laws had been changed in 1971 to restrict college deferments and even fewer discussed the sweeping new policies regarding selective service registration. The border agreement between Canada and the U.S. (yet another roadblock to would-be draft dodgers) received even less press.

I first became interested in this story in July 2002, after reading a letter to the editor of the *Philadelphia Inquirer* regarding pending legislation linking drivers' license applications to selective service registration. At the time, half of all U.S. states had enacted such legislation (with scarce media attention), and as of April 9, 2004, all but 13 states had either passed such legislation or were in the process of doing so (also with scarce media attention).

Since this story broke, presidential candidates Ralph Nader and Representative Dennis Kucinich (D–OH) have raised concerns over conscription's everincreasing likelihood; Senator Chuck Hagel (R–NE) has called for a national debate on the issue; and the Selective Service System's proposal to draft women and extend the draft registration age from 25 to 34 has been uncovered. Yet the mainstream media continues to ignore the larger implications in regard to the 2004 election. (The Internet remains an exception, however. <BuzzFlash.com> has featured several editorials on the subject and in May 2004, conservative columnist Paul Craig Roberts, writing for <antiwar.com>, wrote: "If Bush is reelected, wider war and a draft to feed it seem a certainty.")

This story is important for several reasons, but most notably for the questions it raises. Why did the Selective Service System feel compelled to ensure compliance through new laws? Does this shift have anything to do with the larger, but also underreported agenda to widen the war in the Middle East? Do most Americans comprehend the long-term consequences of President Bush's stated desire to "change the world"?

An informed citizenry is crucial to democracy. Given that our military is already overextended, Americans need to scrutinize this administration's intentions for "dealing with" Iran, Syria, and other countries. And before they vote, they should also understand that extended military commitments would most likely require a return to the draft—and that this time around, neither college nor Canada would provide refuge.

For map of states linking drivers' license applications to Selective Service registration, see <www.sss.gov/PDFs/DriversLicense2004.pdf>. For information on how the draft has changed since Vietnam, see <www.sss.gov/viet.htm>. For more on the U.S.–Canada "Smart Border Agreement," see <www.canadianembassy.org/border/declaration-en.asp>.

UPDATE BY JORGE MARISCAL: My article called attention to the Pentagon's efforts to double the number of Latinos in the U.S. military by 2006 and to the ongoing militarization of public school systems. As popular support for the invasion and occupation of Iraq began to decline throughout early 2004, the Latino/a community became increasingly aware of the negative consequences of military service, the distortions used by military recruiters to seduce young people, and the increasingly limited range of alternatives available to working-class youth.

Counter-recruitment activities in predominantly Latino schools increased as never before. For the first time, activists, students, and educators in Los Angeles held a citywide counter-recruitment conference at Manual Arts High School. The organization formed at that conference continues to leaflet local high schools and hold meetings for parents and teachers. I was able to deliver lectures on militarism and the militarization of public schools at a number of venues throughout the Southwest. In April, activist Fernando Suarez del Solar and I spoke to approximately 300 students at the University of Texas, El Paso. Many of them vowed to begin counter-recruitment projects. Others said they would reconsider their decision to enlist in the military as a way to receive funding for education. We witnessed similar results in Albuquerque, San Antonio, and other cities with large Latino populations. Students at several universities in Puerto Rico organized protests to challenge the use of funding for ROTC programs. Efforts to establish a national network of counter-recruitment groups were successful, and organizers called a national meeting for the summer of 2004 in Philadelphia.

Working with Fernando Suarez del Solar (who lost his son during the invasion of Iraq) and his Guerrero Azteca Project, our organization Project on Youth and Non-Military Opportunities (YANO) visited numerous high schools, colleges, and Latino parents' groups in California. Across the state, students leafleted their schools with information about the truth behind the recruiters' sales pitch. At an antiwar poetry recital in San Diego, poet Jimmy Santiago Baca joined young local poets to raise funds for YANO's important work. YANO continues to produce Spanish-language literature on the realities of military life and the partial truths presented by recruiters. Its director, Rick Jahnkow, advises other groups on how to begin and sustain counter-recruitment activities. YANO and its sister organization Committee Opposed to Militarism and the Draft (COMD) continue to offer sound advice on the possibility of a military draft.

Mainstream coverage of the issues presented in my story was minimal. French, Swiss, and British journalists contacted us on several occasions, but U.S. media outlets did not. In terms of our work in Spanish-language communities, we received a great deal of coverage from Spanish-language radio and television (e.g., *Univision* and *Radio Bilingue*) as well as the Spanish-language print media. Public radio stations with limited Latino programming in English (such as KPFK in Los Angeles) conducted several interviews with YANO members and associates.

Additional information about the issues raised in my story can be found at the following locations: Project on Youth and Non-Military Opportunities (YANO), <www.projectyano.org>; Committee Opposed to Militarism and the Draft (COMD), <www.comdsd.org>; American Friends Service Committee (AFSC), <www.afsc.org/youthmil.htm>; and Guerrero Azteca Project, <www.guerreroazteca.org>.

 # Wal-Mart Brings Inequity and Low Prices to the World

Source:
Multinational Monitor, October 2003
Title: "Welcome to Wal-World"
Author: Andy Rowell

Faculty Evaluators: Phil McGough and Laurie Dawson
Student Researchers: Mariah Wegener-Vernagallo and Doug Reynolds

"Country by country, the world is discovering the great value of shopping at Wal-Mart," says John Menzer, president of the international division of Wal-Mart, the world's largest retailer. Menzer's vision is one where Wal-Mart becomes a global brand, just like McDonald's or Coca-Cola, monopolizing the global retail market.

What Menzer fails to tell shareholders is the fact that Wal-Mart is also facing lots of consumer pressure both at home and abroad for some of their business activities. Wal-Mart's strategy of corporate takeovers in other countries has come into question. When entering a new market, the company never opens directly to the public; instead they buy into an already fully operational company and slowly take control. First, a large competitor is eliminated; then Wal-Mart gains real estate and employees, creating a massive presence in its targeted location.

In addition, by taking over existing stores rather than opening new ones, Wal-Mart avoids the community opposition that it faces in the U.S. Al Norman, the founder of Sprawl-Busters, who has been described by CBS's *60 Minutes*, as the guru of the anti-Wal-Mart movement, says, "What Wal-Mart did in Mexico was very instructive. Mexico was a testing ground for the method of operation. They basically acquired existing stores. They moved into Mexico and that became the theme in other countries like the U.K., Germany, and Japan. They would buy into an existing operation rather than start from scratch."

Wal-Mart opposition overseas has been from unions (over low pay), local regulators (over predatory pricing), and small businesses that face financial ruin. Recently, the company has also come under pressure from the United Food and Commercial

Workers (UFCW) in the U.S. for not allowing union representation in their super-stores. With new superstores opening that contain groceries as well as all other Wal-Mart amenities, competitor supermarket chains with unions are worried about their future revenues.

Just as Wal-Mart exports sprawl, it exports bad labor practices. Uni-Commerce, the global trade union for commercial workers, characterizes Wal-Mart as "an obsessively anti-union company at home and abroad." The company "builds its competitive advantage on low wages, poor benefits, and a squeeze on producers. Through predatory pricing, it can force both large and small competitors out of business," according to Uni-Commerce. "Worldwide, Wal-Mart is the most serious threat to employment, wages, and working conditions in commerce." The problem with unions over low pay is one of the main obstacles the company faces in its international expansion plans. The rift between unions and Wal-Mart, say financial analysts <Fallstreet.com>, is "intensifying with each global step the company makes."

Wal-Mart also threatens small shops in countries in which it does not even operate. In 1998, the Irish government adopted a cap on the size of stores. But companies like Swedish furniture retailer IKEA and Wal-Mart are believed to be pressuring government officials to lift the cap. The only place such large stores would be built would be out of town, creating sprawl. "Any country that has predominantly smaller stores will be shocked by the superstore format," argues Norman.

"In five or six years, you could be talking about 5,000 to 6,000 Wal-Mart stores outside of the United States," says Norman. "Wal-Mart is Americanizing retailing around the world. It is a really undesirable outcome both culturally and economically for a U.S. company to be exercising so much power."

UPDATE BY ANDY ROWELL: Wal-Mart's unstoppable spread continues. In September 2003, Wal-Mart announced the "continuation of its aggressive unit growth for the fiscal year beginning February 1, 2004." In the U.S., Wal-Mart planned to open approximately 50 to 55 new discount stores, 220 to 230 new supercenters, 25 to 30 new neighborhood markets, and 35-40 new Sam's Clubs. Wal-Mart International planned to open 130 to 140 units in existing markets.

In March 2004, Wal-Mart Brazil announced the acquisition of Bompreco, a retail chain in northeastern Brazil with 118 units (hypermarkets, supermarkets, and minimarkets). In April 2004, the company's international operations stood at 1,494 total units: 641 in Mexico, 53 in Puerto Rico, 236 in Canada, 11 in Argentina, 144 in Brazil, 35 in China, 15 in South Korea, 92 in Germany, and 267 in the United Kingdom. Its international sales were $47.5 billion, a 16.6 percent increase over the previous year. International operating profit was $2.3 billion, an increase of 18.6 percent compared to the previous fiscal year.

And so it goes on. Where will the next Wal-Mart be? Will it be in your local community? Do you want a world run by Wal-Mart, where raw economic muscle of a huge global retailer can out-price any local competitor and put them out of business? In this cut price war the consumer will lose, the environment will lose and communities will lose.

In the U.K., Wal-Mart's takeover of Asda has had a devastating effect. Award-wining food journalist Joanna Blythman's new book called *Shopped: The Shocking Power of British Supermarkets*, published May 2004, outlines how Blythman "learned that U.K. supermarkets now jump to the tune of our second largest chain, Asda. Since 1999, when it was taken over by the biggest retailer in the world, the U.S. chain Wal-Mart, Asda's strategy of 'Every Day Low Pricing,' has triggered a supermarket price war in which chains without buying muscle are disadvantaged. In order to keep up with Asda, our leading chains in the U.K. must be ever more ruthless in the way they operate or else risk losing their place at the supermarket superpowers' top table."

This means that suppliers are squeezed, farmers are squeezed, and supermarkets source from the cheapest overseas suppliers where labor, human rights, and environmental standards are the lowest. Every week in the U.K., 50 specialist shops like butchers and bakers are closing, and one farmer or farm worker commits suicide. We enter a race to the bottom where everyone loses, especially the consumer.

For additional information, see Al Norman's Sprawl-Busters, <www.sprawl-busters.com>; Joanna Blythman's *Shopped*, which can be purchased at <harpercollins.co.uk/books/default.aspx?id=27115>; Friends of the Earth supermarket campaign, <www.foe.co.uk/campaigns/real_food/press_for_change/>; a coalition of groups in the U.K. against supermarkets, <www.breakingthearmlock.com>; Wal-Mart and unions, <www.union-network.org/>; and a selection of Andy Rowell articles, <www.andyrowell.com>.

Al Norman, guru of the anti-Wal-Mart movement, also has a new book out called *The Case Against Wal-Mart*. To order, call toll-free (in the U.S.) (877) 386-5925 or e-mail <ruth@raphel.com> or visit <www.raphel.com>.

Censored 2005 Runners-Up

LABOR MOVEMENT WORKS TO REVITALIZE IMMIGRANT RIGHTS

Sources:
Labor Notes, July 2003
Title: "Labor and Allies Seek to Rebuild Momentum for Immigration Reform"
Author: Teo Reyes

Voices from the Earth, Vol. 4, No. 3, Fall 2003
Title: "Farm Workers: Are They Really Protected in the Fields?"
Authors: Ruben Nunez, Olga Pedroza, and Kitty Richard

New Mexico Legal Aid reports that farm workers have shorter life spans and suffer from many health problems because of employment in the fields and poverty. They are inadequately trained about how to avoid the hazards of pesticides and are given insufficient protective gear. They often suffer poor health due to lack of health care insurance. Due to the risk of retaliation or deportation, many farm workers forced to work under inhumane conditions are not willing to file formal complaints with any government agency. Labor and its allies are trying to rebuild awareness about the needs and rights of immigrant workers.

DEPARTMENT OF ENERGY AND THE LOS ALAMOS LAB: A SYMBIOTIC RELATIONSHIP

Sources:
Voices from the Earth, Vol. 4, No. 3, Fall 2003
Title: "Bioterror at Home: Biological Research—A Short Step to Weapon's Production"
Author: Colin King

Voices from the Earth, Vol. 4, No. 3, Fall 2003
Title: "Bombing New Mexico: Nuclear Bomb Facility Proposed"
Author: Amy Williams

The National Nuclear Security Administration (NNSA), a semi-autonomous agency within the Department of Energy (DOE) has proposed two new facilities for Los Alamos National Laboratory as well as a biosafety level 3 lab. This biosafety lab, the first of its kind within the DOE, is setting a precedent for being located at a top secret nuclear weapons research facility. The Department of Homeland Security (DHS), which has already earned a reputation in the halls of Congress for being overly secretive, has inherited this NNSA program.

THE REAL FORCE BEHIND "CITIZENS AGAINST LAWSUIT ABUSE"

Source: *Multinational Monitor*, March 2003
Title: "Corporate Astroturf and Civil Justice"
Authors: Carl Deal and Joanne Doroshow

Major corporations are attempting to escape liability for the harm they cause consumers by restricting the avenue for individuals to bring civil lawsuits against them. One of their strategies is to organize and generously fund ostensibly nonpartisan, "grassroots" citizen groups opposed to "lawsuit abuse."

CORPORATIONS POSE A GROWING THREAT TO CONSTITUTIONAL FREEDOMS

Source: *Dollars and Sense*, May/June 2003
Title: "The Invisible Gag"
Author: Lawrence Soley

Corporations can now impose an almost endless array of restrictions on our Constitutional freedoms. The increased power of corporations to censor and restrict arises from three related factors:

➤ the Supreme Court's deference to private sector property rights over the rights of citizens under the First Amendment;
➤ the gigantic and powerful nature of modern corporations;
➤ and the shrinking of the public sector as the private sector increasingly takes over, resulting in fewer places where citizens can legally exercise their constitutionally protected rights.

The control extends from public spaces to private homes. Homeowners' associations (private corporations that own or govern housing developments and condominiums) have an increasing ability to restrict speech, behavior, and overall actions of their residents.

THE WAR ON CHURCH-STATE BOUNDARIES

Source: *Z Magazine*, July/August 2003
Title: "Faith-Based Finagling"
Author: Bill Berkowitz

Bush's CARE Act is nothing more then a diluted version of Bush's faith-based initiative. The plan allows Christian groups, but not other religions, to compete equally with secular groups for federal funding, challenging the checks and balances between church-state boundaries.

CORPORATE MALFEASANCE REDUCED TO MINOR OFFENSES

Source: *Asheville Global Report (AGR)*, January 22, 2004
Title: "Multiple Corporate Personality Disorder"
Authors: Russell Mokhiber and Robert Weissman

Only two top-level executives are in jail for corporate crime, and yet the problem of corporate fraud is costing American taxpayers billions of dollars. Corporations have taken to cutting deals with the Justice Department for reduced charges and pleading off a few executives as scapegoats, thus avoiding more severe repercussions to the corporation itself.

U.S. EXPANDING ITS ABILITY TO DELIVER MISSILES

Source: *Asheville Global Report (AGR)*, July 10-16, 2003
Title: "U.S.-Based Missiles to Have Global Reach"
Author: Julian Borger

The U.S. military is looking into ways to send non-nuclear missiles from the continental U.S. to any target around the world by 2010. The program, code named FALCON (Force Application and Launch from the Continental U.S.), wants to launch weapons using expendable rocket boosters by 2010 with a reusable unmanned hypersonic cruise vehicle for bombing runs from the continental U.S. to be developed by 2025.

BRITISH INTELLIGENCE EMPLOYEE FACES CHARGES FOR SPEAKING OUT

Source: *Baltimore Sun*, December 14, 2003
Title: "For Telling the Truth"
Author: Norman Solomon

For almost a year, the American press has completely ignored the story of whistle-blower Katharine Gun, a translator at Britain's Government Communications Headquarters (GCH) who had been fired and arrested for leaking a top-secret memorandum to *The Observer* back in February of 2003. This memo outlined an American surveillance strategy to spy on U.N. delegates from Mexico, Chile, Bulgaria, Angola, Cameroon, Guinea, and especially Pakistan in an effort to obtain "the whole gamut of information that could give U.S. policymakers an edge in obtaining results favorable to U.S. goals—support for war on Iraq." This memo requested aid from the staff at Britain's GCH in the surveillance effort. It wasn't until roughly a year later, on the day of Katharine Gun's pretrial hearing, that her name got mainstream attention from the American press.

BOLIVIA'S REVOLUTION

Sources:
Left Turn, March 2004
Title: "Bolivia's October Revolution"
Author: Forrest Hylton

World Press Review, January 2004
Title: "Bolivia's Political Earthquake—Andean Time Bomb"
Author: Maria Elvira Samper

On October 17, 2003, between 250,000 and 500,000 people took control of the political capital of Bolivia, forcing their neoliberal president to flee to Miami. The insurrection was lead by the indigenous Aymara people, supported by miners, coca growers, and peasants in protest of the announcement of plans to export Bolivia's natural gas to California and Mexico.

IRAQI DEATHS DON'T COUNT

Source: *Peace Magazine*, January–March 2004
Title: "The Killing in Iraq Goes On and No One is Counting the Full Cost"
Authors: John Sloboda and Hamit Dardagan

The oft-reported Western death toll in Iraq (under 400 at time of print) is dwarfed by the uncounted Iraqi death toll (around 7,000 to 9,000 civilian deaths to date and an unknown number of military deaths, likely between 10,000 and 45,000). According to U.K. Defense Minister Adam Ingram, "Whilst the Ministry of Defense has accurate data relating to the number of U.K. service personnel that have been killed or injured …we do not propose to undertake a formal review of Iraqi casualties."

STATE DEPARTMENT LISTS "TERRORIST" COUNTRIES

Source: *International Socialist Review*, July/August 2003
Title: "Who's Next On…Bush's Hit List?"
Author: Anthony Arnove

The agenda of the U.S. administration to reshape the Middle East is veiled by the familiar war on terror. The State Department has listed Georgia, Chechnya, Kenya, Sudan, and the Philippines as well as many others as potential targets, though none have been involved in terrorist activities in almost 20 years. Meanwhile, administration officials have warned Iran that the invasion of Iraq could serve as a model for an invasion of their country. The current opposition to the occupation of Iraq is only a precursor to what could be the largest global protest against our country if the administration continues with its current foreign policies.

SUPPORTING OUR TROOPS?

Source: *Eat the State!*, November 19, 2003
Title: "How America Supports Its Veterans"
Author: None Listed

The Veteran's Administration (VA) and the Bush Administration are stonewalling pleas from vet groups to live up to their promises. Generations of vets face extensive service-related health problems as cutbacks in spending and benefits for the VA health care increase. The VA still does not acknowledge Gulf War Syndrome and is ignoring reports of war-related disease and serious maladies from the veterans of the current conflict Iraq, including rising cancer rates.

SUGAR INDUSTRY THREATENS WORLD HEALTH ORGANIZATION FUNDING

Source: *Guardian Weekly*, April 24-30, 2003
Title: "Sugar Industry Threatens to Scupper U.S. Funding of WHO"
Author: Sarah Boseley

Six food industry groups have threatened to lobby congress to remove $406 million worth of funding to the World Health Organization (WHO) if a report by the WHO stating that sugar should account for no more than 10 percent of a healthy diet is not immediately scrapped. The sugar industry supports a finding by the Institute of Medicine that claims a 25 percent sugar intake is acceptable, though the institute warns that the report is being misinterpreted and 25 percent is not the recommended intake. WHO insiders are describing the threat as blackmail and worse than any pressure exerted by the tobacco lobby.

IS YOUR FOOD AT RISK?

Source: *Left Turn*, August/September 2003
Title: "Is Your Food at Risk?"
Author: Monique Mikhail

Although irradiated food needs to be labeled when sold in stores, it has stealthily made its way into the school system. A provision in the 2002 Farm Bill, which the food irradiation industry lobbied for, allows irradiated food to be served in cafeterias at educational institutions. Food-borne illnesses have caused meat companies to utilize food irradiation. Irradiation kills the bacteria that is harbored in the feces, urine, pus, and other contaminants on meat while destroying up to 95 percent of the vitamin content in food.

ISRAELIS SEEN FILMING 9/11 TRAGEDY

Source: *Scotland Sunday Herald*, November 2, 2003
Title: " Five Israelis Were Seen Filming as Jet Liners Ploughed into the Twin
  Towers on September 11, 2001..."
Author: None Listed

Israeli intelligence may have known the attacks on September 11 were going to occur, but did nothing to stop them. Five Israeli intelligence agents were spotted filming and celebrating as the World Trade Center fell. All of them had links to Mossad. A U.S. government report details how Israel may have had a large intelligence organization tracking Arabs in America and many suspected Israeli intelligence members lived near the leaders of the September 11 attack.

A WHOLE NEW WORLD—THE ZAPATISTA WAY

Source: *Left Turn*, March/April 2004
Title: "The Zapatistas Construct Another World"
Author: Mary Ann Tenuto Sanchez

On January 1, 2004, the Zapatista Army of National Liberation (EZLN or Zapatistas) commemorated the tenth anniversary of the Zapatista Uprising in Chiapas, Mexico. They are slowly constructing another world based upon civilian, regional, indigenous self-government (autonomy), and collective work for the community. Utilizing regional governance structures called Juntas de Buen Gobierno, or simply Juntas, autonomous county councils, carry out the usual functions of local government. Zapatista progress is moving slowly, however, in the process of constructing their own world, they have shown that another world with cultural values opposing those of neoliberalism is possible.

BUSH PUSHES TO REVOKE ENDANGERED SPECIES ACT

Source: *Earth First!*, July/August 2003
Title: "Bush Undermines Critical Habitat"
Author: Salmon

The Bush Administration is undermining the Endangered Species Act (ESA) in favor of corporations. Logging, recreational vehicle use, military operations, pollution, livestock grazing, urban sprawl, and other forms of human encroachment have taken a heavy toll on the wildlife during the last 30 years. The Bush Administration is using stalling tactics and loopholes in the ESA to avoid addressing the underlying problems, such as pollution and habitat destruction. Only 406 out of the 1,262 species that are listed as endangered or threatened species have critical habitat designation. Bush has revoked 27 Clinton era Critical Habitat Designations, totaling more than 16 million acres.

CONSTITUTION RESTORATION ACT COULD TRANSFORM U.S. INTO A THEOCRACY

Source: *The Moscow Times*, March 12–14, 2004
Title: "Pin Heads"
Author: Chris Floyd

In February of 2004, close congressional allies of the Bush Administration introduced a bill called the "Constitution Restoration Act of 2004." It was drafted by a group of religious extremists known as "Dominionists," whose aim is to establish "biblical rule" over every aspect of society and is supported by John Ashcroft.

MEDICARE ANALYST THREATENED TO CHANGE STORY

Source: *Philadelphia Inquirer*, March 13, 2004
Title: "Medicare Analyst Confirms Muzzling"
Author: Tony Pugh

The nation's top Medicare cost analyst maintains that his former boss ordered him to withhold from lawmakers unfavorable cost estimates about the Medicare prescription drug bill or be fired. He said the estimates given to Congress were off by more than $100 billion.

U.S. GOVERNMENT FAKED BUSH NEWS REPORTS

Source: *The Guardian* (London), March 16, 2004
Title: "U.S. Government Faked Bush News Reports"
Author: Chris Tryhorn

TV news footage that showed President Bush getting a standing ovation from potential voters has been exposed as fake. The government admitted it paid actors to play journalists in video news releases intended to convey support for a new health benefits and Medicare law. It also prepared scripts to be used by news anchors.

TORTURERS FIND HAVEN IN THE UNITED STATES

Source: *Mother Jones*, May/June 2003
Title: "The Torturers Next Door"
Author: Karen Olsson

According to a recent report by Amnesty International, as many as 1,000 human-rights violators from around the world live in the United States. Like the former Nazis who made headlines in the 1970s and 1980s, most of them lead quiet lives on sub-urban cul-de-sacs and in gated retirement communities. But unlike former Nazis, who for decades have been subject to a concerted federal effort to find and deport them, these retired torturers have little to fear from the U.S. government. The Immigration and Naturalization Service (INS) has stepped up efforts to deport those who violate immigration law, but the agency says it cannot expel people on human-rights grounds alone. And while the Justice Department is required by law to prosecute human-rights violators in the criminal courts under the 1994 Convention Against Torture, the department has not filed one single such case. It has instead helped bring torturers here under a 1949 bill authorizing the CIA to admit up to 100 people a year "in the interest of national security." This authorization was never repealed. Many former torturers now live in southern Florida where they hold real-estate licenses, work at Disney World, win the lotto, and bump into their victims at neighborhood parties.

THIS MODERN WORLD

by TOM TOMORROW

SIR--THE ECONOMY'S *TANKING*... SOLDIERS ARE DYING IN IRAQ ON A *DAILY BASIS*...AND WE *STILL* HAVEN'T FOUND ANY WMD'S!

AND YOUR NUMBERS HAVE BEEN DROPPING LIKE AN *ANCHOR* SINCE YOU ASKED FOR THAT $87 BILLION!

LEADERS OF THE HOUSE INTELLI-GENCE COMMITTEE HAVE DECLARED THAT THE INTEL WE USED TO JUS-TIFY THE WAR WAS *OUTDATED* AND *CIRCUMSTANTIAL*--

--AND THE DEFENSE INTELLIGENCE AGENCY HAS CONCLUDED THAT EXILES LIKE AHMAD CHALABI WHO CLAIMED TO HAVE INSIDE INFORMATION WERE SIMPLY *MAKING STUFF UP* AND TELLING US WHAT WE WANTED TO *HEAR!*

ON TOP OF ALL THIS, WE'RE BEING INVESTIGATED FOR BLOWING THE COVER OF A CIA OPERATIVE AFTER HER HUSBAND EXPOSED OUR YEL-LOWCAKE URANIUM STORY AS A *FICTION!*

CAPTAIN, IT'S A FREAKISH CONFLUENCE OF FACTORS WHICH COULD EASILY COALESCE INTO AN UNBELIEVABLE *TEMPEST!* WE *COULD* BE LOOK-ING AT--

--*THE PERFECT STORM!!*

AH, I'M SURE IT'LL ALL BLOW OVER.

FULL SPEED AHEAD!

AYE, AYE, CAP'N.

WILL THE CREW OF THE S.S. OVAL OFFICE *SURVIVE*? STAY *TUNED!*

TOM TOMORROW©2003 ... www.thismodernworld.com

CHAPTER 2

Censored Déjà Vu

A REVIEW AND UPDATE ON IMPORTANT CENSORED STORIES FROM PRIOR YEARS

By Peter Phillips, Brooke Finley, Christopher Robin Cox, Matthew Hagan, Brittany Roeland, Emilio Licea, Melody Lindsey, Anna Miranda, Lauren Kettner, Timothy Zolezzi, Julie Mayeda, and Ambrosia Pardue

Remembering Yugoslavia: Managed News and Weapons of Mass Destruction

BY BROOKE FINLEY

On March 24, 1999, the United States military along with NATO forces mounted one of the most extensive and devastating aerial bombings in the history of modern warfare on Yugoslavia. NATO's "air campaign" was conducted 24 hours a day, 7 days a week, over a 78-day period and dropped a total of 20,000 tons of bombs. The operations that ended on June 10, 1999 were in response to a alleged humanitarian crisis of genocide and ethnic cleansing.[1]

On March 19, 2003, General Tommy Franks, under the orders of George W. Bush's White House, began the U.S. invasion of Iraq, code-named "Operation Iraqi Freedom." It began with the "Shock and Awe" campaign, an aerial attack over Baghdad consisting of 1,663 U.S. aircraft, including B-52, B-1, and B-2 stealth bombers. It was the first time ever that all three bomber types were used simultaneously. These aircraft flew 20,753 combat missions, dropping 18,467 smart bombs and 9,251 dumb bombs. The Navy also fired 802 cruise missiles.[2] The ground invasion ended April 9, 2003, when the U.S. declared "victory." Yet the occupation of Iraq continues. As of June 10,

2004, between 9,284 and 11,147 innocent civilians have died as a direct result of this military action.[3] This operation is a continuation of the United States' "War on Terror," a response to Saddam's supposed "weapons of mass destruction." The stated goal of this invasion was to free the Iraqi people from a torturous regime.[4]

At first glance, it would seem as though these two acts of war have very little in common. They occurred in two different parts of the world with, ostensibly, two completely different reasons for involvement. But closer examination reveals that in both cases, the real, albeit unspoken, reasons for invading reflected previous invasions: Strategic economic interests as well as military geopolitical positioning were the driving forces behind United States involvement. However, in order to guarantee international support, there were false justifications, and the corporate media was the willing mechanism for spreading the fabrications. The media have always played a large role in shaping public opinion during times of war, but never before had they actually dictated foreign policy (as in Bosnia) or become such an exclusive propaganda arm of the war machine (as in Iraq).

BACKGROUND

Prior to the late 1980s, the Socialist Federal Republic of Yugoslavia—a nation built of six loosely affiliated republics, two autonomous provinces, 25 separate ethnic groups, and a multitude of religions—was an example of a cooperative struggle towards unity. The government of Yugoslavia shared a collective presidency composed of one representative from each of the republics, with the objective of establishing a balance between the leadership of the regional and national interests. Its economy, the system which has come to be known as "self-management," reached its most developed form in the Law of Associated Labor of 1976, under which the means of production and other major resources are not regarded as state property (as in the Soviet Union) but as social property. From this basis of democratic socialism, Yugoslavia was making a bold attempt to push diversity and progress forward.

Among its achievements were a literacy rate that had gone from 55 percent in 1953 to 90 percent in 1986, an infant mortality rate that dropped from 116.5 per 1,000 births to 27.1 per 1,000 births over the same period, free medical coverage, free education, and an evergrowing national identity that crossed traditional boundaries. According to the 1992 *Encyclopedia Britannica*, "Since World War II, largely in Serbo-Croatian speaking areas, there has been the gradual emergence of a sizable section of the population who prefer to describe themselves as 'Yugoslavs.'" It also notes, "their numbers are growing steadily, more as a result of ethnically-mixed marriages than because of high natural increase."[5]

The quotations above describe a vastly different Yugoslavia than the one later depicted by NATO and allied leaders. As early as 1984, the Reagan Administration produced a classified National Security Decision Directive (NSDD 133), entitled "United States Policy Toward Yugoslavia," calling for a "quiet revolution" and then integration into a neoliberal free-market economy.[6] By 1989, Yugoslavia had undergone a drastic shift. Needing to stabilize its economy, it borrowed heavily from creditors including the International Monetary Fund (IMF) and World Bank. A western economic recession lead to an interest-driven spiral of debt, and the IMF demanded "restructuring," including massive cuts in social spending, forced privatization, and wage freezes. In the one-year span of 1989–1990 an estimated 600,000 Yugoslavian workers were laid off due to over 1,000 company bankruptcies.[7]

Michel Chossudovsky provides data that shows how 6.1 percent GDP growth in the 1960s and 1970s became a 7.5 percent decline by 1990, with real wages falling 41 percent. In 1991, the GDP fell 15 percent further, while industrial output shrank by 21 percent. The World Bank stated that an additional 2,435 companies were to be liquidated; "their 1.3 million workers— half the remaining industrial work force—were considered redundant," states Chossudovsky. "The IMF-induced budgetary crisis created an economic fait accompli that paved the way for Croatia's and Slovenia's formal secession in June [25] 1991."[8] Two days later, Bosnia and Macedonia followed. Wanting to remain a united federation, Serbia and Montenegro refused the Western ideals of capitalism and on June 27, 1991, the civil war of the Republics of Yugoslavia began.

WESTERN INTERESTS IN THE BALKANS

Western economic and military interests set the stage for the civil war that peaked with NATO air strikes on Serbian Yugoslavia. *Censored* #6 in 2000 explained specific reasons for U.S./NATO involvement. Since the weakening and collapse of the Soviet Union, the U.S. had been hungrily eyeing an estimated $5 trillion in vast oil reserves in the Caspian Sea. In addition Yugoslavia held valuable resources in the Trepca mines complex in the Balkans—gold, lead, silver, zinc, and coal that was worth in excess of $5 billion. After the war, NATO used trumped-up reports of mass graves and crematories at Trepca in order to take over the mines although no evidence was ever brought forward to prove NATO's accusations. The mines, which were once run by Kosovo with the revenue reinvested in its economy, continue to be controlled under NATO forces by private corporations. The profits from these resources are now denied to the people of Kosovo.

After the destruction of Yugoslavia, the U.S. gained control over the Albanian-Macedonian-Bulgarian Oil pipeline (AMBO), which has become their gateway to the Caspian Sea. AMBO Pipeline Corporation, based in New York, has exclusive rights to the development of the project and is expected to begin construction in 2005 with completion in 2008.[9]

These assets (oil and mineral resources) made Yugoslavia a golden fleece in the eyes of the West. When the U.S. "stick-and-carrot" approach to foreign policy failed to quell the "quiet revolution" so strongly desired and instead ended in civil war, the use of force became a necessity. The problem arose of how to do it within the bounds of international law. We needed a smoke screen. And the media was very effective in providing just that.

MEDIA PROMOTES BIASED COVERAGE

Nothing convinced the public more of Serbian atrocities than the fabricated, Nazi-esque photos of a Bosnian Serb camp at Trnopolji doctored from a videotape shot on August 5, 1992, by a British television team lead by Penny Marshall (ITN). Marshall's team went out of their way to depict the most atrocious images (*Censored* #17, 1999). Coincidentally, another Serbian news team shot the same camp, on the same day, capturing Marshall in much of their footage. The Serbian camera crew filmed Trnopolji as a voluntary refugee camp, as well as Marshall sensationalizing a story that never existed. What was later uncovered was the fact that U.N. forces never found such "death camps" when they gained access to all of Bosnia-Herzegovina. There were no signs of metal cages, cremation furnaces, or mass graves, but even this story went unnoticed in the press. The reports of "rape camps" allegedly maintained by the Serbs were also found to be fabricated. After U.N. troops occupied Bosnia, evidence of such camps was never unearthed, and no medical records of the waves of pregnant victims ever materialized.

Ruder-Finn Global Public Affairs, a Washington, DC-based public relations firm, was hired by the Republic of Croatia, the Republic of Bosnia-Herzegovina, and the parliamentary opposition to Kosovo in order to "manufacture" public opinion during the destabilization of Yugoslavia. When the director of Ruder-Finn, James Harff, was interviewed by Jacques Merlino, associate director of French TV2 in April 1993, he boasted about his company's manipulation of Jewish opinion. "Tens of thousands of Jews perished in Croatian camps, so there was every reason for intellectuals and Jewish organizations to be hostile toward the Croats and the [Muslim] Bosnians. Our challenge was to reverse this attitude, and we succeeded masterfully."[10] Harff explains that by mobilizing the Jewish organizations after reports from a *Newsday* article came out about the reputed Serbian death camps, Ruder-Finn was able to "present a simple story of good guys and bad guys which would hereafter play itself."[11] Ruder-Finn did what most public relations firms do: manipulate images, target key groups, bend information, plant stories, and lobby Congress. But what made Ruder-Finn so successful was the receptivity of the Western media, who had already been creating an anti-Serbian climate.

U.S./KLA CREATE DISINFORMATION

The "Racak massacre" was (as described in *Censored* #12, 2000) "the turning point" in NATO's decision to go to war against Yugoslavia. According to *The New York Times*, U.S. diplomat William Walker led an Associated Press (AP) film crew to the site of a supposed massacre of 45 Albanians at the hands of Serbian forces. Challenges to Walker's massacre story were published in *Le Monde* and *Le Figaro*. Belarusian and Finnish forensic experts were later unable to verify that a massacre had actually occurred in Racak. In his update, author Mark Cook compared the massacre to the stories of the Battleship Maine and the Gulf of Tonkin. War correspondent Renaud Girard remarks, "What is disturbing is that the pictures filmed by the AP journalists radically contradict Walker's accusations."[12]

In January 2004, the Finnish pathologist Helena Ranta, who led forensic investigations into the case, said that Serb security troops were also killed. She questioned why the photographs taken before the arrival of international monitors had not been published. Only the photos taken by the Organization for Security and Cooperation in Europe (OSCE) appeared in public. Ranta claims that the OSCE observers forgot to take necessary steps to secure the crime scene. She also said that the work of the Hague tribunal (against Slobodan Milosevic) regarding the supposed Racak massacre was incomprehensible. Ranta and other forensic experts suggested that the bodies were from a fight the night before involving the Serbian police and the KLA and could have been staged in the manner that they were found.[13] In February 2000, PBS's *Frontline* reported the "Racak massacre" exactly as the media had originally, posing no questions or further investigations.[14] Once again, in the face of substantial evidence to the contrary, with mounting questions as to its validity, the mainstream media of the West towed the government story line, forsaking journalistic integrity and objectivity.

In Athens, Greece, a tribunal of over 10,000 declared President Clinton a war criminal in November 1999.[15] In June 2000, an international panel of judges gathered in New York and found U.S. and NATO political and military leaders guilty of war crimes against Yugoslavia during and before the assault on that country from March 24 to June 10, 1999. Former U.S. Attorney General Ramsey Clark was the lead prosecutor in the tribunal on U.S./NATO war crimes against Yugoslavia. Witnesses described the use of media to demonize Serbs, demonstrated how Washington had rigged the Racak massacre for the media, and recounted how the Rambouillet accord (*Censored* #10, 2000) had been used to force war and occupation. Testimony included material illustrating the deliberate targeting of civilians in the bombing of a Belgrade television station, the bombing of refugees, and the bombing of the Chinese Embassy (*Censored* #4, 2001). While the Western media has extensively covered Slobodan Milosevic's indictment for war crimes, there has been barely any mention of Clinton's violation of the War Powers Act during the invasion of Yugoslavia or of either of his two civil indictments.

IRAQ BACKGROUND

In July of 1979, a CIA "asset" by the name of Saddam Hussein gained control of the Baath party and became president of Iraq. In September 1980, fearing Ayatollah Khomeini's influence on the Shiite majority, Hussein invaded Iran. But by early 1982, Iran was winning. Fearing the spread of Islamic fundamentalism throughout the Middle East, the U.S. launched covert operations to arm and aid Iraq. By the end of 1983, the U.S. was providing satellite images of Iran forces and funneling $5.5 billion in loans intended to "promote American farm exports" to assist Iraq in purchasing weapons. In December 1983 and again in March 1984, Reagan sent his personal envoy Donald Rumsfeld to meet with Hussein. The latter visit came at a time when the U.N. was accusing Iraq of using chemical weapons against Iran. From 1986 to 1989 (two years after diplomatic relations had been officially restored), "73 [weapons] transactions took place that included bacterial cultures to make weapons grade anthrax..." In 1988, Iraq gassed 5,000 Kurds, using helicopters purchased from the U.S. On August 2, 1990, Iraq invaded Kuwait, and Hussein's honeymoon with the U.S. ended. Desert Storm, an operation of 573,000 U.S. troops, 100,000 sorties, and 85 tons of bombs, was launched on January 16, 1991, and declared over, barely one month later, on February 28. Saddam

Hussein, however, remained in power. During the Clinton years, despite U.S. imposed economic sanctions that, according to the U.N., took the lives of over 500,000 Iraqis (*Censored* #5, 2003), the "Neocons," newly deposed from power, formed the Project for the New American Century (PNAC). In a letter written by Trent Lott and Newt Gingrich and signed January 26, 1998, the PNAC called for "the removal of Saddam Hussein's regime from power." The signers included Donald Rumsfeld, Paul Wolfowitz, Elliot Abrahams, Richard Armitage, Richard Pearle, and John Bolton. Other PNAC members include Dick Cheney, I. Lewis Libby, and Stephen Cambone (*Censored* #1, 2004). Two years later, all of these men would have positions in George W. Bush's White House and war would become unavoidable.[16]

U.S. INTERESTS IN IRAQ

Since the end of World War II, the U.S. has displayed profound interest in the Middle East. CIA operations in Iran, the support of Iraq during the Iran/Iraq wars, and the first Gulf War are only a few examples of the extent we have been willing to go to secure a compliant Middle East. The afore-mentioned letter by Lott and Gingrich also stated that "we should establish and maintain strong military presence in the region and be prepared to use that force to protect our vital interests in the [Persian] Gulf." The Joint Chiefs of Staff's *Strategic Assessment 1999* stated an "oil war" could be necessary and that "U.S. forces might be used to ensure adequate supplies."[17] Iraq has the second largest oil reserves on earth, only behind those of Saudi Arabia. It also provides strategic placement of military bases, as it borders Iran, Syria, Turkey, and Kuwait. Bases in a post-Saddam, submissive Iraq would ensure protection of U.S. interests in the Persian Gulf for many years to come. To this line of reasoning, author Chalmers Johnson stated, "It would be hard to deny that oil, Israel, and domestic politics all played crucial roles in the Bush Administration's war against Iraq, but I believe the encompassing explanation for our second war with Iraq is no different from that of our wars in the Balkans in 1999 or in Afghanistan in 2001 and 2002: the inexorable pressures of imperialism and militarism."[18]

MEDIA MANIPULATION IN IRAQ

During the toppling of a statue of Saddam Hussein in Firdos Square in Baghdad, the media turned a stage-managed affair into a "feel-good" story with commentary comparing the scene to the fall of the Berlin Wall in 1989. A cropped photo created the appearance of a crowd surrounding the statue and cheering as it fell. Of the crowd assembled, the majority were American soldiers and journalists. A report from the BBC stated that only "dozens" of Iraqis were in the crowd. Others were Iraqi political agents of the American military.[19]

While Americans were left with warm hearts after being told that the U.S. military was "freeing" the Iraqi people, what was never mentioned was that, by Pentagon figures, more Iraqis were killed in Baghdad on Saturday, April 5, than Americans killed at the World Trade Center on September 11, 2001. What was also never mentioned was that the total number of Iraqis killed in three weeks of war exceeded the 50,000 Americans killed over 12 years in Vietnam.[20]

While the media had helped create the reasons for U.S. involvement in Yugoslavia, the media was now transmitting government perspectives about its motives for invading Iraq. As before, the press preferred to passively receive and relay misinformation, as opposed to actively pursuing facts. During the period from September 2002 to June 2003, national paper headlines were filled daily with stories about weapons of mass destruction, and on the nightly news, the Bush Administration claimed to have conclusive evidence of those weapons in Iraq.

Nearly one year later, with the promised "smoking gun" still not found, *The New York Times* finally issued a statement of apology. On May 26, 2004, a letter from the editors was published in the *New York Times* on page A10, acknowledging the lack of investigation and objectivity of their stories dealing with the war in Iraq. They claimed to have rushed for "scoops," using unsubstantiated evidence and single-person testimonies in above-the-fold stories. Follow-up articles questioning the validity of the originals were buried on back pages or never mentioned at all. Many times, useful information was hidden in the middle of an article rather than presented at the beginning. In most cases, information presented by the government was allowed to stand unchallenged.[21] Specific disinformation from *The New York Times* about instances in the war on Iraq are also mentioned in the letter from the editors and can be found online at <nytimes.com/critique>.

In an op-ed in the Sunday, May 30, 2004, edition of *The New York Times*, a letter to editor Daniel Okrent, asked, "Will your column this Sunday address why *The New York Times* buried its editors note—full of apologies for burying apologies on A10—on A10?"[22] According to *Harper's Index*, at least 237 misleading statements on Iraq were made by the Bush Administration's top officials since March 2002. One hundred percent of these statements contradicted, made selected use of, or mischaracterized existing government intelligence. This stands in sharp contrast to "the number of articles in major U.S. newspapers that have called any White House statement on Iraq a lie: zero."[23]

As with Clinton in Kosovo, the Bush Administration has been managing the news and feeding the public disinformation about U.S. involvement in Iraq. Instead of verifying, questioning, or investigating these stories, corporate media has eagerly published every shaky claim in a rush to be the first to cover the next front-page scoop. In the world of journalism, disseminating unverified information is an equal sin, with the same overall effect of skewing public opinion as fabricating a story in its entirety. No matter how you split hairs, a lie is still a lie. The rush to print, which shaped public opinion, is now partially responsible for a situation that has cost thousands of lives.

CENSORED #1 2004
THE NEOCONSERVATIVE PLAN FOR GLOBAL DOMINANCE

The corporate media have made much of Saddam Hussein and his stockpile of weapons of mass destruction. Rarely have the press addressed the possibility that larger strategies might also have driven the decision to invade Iraq. Broad political strategies regarding foreign policy do indeed exist and are part of public record.

In the 1970s, American military presence in the Gulf was minimal, so gaining control of Arab oil fields by force was unattainable. Still, the idea of full domination was very attractive to a group of hard-line, pro-military Washington insiders that included both Democrats and Republicans. Eventually labeled "neoconservatives," this circle of influential strategists played important roles in the Defense Departments of Gerald Ford, Ronald Reagan, and George Bush Sr., and in conservative think tanks throughout the 1980s and 1990s. Today this same circle occupies several key posts in the White House, Pentagon, and State Department. The principals among them are:

➤ Vice President Dick Cheney, and Defense Secretary Donald Rumsfeld, who have been closely aligned since they served with the Ford Administration in the 1970s;

➤ Deputy Defense Secretary Paul Wolfowitz, the key architect of the postwar construction of Iraq;

➤ Richard Perle, former chairman and current member of the Pentagon's Defense Policy Board, which has great influence over foreign military policies;

➤ and William Kristol, editor of *The Weekly Standard* and founder of Project for the New American Century, the powerful, neoconservative think tank.

Since the first Gulf War, the U.S. has built a network of military bases that now almost completely encircle the oil fields of the Persian Gulf.

In 1989, following the end of the Cold War and just prior to the Gulf War, Dick Cheney, Colin Powell, and Paul Wolfowitz produced the Defense Planning Guidance Report advocating U.S. military dominance around the globe. The plan called for the United States to maintain and grow in military superiority and prevent new rivals from raising up to challenge us on the world stage. Using words like "preemptive" and military "forward presence," the plan called for the U.S. to be dominant over friends and foes alike. It concluded with the assertion that the U.S. can best attain this position by making itself "absolutely powerful."

On August 2, 1990, President Bush called a press conference. He explained that the threat of global war had significantly receded, but in its wake, a new danger arose. This unforeseen threat to national security could come from any angle and from any power.

Iraq, by a remarkable coincidence, invaded Northern Kuwait later the same day.

Cheney et al. were out of political power for the eight years of Bill Clinton's presidency. During this time, the neoconservatives founded the Project for the New American Century (PNAC). The most influential product of the PNAC was a report entitled "Rebuilding America's Defense," <www.newamericancentury.org>, which called for U.S. military dominance and control of global economic markets.

With the election of George W. Bush, the authors of the plan were returned to power: Cheney as vice president, Powell as secretary of state, and Wolfowitz in the number-two spot at the Pentagon. With the old Defense Planning Guidance as the skeleton, the three went back to the drawing board. When their new plan was complete, it included contributions from Wolfowitz's boss Donald Rumsfeld. The old "preemptive" attacks have now become "unwarned attacks." The Powell-Cheney doctrine of military "forward presence" has been replaced by "forward deterrence." The U.S. stands ready to invade any country deemed a possible threat to our economic interests.

UPDATE BY CHRISTOPHER ROBIN COX: The neoconservative contingent within the Bush Administration remains small in number, highly elusive, and full of influence. After the overthrow and capture of Saddam Hussein, the fabled weapons of mass destruction (WMD), which were given as the main reason for preemptive, unilaterally-led war in the region, still have not been found. The first chore on the list of the neoconservative plan for global dominance was accomplished when the U.S. occupied Iraq and took control of its oil reserves.

We now know that much of the information that was used to gain consent for going to war in Iraq originated not from the CIA or the intelligence gathered by weapons inspectors, but from a small cadre of very powerful and secretive government organizations whose sole job was to develop evidence of Iraq's connection to 9/11 and its possession of WMDs. Primarily, neoconservative hawks manned these organizations. In the last year, there has been official testimony by David Kay, former top U.S. weapons inspector, stating, "We were all wrong." Additional devastating statements were made about the actions of this administration by Paul O'Neill, former secretary of the treasury, and Richard Clarke, former counterterrorism czar under the past four presidential administrations. Senator Edward M. Kennedy (D–MA) said in *The Nation*, "What happened was not merely a failure of intelligence; it was the result of manipulation of intelligence and selective use of questionable intelligence to justify a decision already made."

What follows is a brief analysis of the various governmental and nongovernmental offices, run primarily by neoconservatives, responsible for providing the "strategic intelligence" necessary to build the case for war in Iraq:

The two most active offices in the quest of gathering intelligence outside of the normal official channels were the Office of Special Plans (OSP) and its parallel, the Counter-Terrorism Evaluation Group (CTEG). Both the OSP and the CTEG were organized, by Undersecretary of Defense Douglas Feith and his superior Donald Rumsfeld, literally days after 9/11. They were charged with finding any evidence that the CIA, NSA, FBI, and DIA may have missed in regard to Iraq's connections to 9/11 and/or Al Qaeda, a tall order indeed. These organizations under Feith commonly chose the "worst-case scenarios" due to a lack of "actionable" evidence.

The Defense Policy Board, also known as the Defense Policy Group (DPG) was chaired by Richard Perle, Feith's mentor, long-time member of the PNAC and a close personal friend to Iraqi National Congress (INC) leader Ahmed Chalabi. The DPG worked closely with the OSP. The DPG was so bold as to meet with Chalabi to "discuss ways in which the terrorist attacks could be tied to Hussein," says Jim Lobe of Inter Press Service News Agency. Chalabi will be devastating to the administration and its neocons if his intimate involvement in their cadre is made public in congressional hearings. In response to accusations that he and the INC had provided misleading intelligence to George W. Bush, Chalabi said: "What was said before is not important. The Bush Administration is looking for a scapegoat. We're ready to fall on our swords if he wants."

The OSP and the CTEG operated a number of small offices outside of the official United States intelligence apparatus, producing the "strategic intelligence" that was often utilized by neoconservative hard-liners and hawks. The building up and breaking down of these small offices, often with only a handful of full-time staffers, shows an organized and versatile network. The goal of the OSP and CTEG was to gather the intelligence necessary to get the U.S. legally into Iraq and quickly in control of its oil reserves. Upon the "end of official hostilities" in Iraq, the OSP and CTEG quickly disappeared and very little mention was ever made in corporate news.

The most clear and present danger of the neoconservative clique is the nearly direct line of influence they continue to have on national and international governmental policy making. It is important to note that the vice president, secretary of state, attorney general, secretary of defense, and the deputy secretary of defense all defiantly support unilateral United States global supremacy, by both economic and military means, clearly shown to be contrary to the mind of the majority of Americans.

The tenets of neoconservatism also provide the basis for our close strategic alliance with Israel, an important aspect of the so-called "war on terror." Without the total support of Israel, there is little chance of controlling the Gulf region and its famed oil reserves. The reliance we have on the Israelis as a strategic alliance and the reliance they have upon us for massive financial support, makes for an extremely codependent relationship. For 30 years, the majority of the world's civilized countries, including many of our allies, have been calling for the withdrawal of Israeli troops from Gaza and the West Bank, while the United States sheepishly supports Israel in their unpopular devastation of the Palestinians. There are many Israelis who protest this, but to no avail. This is largely due to the intense influence of the neocons in current and past administrations. "No group in Israel can gain much credibility within unless it has strong support from the society of the boss-man," said Noam Chomsky in an interview with M. Junaid Alam.

The size and funding of PNAC is absolutely miniscule when compared with the think tanks that are associated with the neoconservative agenda. Since 9/11 a few of these tanks have come forward in transparent support of the "global war on terrorism." The most powerful is certainly the American Enterprise Institute (AEI), with a member list that includes well over 20 neocons who have done work for the Bush Administration in various capacities. Richard Perle, Dick Cheney, Paul Wolfowitz, William Kristol, Newt Gingrich, and Elliot Cohen are but a few on the AEI roster. The Hudson Institute and the Heritage Foundation are also widely known for their neoconservativist slant.

Organizations similar to PNAC have also cropped up, but only long enough to stay clear of congressional oversight. One of those was the Committee for the Liberation of Iraq (CLI), which was founded by Bruce P. Jackson, one of the directors of PNAC and former vice president for strategy and planning at Lockheed Martin Corporation. Like the OSP, the CLI quickly disappeared after the fall of the Hussein regime.

The neoconservative plan for global dominance has reached a point of no return. The secret offices that facilitated the propaganda for the war in Iraq and the government officials who ran them are quite visible now. Both David Kay and most of the administration have been quick to lay blame upon George Tenet and the CIA for providing false or misleading intelligence. Increasingly less mention of the intelligence supplied by OSP and CTEG is being made by the neocons in the administration. On the other hand, Representative Jane Harmon (D–CA), in a speech at AEI of all places, said, "disclaimers notwithstanding, many in Congress and intelligence operatives in the field now believe these entities fed unreliable and 'unvetted' intelligence to [Pentagon] policymakers and the office of the vice president."

SOURCES: M. Junaid Alam, "An Interview with Noam Chomsky on Bush and the Left's Strategy for the Elections, " <www.dissentvoice.org >, February 6, 2004; Jim Lobe, "Bush Lies Uncovered," *AlterNet,* February 23, 2004, <www.AlterNet.org>; Jim Lobe, "CIA Chief Clueless on Neo-Con Intelligence Channel," Inter Press Service News Agency, March 10, 2004; and Edward M. Kennedy, "Iraq and U.S. Leadership," *The Nation,* March 29 2004.

CENSORED #2
HOMELAND SECURITY THREATENS CIVIL LIBERTY

The new Department of Homeland Security (DHS) combines over 100 separate entities of the executive branch, including the Secret Service, the Coast Guard, and the Border Patrol, among others. The DHS employs over 170,000 federal workers and commands a total annual budget of $37 billion. One DHS mandate largely ignored by the press requires the FBI, CIA, state, and local governments to share intelligence reports with the department upon command, without explanation. According to the American Civil Liberties Union (ACLU), the Department of Homeland Security will be "100 percent secret and 0 percent accountable." Meanwhile, the gathering, retention, and use of information collected are central focuses of the Bush Administration's new agenda. Officially established to track down terrorists, information can be collected on any American citizen.

No member of Congress was given sufficient time to study the first Patriot Act that was passed by the House on October 27, 2001. In some cases, while driving the act through Congress, Vice President Cheney would not allow the legislation to be read; publicly threatening members of Congress that they would be blamed for the next terrorist attack if they did not vote for the Patriot Act.

SOURCES: Frank Morales, "Homeland Defense: Pentagon Declares War on America," *Global Outlook,* Winter 2003; Alex Jones, "Secret Patriot II Destroys Remaining U.S. Liberty," <Rense.com>, February 11, 2003 and *Global Outlook*, Vol. 4; and Charles Lewis and Adam Mayle, "Justice Department Drafts Sweeping Expansion of Terrorism Act," Center for Public Integrity, <publicintegrity.org>.

UPDATE BY ANNA MIRANDA: Hastily and stealthily passed in October 2001, the USA Patriot Act continues to undermine rights of American citizens. From libraries and booksellers to financial and educational institutions to our rights to travel and to live in the United States, every single American is affected by the intrusion of the government's right to conduct surveillance on our personal lives as if we were each potential terrorists.

Since 2001, many of the Patriot Acts potential effects have become reality. Applying for credit? Read the fine print. "To help the government fight the funding of terrorism and money laundering activities, federal law requires all financial institutions to obtain, verify, and record information that identifies each person who opens an account. What this means for you: When you open an account, we will ask for your name, address, date of birth, and other information that will allow us to identify you."

Buying or selling property? Considered a "financial institution," title companies are required to check your background against a list of people who have been identified as potential terrorists known as "specifically designated nationals."

Traveling? Once you've been placed on the government's "no-fly list" through a program called CAPPS II, you can be banned from flying within or outside of the United States. Those who have been identified and placed on the list are finding difficulty determining how it was they were placed on the list in the first place or how they will get off.

Legal resident of the United States with a green card? According to the Department of Homeland Security, over 63,000 immigrants—many of whom possessed green cards and have been living in the United States for years—have been detained, with up to 70 percent having already been deported.

The Patriot Act, however, is receiving resistance in many circles, including bipartisan groups. The Campaign for Reader Privacy combines Republicans, Democrats, and Independents in sponsoring the Freedom to Read Protection Act (H.R. 1157) and the Security and Freedom Ensured (SAFE) Act (S. 1709) to amend Section 215 of the Patriot Act which gives the FBI unlimited access to bookstore and library records.

Together, the Electronic Frontier Foundation and the American Civil Liberties Union (ACLU) are challenging the constitutionality of National Security Letters (NSL). Finally, a bipartisan group of senators have introduced the SAFE Act (S. 1709) that calls for revisions of Section 213, the "sneak and peak" provision, which allows searches to be conducted and property seized without prior notification. The SAFE Act requires a warrant to be issued and protection of the person being searched.

SOURCES: <www.washingtondispatch.com/article_7571.shtml> and <www. white-house.gov/news/releases/2004/04/20040419-4.html>.

U.S. ILLEGALLY REMOVES PAGES FROM IRAQ U.N. REPORT

On December 19, 2002, a Berlin newspaper, *Die Tagezeitung*, broke the story that the U.S. had illegally removed pages from an Iraq U.N. report. Iraq had sent copies of the complete report to journalists throughout Europe. There were 8,000 pages missing from the 11,800 page original report. The question is why did the U.S. remove these pages?

Michael Niman says, "The missing pages implicated 24 U.S.-based corporations and the successive Ronald Reagan and George Bush Sr. Administrations in connection with illegally supplying Saddam Hussein's government with myriad weapons of mass destruction and the training on how to use them." The U.S. convinced Colombia, chair of the Security Council and current target of U.S. military occupation and recipient of financial aid, to look the other way while the report was removed, edited, and returned. Other members of the Security Council, such as Britain, France, China, and Russia, were implicated in the missing pages as well (China and Russia were still arming Iraq) and had little desire to expose the U.S.'s transgression. So all members accepted the new, abbreviated version.

Perhaps most importantly, the missing pages contain information that could potentially make a case for war crimes against officials within the Reagan and the Bush Sr. Administrations. This includes the current Defense Secretary Donald Rumsfeld—for his collaboration with Saddam Hussein leading up to the massacres of Iraqi Kurds and for acting as liaison for U.S. military aid during the war between Iraq and Iran.

SOURCES: Michael I. Niman, "What Bush Didn't Want You to Know About Iraq," *The Humanist* and *ArtVoice*, March/April 2003. First covered by Amy Goodman on *Democracy Now!*

UPDATE BY MATTHEW HAGAN: There is no update to this story. Searching numerous databases (LexisNexis, Proquest, Factiva, JSTOR, and Alt-Press Watch) as well as contacting people originally involved with the story resulted in the discovery that no media attention has been given to this story. Not one development or even the smallest blurb of information was uncovered.

Not only was nothing new exposed, but also coverage of the original story was limited. It is as if the mystery of the missing papers has conveniently evaporated in the year since it was covered in the pages of *Censored*.

RUMSFELD'S PLAN TO PROVOKE TERRORISTS

Secretary of Defense Donald Rumsfeld's Defense Science Board (DSB) has created a new organization called the Proactive Preemptive Operations Group (P2OG) to thwart potential terrorist attacks on the United States. A group of 100 counterintelligence agents are responsible for secret missions designed to "stimulate reactions" among terrorist groups, in order to provoke them into committing violent acts, exposing them to a counterattack by U.S. forces. At least $100 million a year is needed for these secret missions and other strategies, including tricking terrorist cells with fake communication and stealing money from the terrorist cells.

SOURCE: Chris Floyd, "Into the Dark," *CounterPunch*, November 1, 2002, <www.counterpunch.org/floyd101.html>.

UPDATE BY BROOKE FINLEY: Although there have been no signs of action from Rumsfeld's Proactive Preemptive Operations Group (P2OG) in the past year, there has been more information available about what the P2OG entails.

When the Defense Science Board (DSB) recommended the P2OG to Secretary of Defense Donald Rumsfeld, they suggested that a special operations executive within the National Security Council (NSC) be responsible for the P2OG. The NSC would be in charge of planning operations, but would then hand over the duty of executing the plans to the Pentagon and the CIA, in order to avoid repeating past abuses. One person would oversee the NSC and would answer directly to the White House. This special operations executive is John A. Gordon, the current deputy assistant national security advisor on combatting terrorism. During Gordon's career, he helped in the research and development of the Peacekeeper intercontinental ballistic missiles and later commanded the 90th missile wing (the only Peacekeeper unit). As special operations executive, Gordon's position would entail defining national strategy, enunciating policy, and holding accountability and responsibility for the entirety of the P2OG.

The entire package of the P2OG will cost close to $7 billion. Over a five-year period beginning in 2004, $1.7 billion would be used for an intelligence community's ability to penetrate terrorist cells in order to collect information. Over the next six years, $1.6 billion would go toward intelligence, surveillance, and reconnaissance enhancement. Research and development of sensor and agent defeat technologies would cost $1 billion per year. Paying an additional 500 people needed for the reporting of the effects of globalization, radicalism, economics, religions, and cultures in order to be able to characterize potential enemies would cost $800 million. A special team of specifically trained forces, able to take action against suspected weapons sites and to offer force protection for nearby soldiers, would cost $500 million. A force consisting of former intelligence retirees would need $100 million in order to meet once a year to participate in counterterrorist exercises. Finally, for $20 million, the DSB suggests creating a panel of two dozen analysts, who would conger up ways in which a terrorist might attack and then report their findings to the CIA director.

SOURCES: "Pentagon Takes Quiet Aim at Terror; Military Amassing More Secret Warriors," Catche File, November 13, 2002, <www.CNN.com>; Bill Berkowitz, "Hellzapoppin' at the Pentagon," *Working for Change*, November 13, 2002, <www.workingforchange.com/article.cfm?ItemID=14076>; Pamela Hess, "Panel Wants $7 Billion Elite Counterterror Unit," United Press International, September 26, 2002, <www.cooperativeresearch.org/timeline/2002/upi092602.html>; and David Isenberg, "'P2OG' Allows Pentagon to Fight Dirty," *Asia Times*, <www.atimes.com/atimes/Middle_East/DK05 Ak02.html>.

CENSORED #7 2004
TREATY BUSTING BY THE UNITED STATES

The U.S. is a signatory to nine multilateral treaties that it has either blatantly violated or gradually subverted. The Bush Administration is now outright rejecting a number of those treaties, and in doing so, places global security in jeopardy, as other nations feel entitled to do the same. The rejected treaties include: The Comprehensive Test Ban Treaty (CTBT), the Treaty Banning Antipersonnel Mines, the Rome Statute of the International Criminal Court (ICC), a protocol to create a compliance regime for the Biological Weapons Convention (BWC), the Kyoto Protocol on global warming, and the Anti-Ballistic Missile Treaty (ABM). The U.S. is also not complying with the Nuclear Non-Proliferation Treaty (NPT), the Chemical Weapons Commission (CWC), the BWC, and the U.N. framework Convention on Climate Change.

This unprecedented rejection of and rapid retreat from global treaties that have in effect kept the peace through the decades will not only continue to isolate U.S. policy, but will also render these treaties and conventions invalid without the support and participation of the world's foremost superpower.

SOURCES: Marylia Kelly and Nicole Deller, "Rule of Power or Rule of Law?", *Connections*, June 2002; John B. Anderson, "Unsigning the ICC," *The Nation*, April 2002; Eamon Martin, "U.S. Invasion Proposal Shocks the Netherlands," *Asheville Global Report (AGR)*, June 20-26, 2002; and John Valleau, "Nuclear Nightmare," *Global Outlook*, Summer 2002.

Additional Information from: Dr. Robert Bowman, Lt. Col., USAF (ret), "The ABM Treaty: Dead or Alive?" *Space and Security News*, February 2002.

UPDATE BY BRITTANY ROELAND: Current U.S. trends concerning foreign policy represent a lack of acknowledgment and violations of nine international treaties. This truth may be a crucial explanation for the way the rest of the world considers the United States.

In November 2002, the Bush Administration announced their plans to construct biowarfare agent facilities at the Lawrence Livermore lab in northern California and at the Los Alamos lab in New Mexico. These plans are in violation of the Biological Weapons Convention (BWC). In response to the Bush Administration's proposed plans, the Nuclear Watch of Santa Fe, New Mexico, and Tri-Valley CAREs of Livermore, California, filed litigation on August 26, 2003, in the federal district court in northern California. The suit is charging the U.S. Department of Energy (DOE) with violating the National Environmental Policy Act (NEPA). The DOE approved advanced research on bioweapon agents at Los Alamos and Livermore labs without performing a detailed evaluation of the environmental hazards and influence on international non-proliferation agreements. The lawsuit asks the court to require specific Environmental Impact Statements (EISs) and public hearings before the DOE can begin operating at either lab.

The DOE announced that it has cancelled approval for its newly constructed biowarfare agent research facility at the Los Alamos lab. The DOE withdrew the original Finding of No Significant Impact (FONSI) and Environmental Assessment (EA) that it had issued before the construction of the labs. The Los Alamos facility, a "Biosafety Level-3" (BSL-3), would have been used for experiments—including genetic modification—with live anthrax, botulism, bubonic plague, and other agents. As of now, the Lawrence Livermore National lab in California still remains under construction. A DOE press release admits that "it will now need to go back to square one, produce a new environmental assessment, and review anew whether the agency will undertake a full Environmental Impact Statement, a key demand in the lawsuit."

"We remain concerned that construction continues on the extremely dangerous Livermore biolab," stated Marylia Kelley, the executive director of Tri-Valley CAREs. "The risks to public health and safety posed by the deadly pathogens DOE proposed to use in Los Alamos are even greater here in Livermore. The Livermore site is adjacent to the active Los Positas earthquake fault and next to a large metropolitan area," explained Kelley. "Surely, we deserve no less than an immediate halt to the construction of the Livermore biowarfare agent facility and for DOE to withdraw its approval."

Responding to congressional pressure, the DOE announced on January 28, 2004, that it would postpone plans for the Modern Pit Facility (MPF). MPF is a new plutonium bomb factory capable of mass-producing 250 to 900 bomb cores, called pits, each year.

The Alliance for Nuclear Accountability announced the delay, referring to "the inevitable health and environmental risks of plutonium manufacturing" and the simple lack of need, as well as the possibility of causing destructive international relations in regards to the facility. "The MPF is one project America can live without," declared the national alliance of groups, including Tri-Valley CAREs. Senator Feinstein (D–CA) said she welcomed the delay and pointed out that if the new bomb factory were to operate at only half of its capacity, it could equal or exceed China's entire nuclear arsenal in a single year. "I believe the development of new nuclear weapons will hurt our relations with other nations around the globe, our non-proliferation efforts, and the environment," Feinstein concluded. DOE's draft EIS made it clear that the MPF would include the capability to make new design pits, meaning that it could facilitate production of entirely new types of nuclear weapons. The MPF facility would be in opposition to the Non-Proliferation of Nuclear Weapons (NPT).

According to Tri-Valley CAREs, "The U.S. has deployed an estimated 150 to 180 nuclear weapons on seven European NATO states, six of which are non-nuclear weapon states. As long as these policies endure, NATO countries cannot in good faith claim they are making the progress towards disarmament that has been demanded as an NPT Article VI obligation since 1995. The 2005 Review Conference of the NPT is likely to be chaotic even if the U.S. does change its nuclear policy for the better. All NATO states, except the U.S., have ratified the Comprehensive Test Ban Treaty (CTBT) and have committed to ensuring its enforcement. The test ban is intimately linked with the nuclear non-proliferation and disarmament goals of the NPT."

The 2005 fiscal-year budget specifies that the Bush Administration will make plans to increase and speed up its strategy to organize a missile defense, plus a possible third deployment site. Despite previous claims that the Missile Defense Agency would put off space-based missile defense activities due to technical challenges, the 2005 fiscal-year budget incorporates development activities on a space-based interceptor test bed. This is in violation of the Anti-Ballistic Missile Treaty (ABM).

The International Criminal Court (ICC) has recently come into full operation with the selection of its chief prosecutor, Oscar Moreno-Ocampo of Argentina. Most of the 199 nations of the U.N. are celebrating this long sought accomplishment. Of the 134 signatories of the Rome statute, 92 have already ratified their commitment to the ICC. The U.S. surprised the world by un-signing the ICC. Ambassador David Scheffer, the U.S. representative, declared that he worried the document would hinder U.S. military duties and that the U.S. service personnel might be vulnerable. Of the first 499 communications from 66 countries that were received by the new court, more than 100 of them were allegations against the U.S., 16 related to acts allegedly committed by U.S. troops in Iraq, but neither Iraq nor the U.S. had become a party to the Rome statute, so the court has no jurisdiction over either of them at this time. As the court struggles with difficult decisions, nations, groups, and individuals are saluting it as a hope for a peaceful, nonviolent world.

The Kyoto Protocol was catapulted back onto the global agenda as Russia committed to signing the climate treaty in the spring of 2004, at the same time as Hollywood released a blockbuster in which rising temperatures trigger an ice age that freeze-dries New York. Europe, Canada, and Japan have ratified the Kyoto Protocol. While it now appears that Russia will sign, the Bush Administration has ruled out U.S. participation. "Even if Russia joins and the Kyoto Protocol takes effect, the absence of the world's largest greenhouse gas (GHG) emitters, the U.S. and China, means that Kyoto will have little impact on future climate change," explains Richard B. Stewart and Richard B. Weiner in their *Science and Technology* article "The Practical Climate Change." China will not act without the U.S. both because of perceived unfairness if the U.S. does not adopt limitations and because its major incentive for joining the climate management agreement is selling pollution allowances to U.S. companies. Though it may be in our planet's best interest for the Kyoto Protocol to be ratified, it appears that the capitalistic priorities of the U.S. are standing in the way of long-term survival.

SOURCES: "Russia Warms to Kyoto," *The Weekend Australian*, May 29, 2004; Beth Lamont, "The ICC Promise Without the U.S.," *Humanist*, November/December 2003; Richard B. Stewart and Richard B. Weiner, "The Practical Climate Change Policy," *Science and Technology*, Winter 2003–2004; <www.trivalleycares.org>; <www.ucs usa.org>; and <www.ieer.org>.

CENSORED #8 2004

U.S./BRITISH FORCES CONTINUE USE OF DEPLETED URANIUM WEAPONS DESPITE MASSIVE EVIDENCE OF NEGATIVE HEALTH EFFECTS

British and American coalition forces used depleted uranium (DU) shells in the war against Iraq and deliberately flouted a U.N. resolution that classifies the munitions as illegal weapons of mass destruction. An August 2002 U.N. report states that the use of DU weapons is in violation of numerous laws and U.N. conventions. Maj. Doug Rokke, ex-director of the Pentagon's DU project says, "We must do what is right for the citizens of the world—ban DU." Reportedly, more than 9,600 veterans have died since serving in Iraq during the first Gulf War, a statistical anomaly. The Pentagon has blamed the extraordinary number of illnesses and deaths on a variety of factors, including stress, pesticides, vaccines, and oil-well fire smoke. However, according to top-level U.S. Army reports and military contractors, "short-term effects of high doses (of DU) can result in death, while long-term effects of low doses have been implicated in cancer and birth defects."

SOURCES: Dan Kapelovitz, "Toxic Troops: What Our Soldiers Can Expect in Gulf War II," *Hustler*, June 2003; Reese Erlich, "The Hidden Killer," *Children of War*, March 2003.

UPDATE BY LAUREN KETTNER: For years, the U.S. government has known the danger of depleted uranium (DU). Even after reports of increased cancer rates in the Middle East and a mysterious illness known as the Gulf War Syndrome, the U.S. used DU during the 2003 bombing of Baghdad.

DU is used to harden bombs, shells, and tanks. It is both toxic and radioactive, affecting an individual's DNA, so the consequences will last for generations. The childhood leukemia rate in Iraq tripled after 300 tons of DU was dispersed into the air, soil, and water during the 1991 Gulf War. Since then, statistical evidence of increased cancer cases in Iraq correlates with the use of depleted uranium and nuclear arms in the Gulf War. In 1989, there were 11 abnormalities per 100,000 births; in 2001, there were 116 per 100,000. In 1988, 34 people died of cancer; in 1998, 450 people died of cancer; in 2001, there were 603 cancer deaths. The use of depleted uranium is illegal by international law and, at a meeting of the International Court Tribunal for Afghanistan, the court ruled the U.S. guilty of this war crime.

While medical research connecting DU exposure to cancer and other adverse health conditions exists, the U.S., British, and NATO officials continue to refuse to acknowledge the relationship. Despite continued contamination in Iraq, for political and economic reasons, the U.S. and Great Britain have ignored the environmental and health hazards. Gulf War soldiers, and Iraqi and Serbian representatives, along with health care professionals, continue to request medical care and environmental decontamination.

Washington continues to deny the impact of DU weapons on either the Iraqi people or U.S. and British soldiers. Currently, the U.S. has refused to disclose specific information about the use of DU in Iraq. It also refuses to let a group from the United Nations Environmental Program (UNEP) study the environmental impact of DU in Iraq. In a report by UNEP, dated October 20, 2003, officials claim that immediate attention is necessary. It suggests that residents should be tested and monitored and that awareness of the danger should be raised among the Iraqi people. However, there are no plans for the removal of debris.

Deliberate denial of medical screening and health care to individuals exposed to DU continues in 2004. In a landmark case, a Gulf War veteran from Scotland was awarded the first war pension for the effects of DU. Other suits are being reconsidered as substantial scientific evidence is questioned. Although this one case gives hope to veterans fighting for compensation, many other U.S. soldiers have been denied health benefits or recognition of their diseases.

Reports by the *Christian Science Monitor* of children playing on and around bomb sites proves that the Iraqis have not received proper warning of the danger of DU. The *Los Angeles Times* along with other mainstream media sources have featured stories related to the impacts of DU, but these stories have not created enough widespread demand for U.S. responsibility.

Ten thousand Americans have already been evacuated from Iraq, many reporting illnesses similar to those suffered by veterans from the first Gulf War. Despite documented respiratory problems, miscarriages, hair loss, and other health problems plaguing residents surrounding Baghdad, the U.S. and Great Britain refuse to allow the International Atomic Energy Agency to conduct systematic monitoring of the effects of uranium contamination.

SOURCES: Paul Rockwell, "Depleted Uranium: The War Crime That Has No End," <YellowTimes.org>, February 2004; Robert Tomsho, "Veterans Say Military Keeps Poor Health Records on Troops," *Wall Street Journal*, February 2004; Ed Kinane, "I Wish Soldiers Could Hear My Voice Now," *The Post Standard/Herald-Journal*, January 2004; "War in Iraq Devastating Environment—U.N. Report," *Kyodo News*, January 2004; John Pilger, "American Terrorist: Forget Hutton. He Will Not Reveal What the U.S. and U.K. Authorities Really Don't Want You to Know: That Radiation Illnesses Caused by Uranium Weapons are now Common in Iraq," *New Statesman*, January 2004; Dr. Doug Rokke, "Immediate Action Required on Depleted Uranium," *Health NOW!*, January 2004, <www.health-now.org/site/article.php?menuId=16& articleId=94>; and "Another War Crime? Iraqi Cities 'Hot' With Depleted Uranium," <www.iacenter.org>.

CENSORED #9 2003

IN AFGHANISTAN: POVERTY, WOMEN'S RIGHTS, AND CIVIL DISRUPTION WORSE THAN EVER

While all eyes have turned to Iraq, the people of Afghanistan continue to silently suffer what is considered their worst poverty in decades. The promised democratic government is too concerned with assassination attempts to worry about the suffering of the people. They still have no new constitution, no new laws, and little food. Ethnic and political rivalries plague the country and the military power of the warlords has increased. While the International Security Assistance Force (ISAF), the 4,500-strong foreign peacekeeping unit, is assigned to defend only the capital, private armies of an estimated 700,000 people roam the country continuing a traditional system of fiefdoms.

Despite the fanfare (stripping the burqa and the signing of the new Declaration of Essential Rights of Afghan Women), little has changed for the average Afghani. The new Interior Ministry still requires women to receive permission from their male relatives before they travel. As for the future *loya jirga*, or grand council, that will help determine governmental policies, only 160 seats out of 1,450 have been guaranteed to women.

As of July 2002, the average life expectancy for the people of Afghanistan is 46 years. The average yearly income per capita is $280. As for the children, 90 percent are not in school. More than one out of every four children in Afghanistan will die before the age of five. A UNICEF study found that the majority of children are highly traumatized and expect to die before reaching adulthood. Beyond this, the region is just overcoming a three-year drought, which killed half the crops and 80 percent of livestock in some areas.

SOURCES: Ahmed Rashid, "Afghanistan Imperiled," *The Nation*, October 14, 2002; Pranjal Tiwari, "Afghanistan: Lies and Horrible Truths," *Left Turn*, February/March 2003; Jan Goodwin, "An Uneasy Peace," *The Nation*, April 29, 2002; and Scott Carrier (text) and Chien-Min/Saba (photo essay), "Childhood Burdens," *Mother Jones*, July/August 2002.

UPDATE BY PATRICK CARLSON: The United States invasion of Afghanistan ousted the Taliban but instead of aiding the country, U.S. resources were turned to Iraq. In place of the Taliban, the U.S. placed "friendlier" President Hamid Karzai in charge along with the mujahideen warlords who helped the U.S. fight against the Taliban. "The problem with the mujahideen warlords is that they are just as bad if not worse than the Taliban. Thieves in their own right, these men loot, extort money, and have little care for the people of Afghanistan," said John Sifton, the Afghanistan researcher at Human Rights Watch, in an interview with Terry Gross. "The country is in disarray as corrupt warlords sit idle as chaos reigns. There is no justice, no laws, and no help as the looting, raping, and overall poverty continues on. No real progress on the reconstruction of cities has been made. Many buildings and cities are still completely devastated. Part of it is that the country's economy is barely existent, so the weakened country has become a wasteland. The only accomplishment being a road constructed from Kabul to Kandahar. On top of all this is the pollution from the uranium bullets."

High numbers of the population are exposed to uranium dust and debris from the fighting. Scientists found medically significant levels of non-depleted uranium in the urine of 100 percent of civilians tested, who live near bombsites, 400 percent to 2,000 percent higher than the normal population baseline. Eight million people face food shortages. People are starved, exhausted, hurt, incapacitated, and suffering. There are at least 500,000 disabled orphans and hundreds of thousands of widows. Shells in the major cities have hit many walls, buildings, and landmarks. One in every 10 land mines in the world is littered in Afghanistan, claiming an average of 25 victims a day. Children are forced to help their families by working horrific jobs for little to no pay.

Life for Afghan women has not improved. Fear for safety still plagues their lives, as they get harassed by men for not wearing the burqa, and parents, afraid their daughters will be kidnapped or sexually assaulted if not supervised at all times, refuse to allow them to attend school. Afghan women have little to no access to obstetric or postnatal care in the postwar chaos. Reproductive health care is completely unavailable in two-thirds of the country's provinces. Many clinics have been closed or bombed.

Afghanistan's hopes lie in a constitutional draft written by President Karzai at the loya jirga convention. "The constitutional draft was finally approved in January of this year but the document is full of poorly crafted promises, missed opportunities, and does not address some key issues," explained Sifton. Vote buying, bullying, and even death threats by certain powerful criminals who are now the "appointed" leaders of the country overshadowed the entire process. These leaders are not recognizing women or the poor.

SOURCES: "Human Rights and Afghani Women Since the Regime Change," <www.indymedia.org>, June 15, 2003; Davey Garland, "Afghanistan: The Nuclear Nightmare Begins," January 16, 2003, <www.indymedia.org.uk/en/ 2003/01/50059. html>; <www.savingwomenslives.org>; <www.salaam.co.uk>; <www.development-gateway.org>; "Betrayal," *Ni* magazine, Issue 364, January/February 2004, <www.newnt.org>; Terry Gross, "Interview of John Sifton," *Fresh Air*, December 22, 2003; Hamid Hussain, M.D., "Forgotten Ties," *CovertAction Quarterly*, Vol. 72; Stephanie Hiller, "Scientists Uncover Radioactive Trail in Afghanistan," *Awakened Woman* e-magazine, January 7, 2004, <www.awakenedwoman.com/umrc.htm>; Sonali Kolhatkar, "Replacing One Terrorist State with Another," *Foreign Policy in Focus*, October 6, 2003; John Sifton, "Afghanistan: Flawed Charter for a Land Ruled by Fear," *International Herald Tribune*, June 6, 2003; and Pranjal Tiwari, "Afghanistan Warlord Bids for High-Level Position," *The Newstandard*, February 23, 2004.

CENSORED #10 2004
AFRICA FACES THREAT OF NEW COLONIALISM

In June 2002, leaders from the eight most powerful countries in the world (the G8) met to form the New Partnership for Africa's Development (NEPAD), an agency intended to get the countries of Africa "on track" with the global economy. Not one of the eight leaders, however, was from Africa. NEPAD's objective is to provide aid to African countries that embrace the required development model. The danger of NEPAD is that it fails to protect Africa from exploitation of its resources. If this game plan sounds familiar to the structural adjustment programs implemented by the International Monetary Fund (IMF), that is because they are essentially the same, and NEPAD is essentially controlled by the same neoliberal interests.

The African countries that have officially embraced NEPAD membership are Algeria, Nigeria, Senegal, South Africa, Congo-Brazzaville, Cameroon, Ghana, Mauritius, Kenya, Mozambique, Rwanda, Ethiopia, Gabon, Uganda, Burkina Faso and Mali. Angola also joined the group at the most recent summit meeting held in Kigali, Rwanda, in February of this year. This brings the membership total up to 17 African nations. Protests against NEPAD have, however, continued to erupt all over Africa. One exceptionally large demonstration took place at the World Summit on Sustainable Development in Johannesburg.

While the ongoing wars in the Middle East have lowered the new colonization of Africa on the list of U.S. priorities, disease, war, poverty, and political instability are still reeking havoc on the African continent. More than 5 million people have died in the Congo Wars since 1998, and Uganda has suffered over 11,400 deaths due to war, disease, and starvation.

SOURCES: Michelle Robidoux, "NEPAD: Repackaging Colonialism in Africa," *Left Turn*, July/August 2002; Asad Ismi, "Ravaging Africa," *Briarpatch*, Vol. 32, No. 1, excerpted from *The CCPA Monitor*, October 2002; Dena Montague, "Africa: The New Oil and Military Frontier," *Peacework*, October 2002; and Dr. Tewolde Berhan Gebre Egziabher, "How (Not) to Feed Africa," *New Internationalist*, January/February 2003.

UPDATE BY TIMOTHY ZOLEZZI: Little has transpired in terms of "progress" since our story on NEPAD was published in *Censored 2004*, and even less transpired in terms of media coverage. At the beginning of 2003, Canada was due to hand over a highly publicized $500 million in aid, but only $70 million ever materialized. What the Canadian government, along with the IMF, World Bank, and the G8, fail to address, is that a simple cancellation of Africa's imposed debt would go a long way to initiating recovery.

Most of the aid promised to Africa in 2001 has been withheld because of "unfavorable political, economic, and/or social conditions" in the participating countries. In March 2003, under the recommendation of the G8 countries, the members of NEPAD decided to erect the African Peer Review Mechanism (APRM). APRM was established as an internal watchdog, assessing the performance and progress of participating countries. At the NEPAD summit conference held in February 2004, it was decided that countries the APRM found to be in compliance with colonizer-friendly NEPAD standards should receive the bulk of the meager aid.

Currently, the only aid offered to Africa by the G8 is $15 billion to establish the Rapid Development Force, which is essentially an army that enforces the policies established by NEPAD. Furthermore, the $15 billion in aid President Bush offered is conditional upon Africa's acceptance of genetically modified crops.

The fact that the main motive behind the G8's construction of NEPAD was to secure colonial-style commerce for Western profit is no secret; yet in a recent interview with the BBC, NEPAD secretary chairman Professor Wiseman Nkuhlu stated, "Through NEPAD, we now have a platform to tackle the G8 countries on a level playing field. The number of African countries actively talking with G8 countries has increased from 5 to 20. There has also been a rise in the number of international organizations funding NEPAD projects."

Many analysts, both those in favor of and those opposed to NEPAD, speculate that even in light of the newly instituted APRM, NEPAD is on its last legs. With or without NEPAD, however, one thing is certain; Africa is still being ravaged and exploited by the same foreign menaces that have been raping its landscape and people for the last three centuries.

SOURCES: "Monitoring Africa," BBC London, February 18, 2004; Dennis Brutus, "Africa's Struggles Today," *International Socialist Review*, September/October 2003; Yves Engler and Bianca Mugyenyi, "G8 and Africa: A High Price to Pay For a Lot of Talk," *Z Magazine*, June 6, 2003; Robyn Dixon, "The World: Cancel Iraqi Debt? What About Africa?," *Los Angeles Times*, January 26, 2004; and Africa Infoserv <www.africafiles.org?articles/ 4413.asp>.

CENSORED #11 2004
U.S. IMPLICATED IN TALIBAN MASSACRE

A documentary entitled *Massacre at Mazar*, released in 2002 by Scottish film producer Jamie Doran, implicates U.S. troops in the torturing and deaths of approximately 3,000 men from Mazar-i-Sharif, Afghanistan. In the documentary, two witnesses claim that they were forced to drive into the desert with hundreds of Taliban prisoners sealed in cargo containers. The witnesses said that the orders came from a local U.S. commander.

When they reached their destination, Northern Alliance gunmen shot the prisoners who had not yet suffocated to death inside the vans, while 30 to 40 U.S. soldiers stood watching. "They crammed us into sealed cargo containers. We had no water for 20 hours. We banged on the side of the container. There was no air and it was very hot.

There were 300 of us in my container. By the time we arrived in Sheberghan, only 10 of us were alive," described one survivor. Another witness stated that he observed a U.S. soldier break an Afghani prisoner's neck and pour acid on others.

Afghani warlord General Abdul Rashid Dostum, the man whose forces allegedly carried out the killings, said there were only 200 such deaths and that the prisoners died before the transfer.

"They're hiding behind a wall of secrecy, hoping this story will go away, but it won't," said director Jamie Doran.

SOURCES: Kendra Sarvadi, "Documentary Implicates U.S. Troops in Taliban Prisoner Deaths," *Asheville Global Report (AGR)*, No. 179, June 20-26, 2002.

UPDATE BY EMILIO LICEA: The documentary by Jamie Doran, which implicates American soldiers in the massacre, has been shown throughout Europe, but has yet to be shown in the U.S. The only media attention the massacre has received is from *Newsweek* magazine in the August 26, 2002, issue. Although *Newsweek* did break the story to the U.S. audience, they did not report any information of U.S. involvement.

Jamie Doran was interviewed for the *Newsweek* piece, and the article was based solely on Doran's documentary, yet when the story was published there was no mention of Jamie Doran or any U.S. implication in the massacre. The article stated that, "nothing *Newsweek* learned suggests that American forces had advance knowledge of the killings, witnessed the prisoners being stuffed into unventilated trucks, or were in a position to prevent that." Doran claims that the original article contained much more information, but when the final publication was released, the U.S. involvement portion had been deleted.

The *Newsweek* piece did verify a crucial fact: that there was an American presence at Sheberghan Prison. U.S. presence near the massacre reveals that it would have been nearly impossible for U.S. soldiers not to have had knowledge of, or to have been involved in, the massacre. The Pentagon has yet to answer any specific questions about a presence in the area, but claims U.S. troops were not involved in the killings.

The most compelling evidence was provided by a U.N.-backed investigation by American forensic anthropologist William Haglund, published in *The Observer* on March 21, 2004. In the article "U.S. Afghan Allies Committed Massacre," Haglund reported that he "exhumed 15 bodies, a tiny sample of what may be a very large total." Luckily, the cold, dry climate of Dast-I-Leili provided a great environment for the preservation of the bodies. This gave Haglund the opportunity to perform thorough autopsies. Haglund concluded that they died from suffocation, which exactly corroborates the stories provided by eyewitness accounts. The combination of Haglund's investigation and eyewitness accounts reveals that the slaughter of thousands of people occurred. The killing of these Taliban prisoners (even if indirectly by asphyxiation) is a violation of the Third Geneva Convention, and the next step should be a full and thorough investigation of the Afghan massacre.

General Dostum, the suspected leader of the brutal and ruthless massacre, has become even more powerful in the area of Mazar-i-Sharif, due in large part to his alliance with the U.S. military. Dostum's production of opium has greatly increased, and he continues to control much of northern Afghanistan. The most crucial evidence of the massacre is still under the control of General Dostum: a videotape, which contains footage of U.S. soldier's direct involvement. It appears that General Dostum is keeping the tape for leverage with U.S. forces.

The hypocrisy of U.S. policy and corporate media complicity is evident in the coverage of Donald Rumsfeld's stopover in Mazar-i-Sharif, Afghanistan, on December 4, 2003, to meet General Abdul Rashid Dostum and his rival General Ustad Atta Mohammed. Rumsfeld was there to finalize a deal with the warlords to begin the decommissioning of their military forces in exchange for millions of dollars in international aid and increased power in the central Afghan government.

During the meeting with Dostum, Donald Rumsfeld is quoted as saying, "I spent many weeks in the Pentagon following closely your activities, I should say your successful activities" (*Washington Post*, December 5, 2003). The *Post* reported the fact that General Dostum had been instrumental in routing Taliban forces from northern Afghanistan in the early weeks of the war two years ago, but said nothing about General Dostum's brutal past.

SOURCES: Barry Gutman Dehghanpisheh, "The Death Convoy of Afghanistan," *Newsweek*, August 2002; L. Harding, "Afghan Massacre haunts Pentagon," *The Guardian*, September 2002; D. Rose, "U.S. Afghan Allies Committed Massacre," *The Guardian*, March 21, 2004; and "Did U.S. Forces Allow a Massacre of 3,000 Taliban Prisoners to Occur?" <Buzzflash.com>, September 2003, <www.buzz flash.com/interviews/03/09/23_doran.html>; and Stefan Steinberg, "Interview with Jamie Doran, Director of *Massacre at Mazar*," June 2002, <www.wsws.org/articles/ 2002/dora-j17.shtml>.

CENSORED #13 2004
CORPORATE PERSONHOOD CHALLENGED

When the founding fathers wrote the Bill of Rights—especially the First Amendment—they did not have corporations in mind. They were leery of dominating interest groups and factions that could undermine democracy and were adamant in bestowing power to the people. Yet today, corporations claim that rights intended for physical persons somehow pertain to them. It seems like it should just be a matter of common sense. Is a corporation a person?

The claim that corporations use to assert that they have rights as "persons" comes from a defunct 1886 Supreme Court case summary from *Santa Clara County v. the Southern Pacific Railroad Company* that says "the defendant corporations are persons within the intent of the clause in Section 1 of the Fourteenth Amendment to the Constitution of the United States, which forbids a state to deny any person within its jurisdiction the equal protection of the laws." The summary came from a court clerk—a former railroad president—and was not really legal, but because it was on the case document, it was treated as such. The notion that corporations have the same rights as people is called corporate personhood. The main use of corporate personhood by corporations is to be exempt from the laws that would normally hold them responsible for their actions. Through the claim that they are persons deserving of equal protection under the Constitution, including free speech, corporations gain the liberty to deceive at will. Since the 1886 case, courts have been reluctant to make a decisive ruling on the legality of corporate personhood itself, but rather have chosen to concentrate on the individual context of each court case.

In 1998, Mark Kasky, an amateur marathon runner and labor activist, sued Nike Inc. over their statements in a PR campaign that misrepresented the work conditions of its overseas factories. In 2002, the California Supreme Court ruled 4-3 that Nike was accountable for its speech and that the corporation's right to misrepresent itself was not protected by the Constitution. Because Nike's statements could affect consumers' choices, their speech was declared commercial expression, for which the corporation is accountable. Nike appealed the free speech case, and it was sent to the Supreme Court for review.

On December 9, 2002, Porter Township, Pennsylvania, became the first municipality to deny corporations personhood and passed an ordinance declaring that "the judicial bestowal of civil and political rights upon corporations interferes with the administrations of laws within Porter Township and usurps the basic human and Constitutional rights exercised by the people of Porter Township." Because Porter Township and other small municipals in Pennsylvania are near dumping sites for corporations' waste and sludge, they are tremendously affected by corporate personhood. Assuming the same Constitutional rights meant for actual persons gives these corporations exemption from responsibility for the people and environments they harm.

SOURCES: Thom Hartmann, "Americans Revolt in Pennsylvania: New Battle Lines are Drawn," *Wild Matters*, February 2003.

UPDATE BY MELODY LINDSEY: The *Nike v. Kasky* case, named as such because Nike was the party appealing, should have set the new precedent in the courts that corporations would no longer be considered persons with constitutional rights to deceive and injure the public. Instead, the case was settled out of court on September 12, 2003, in California after being refused by the Supreme Court in June 2003. Nike, the multinational corporation that pulls in about $10.7 billion in annual sales, agreed to pay $1.5 million to the Fair Labor Association (FLA) for "program operations and worker development programs focused on education and economic opportunity." The donation to the FLA may be beneficial to overseas labor, but the concept of corporate personhood went unchecked.

In Pennsylvania, there is a new battle with corporations concerning genetically modified seeds grown on family farms in rural townships. In Second-Class Township, Pennsylvania, an ordinance was recently passed to protect the township's democracy from corporate influence and to protect their farmers from being forced to use genetically modified seeds produced by corporations. The ordinance declares in unison with Porter Township and Licking Township that corporations are not people and that being forced to legally consider them as such hinders the welfare of citizens, environment, and democracy.

SOURCES: <NikeWatch.com>; < www.nikewatch.com >; Clean Clothes Campaign, <www.cleanclothes.com>; Reclaim Democracy, < www.reclaimdemocracy.org>; Fair Labor Association, <www.fairlabor.org>; Community Environmental Legal Defense Fund, <www.celdf.org/cdp.htm>; and Program on Corporations Law and Democracy (POCLAD), < www.poclad.org>.

CENSORED #14 2004
UNWANTED REFUGEES A GLOBAL PROBLEM

According to the 2002 World Refugee Survey, there are as many as 40 million displaced people throughout the world. Fifteen million are seeking asylum in other countries. In addition, there are at least 22 million "internally displaced" within their country of origin who are not protected by international law and are therefore at even greater risk of oppression and abuse.

Living in the margins of unwilling host communities, long-term refugees are victims, not only of the war and persecution that forced them from their homes, but of the neglect of an international community, unwilling to devote attention and resources this social and humanitarian issue. Herded into huge refugee camps, where the prospect of emigration is slim, they can be deported at any time.

Corporate profiteers from developed countries are finding ways of benefiting from this global misfortune. Wackenhut, one of the largest operators of for-profit prisons, is now setting up, with local subsidies, for-profit internment camps that charge penniless exiles a daily fee and then deport them when they are unable to pay.

SOURCES: Daniel Swift, "The World Isn't Watching—The Forgotten Refugee Crisis," *In These Times*, October 14, 2002; Charles Bowden, "Outback Nightmares and Refugee Dreams," *Mother Jones*, March 2003; and Bill Frelick, "Neglect is Never Benign," *Bulletin of Atomic Scientists*, November/December 2002.

UPDATE BY LAUREN KETTNER: Across the globe, increasing numbers of unwanted people are fleeing their homelands and seeking safety in foreign lands. These refugees, in attempts to escape hostile homeland environments, often encounter an unwelcome reception. Most nations are unwilling to accept the responsibility of housing these immigrants, resulting in abuse and neglect of those seeking help.

Mainstream media outlets generally fail to communicate the suffering of these many millions of people. Recently, however, there was coverage of floods of Haitian refugees attempting to enter the U.S. as the Bush Administration denied them political asylum. The Human Rights Organization fears the return of these individuals to Haiti will result in persecution, torture, and death. Similar denials of asylum are occurring around the world, and many refugees are experiencing inhumane treatment.

Studies have shown that children in detention camps suffer from psychological damage and often may need a lifetime of counseling. The Woomera Detention Center in Australia was the site of a research study in which experts compared the practice of detaining children to "child abuse." Despite the closing of Woomera, other detention centers in Australia have come under fierce fire by critics who claim that they serve as for-profit prisons. Inhabitants of Woomera were moved to Baxter, where an electric fence surrounds the area and the compounds face inward, preventing communication with the outside world. In Baxter, Nauru, and Papua New Guinea, refugees can be detained for an indefinite period of time, and individuals often spend years without placement in the community.

Australia's harsh refugee policies are reflected in similar adaptations by the U.S., Great Britain, and other European countries. Northern Ireland houses refugees in actual prisons. Locked in cells like convicts, many are suffering mental as well as physical health problems. Austria's largest refugee center, Traiskirchen, is familiar to controversy, and the United Nations High Commissioner for Refugees (UNHCR) has urged an investigation into the center. Austria's hostile attitude toward foreigners includes allegedly rampant racism, sexual assault, and abuse in detention centers where police practice brutal tactics.

The Sudan government has been accused of targeting its own displaced civilians using air strikes and ground attacks on villages. The UNHCR is seeking $16 million to help the refugees cross the boarder into Chad where lack of water and resources hinder the process. With little or no cooperation from the broader international community, the UNHCR and watchdog groups are struggling to ease conditions for refugees.

SOURCES: Jonathan Fowler, "U.N. Aid Agencies Face Massive Shortfall for Sudanese Refugees in Chad," Associated Press Newswires, January 2004; "U.S.: Don't Turn Away Haitian Refugees," *Human Rights News*, February 2004; David Fickling, "Notorious Australian Refugee Camp Shut," *The Observer*, April 2003; Melissa Marino, "Detention is Child Abuse, Says Study," *Sunday Age*, January 2004; Michael Gordon, "A 'Solution' That Has Given Rise to Many Unwelcome Problems," *The Age*, December 2003; Emsie Ferreira, "Rights Bodies Lament Treatment of Foreigners in Austria," Agence France-Presse, February 2004; and Nina Bernstein, "Detention for Asylum-Seekers is Routine, but U.S. is Taking Another Look," *The New York Times,* January 2004.

CENSORED #15 2004
U.S. MILITARY'S WAR ON THE EARTH

The U.S. military is the world's largest polluter, generating 750,000 tons of toxic material annually. In the U.S., there are 27,000 toxic hot spots on 8,500 military properties. The U.S. military's pollution also occurs globally, as the U.S. maintains bases in dozens of countries. The military is emitting toxic material into the air and water, poisoning nearby communities, resulting in increased rates of cancer, kidney disease, birth defects, low birth rate, and miscarriage.

Rather than cleaning up the problem, the Pentagon claims that focusing on this issue stands in the way of troop readiness. A December 10, 2002, document entitled *Sustainable Ranges 2003 Decision Briefing to the Deputy Secretary of Defense*, unleashed a three-year campaign to exempt all U.S. military activity from all environmental restrictions. The Pentagon already operates military bases as "federal reservations," which fall outside of normal restrictions. Now the Department of Defense is seeking further exemptions from the Endangered Species Act, the Migratory Bird Treaties Act, the Wildlife Act, the National Environmental Policy Act, and the Clean Air Act.

SOURCES: Bob Feldman, "War on the Earth," *Dollars and Sense*, March/April 2003; David S. Mann and Glen Milner, "Disobeying Orders," *Washington Free Press*, September/October 2002; and John Passacantando, "Military Dumping," *Wild Matters*, October 2002.

UPDATE BY BROOKE FINLEY: Although it seemed that the military couldn't get any worse in the destruction of our planet, the Bush Administration is now trying to make the military exempt from responsibility for the pollution it causes. The Readiness and Range Preservation Initiative has been submitted to Congress by the Pentagon. Congress has already passed portions of this initiative, including exemptions from the Endangered Species Act, the Marine Mammals Act, and the Migratory Birds Act. The military can now redefine "harassment" of mammals during sonar testing under the Marine Mammals Act and not be concerned with endangered species or migratory birds when training for war.

Undermining local, state, and federal agency oversight, the next military exemptions planned for discussion with Congress have to do with the Clean Air Act and two pollution laws. These would excuse military bases from toxic dumping restrictions, from mandatory cleanup of unspent munitions, and from restrictions on emissions from military vehicles written into the Clean Air Act.

While the Bush Administration claims that these exemptions will boost the readiness of our military in our time of "war and crisis," experts disagree. "I don't believe that there is a training mission anywhere in the country that is being held up or not taking place because of environmental protection regulations," stated Christine Todd Whitman, former Environmental Protection Agency chief, before she retired from her position. Shortly after Whitman's retirement, Bush appointed his "old friend" Mike Leavitt to the job. Leavitt, the former governor of Utah, has been involved with some environmental exemptions of his own. Leavitt downplayed the seriousness of toxic releases produced by the Utah mining industry and failed to bring U.S. Magnesium, one of the nation's top polluters, under control, allowing 42 million tons of chlorine emissions per year into Utah's environment. Eventually, the EPA had to sue U.S. Magnesium to stop the pollution.

The hazardous waste proposal failed to pass Congress, but it will be reintroduced. A report from the EPA's staff to the president's Office of Management and Budget warned against relaxing hazardous-waste regulations, noting that munitions residue could present "an imminent and substantial endangerment of health and the environment." John Suarez, the EPA's enforcement chief, however, assured Congress that the easing of the hazardous waste regulations were "appropriate." If the Bush Administration furthers the military exemptions of hazardous waste cleanup and Congress decides to take advice from John Suarez, per chlorate, a rocket-fuel additive that has been found in ground water and surface water of 27 Defense Department facilities, will continue to contaminate drinking water supplies. Per chlorate has seeped into the Colorado River and has contaminated crops of lettuce and supermarket milk.

In addition to environmental degradation at home, the U.S. military is perpetrating this lack of responsibility globally. U.S. District judge James Ware recently ruled that the nation's toxic cleanup laws and the 1980 Superfund law do not apply to any U.S. military bases. This ruling, specifically pertaining to two former bases in the Philippines, sets a dangerous precedent, allowing U.S. armed forces freedom to contaminate foreign nations without being held liable for their actions.

SOURCES: Jon R. Lusma, "Toxic Immunity," *Mother Jones*, November/December 2003; Brad Knickerbocker, "Military Gets Break From Environmental Rules," *Christian Science Monitor*, November 24, 2003; Jan Hollingsworth and Keith Epstein, "The Other War," *Tampa Tribune*, August 31, 2003; Elizabeth Shogren, "The Nation; Pentagon Appeals to White House on Pollution Limits; Congress Has Denied the Clean Air and Toxic Waste Exemptions. But the Department of Defense Says the Laws Could Inhibit Readiness," *Los Angeles Times*, January 15, 2004; "At War With the Environment," *San Francisco Chronicle*, April 3, 2003; Donovan Webster and Michael Scherer, "No Clear Skies," *Mother Jones*, September/October 2003; Jeffrey St. Clair and Alexander Cockburn, "Biowarfare in the Andes," *Terrain*, Spring 2003; and Bob Egelko, "Judge Kills Suit Seeking Toxic Survey," *San Francisco Chronicle*, December 12, 2003.

CENSORED #17 2004
CLEAR CHANNEL MONOPOLY DRAWS CRITICISM

Clear Channel Communications of San Antonio, Texas, may not yet be a household name, but since 1996, the radio station conglomerate has rocketed to a place alongside NBC and Gannett as one of the largest media companies in the United States.

Before passage of the 1996 Telecommunications Act, a company could not own more than 40 radio stations in the entire country. With the act's sweeping relaxation of ownership limits, the cap on radio ownership was eliminated. As a result, Clear Channel has dominated the industry by growing from 40 radio stations nationally in the mid-'90s, to approximately 1,225 stations nationally by 2003. The station also dominates the audience share in 100 of 112 major markets. In addition to its radio stations, Clear Channel also owns television station affiliates, billboards, and outdoor advertising and owns or exclusively books the vast majority of concert venues, amphitheaters, and clubs in the country. In 2000, Clear Channel purchased the nation's largest concert and events promoter, and in 2001, Clear Channel did 70 percent of national ticket sales.

SOURCES: Jeff Perlstein, "Clear Channel Stumbles," *MediaFile*, September 2002; *NOW With Bill Moyers*, April 26, 2002, and April 4, 2003; *The New York Times*, January 30, 2003, and February 3, 2003; and *Wall Street Journal*, January 31, 2003.

UPDATE BY JULIE MAYEDA: Clear Channel Communications is now a $27-billion corporation. Clear Channel operates in 65 countries worldwide. One hundred million listeners tune in daily. Clear Channel makes up 20 percent of all radio industry revenues, controlling 11 percent of all the stations in the country, and owns five times as many stations as its closest competitor.

Clear Channel owns 106 live entertainment venues, including Broadway touring businesses and sporting events, and controls 70 percent of live music venues in the country. In 2002, Clear Channel sold upwards of 30 million concert tickets, 23 million more than the closest competitor, leading to accusations of anticompetitive behavior. Worldwide, the company owns, leases, operates, or books a total of 135 venues. They stage over 135 live entertainment venues across the country.

The third largest revenue maker for the conglomerate is outdoor advertising. They own 716,000 displays, 114,094 in the U.S. and 571,942 in 65 other countries. A significant portion of the outdoor business is in foreign markets. These include billboards, taxi tops, mobile truck panels, and bus, train, shopping mall, and airport displays. Through these displays, the company boasts to reach over half of the overall U.S. population and 75 percent of the nation's Hispanics.

Clear Channel owns 39 TV stations including affiliates of ABC, CBS, NBC, Fox, WB, PAX, and UPN, and is within the top 15 TV groups in terms of audience reach. Clear Channel has ties to Hispanic Broadcasting Corporation (HBC), the largest Hispanic radio network in the U.S. HBC has recently merged with Univision Communications, the largest Hispanic television network in the country.

Clear Channel's ultimate goal is to dominate broadcast programming and control concert promotion. The company has effectively shut down local competition nationwide, reducing local on-air talent and regionally relevant news and views.

As explained by Clear Channel's CEO Lowry Mays, "this company is not in the business of providing music, news or information, but rather in the business of selling advertising to its customers."

SOURCES: Christine Y. Chen, "The Bad Boys of Radio," *Fortune*, March 3, 2003; Bob Williams and Morgan Jindrich, "On the Road Again—and Again: FCC Officials Rack Up $2.8 Million Travel Tab with Industries They Regulate," May 22, 2003, <www.openairwaves.org>; "Clear Channel's Practices Show What's Wrong with Media Monopolies," AFL-CIO, January 30, 2004, <www.aflcio.org>; <www.media-aliance.org/mediafile/21-3/clearchannel. html>; <www.indypgh.org>; <www.oligopoly watch.com/ 2003/05/01>; <www.alenet. org/members/story>; <www.mediaaccess. org/programs/diversity/Business NorthExclusives.htm>; and Maria Figueroa, Damone Richardson, and Pam Whitefield, "The Clear Picture on Clear Channel Communications, Inc. A Corporate Profile," <www.dpeaflcio.org>.

U.S. DOLLAR VS. THE EURO: ANOTHER REASON FOR THE INVASION OF IRAQ

President Richard Nixon removed U.S. currency from the gold standard in 1971. Since then, the world's supply of oil has been traded in U.S. fiat dollars, making the dollar the dominant world reserve currency. Countries must provide the U.S. with goods and services for dollars—which the U.S. can freely print. To purchase energy and pay off any IMF debts, countries must hold vast dollar reserves. This means that in addition to controlling world trade, the United States is importing substantial quantities of goods and services for very low relative costs.

The euro has begun to emerge as a serious threat to dollar hegemony and U.S. economic dominance. The dollar may prevail throughout the Western Hemisphere, but the euro and dollar are clashing in the former Soviet Union, Central Asia, sub-Saharan Africa, and the Middle East.

In November 2000, Iraq became the first OPEC nation to begin selling its oil for euros. Since then, the value of the euro has increased 17 percent, and the dollar has declined. One important reason for the invasion and installation of a U.S. dominated government in Iraq was to force the country back onto the dollar. Another reason for the invasion was to dissuade further OPEC momentum toward the euro, especially from Iran, the second largest OPEC producer, which was actively discussing a switch to euros for its oil exports.

Because of huge trade deficits, it is estimated that the dollar is currently overvalued by at least 40 percent. Conversely, the euro-zone does not run huge deficits, uses higher interest rates, and has an increasingly larger share of world trade. As the euro establishes its durability and comes into wider use, the dollar will no longer be the world's only option. At that point, it would be easier for other countries to exercise financial leverage against the United States without damaging themselves or the global financial system as a whole.

Faced with waning international economic power, military superiority is the United States' only tool for world domination. Although the expense of this military control is unsustainable, says journalist William Clark, "one of the dirty little secrets of today's international order is that the rest of the globe could topple the United States from its hegemonic status whenever they so choose with a concerted abandonment of the dollar standard. This is America's preeminent, inescapable Achilles' heel." If American power is ever perceived globally as a greater liability than the dangers of toppling the international order, the U.S. systems of control can be eliminated and collapsed. When acting against world opinion—as in Iraq—an international consensus could brand the United States as a "rogue nation."

SOURCES: William Clark, "The Real Reasons for the Upcoming War with Iraq," *The Sierra Times*, February 9, 2003; Coilin Nunan, "Oil, Currency, and the War on Iraq," *Feasta*, January 2003; and William Greider, "The End of Empire," *The Nation*, September 23, 2002.

UPDATE BY AMBROSIA PARDUE: The U.S. is still battling OPEC and other countries that are considering using the euro as a payment for petrol. A trader at the Rothschild bank in London notes, "If the dollar loses its role as a currency of reference, the United States, the world's largest oil importer, will no longer be able to have outside countries finance its abyssal trade deficit." The dollar is in fact becoming less and less stable against the euro. On February 12, 2004, the euro was at $1.2804 versus the dollar.

As it stands, oil can only be bought from OPEC in dollars. Non-oil-producing countries sell their goods in order to earn dollars with which to purchase oil. If a country does not have enough dollars, they must borrow them from the World Bank/IMF, incurring debt to be paid back, with interest, in dollars. This increases the demand for dollars, which boosts the U.S. economy. Foreign deposited dollars strengthen the U.S. dollar and give the United States enormous power to manipulate the world economy, set rules, and prevail in the international market. Allowing the U.S. to act as the "world's central bank," the dollar becomes oil-backed, rather than gold-backed.

In December 2003, OPEC held a meeting in Vienna, in which its members voiced complaints that oil profits were down 25 to 30 percent due to primarily to attachment to the dollar. Several members are considering a move away from the dollar, including Venezuela, Russia, Indonesia, and Malaysia. Japan has shifted a modest amount of dollar bonds to euro bonds. China announced in July 2003 that it would switch part of its dollar reserves into the euro. After September 11, 2001, Islamic financiers repatriated their investments, which were worth billions of dollars, to Arab banks because there was worry of the possible seizure of assets under the USA Patriot Act. Much of Iran's reserve fund has also switched to the euro. Some suggest that European countries will pressure OPEC to trade in euros to reduce currency risks.

The Bush Administration presented the U.N. Security Council with "Resolution 1483" on May 9, 2003, which proposed dropping all sanctions against Iraq and giving the U.S./U.K. complete control of Iraq's oil production revenue. Iraq's oil was to remain under U.N. control under the "oil for food" program until the U.N. sanctions were lifted but Resolution 1483 establishes a U.S./U.K. administered "Iraqi Assistance Fund" instead. According to William Clark, the "Iraqi Assistance Fund provided the mechanism to quietly and legally reconvert Iraq's oil exports back to the dollar." With U.S. control over Iraq, the Bush Administration does not have to worry about that government switching to the euro.

Z Magazine reported in February 2004 that the "shock and awe" attack on Iraq served several economic purposes: "(1) Safeguard the U.S. economy by resecuring Iraqi oil in U.S. dollars, instead of the euro, to try to lock the World Bank into dollar oil trading so the U.S. would remain the dominant world power—militarily and economically. (2) Send a clear message to other oil producers as to what will happen to them if they abandon the dollar matrix. (3) Place the second largest oil reserve under direct U.S. control. (4) Create a state where the U.S. can maintain a huge force to dominate the Middle East and its oil. (5) Create a severe setback to the European Union and its euro, the only trading block and currency strong enough to attack U.S. dominance of the world through trade. (6) Free its forces (ultimately) so that it can begin operations against those countries that are trying to disengage themselves from the U.S. dollar imperialism—such as Venezuela, where the U.S. has supported the attempted overthrow of a democratic government by a junta more friendly to U.S. business/oil interests."

The U.S. has been encouraging Nigeria with offers of expanded aid to withdraw from OPEC. The U.S. would like to create a new oil cartel in the Middle East and Africa in order to replace OPEC. The U.S. is also pressuring non-OPEC producers to flood the oil market in order to retain the domination in dollars in an attempt to weaken OPEC's market control.

SOURCES: "OPEC Considers Ditching the Dollar," *Free Republic*, February 9, 2004, <www.freerepublic.com/focus/f-news/1074714/posts>; Steve Goldstein, "Europe Finishes Flat, Unilever High," *CBS Market Watch*, February 12, 2004, <www.cbs.marketwatch.com/news/story.asp>; Mariko Hayashibara, "Dollar Steady vs. Major on Capital Inflow," *Boston Globe*, January 19, 2004, <www.boston.com/news/world/asia/articles/2004/01/19>; Patrick Brethour, "OPEC Mulls Move to Euro for Pricing Crude Oil," *Globe and Mail*, January 12, 2004<www.globalandmail.com>; Sharma, Tracy, and Kumar, "The Invasion of Iraq: Dollar vs. Euro", *Z Magazine*, February 2004; and William Clark, "Post-War Commentary," January 1, 2004, <www.ratical.org/ratville/CAHRr iraqWar.html>.

CENSORED #24

U.S. AID TO ISRAEL FUELS REPRESSIVE OCCUPATION IN PALESTINE

During the last 25 years, U.S. aid to Israel has been about 60 percent military aid and 40 percent economic aid. There is a new plan to phase out all economic aid by 2008 in order to have all the aid going to military. Israel receives about $3 billion a year in direct aid and $3 billion a year in indirect aid in the form of special loans and grants.

It is with this aid that Israel has been able to continue the comprehensive and unrelenting occupation of the West Bank and Gaza. Now, Israel is building a 30-foot high cement wall with gun towers and electric fencing to imprison Palestinians and the entire West Bank.

SOURCES: John Steinbach, "Palestine in the Crosshairs: U.S. Policy and the Struggle for Nationhood," *CovertAction Quarterly*, Spring 2002, No. 72; Matt Bowles, "U.S. Aid Lifeblood of the Occupation," *Left Turn*, March 2002; and Bob Wing, "Israel Erecting 'Great Wall' Around Palestine," *Wartimes*, April 2003.

UPDATE BY ANNA MIRANDA: Billions of dollars continues to flow to Israel every year from the U.S. In December 2003, in a move that undermined and threatened the "roadmap to peace," Ariel Sharon's unilateral disengagement speech proposed to create an independent Palestinian state. The plan includes redrawing Israel's border, relocating Israeli Arabs to Palestine, and the removal of some of the Jewish settlements in the occupied territories. Sharon's "generous offer" is contingent on the Palestinian's agreement to come to the table and negotiate a final settlement.

Concerns over the plan include the redrawing of the border, which would "relocate" Israeli Arab towns and villages into Palestine. The reduction of the Arab population in Israel would reduce the impact and representation of their voice in elections. In addition, Palestinians fear the apartheid wall will become a de facto border where nearly half of the West Bank would be ceded to Israel. The Palestine National Authority has rejected the disengagement plan and views it as "a serious violation and an attempt to destroy the peace process." Sharon threatens he will not wait for the Palestinians to come to a decision. If they are unable to come to an agreement, Israel will proceed with unilateral disengagement from the Palestinians "politically and militarily to prevent any contact between them and us."

Sharon's oppressive policies continue to devastate the lives of Palestinians. In October 2003, the U.N. General Assembly approved a resolution demanding that the construction of the wall be stopped and reversed and that the killings of both Israelis and Palestinians end. Sharon ignored the resolution and continues to build the wall. According to Israel's Vice-Premier Ehud Olmert, "The fence will continue to be built. We have to worry about Israel's security, and it is clear that we will not act according to the instructions of a hostile, automatic majority...which has always acted against Israel."

Another issue is the continued development of settlements despite its conflict with the road map. The U.S. State Department has stated, "We have made our policy clear, which is that under the road map, Israel has made a commitment to stop settlement activity. Sticking to that commitment is important." In October 2003, an announcement was made by the Israeli government that 300 new apartments would be built in the west Bank in two settlements—one in Nablus, the other in Jerusalem. More settlers result in more soldiers. More soldiers result in more violence.

In December 2003, 200 people were left homeless in Khan Yunis when the Israeli occupation army destroyed 22 Palestinian homes. In October 2003, the military destroyed 100 homes, leaving 1,500 people homeless and eight people dead, including two children.

Death and violence is not limited to the Palestinian people. In April 2003, Tom Hurndall, an activist with the International Solidarity Movement, was shot in the head while shepherding children from the line of fire of Israeli soldiers. Hurndall passed away in January 2004 after being in a coma for nine months. The soldier who shot him was charged with manslaughter, a charge Hurndall's family says should have been murder. Although violent incidences with the army continue to escalate, there is also a rise in military dissent.

A group of air force pilots, soldiers, and would-be draftees have openly expressed their disagreement with the government's policies and object to taking part in killing innocent Palestinians. Black Hawk helicopter and F-16 fighter pilots have been dismissed from the air force and denounced as traitors. These "refuseniks" have been joined by over 30 other pilots who have endorsed a letter refusing to bomb Palestinian cities. Sayaret Matka, an elite commando unit, has received a letter from 13 reserve soldiers who refuse to serve in the West Bank and Gaza strip. A petition supporting the Israeli pilots' refusal to serve was signed by 64 Israeli movie directors and producers. As protests within the military rise, unprecedented dissent outside the ranks among would-be draftees is causing more trouble for the military.

Five young men have refused to be drafted, not only to serve in the occupied territories, but also to serve in the military altogether. They have been sentenced to serve one-year sentences in jail as well as an additional 14 months while they wait for their trial, a sentence longer than those served by previous dissenters who have only spent one month in jail. These dissenters are unique because instead of avoiding the draft by faking an illness or lying, they have chosen to speak the truth and openly express their disagreement with their government's policies.

SOURCES: <www.arabicnews.com/ansub/Daily/Day/040113/2004011337. html>; Peter Hirschberg, *Irish Times (Dublin)*, January 6, 2004; <www.mercury news.com/ mld/mercurynews/news/7069685.htm>; <www.motherjones.com/ news/dailymojo/ 2003/10/we_599_01b.html>; <www.commondreams.org/ headlines03/1203-07.html; <www.commondreams.org/headlines04/0105-03. html>; and <www.motherjones. com/news/dailymojo/2003/07/we_490_05. html>.

NOTES:

1. Michael Parenti, *To Kill a Nation: The Attack on Yugoslavia* (New York: Verso, 2000): 9.
2. James Dunnigan, *The Air Campaign in Iraq*, <www.StrategyPage.com>, May 21, 2003.
3. <Iraqibodycount.com>, June 10, 2004.
4. Chalmers Johnson, *The Sorrows of Empire: Militarism, Secrecy, and the End of the Republic* (New York: Metropolitan Books, 2004): 221.
5. "Yugoslavia," *Encyclopedia Britannica: Macropaedia*, 1992.
6. Michel Chossudovsky, *NATO in the Balkans* (New York: International Action Center, 1998): 82.
7. Parenti, *To Kill A Nation*, 19–21.
8. Chossudovsky, *NATO in the Balkans*, 82–87.
9. David Correl, *Balkans Region: Oil and Gas Act Sheet*, *Balkans Regional Country Analysis Brief*, <www.eia.doe.gov>, January 2004.
10. Parenti, *To Kill a Nation*, 92.
11. *Ibid.*
12. Peter Phillips and Project Censored, *Censored 1999* (New York: Seven Stories Press, 1998): 58–62.
13. Michel Collon, *Revelations: Racak, the Timisoara of Kosovo 99*, <michel.colon@skynet.be>, January 20, 2004.
14. Parenti, *To Kill a Nation*, 107.
15. John Catalinotto, "U.S./NATO Guilty of War Crimes in Yugoslavia," *Workers World*, June 22, 2000.
16. Johnson, *The Sorrows of Empire*, 224–225.
17. *Ibid.*, 236.
18. *Ibid.*, 226.
19. Patrick Martin, "The Stage Managed Event in Baghdad's Firdos Square: Image Making, Lies, and the 'Liberation' of Iraq," *World Socialist Web* site, April 12, 2003, <www.wsws.org/articles/2003/apr2003/fird-a12.shtml>.
20. *Ibid.*
21. Editorial, "The Times in Iraq," *The New York Times*, May 26, 2004.
22. Daniel Okrent, "Weapons of Mass Destruction? Or Mass Distraction?," *The New York Times*, May 30, 2004.
23. *Harper's Magazine*, <www.harpersindex.com>, May 5, 2004.

THIS MODERN WORLD

by TOM TOMORROW

Panel 1: IT'S TIME FOR ANOTHER EXCITING EPISODE OF EVERYONE'S FAVORITE CRIME DRAMA--

PARTISAN INVESTIGATIONS UNIT

"If we're not looking into it-- It's not worth looking into!"

THIS WEEK: THE TEAM TRIES TO FIND SOMETHING TO DO.

Panel 2: BOSS--THEY STILL HAVEN'T FOUND OUT WHO TOLD ROBERT NOVAK THAT VALERIE PLAME WAS A CIA OPERATIVE! YOU WANT **US** TO CHECK IT OUT?

NAH! I'M **SURE** THE MISCREANT WILL STEP FORWARD EVENTUALLY.

SNICKER!

Panel 3: THE 9/11 COMMISSION SAYS THEY CAN'T FINISH THEIR WORK IN THE TIME ALLOTTED! SHOULD WE SEND SOME PEOPLE OVER TO HELP **OUT**?

HEY--IT'S NOT **MY** PROBLEM IF THEY'RE A BUNCH OF DAMN **PROCRASTINATORS**!

WHAT **ELSE** HAVE WE GOT?

Panel 4: THE PRESIDENT'S SETTING UP A COMMISSION TO INVESTIGATE PRE-WAR INTELLIGENCE FAILURES! WE **COULD** LEND THEM A HAND!

AHEM! YES, WELL-- WE'LL CERTAINLY PUT AS MUCH EFFORT INTO THAT AS THE PRESIDENT **WANTS** US TO!

WINK!

Panel 5: **BOSS**! JANET JACKSON'S NIPPLE WAS **BRIEFLY VISIBLE** DURING THE SUPER BOWL HALFTIME SHOW! THE FCC IS CALLING FOR A **FULL INVESTIGATION**!

A **NIPPLE**? ON **NATIONAL TELEVISION**?!

YES, SIR.

Panel 6: WELL WHAT THE HELL ARE YOU **WAITING** FOR? GET A **MOVE** ON! THE AMERICAN PEOPLE DESERVE **ANSWERS**!

I'LL COMPILE A LIST OF **WITNESSES**!

I'LL REVIEW THE **TAPE**!

LET'S **ROLL**!!

NEXT: AN INNOCENT **BREAST**--OR A THREAT TO **NATIONAL SECURITY**? THE P.I.U. IS **ON THE CASE**!

TOM TOMORROW©2004... www.thismodernworld.com

CHAPTER 3

Junk Food News and News Abuse

By Ambrosia Pardue and Joni Wallent, Student Researchers,
Censorship in Media, Sonoma State University, Spring 2004

Each year, the researchers at Project Censored devote some of their time to unearthing—and discussing—the most frivolous, time-consuming news pieces covered by the corporate media. This year's selections were voted on by the 200 students, faculty, and media researchers who work with Project Censored and hundreds of others worldwide who are members of our weekly independent news listserv. We have two categories: "Junk Food News" and "News Abuse." The Junk Food News section focuses on empty calorie news, while News Abuse details the way in which mainstream media misuse and obsess over tragic or horrific events.

As usual, the Junk Food News chapter is filled with celebrity gossip and drama. Due to the recent rise in reality entertainment now considered newsworthy, we also felt it necessary to pay some attention to the genre of reality television. This year, we examine the list of top reality shows that have begun to invade our mainstream news programs.

While there is nothing wrong with enjoying entertainment, when entertainment starts consuming the limited time and space for critical news stories, it becomes a problem. Entertainment, disguised as news, increasingly infects limited and valuable news space. We believe that real news—news about our leaders and the choices they make that impact our daily lives— ought to have first-place priority in news programming. Unfortunately, this kind of news seems to get less and less attention each time we put this chapter together. The more Junk Food News desensitizes viewers, listeners, and readers, the more Americans are coaxed into accepting programs or news clips that have no real meaning or substance.

Our nation has become one that would rather sit down and tune off—and our waistlines show it. We love to know everything about those famous few, reveling in their glories and disasters, but claim that news about what is happening to people throughout the world is either too boring or "too depressing." Television has become a way to detach from reality while, at the same time, somehow convincing the viewer that it is reality.

With so much competing for our attention on radio and TV, it is easy to become hypnotized by a media bombarding us with unnecessary babble. Yet as we become subjected to more and more of this type of programming, it is important to remember that a healthy media is crucial to a fully functioning democracy. While some may feel that the Junk Food News chapter is itself junk food news, this is an influential part of our culture that cannot—and should not—be ignored. These stories can tell us a little bit about what the majority values, and it gives some insight into how people think. In order to change people's ideas, we must be able to understand them. If individuals do not look at the whole of what media has become, we cannot effectively understand or work to shift the current paradigms.

And so, every year, Project Censored spends some time documenting the most striking examples of Junk Food News and News Abuse, in an attempt to get a better understanding of what makes up our press and how it influences us.

Junk Food News

The Junk Food top 10 are always filled with celebrity gossip. Holding true to tradition, this year's list is made up of the biggest celebrity happenings that were deemed important enough for coverage on your nightly news program. It is composed of many familiar names—several of which were on our list last year. Here are the top 10 Junk Food News stories of the year:

1. Janet's Super Bowl Exposure
2. Ben and J.Lo's breakup
3. the Hilton sisters (especially Paris Hilton)
4. Britney Spears' wedding
5. Martha Stewart
6. Britney and Madonna's kiss
7. Trista and Ryan's wedding
8. *American Idol*

9. the last episode of *Friends*

10. Ashton and Demi

Ashton Kutcher and Demi Moore's relationship, with a 15-year difference between them, created quite a stir in the headlines on paper, radio, and television. They turned heads and raised brows as the "young man, older lady" duo. At Project Censored, votes were counted, and the results showed that the couple made spot number 10 on this year's Junk Food News list.

Number 9 this year includes the six guys and gals from the famous television show *Friends*. 2004 closed out the tenth year for the folks, creating a buzz among those who religiously watched the show every week and even for those who caught a show occasionally. Some called the finale the "Thursday Night Super Bowl." *Friends* was a social phenomenon, and Monica, Chandler, Ross, Rachel, Joey, and Phoebe became the icons of a generation. As news of the show's last episode made its way around, it dominated media attention and news headlines. Now that the show is over, what will everyone do? As the cast members adjust to their new life without *Friends*, they should have no trouble finding spare cash, considering the $1 million they made per episode toward the end. As for the rest of the people out there in the world, they will have to be satisfied with what was (and catching the reruns and buying the DVDs).

American Idol made number 4 on the Junk Food list last year, but slipped down a few notches to Number 8 for 2005. The show has remained a favorite for many, despite the cruel words from Simon...perhaps that is what draws so many. Even after several seasons of this show, people still flock to their TV screens to vote for their favorite "Idols" and to see who will be kicked off next. *American Idol* results are often seen and heard on the morning news, updating the viewers on participants' progress. Whether it is Simon or the "Idols" themselves, *American Idol* has become an instant "success" throughout America—and the media.

On the list for number 7 is the wedding of Trista Rehn and Ryan Sutter. Who would have known that a reality show would ever have produced true love and a million-dollar wedding? One must wonder why their relationship lasted while so many other television reality-show hookups floundered. It seems to be that the lovebirds were made for each other as much as they were for television. Millions across the world viewed their wedding. Ryan and Trista have been on countless television shows and magazine covers. Even Trista's ring was star-for-a-day.

Landing on our list at number 6 is the kiss between Britney Spears and Madonna. Controversy seems to be their forté, and they created quite a stir with their lip-to-lip at the *2003 MTV Video Music Awards* show in New York. These two have separately been in the headlines for their entire careers—what better move than to create a headline with the both of them! Whoever thought this one up was a true genius of media hype and self-promotion. (Reportedly, it was Madonna herself.)

Amazingly, Martha Stewart moved up the list one spot from last year to number 5 this year. She is still an everpresent face in our court system, and her products can be found on the shelves at Kmart. This high profile case was dragged out by the media and has proven to be a guilty case of Junk Food News.

Britney Spears makes this year's list again, coming in at Number 4 with her marriage to childhood friend Jason Alexander. The two were married on a Saturday in Las Vegas and had their marriage annulled the next Monday. Every move of Britney's seems made to create attention. The media loves her and her headlines dominate the news as well as the tabloids.

At number 3 are the Hilton sisters. Not many people had heard of them before this past year, but now it seems that wherever one looks on mainstream media, there they are, especially Paris Hilton. From her sex video to her appearance on *The Simple Life*, she's demanded a lot of attention. Could it be that so many care about a rich girl who doesn't even know what Wal-Mart is?

Coming in at number 2 is Ben Affleck and Jennifer Lopez's breakup. They were making news even before they called their relationship off. For the second year in a row, J. Lo was in the news and on our top 10. From Ben and J. Lo's on-again, off-again relationship, plenty of people were all over their every move. They graced the covers of magazines and tabloids, with people waiting anxiously and holding their breaths over what the couple would do next. The "rock" for "Jenny from the block" sat pretty on her finger for only so long. Even though Ben and J. Lo are over, they have not faded from celebrity gossip.

And the number 1 story is...Janet Jackson and her Super Bowl exposure. Sexuality was a topic discussed in last year's Junk Food News chapter, and it remains a hot topic this year, as Janet's Super Bowl exposure has shown us. It shocked our nation, and so did the FCC with their tizzy over a nipple. To reiterate last year's chapter, "Nobody at the project would be averse to the media having a healthy, educational public discussion of the evolution of human sexuality within our culture"—or, for that matter, an in-depth public discussion about the problems with the FCC. But once again, most of the debate sparked by this event never rose above the level of the shallow or the inane.

The vulgarity and sleaziness of the rest of the Super Bowl half-time show seemed to slither back into the dark, not making headlines or an outrage. What about Kid Rock, who desecrated the American flag, flouncing around the stage with it on his back? Why was that not attacked by our media? There was also an "in your face" sexual overtone throughout the entire show, which was quickly overlooked. The issue of nudity, or slight nudity, remains a topic with varied opinions, and as a result, has produced much controversy and headlines. Some see it as nothing terrible, while others cover their children's eyes over a "fluke" exposure. Meanwhile, dancers rip off their costumes to such lyrics as " it's getting hot in here so take off all your clothes," from a song that's everpopular with teens and preteens and is shown regularly on MTV. Others see incidences like the Super Bowl exposure as sexist, questioning why it was Janet, a woman, who created the controversy, while little attention was paid to her partner in crime, Justin Timberlake. Was the whole idea of "exposure" sexist? Could it be that the exposure of a single nipple has more importance than the issues of our nation and world that daily impact millions, or billions, of people? More weight is given to celebrity cries for attention than to the millions of children who are starving each day or to the men and women dying on foreign soil. As the Junk Food News section shows, media priorities are a bit warped.

News Abuse

Not to be confused with Junk Food News, News Abuse seeks to examine those stories that were manipulated and dragged out by the mainstream media. While all true news stories deserve mention, it is important to move on in a reasonable time frame. When the media attempt to attract viewers by repeating headlines ad nauseam, this is news abuse. News Abuse stories may be tragic in nature, as the Scott Peterson case has proved. They can also be events twisted into minireality soaps like the Michael Jackson saga or the Bush aircraft carrier landing. Whatever the event, all are examples of our nation's corporate media abusing the limited space and time that should be allotted to the very current critical news of our world. Here is the News Abuse top 5 for 2005:

1. Jessica Lynch
2. Mel Gibson's movie *The Passion of the Christ*
3. Michael Jackson
4. Bush's aircraft carrier landing
5. Scott Peterson

This year's News Abuse theme is the "soap-like" way in which the media manipulates tragedies and elitist publicity stunts. The section illustrates the ways in which our media has manipulated and distracted the public from reality. The Scott Peterson case, coming in at number 5, made the perfect example of "soap-like" news. The media focused on a brutal crime in which Scott Peterson stands accused of murdering his attractive and pregnant wife. Mixed with a long drawn-out trial, the result is a TV news frenzy. The stations jumped on this from the very moment Laci went missing, and they have not backed off yet. This case has received so much attention that it has proved difficult to find an impartial jury.

At number 4 on this year's News Abuse list is Bush's aircraft carrier landing. In a publicity stunt, George W., dressed in a bomber suit, landed on an aircraft carrier, receiving major press coverage. Under a patriotic guise, the presidential outing at the height of the Middle East conflict dominated the news, distracting the public from the real news stories taking place at the same time.

Also surrounded by controversy is the Michael Jackson hoopla, which comes in at the number 3 spot. Fans held candlelight vigils in the star's honor; it seemed that Jackson was trying to win points in court through the opinion of his fans. He and his family spoke out on television, creating more emotion, attention, and drama. With so much else going on in our modern times, it seems a shame to spend so much time on one person.

The Passion of the Christ received an enormous amount of press coverage over its opening. The movie proved to be controversial, stirring the audience with its emotional accounts of the death of Christ. It fueled debate and pitted our nation against itself, making Mel Gibson the most loved—and most hated—man in America.

At the number 1 spot for 2005 is the Jessica Lynch ordeal. As a soldier stationed in Iraq, her dramatic rescue was filmed by a Special Forces unit, and she became a war hero. During her time as a prisoner of war, Jessica was abused and assaulted and was not able to remember much. Her story is a tragic tale with a happy ending. Blown up on the news and then floating away out of sight, Jessica's story is a testament to consequences of war and is a great example of a patriotic rescue manipulated by film.

Reality Television

During a brainstorming session early last year, the Project Censored team found that reality television shows, such as *American Idol*, were creating such a stir that they were finding their way onto the news and radio channels.

Unfortunately, reality television shows are now considered newsworthy. People migrate to their television sets on a weekly basis to catch the latest update on their reality shows. This spawned our curiosity. We wanted to find out what the top 3 reality television shows were and how people felt about them. As a response to this evergrowing genre of television shows invading the airwaves, we have included the results in this year's Junk Food News chapter. Separate from both Junk Food News and News Abuse, the reality television phenomenon demands its own mention. Here are the top 3 reality television shows:

1. *Temptation Island*
2. *American Idol*
3. *The Bachelor*

A dating show for the modern age, number 3's *The Bachelor* has truly transformed the meaning of a "hookup." Gone are the days of introductions by friends and family members. In today's world, it takes a television show to bring two strangers together—that and a hefty budget and viewing audience. Once again, this television show invades a person's life, cutting it open and exposing intimate moments to all. People still run to the casting calls and to their television sets. Our society is fascinated by it. The allure of finding "true love" surrounded by breathtaking scenery and a gorgeous house is still alive in the minds of many. It could happen. The likelihood of this dream happening, as the lives of those lucky guys and gals show, is not too inconceivable. This show spawns false hope and an emotional roller coaster, possibly the two most important components of the reality television formula.

American Idol is reality television show number 2. The show has drawn millions of viewers each night for the last two years. It has made "average" Americans stars and has crushed many more Americans' hearts as they have been rejected and told that they were no good. This show takes the meaning of "audition" to a whole new level. Rather than feel the burn of humiliation in front of a selected few people, *American Idol* contestants feel humiliation in front of millions of viewers. This show has added yet another option to the reality television lineup. It has become typical for Americans to be engrossed in the lives of these contestants—their winnings and their misfortunes. As Americans, we must ask ourselves why a show like *American Idol* has taken center stage in our lives, becoming the highlight of our week.

Ringing in at number 1 is *Temptation Island*. The temptation to watch this show is reality television at its finest. While writing this blurb about *Temptation Island*, we were trying to figure out just what the show was. No one seemed to know; we got several shows confused, not knowing what *Temptation*

Island was really about and how it worked. Case in point: Reality television has become such an enormous phenomenon that show after show is developed, with few even understanding where one leaves off and the next begins. This genre is intertwined, and many reality television shows mimic each other. Perhaps the temptation should be to scratch reality TV from our selection of television viewing all together.

Reality television shows are considered to be Junk Food because of the enormous audiences they attract and the fact that they have no real value for viewers. The funny part about it is, reality shows are not really reality. There are no scripts in real life or consolation prizes at the end of a day or millions of people watching. Reality shows have tricked people into believing that those shown are portraying their real selves. In reality, they are presenting a front, going along with the game to get their 15 minutes of fame. Our society has become such that we are driven to fit into a cookie-cutter mold, to do what others expect—and the reality show phenomenon epitomizes this trend.

In our current political climate, it is curious to be spending so much time devoted to celebrities. Most of these Junk Food News stories were on both the morning and nightly news. Junk Food News seems to be counterproductive, yet continually uses our news space. Many people neglect to watch or listen to corporate news, let alone the real news, because it is seen as depressing. News is more or less full of fluff, and even entertainment is taking on that trend. The media is misusing the mainstream space, which is a national resource belonging to us all. Quality media with diversified ideas is desperately needed in a free and democratic society in order to guarantee the continuance of a democracy.

As this chapter illustrates, much of that sacred and rare space is taken up by programming that is essentially garbage. Americans seem to be less and less concerned about real issues, about the real reality. While perhaps initially unpleasant, concerning oneself with what is really going on will allow more individuals to gain a unified voice, increasing the chance to change and further the concept of equality for all. People need to become outraged at the complacency the majority of individuals and our corporate media feel towards the discrepancies around this world. If the Junk Food chapter is a window into the soul of America, the sight is not pretty. Our country should be sick and tired of the trash that is filling our airwaves. It is time that Americans get out of their comfort zone and stop tuning out the real truth and real reality that is happening around them. And it starts with you.

CHAPTER 4

The Big Media Giants

BY MARK CRISPIN MILLER
Media Map Research by Project Censored intern Emilio Licea

Ten years ago, when media activists—and there were not that many of us
then—had just begun to call for national debate about the impact of corporate concentration, our arguments against consolidation tended to be less
empirical than inferential, hypothetical, prophetic. The evidence was too
complex and scattered to arouse a general feeling of emergency (and of
course, the impact of that evidence was further muffled by the media's reluc-
tance even to perceive the problem, much less to properly report it). We had
to make a powerful case for *what was missing*: missing from TV, radio, and
the multiplexes, from the daily papers and national magazines, from the music
scene, the book business and even cyberspace. We highlighted those
instances when managerial suppression of the news had been so blatant as
to get some press: CBS's spiking of the *60 Minutes* story about Brown &
Williamson; Phillip Morris forcing ABC News to apologize for airing news
that was entirely accurate; and Rupert Murdoch's dropping BBC News from
his Asian satellite TV system to mollify a Chinese government outraged by
the network's tough reporting on the massacre in Tiananmen Square.

Because you can't prove a negative, it would be hard in any case to base
a rousing argument on stories that were *not* reported, movies that were *not*
released, books that were *not* on the shelves, etc. That job was, moreover,
made still harder by the grand illusion of unbounded "choice" implicit in the
glittering multitude of items proffered by our cable guides and newsstands
and chain bookstores. What could consumers possibly be missing? Surely

what you want is out there somewhere, at the market price. And as the most notorious strokes of corporate censorship were too few, evidently, not to seem to be exceptional, so were the copious statistics on our cultural losses not stark enough to get a movement going. The end of radio and television journalism, the near-disappearance of foreign films from U.S. movie screens, the vanishing of genres from, and the dire shrinkage of, the play-lists on commercial radio, the death of Broadway as a place of innovation and variety, and so on, are all losses that, while keenly felt by persons old enough to have some memories of the prior world, are too abstract to bother younger people, who know boredom but, they think, not deprivation. We don't know what we don't know: that tragic, all-too-human limitation has, until recently, made media reform seem like a really nice idea, and nothing more.

All that has now changed. The rise of Bush & Co. and the regime's imposition of its catastrophic policies have finally made quite clear how dangerous it is to have a media system dominated by a few gigantic advertisers, all working in collusion with the federal government. It is now clear to millions of Americans that what currently confronts us is not just cultural loss, our choices ever cruder and more stupid, but that our lives as "media consumers" have grown poorer. For those of us who care about democracy are *not* merely "consumers" after all, but *citizens*, obliged to take part in our government; and in a democracy, "the media" must serve as more than a distraction or narcotic. On the contrary, the U.S. press, according to the First Amendment, bears a constitutional responsibility to clue us in, not knock us out: to tell us what our government is doing to us here and what it's doing elsewhere in our name. Rather than demand a tense conformity, media should enable healthy

THIS MODERN WORLD
by TOM TOMORROW

public argument as to our proper course. The media's dismal failure to fulfill that obligation—a failure that is largely (but not only) due to the commercial concentration of the press and of the arts—has now had civic consequences whose disastrousness is obvious to those Americans who want to help this great republican experiment succeed at last.

Those consequences have become especially apparent in this sudden season of preemptive war. Indeed, the war itself *is* such a consequence, the media having all along served this regime and *not* the people. The huge commercial system profiled in these charts of corporate ownership is far too close to those in power, and, therefore, far too powerful itself, to bother with the First Amendment, other than to use it as a profitable license to offend. Notwithstanding the psychotic (and convenient) myth of "liberal bias" in the media, the institution roughly portrayed here has consistently endorsed the Bush/Cheney line, from its routine derision of Al Gore (and general erasure of Ralph Nader) to the moment when it closed the books on the election of 2000, and up through its long collusion with the White House and the Pentagon in pushing Bush's "war on terror" and the pointless and calamitous invasion of Iraq.

Take, for example, Clear Channel Communications, the largest radio station owner in the nation and the world. A big contributor to Bush & Co.'s coffers managed by a tight cabal of staunch Republicans long close to the Bush dynasty ("I see him all the time," CEO Lowry Mays said of Bush Jr. in 2000), Clear Channel has done all it can to keep the public misinformed. The corporation has been quick to mute those voices that have spoken against Bush. In late February of 2004, Clear Channel abruptly dropped Howard Stern's show from its stations, which left Stern off the air in six major markets.

Although the corporation claimed that Stern was sacked because of his "inde-cency" (specifically, a riff on anal sex), it is far likelier that he was cancelled for his dissidence. While Stern has talked "indecently" for years, it was only after he began to knock the Bush administration that Clear Channel found his "indecency" intolerable. Other, lesser figures have been similarly dumped—and none with any of the national publicity that surged around the firing of the famous Stern. Roxanne Walker—"South Carolina Broadcasters Association 2002 radio personality of the year"—was let go for her criticisms of the pres-ident, as was Phoenix talk show host Charles Goyette (a local GOP stalwart, who calls himself "a Goldwater Republican"). Meanwhile, Rush Limbaugh vents day after day under the rubric of Clear Channel, which has also catered to the White House by arranging pro-war rallies in some 20 U.S. cities.

That those seeming surges of spontaneous grassroots approval were only propaganda for the White House, set up under the auspices of a mammoth media concern with a big interest in prolonging Bush & Co.'s cartel-friendly rule, would seem to indicate a threat to our democracy. That threat is grave—and yet, in this case as in many others, it happened *not* to be a case of mere top-down manipulation. Clear Channel's rallies, reported S.C. Gwynne in *Texas Monthly*, "were tolerated but not did not originate at corporate head-quarters; they were also replicated at stations owned by Federated Media and Susquehanna Media, as well as at Infinity." Thus do all the media giants tend, as if naturally, to favor state and corporate power and to shout down the protests of the people without having to be given orders from on high? Under Bush & Co., that collective drive will surely stifle what is left of our democ-racy, unless we act to cut these giants down to size.

Mark Crispin Miller is a professor of media ecology at New York University and director of the Project on Media Ownership.

NEWS CORPORATION

TELEVISION

Fox Broadcasting Company: Atlanta, GA: WAGA; Austin, TX: KTBC; Baltimore, MD: WUTB; Birmingham, AL: WBRC; Boston, MA: WFXT; Chicago, IL: WFLD and WPWR; Cleveland, OH: WJW; Dallas, TX: KDFI and KDFW; Denver, CO: KDVR; Detroit, MI: WJBK; Greensboro, NC: WGHP; Houston, TX: KRIV and KTXH; Kansas City, MO: KDAF; Los Angeles, CA: KCOP and KTTV; Memphis, TN: WHBQ; Milwaukee, WI: WITI; Minneapolis–St. Paul, MN: KMSP and WFTC; New York, NY: WNYW and WWOR; Ocala, : WOGX; Orlando, FL: WOFL and WRBW; Philadelphia, PA: WTXF; Phoenix, AZ: KSAZ and KUTP; Salt Lake City, UT: KSTU; St. Louis, MO: KTVI; Tampa, FL: WTVT; and Washington, DC: WTTG.

BSkyB-FOXTEL, Fox Movie Channel, Fox News Channel, Fox Sports Arizona, Fox Sports Bay Area (with Rainbow Media Holdings), Fox Sports Chicago (with Rainbow Media Holdings), Fox Sports Detroit, Fox Sports Intermountain West, Fox Sports Midwest, Fox Sports Net, Fox Sports New England (with Rainbow Media), Fox Sports New York (with Rainbow Media), Fox Sports Northwest, Fox Sports Ohio (with Rainbow Media), Fox Sports Pittsburgh, Fox Sports Rocky Mountain, Fox Sports South, Fox Sports Southeast, Fox Sports West, Fox Sports West #2, FX, National Geographic Channel, SKYPerfecTV, SPEED Channel, STAR, and Stream.

MAGAZINES

donna hay, InsideOut, SmartSource, TV Guide, and *The Weekly Standard.*

FILM

20th Century Fox, Fox Searchlight Pictures, and Fox Television Studios.

BOOKS

HarperCollins Publishers: Access Travel, Amistad Press, Avon, Branded Books Program, Cliff Street Books, The Ecco Press, Eos, HarperAudio, HarperBusiness, HarperCollins, HarperCollins General Book Group, HarperEntertainment, HarperInformation, HarperResource, HarperSanFrancisco, HarperTorch, Morrow/ Avon, Perennial, Regan Books, Quill, William Morrow, William Morrow Cookbooks, and Zondervan. **HarperCollins Children's Book Group**: Greenwillow Books, HarperFestival, HarperTrophy, Joanna Cotler Books, and Laura Geringer Books.

NEWSPAPERS

United States: *New York Post.* **United Kingdom**: *News of the World, News International, Sun, Sunday Times,* and *The Times.* **Australia**: *Advertiser, Australian, Courier-Mail, Daily Telegraph, Fiji Times, Gold Coast Bulletin, Herald Sun, Mercury, Newsphotos, Newspix, Newstext, NT News, Post-Courier, Sunday Herald Sun, Sunday Mail, Sunday Tasmanian, Sunday Telegraph, Sunday Territorian, Sunday Times,* and *Weekly Times.*

Researcher: Emilio Licea
Sources: U.S. Securities and Exchange Commission, <sec.gov/edgar/search edgar/webusers.htm> and *Columbia Journalism Review,* <www.cjr.org/tools/owners>.

TIME WARNER

TELEVISION

Cartoon Network, Cartoon Network in Europe, Cartoon Network in Latin America, Entertainment Networks, TBS Superstation, TNT & Cartoon Network in Asia/Pacific, Turner Classic Movies, Turner Entertainment, Turner Network Television (TNT), and Turner South.

CABLE

CNN, CNN Airport Network, CNN en Español, CNN fn, CNN Headline News, CNN Interactive, CNN International, CNN Radio, Court TV (with Liberty Media), HBO, Kablevision (cable television in Hungary—53.75%), New York 1 News (24-hour news channel devoted only to NYC), Road Runner, and Time Warner Cable.

FILM & TV PRODUCTION/DISTRIBUTION

Castle Rock Entertainment, Warner Brothers, Warner Brothers Domestic Pay TV, Warner Brothers Domestic Television Distribution, Warner Brothers International Television Distribution, Warner Brothers International Theaters (owns/operates multiplex theaters in over 12 countries), Warner Brothers Studios, Warner Brothers Television (production), Warner Brothers Television Animation, The Warner Channel (Latin America, Asia-Pacific, Australia, and Germany), Warner Home Video, The WB Television Network, Hanna-Barbera Cartoons, Telepictures Production, and Witt Thomas Productions.

FILM

Film Production: Fine Line Features, New Line Cinema, and Turner Original Productions.

THEME PARKS

Warner Brothers Recreation Enterprises (owns/operates international theme parks).

MERCHANDISE/RETAIL

Warner Bros. Consumer Products.

MAGAZINES

All You, *Asiaweek* (Asian news weekly), *Business 2.0*, *Dancyu* (Japanese cooking), *Entertainment Weekly*, *EW Metro*, *Field & Stream*, *Fortune*, *Freeze*, *Golf Magazine*, *Inside Stuff*, *In Style*, *Life*, *Money*, *Outdoor Life*, *People*, *People en Español*, *Popular Science*, *President* (Japanese business monthly), *Progressive Farmer*, *Real Simple*, *Ride BMX*, *Salt Water Sportsman*, *SI for Kids*, *Ski*, *Skiing Magazine*, *Skiing Trade News*, *SNAP*, *Snowboard Life*, *Southern Accents*, *Southern Living*, *Sports Illustrated*, *Sports Illustrated International*, *Sunset*, *Sunset Garden Guide*, *Teen People*, *This Old House*, *The Ticket*, *Time*, *Time Asia*, *Time Atlantic*, *Time Canada*, *Time for Kids*, *Time Latin America*, *Time Money*, *Time South Pacific*, *Today's Homeowner*, *TransWorld Skateboarding*, *TransWorld Snowboarding*, *Verge*, *Wallpaper* (U.K.), *Warp*, *Weight Watchers*, *Who Weekly*, *Yachting Magazine*, and *Your Future*. **American Express Publishing Corporation** (partial ownership/management): *Departures*, *Food & Wine*, *SkyGuide*, *Travel & Leisure*, and *Your Company*. **The Health Publishing Group**: *Health*, *Hippocrates*, *Coastal Living*, and *Cooking Light*. **The Parent Group**: *Parenting*, *Baby on the Way*, and *Baby Talk*. **Magazines listed under Warner Brothers label**: *DC Comics*, *Mad Magazine*, *Milestone*, *Paradox*, and *Vertigo*.

TIME WARNER

MUSIC

Recording Labels: American Recordings, Asylum, Atlantic Classics, The Atlantic Group, Atlantic Jazz, Atlantic Nashville, Atlantic Theater, Big Beat, Blackground, Breaking, CGD East West, China, Coalition, Continental, DRO East West, EastWest, East West ZTT, Elektra, Elektra Entertainment Group, Elektra/Sire, Erato, Fazer, Finlandia, Giant, Igloo, Lava, Magneoton, Maverick, MCM, Mesa/Bluemoon, Modern, Nonesuch, 1 43, Qwest, Reprise, Reprise Nashville, Revolution, Rhino Records, Teldec, Warner Alliance, Warner Brothers, Warner Brothers Records, Warner Music International, Warner Nashville, Warner Resound, Warner Sunset, and WEA Telegram. **Other Recording Interests**: Ivy Hill Corporation (printing and packaging), Warner/Chappell Music (publishing company), Warner Special Products, and WEA, Inc. (sales, distribution, and manufacturing). **Joint Ventures**: Channel V (with Sony, EMI, Bertelsmann, and News Corp.), Columbia House, Heartland Music (direct order of country and gospel music—50%), Music Choice and Music Choice Europe (with Sony, EMI, and General Instrument), MusicNet (with RealNetworks, EMI, and BMG), Music Sound Exchange (direct marketing—with Sony), and Viva (German music video channel—with Sony, Polygram, and EMI).

BOOKS

Back Bay Books; Book-of-the-Month Club, Bulfinch Press, Children's Book-of-the-Month Club, Crafter's Choice, History Book Club, HomeStyle Books, Leisure Arts, Little, Brown and Company, Little Brown and Company (U.K.), Money Book Club, The Mysterious Press, One Spirit, Oxmoor House (subsidiary of Southern Progress Corporation), Paperback Book Club, Sunset Books, Time Life AudioBooks, Time Life Books, Time Life Education, Time Life International, Time Life Music, TW Kids, Warner Aspect, Warner Books, Warner Treasures, and Warner Vision.

OTHER OPERATIONS

<Amazon.com> (partial), AOL MovieFone, CNN Newsroom (daily news program for classrooms), iAmaze, Netscape Communications, Netscape Netcenter portal, <Quack.com>, Streetmail (partial), Switchboard (6%), Turner Adventure Learning (electronic field trips for schools), Turner Home Satellite, Turner Learning, and Turner Network Sales.

SPORTS

Atlanta Braves, Atlanta Hawks, Atlanta Thrashers, Good Will Games, Philips Arena, and Turner Sports.

ONLINE SERVICES

<AOL.com> portal, AOL Europe, AOL Instant Messenger, CompuServe Interactive Services, Digital City, <DrKoop.com>, ICQ, The Knot, Inc. (wedding content—8% with QVC 36% and Hummer), WinbladFunds, <MapQuest.com> (pending regulatory approval), <Spinner.com>, Winamp, and Legend (Internet service in China—49%). **Online/Other Publishing**: <Africana.com>, American Family Publishers (50%), Pathfinder, Road Runner, and Warner Publisher Time Distribution Services.

VIACOM

TELEVISION

CBS Stations: Austin, TX: KEYE; Baltimore, MD: WJZ; Boston, MA: WBZ; Chicago, IL: WBBM; Dallas–Fort Worth, TX: KTVT; Denver, CO: KCNC, Detroit, MI: WWJ; Green Bay, WI: WFRV; Los Angeles, CA: KCBS; Miami- –Ft. Lauderdale, FL: WFOR; Minneapolis, MN: WCCO; New York, NY: WCBS; Philadelphia, PA: KYW; Pittsburgh, PA: KDKA; Salt Lake City, UT: KUTV; and San Francisco, CA: KPIX. **UPN Stations**: Atlanta, GA: WUPA; Bo ston, MA: WSBK; Columbus, OH: WWHO; Dallas, TX: KTXA; Detroit, MI: WKBD, Indianapolis, IN: WNDY; Miami, FL: WBFS; New Orleans, LA: WUPL; Norfolk, VA: WGNT; Oklahoma City, OK: KAUT; Philadelphia, PA: WPSG; Pittsburgh, PA: WNPA; Providence, RI: WLWC; Sacramento, CA: KMAX; San Francisco, CA: KBHK; Seattle, WA: KSTW; Tampa, FL: WTOG; and West Palm Beach, FL: WTVX. **Others**: Alexandria, MN: KCCO; Escan- aba, WI: WJMN; Los Angeles, CA: KCAL; Walker, MN: KCCW; and Washing- ton, UT: KUSG.

PUBLISHING

Simon & Schuster, Pocket Books, Scribner, Free Press, Fireside, Touchstone, Washington Square Press, Archway, Minstrel, and Pocket Pulse.

FILM

Paramount Home Entertainment and Paramount Pictures.

CABLE

MTV, MTV2, Nickelodeon, BET, Nick at Nite, TV Land, NOGGIN, VH1, Spike TV, CMT, Comedy Central Showtime, The Movie Channel, Flix, and Sundance Channel. **Television Production and Distribution**: Spelling Tele- vision, Big Ticket Television, and King World Productions.

VIACOM

RADIO

Infinity Broadcasting: Atlanta, GA: WAOK, WVEE, and WZGC; Austin, TX: KAMX, KJCE, KKMJ, and KQBT; Baltimore, MD: WBGR, WBMD, WJFK, WLIF, WQSR, WWMX, and WXYV; Boston, MA: WBCN, WBMX, WBZ, WODS, and WZLX; Buffalo, NY: WBLK, WBUF, WECK, WJYE, and WYRK; Charlotte, NC: WBAV, WFNZ, WGIV, WNKS, WPEG, WSOC, and WSSS; Chicago, IL: WBBM, WCKG, WJMK, WSCR, WUSN, and WXRT; Cincinnati, OH: WAQZ, WGRR, WKRQ, and WUBE; Cleveland, OH: WDOK, WNCX, WQAL, and WXTM; Columbus, OH: WAZU, WHOK, and WLVQ; Dallas, TX: KLUV, KOAI, KRBV, KRLD, KVIL, and KYNG; Denver, CO: KDJM, KIMN, and KXKL; Detroit, MI: WKRK, WOMC, WVMV, WWJ, WXYT, and WYCD; Fresno, CA: KMGV, KMJ, KOOR, KOQO, KRNC, KSKS, and KVSR; Greensboro/Winston-Salem, NC: WMFR, WSJS, and WSML; Hartford, CT: WRCH, WTIC, and WZMX; Houston, TX: KIKK and KILT; Kansas City, MO: KBEQ, KFKF, KMXV, and KSRC; Las Vegas, NV: KLUC, KMXB, KMZQ, KSFN, KXNT, and KXTE; Los Angeles, CA: KCBS, KEZN, KFWB, KLSX, KNX, KROQ, KRTH, and KTWV; Memphis, TN: WMC and WMFS; Minneapolis–St. Paul, MN: KDOW, WCCO, WLTE, and WXPT; Orlando, FL: WJHM, WOCL, and WOMX; New York, NY: WCBS, WFAN, WINS, WNEW, and WXRK; Philadelphia, PA: KYW, WIP, WOGL, WPHT, and WYSP; Phoenix, AZ: KMLE, KOOL, and KZON; Pittsburgh, PA: KDKA, WBZZ, WDSY, and WZPT; Portland, OR: KINK, KLTH, KUFO, KUPL, and KVM; Riverside, CA: KFRG, KVFG, KVVQ, and KXFG; Rochester, NY: WCMF, WPXY, WRMM, and WZNE; Sacramento, CA: KHTK, KNCI, KSFM, KXOA, KYMX, and KZZO; St. Louis, MO: KEZK, KMOX, and KYKY; San Antonio, TX: KTFM and KTSA; San Diego, CA: KPLN and KYXY; San Francisco ,CA: KCBS, KFRC, KITS, KKWV, KLLC, and KYCY; San Jose, CA: KBAY and KEZR; Seattle, WA: KBKS, KMPS, KYCW, KYPT, and KZOK; Tampa, FL: WLLD, WQYK, WRBQ, WSJT, and WYUU; Washington, DC: WARW, WHFS, WJFK, and WPGC; and West Palm Beach, FL: WEAT, WIRK, WJBW, WMBX, and WPBZ.

OTHER

Blockbuster, Paramount Parks,
Famous Players theater chain,
United Cinemas International (50%),
and Famous Music.

WALT DISNEY COMPANY

BROADCASTING (INCLUDES THE CAPITAL CITY/ABC SUBSIDIARY)

Television: ABC Television Network. **Owned and Operated Television Stations**: Chicago, IL: WLS; Flint, MI: WJRT; Fresno, CA: KFSN; Houston, TX: KTRK; Los Angeles, CA: KABC; New York, NY: WABC; Philadelphia, PA: WPVI; Raleigh-Durham, NC: WTVD; San Francisco, CA: KGO; and Toledo, OH: WTVG. **Radio Stations**: ESPN Radio (syndicated programming); Albany, NY: WPPY; Atlanta, GA: WDWD, WKHX, and WYAY; Boston, MA: WMKI; Charlotte, NC: WGFY; Chicago, IL: WLS, WMVP, WRDZ, and WZZN; Cleveland, OH: WWMK; Dallas, TX: KESN, KMEO, KMKI, KSCS, and WBAP; Damascus, MD: WDMV; Denver, CO: KADZ and KDDZ; Detroit, MI: WDRQ, WDVD, and WJR; Flint, MI: WFDF; Fremont, OH: WFRO; Hartford, CT: WDZK; Houston, TX: KMIC; Jacksonville, FL: WBML; Kansas City, MO: KPHN; Los Angeles, CA: KABC, KDIS, KLOS, and KSPN; Louisville, KY: WDRD; Miami, FL: WMYM; Minneapolis–St. Paul, MN: KDIZ, KQRS, KXXR, WGVX, WGVY, and WGVZ; Mobile, AL: WQUA; New York, NY: WABC, WEVD, WPLJ, and WQEW; Norfolk, VA: WHKT; Oakland, CA: KMKY; Orlando, FL: WDYZ; Philadelphia, PA: WWJZ; Phoenix, AZ: KMIX; Pittsburgh, PA: WEAE; Providence, RI: WDDZ; Radio Disney; Richmond, VA: WDZY; Sacramento, CA: KIID; San Francisco, CA: KGO and KSFO; Seattle, WA: KKDZ; St. Louis, MO: WSDZ; Tampa, FL: WWMI; Washington; DC: WJZW, WMAL, and WRQX; West Palm Beach, FL: WMNE; and Wichita, KS: KQAM.

CABLE

A&E Television (37.5% with Hearst and GE); ABC Family; The Disney Channel; E! Entertainment (with Comcast and Liberty Media); ESPN, Inc., which includes Classic Sports Network, ESPN, ESPN2, ESPN News, ESPN Now, and ESPN Extreme (80%; Hearst Corporation owns the remaining 20%); SoapNet; Toon Disney; The History Channel (with Hearst and GE); Lifetime Movie Network (50% with Hearst); and Lifetime Television (50% with Hearst). **International Broadcast**: The Disney Channel Australia; The Disney Channel France; The Disney Channel Italy; The Disney Channel Malaysia; The Disney Channel Middle East; The Disney Channel Spain; The Disney Channel Taiwan; The Disney Channel U.K.; ESPN, Inc., International Ventures; ESPN Brazil (50%); ESPN STAR (sports programming throughout Asia—50%); Net STAR (33%), owners of The Sports Network of Canada; and Sportsvision of Australia (25%).

BOOKS

Hyperion Books, Miramax Books, and Walt Disney Company Book Publishing.

MAGAZINES

Magazine Subsidiary Groups: ABC Publishing Group; Disney Publishing, Inc.; Diversified Publications Group; Financial Services and Medical Group; Miller Publishing Company. **Magazines:** *Automotive Industries*, *Biography* (with GE and Hearst), *Discover*, *Disney Adventures*, *Disney Magazine*, *ECN News*, *ESPN Magazine* (distributed by Hearst), *Family Fun*, *Institutional Investor*, *JCK*, *Kodin*, *Quality*, *Top Famille* (French family magazine), *US Weekly* (50%), and *Video Business*.

WALT DISNEY COMPANY

MULTIMEDIA

Walt Disney Internet Group: <ABC.com>, ABC Internet Group, <ABCNEWS.com>, <Disney.com>, Disney Interactive (develops/markets computer software video games, and CD-ROMs), Disney Online (Web sites and content), Disney's Daily Blast, ESPN Internet Group, <ESPN.sportzone.com>, <Family.com>, Go Network, Mr. Showbiz, <NASCAR.com>, <NBA.com>, <Oscar.com>, Skillgames, <Soccernet.com> (60%), <Toysmart.com> (educational toys—majority stake), and Wall of Sound.

THEME PARKS & RESORTS

Disney Cruise Line, The Disney Institute, Disneyland (Anaheim, CA), Disneyland Paris, Disneyland Resort, Disney MGM Studios, Disney Regional Entertainment (entertainment end theme dining in metro areas), Disney's Animal Kingdom, Disney Vacation Club, Epcot, Magic Kingdom, Tokyo Disneyland (partial ownership), Walt Disney World (Orlando, FL), and Walt Disney World Sports Complex (golf course, auto racing track, and baseball complex).

FILM PRODUCTION AND DISTRIBUTION

Buena Vista Home Entertainment, Buena Vista Home Video, Buena Vista International, Caravan Pictures, Hollywood Pictures, Miramax Films, Touchstone Pictures, and Walt Disney Pictures.

FINANCIAL AND RETAIL

Financial: Sid R. Bass (crude petroleum and natural gas production—partial interest). **Retail**: The Disney Store.

MUSIC

Buena Vista Music Group, Hollywood Records (popular music and soundtracks for motion pictures), Lyric Street Records (Nashville-based country music label), Mammoth Records (popular and alternative music label), and Walt Disney Records.

THEATER AND SPORTS

Theatrical Productions: Walt Disney Theatrical Productions (productions include stage versions of *The Lion King*, *Beauty and the Beast*, and *King David*). **Professional Sports Franchises**: Anaheim Sports, Inc. and Mighty Ducks of Anaheim (national hockey league).

OTHER INTERNATIONAL VENTURES

Hamster Productions (French television production), Japan Sports Channel, RTL-2 (German television production and distribution), Scandinavian Broadcasting System, Tele-Munchen (German television production and distribution), Tesauro of Spain, and TV Sport of France. **Television Production and Distribution**: Buena Vista Television, Touchstone Television, Walt Disney Television, Walt Disney Television Animation (has three wholly owned production facilities outside the United States—Japan, Australia, and Canada).

VIVENDI UNIVERSAL

FILM AND TELEVISION

Universal Studios, Universal Pictures, October Films (majority interest), Universal Studios Home Video, United International Pictures (international distribution—33%), and Cinema International BV (video distribution—49%). **Television Production and Distribution**: CANAL+ (European pay-TV provider—51%), Universal Television Group (production and distribution), Brillstein-Grey Entertainment (50%) production, Multimedia Entertainment, USA Networks Inc. (43%), and Universal Pay Television (international distribution). **Partial ownership**: HBO Asia Telecine (Brazil), Cinecanal (Latin America), Showtime (Australia), Star Channel (Japan), and Telepiu (Italian pay television).

PUBLISHING

Rolling Stone, Larousse, Nathan, Anaya, Coktel, Atica, Scipione, Bordas, Retz, Robert L affont, Plon-Perrin, Les Presses—Solar—Belfond, La Decouverte & Syros, Les Presses de la Renaissance, Pocket Jeuness 10/18, Fleuve Noir, Sierra, and Blizzard Entertainment.

INTERACTIVE

Universal Studios New Media Group, Universal Studios Online, <Universal.com>, Universal Interactive Studios (software and video games), Universal Digital Arts, Interplay (video game producer—majority ownership), GetMusic (online music retailer), Vizzavi (European multiaccess portal), <Education.com>, <Flipside.com>, @viso (50% with Softbank), AlloCiné, <Bonjour.fr>, Ad2-One, Atmedica, Scoot, <EMusic.com>, Duet (with Sony), and <MP3.com>.

MUSIC

Universal Music Group: All Nations Catalog, Decca Records, Deutsche Grammophon, Geffen/DGC Records, GRP Recording Company, Hip-O Records, Interscope Music Publishing, Interscope Records, MCA Music Publishing, MCA Records, MCA Records Nashville, Motown, Polygram, Rising Tide, Universal Concerts (concert promotion), Universal Music and Video Distribution, Universal Music International, and Universal Records.

OTHER

Cinema International Corporation (international theaters—49%), Cineplex Odeon Corporation (theaters—42%), Duet (music-subscription service with Yahoo! and Sony), United Cinemas International (international theaters—49%), Vivendi Environnement (the world's #1 water distributor), Vivendi Universal (owns 26.8 million shares in Time Warner), and Viventures (venture capital fund).

RETAIL

Spencer Gifts.

THEME PARKS/RECREATION/RETAIL

Universal Studios Hollywood: CityWalk. **Universal Orlando Resort**: CityWalk, Hard Rock Hotel, Portofino Bay Hotel, Royal Pacific Resort, Universal's Islands of Adventure Theme Park, Universal Studios Theme Park, CityWalk, Hotel Port Aventura, Universal Mediterranea (Spain), Universal Mediterranea Theme Park, Universal Studios Japan, and Wet-n-Wild Orlando.

TELECOMMUNICATION

Vivendi Telecom International, and Cegetel.

Lifestyles of the Media Rich and Oligopolistic

BY STEPHANIE DYER with research assistance from the Sonoma State University students of Liberal Studies 320A (Spring 2004)

In a country committed to the concept of "shareholder democracy," corporate boards of directors are our elected representatives, the public face of private industry. Such individuals represent the will of the shareholders in governing the business practices of corporations, setting long-term strategy and exercising veto power over the decisions of the top corporate executives. They hold legal responsibility for the actions of firms, taking on the role of "in loco parentis" to corporate management. To sit on the board of directors of a corporation is to take on a heavy responsibility for the financial success of that company, the future direction of that industry, the treatment of its clients and consumers, and its relations to other governing structures of society.

In the case of media conglomerates, corporate boards of directors hold an even greater responsibility not only to their shareholders, but also to the public at large. Their governance is the gateway to the information that citizens need to make decisions in a democracy. They hold the power to choose what we know, when we know it, and—to a large extent—how we think about the world we live in. With the increasing concentration of media ownership, the members of these boards tighten the reigns over our access to information. Yet the American public—the broader public beyond the shareholder democracy—knows very little about these individuals who exert so much power over their lives. In the spirit of educating the public, my students and I decided to investigate the individuals who make up what has effectively become the governing body of American culture, the boards of directors of the five leading media conglomerates: Disney, General Electric, News Corporation, Time Warner, and Viacom.

The total membership of these boards consists of 71 people, a combination of senior executives of the conglomerates, their largest shareholders, and "independent directors" (those who have no material interest in the firm). Regardless of whether they are independent or not, most everyone who sits on these boards has extensive investments and board memberships in other leading corporations, creating a powerful web of interlocking corporate directorates, connecting business leaders in media to virtually all other leading economic sectors. It is not surprising that such individuals would tend to vote their pocketbook by endorsing corporate strategy that helps their own stock portfolio. But does this material relationship sufficiently explain board members' unwillingness to criticize the status quo of corporate America? Stock ownership and board membership are part of the lifestyles of the rich and oligopolistic—what Pierre Bourdieu called the *habitus* of social life. The habitus expresses not merely one's material interest; its effect run deeper, forming one's worldview on virtually every aspect of society, from personal morality to cultural taste to politics. The members of media conglomerates' boards of directors inhabit the habitus of the economic elite, making them incapable of questioning the orthodoxies of capitalism and the political establishment.

Education is perhaps the greatest markers of class position—and also the single most important factor in class mobility—in First World countries. It's hardly surprising to find that all of the media board members attended college; indeed, we were pleasantly surprised by the diversity of undergraduate institutions they attended, which ranged from Long Beach City College to Harvard. What quickly became apparent, however, was that regardless of which college they started at, many board members end up finishing their education at a handful of elite private universities, usually majoring in law or business administration. Out of approximately forty-four graduate degrees obtained, 18 percent attended Harvard Business School, 13.6 percent attended Harvard Law School, and 11.3 percent attended Yale Law School. Even if some came from remote corners of the country, their experiences and professional training were certain to acculturated them people to an Ivy League perspective on world issues.

This conformity of mind carries over despite the superficial presence of social diversity on these boards of directors, whose members include women as well as people of color. It is hard to avoid the conclusion that such diversity is cosmetic and deeply tokenistic. While dominated by white men of the business elite, each board contains one or two women and/or people of color, sometimes the same person. Shareholders choose "diverse" individuals who display little risk of actually bringing diverse perspectives to their boards. Eight women sit on the boards of the five media conglomerates—11.2 percent of the members compared to an average of 15.7 percent in the Fortune 500 as a whole. All of these women are corporate presidents, business entrepreneurs, or philanthropists deeply enmeshed in the culture of big business. Some were even born into it. Shari Redstone, daughter of Sumner Redstone and member of the Viacom board, is a perfect example of the nepotism that is part-and-parcel of big business, inheriting her position as president of the family's National Amusements chain of movie theaters after divorcing her husband. While she is not the only example of nepotism here—Lachlan Murdoch, daughter of Rupert, sits on the board of News Corporation—her presence means one less independent female voice among the few women represented on these boards. Sumner himself characterizes her as his "clone" in business: "It's like father, like daughter....She is a great businesswoman."[1] Not surprisingly, the two are usually in sync on business decisions.

Even women who have worked their way to the top tend to assimilate easily to the old-boy network and its sometimes-corrupt business practices. Judith Estrin, a hi-tech entrepreneur who founded two companies, has emerged as one of Michael Eisner's biggest cronies on the Disney board of directors. She has recently become the target of a shareholder revolt due to her role in authorizing millions of dollars in bonuses to the embattled CEO while the company was struggling in a financial slump. Roy Disney has characterized Estrin's business decisions, which she defended with optimistic double-digit growth projections, as "eerily familiar to the pro forma talk of Internet executives" during hi-tech bubble of the late 1990s.[2]

Other female board members work to establish an old-girl network. Shelly Lazarus of the GE board became CEO of Ogilvy and Mather Advertising Agency after working her way up through the ranks of the company for more than 25 years. Before her business success, Lazarus was already a member of the cultural elite, having graduated Smith College and Columbia Business School. In fact, she claims she chose to attend Columbia in the late 1960s because "she didn't want to type," as if working women simply made the choice to become stenographers rather than business executives. Lazarus is a strong feminist; she is a great proponent of increasing female representation among the business elite and a believer that the inclusion of female voices can lead to great innovations in business. She herself is an example of this, being one of the innovators of the "total brand stewardship" strategy that characterizes corporations such as Nike, Disney, and even NBC's "Must See TV" campaign. Yet Lazarus's feminist love of economic empowerment prevents her from acknowledging the ways in which capitalism can hurt the powerless. When asked about critics such as Naomi Klein who have criticized her branding strategy as cultural imperialism, Lazarus demurs:

Brands are actually the way to increase accountability and responsibility among multinational corporations! If companies have to put their names on a product, they have to be accountable for it. Brands are becoming global because they promise quality and performance—that's why a product is chosen anywhere it's available.... Brands communicate value directly to the consumers. It's not that brands are evil or are what's behind globalization—it's that what brands promise is desired all over the globe.[3]

Other female directors of media conglomerates are willing to admit that economic globalization is a political issue and even engage in activism on the subject. Patty Stonesifer of Viacom was a senior vice president at Microsoft before becoming president and co-chair of the Bill and Melinda Gates Foundation. She oversaw the Gates Foundation's attempt to redress the "technology gap" between rich and poor school children as well as the foundation's current program of vaccine distribution in Africa. Seeking to redress the "market failure" of pharmaceutical companies to supply needed drugs to impoverished nations, Stonesifer works toward a market correction by using "Bill and Melinda's visibility in the world"—not to mention their money—to "create a sense of urgency" about global health problems.[4] As laudable as the program is, Stonesifer's approach is classically philanthropic and reformist rather than trying to effect systematic change to the global capitalist system that did nothing to help the devastating health crisis in sub-Saharan Africa in the first place.

Seeking solutions to global problems through the global marketplace is the purview of Time Warner's Carla Hills, former U.S. trade representative under the first George Bush and the primary negotiator of NAFTA. She was joined across the table by General Electric board member Claudio X. Gonzales, then an advisor to Mexican President Ernesto Zedillo. Hills is an unabashed advocate for a Free Trade Agreement for the Americas who credits NAFTA with keeping the peace in the Americas throughout the War on Terror. Hills advocates using the media to export the concept of free trade to the world:

> The effort to explain the merits of trade is not something that government can, or even should, be expected to do alone. Universities, think tanks, the media, businesses, and groups like this must invest the time to educate their own nationals about the benefits of trade lest we lose the consensus favoring open markets that is a key driver to our economic growth.[5]

Hills' activism in support of economic globalization is extensive. She is chair of the National Committee on U.S.-China Relations; vice chair of the Council on Foreign Relations; trustee of the Forum for International Policy; director of the Institute for International Economics; board member of the International Crisis Group; and member of the Trilateral Commission. We can only speculate how Hills may be using Time Warner as a vehicle for her proselytizing.

If white women provide little in the way of a critical voice on the global economic system, can women of color do any better? There are three women of color on media conglomerate boards of directors, following the philosophy that when it comes to token representation, it's easier to kill two birds with one stone. Monica Lozano of the Disney board of directors is the only U.S. national of Latino descent among media conglomerate directors. She runs her own media empire as president of *La Opinion*, the largest circulation Spanish-language daily newspaper in the United States with nearly half a million readers. Like Shari Redstone, Lozano inherited her position, taking over the paper her grandfather founded and her father published. She also inherited her seat on the Disney board, which she took over from her father in 2000. Unlike Redstone, Lozano is quite vocal about the responsibility of being a public servant. "I understood the power of the press and I had a strong belief that with information and news you can improve people's lives and empower them," Lozano has stated. "We wanted the paper to be a conduit and bridge between our readers and the institutions of power and influence in our communities and our nation." The integrity of her newspaper has been recognized in the Latino community by numerous awards. The Lozano family takes their desire to remain an independent media voice so seriously that they dissolved their 14-year partnership with the Times Mirror Company in 2003 after it was bought out by the Tribune Company. To combat the Tribune's forthcoming national expansion of its Spanish-language tabloid *Hoy*, the Lozano family recently created a competing newspaper chain with El Diario/La Prensa called *Impremedia*, of which Monica is currently Vice President[6] Despite Lozano's aggressive pursuit of her own media's autonomous voice and communal responsibility, she has yet to demonstrate such independent thinking on the Disney board. Lozano has recently come under fire for her role on the board's audit committee, which pension fund shareholders charge with unethical auditing practices.

The two other women of color, Ann Fudge and Andrea Jung—both on the General Electric board—are career business executives with only the requisite involvement in philanthropy or politics. Fudge's career trajectory is singular among African-American women, moving from Harvard Business School to CEO of Young & Rubicam advertising agency within 25 years. Andrea Jung's ascent is even more impressive: at age 40, she became CEO of Avon Products, one of only eight women to head Fortune 500 companies. Both Fudge and Jung are directors of Catalyst, a non-profit organization that supports women in business alongside GE CEO Jeffrey Immelt and Time Warner director Reuben Mark. Both Fudge and Jung see themselves as role models for young minority women. Jung speaks of her career as "clearly inspirational" to women who "see that the glass ceiling has been broken at Avon."[7]

Yet neither has publicly demonstrated any willingness to critique the systemic inequalities of capitalism that exist below the glass ceiling. As Arianna Huffington remarked on Ann Fudge's ascent to power at Young and Rubicam, "Clearly, the mere presence of more women in positions of power will not, by itself, be enough to guarantee a change in corporate behavior."[8]

Representation of nonwhites on media corporate boards is low—11.2 percent of all directors—but it's not as low as for the Fortune 1000 as a whole, in which they are a mere 6.9 percent of all directors. Of nonwhite men, the media boards contain three African-Americans and two Asian-Americans. Like Fudge and Jung, most are career executives who have embedded themselves in the habitus of corporate America. Aylwin Lewis and John Chen, both of the Disney board, are single-minded business people, Lewis as president of the Yum! Brands fast-food conglomerate and Chen as CEO of Sybase. James Cash, Jr., a Professor at the Harvard Business School, has made something of a side career sitting on the board of Fortune 500 companies. Cash is one of only seven African-Americans who sit on five or more corporate boards, including General Electric. "Calling on the same names again and again raises questions and suggests that corporate America finds it easier to retread the same faces than reaching out to different African Americans," states the Business Women's Network in their latest industry almanac.[9]

Richard Dean Parsons, chairman and CEO of Time Warner, is one African American whose presence certainly is not just for show. He is a trusted industry insider with extensive executive experience. He is also one of the very few African Americans leaders with deep ties to Republican Party politics. Parsons began his career as legal counsel to Nelson Rockefeller and aide to Gerald Ford before moving into banking, eventually becoming president of Time Warner in 1995. Parsons recently donated the maximum personal contribution to the Bush/Cheney reelection campaign, much to the chagrin of Ted Turner. Parsons is an advocate of multinational corporate expansion who views the worldwide consolidation of the media industry to be an "ineluctable" process. While citizens mobilize worldwide to lobby for regulations to stop this "ineluctable" process, Parsons remains firmly convinced of the essential correctness of the consolidation trend: "The answer...won't be found in government, but in the market." Parsons sees globalization as the gateway to finally bringing real diversity into the boardrooms of corporate America because conglomerates need people from diverse cultural backgrounds who can expand the firm into new markets. "You have to bring globalization into your organization if you want to develop the ability to appreciate a new culture. You have to be a step ahead of change," says Parsons. Globalization will allow diverse executives to break through the glass ceiling in the name of searching out consumers in every corner of the earth.[10]

Viet Dinh is a recent addition to the board of directors at News Corporation who has simultaneously broken the glass ceiling for both racial minorities and right-wing ideologues. Dinh, the first nonwhite member of the News Corp board of directors—which still does not contain any women—is a young law professor at Georgetown University who is enormously popular in conservative political circles. He first came to prominence as associate special council to the Senate Committee investigating Whitewater, and then as special council to Senator Pete Domenici (R–NM) during the Clinton impeachment trial. As an assistant attorney general under John Ashcroft, Dinh was the primary architect of the Patriot Act, which allows for the use of secret wiretaps and monitoring "third-party record holders," such as library accounts and media purchases, in the name of national security. Dinh is sanguine about this infringement on the privacy of American citizens and foreign nationals alike, refusing to see the act as compromising civil liberties. "There is no question that the Patriot Act has dramatically increased the [government's] ability to protect America," he has stated. Dinh is quick to use the old saw of media bias in explaining widespread criticism of the act, stating that the mainstream media news coverage "has [made it] a brand of all that is wrong with the government's war on terror."[11] There's no reason to expect Dinh to be an independent voice on Rupert Murdoch's board because he already parrots the politics of Fox News Channel so effectively.

Other career politicians and public figures sit on these boards: William S. Cohen of Viacom, a Republican who served as President Clinton's secretary of defense; Sam Nunn of General Electric, former Democratic senator from Georgia who chaired the Senate Armed Services Committee; Disney chairman George Mitchell, a former Democratic Senate Majority Leader who sat on the Iran-Contra investigating committee and was a major advocate of NAFTA; and Joseph Califano of Viacom, a Democrat who served as an assistant to Secretary of Defense Robert McNamara in the Johnson Administration and as secretary of health, education, and welfare in the Carter Administration. What characterizes the politics of all of these men is that they are "establishment," powerful centrists who are neither critical of the military-industrial complex nor of American global corporate dominance in general. Even Califano, probably the most liberal of those listed here, has become most well-known in recent years for his promotion of family values. Califano runs the National Center of Addiction and Substance Abuse at Columbia University, which has conducted research into the connection between lack of parental attention and increased use and abuse of alcohol, drugs, and cigarettes among teenagers. Califano advocates families eating dinner together as a way to solve these problems, bypassing thornier questions of economic hardship, longer workdays, and single parenthood. President Bush fully supports Califano's initiative, inaugurating the first national "Family Day" in 2003. So much for the political diversity of Democrats and Republicans.

The world within which media conglomerate board members exist is very small and very elite. It's a world of individuals who have succeeded within the capitalist system and want to export America's stewardship of that system across the globe. It is a world in which people believe in the rewards of individual effort, even when they've inherited their positions or have been groomed for it by attending elite educational institutions. It is a world in which political and business connections are proof that one is fit to govern media content. It's not that these boards consciously operate as a cabal conspiring to shape media content towards specific political ends; indeed, anyone who would question the transparent correctness of their decisions would never be allowed a seat at the table. Perhaps the greatest irony here is that looking to identity politics for a solution—stacking the deck with more women and minorities or greater political "balance" based on party affiliation—will merely perpetuate the current arrangement under a different face.

Stephanie Dyer is an assistant professor at Hutchins School of Liberal Studies at Sonoma State University and a Project Censored faculty evaluator. She can be reached at <stephanie.dyer@sonoma.edu>.

The students in LIBS 320A.1 (Spring 2004) at SSU who worked on this project were: Kate Bates, Ian Elrick, Jamie Husary, Heidi Jobe, Cathy Keeble, Celeste King, Annie Lapinski, Jessica Liparini, Tiffany Perkins, Nicole Stauffacher, Jane Sublett, Michelle Swift, Stephanie Thompson, and Meredith Wilson.

NOTES:
1. Dyan Machan, "Redstone Rising," *Forbes* Online, May 13, 2002.
2. "Roy Disney Offers Info to Step Up Shareholders Revolt," Reuters, March 26, 2004.
3. Deb Arnold, "Shelly Lazarus, CBS Success Story, Recruits for WPP," "An Interview with Shelly Lazarus," Fall 2001, <www3.gsb.columbia.edu/botline/fall01/1108/Lazarus.html>.
4. "A Conversation with Patty Stonesifer," Global Giving Matters, December 2003–January 2004, <www.synergos.org/globalgivingmatters/features/0401gates.htm>.
5. Carla Hills, "Free Trade Agreement for the Americas," December 2003 speech at the Inter-American Dialogue Conference, <www.thedialogue.org/publications/program_reports/trade/ftaa_hills.pdf>.

6. "Monica Lozano: The Independent Communicator," *Hispanic Trends*, Spring 2003.

7. "Meet the Avon Ladies-in-Chief," *Business Week* Online, January 22, 2002.

8. Arianna Huffington, "She.E.O.," TomPaine.com, May 16, 2003, <TomPaine.com>.

9. "Corporate Boards and Diversity," *Women and Diversity WOW! Facts 2003.*

10. Richard Dean Parsons, "Why—and How—Companies Must Go Global," Knowledge@Wharton online, May 5, 2004.

11. Aliya Kahlidi, "Patriot Act Contributor Viet Dinh Informs Students," *Wellesley News*, April 1, 2004.

THIS MODERN WORLD
by TOM TOMORROW

CHAPTER 5

Media Democracy in Action

PACIFIC NEW SERVICE, MEDIA ALLIANCE, WHISPERED MEDIA, YOUTH MEDIA COUNCIL, WE INTERRUPT THIS MESSAGE, SAN FRANCISCO BAY VIEW, <MEDIACHANNEL.ORG>, INDYMEDIA, AND NEWS WITHOUT BORDERS

By Norman Solomon, Alycia Cahill, Lauren Kettner, Melody Lindsey, Anna Miranda, Emilio Licea, and Ambrosia Pardue

Introduction: Cracking the Media Walls

BY NORMAN SOLOMON

The major news outlets are like walls with cracks. The confining structures of big media loom large every day—yet progressives have countless opportunities to find, utilize, and widen the cracks in the corporate media's barriers to democratic communication.

Steadily worsening concentrations of ownership and the hefty clout of advertising combine to severely limit the range of information and debate in news media. Ongoing pressures—economic, ideological, and governmental—constrain the work of mainline journalists, whose efforts routinely suffer from skewed priorities and self-censorship. A profit-driven ideology of the "free market" is in sync with the agendas of top management and advertisers.

In recent years, progressive media projects have gained momentum. But the tilt against truly independent media and wide-ranging discourse is extreme in the United States. While no individual or single organization can take on more than a fraction of the necessary endeavors, the overall work to create a democratic media environment must run a gamut.

Sustained efforts to challenge the corporate media and support alternative media outlets can reinforce each other with continuous synergy—to establish and expand progressive media organizations; to spread deft criticism of rancid mass media; to push for better reporting and much wider debate in mainstream media; to fight for structural reform of agencies like the FCC; to lambaste, debunk, and satirize the insidious junk that so often passes for journalism and cultural uplift.

The horrendous media problems are multifaceted. Our solutions must be as well.

In the long run, no campaign for basic media reform can succeed apart from a broader progressive movement—and vice versa. The degradation of journalism and mass entertainment is entwined with pervasive corporate power that chokes virtually every facet of this country's political and social life.

Media criticism becomes profoundly useful in combination with media activism. Too often we've held onto theories about what is and is not possible. But analysis and action become much more powerful when they constantly inform each other—when assessments shift because of on-the-ground experiences that benefit not only from the results of trial and error, but also from insightful up-to-date analysis.

Along with theory and practice that keep enhancing each other, we need a lot more resources for the media tasks ahead. Many left-leaning foundations remain hesitant or unwilling to fund media work, and the ones that do are often leery of backing media endeavors that seem overly combative or ideological. Not so the right-wing foundations and corporations that sink millions of dollars a week into aggressive media-savvy propaganda outfits like the Heritage Foundation, the American Enterprise Institute, and the Manhattan Institute. Likewise, intensely ideological media organs like the Murdoch-owned *Weekly Standard* magazine are able to gain national prominence and maintain influence thanks to large subsidies from right-wing backers.

As a fundamental matter of social-change strategy, progressive media institutions—including groups that focus on improving mainstream media coverage as well as on building radio, TV, video, print, and Internet projects—merit support to narrow the gaps between their skimpy resources and the huge budgets for right-wing media. This is especially important because the left has to navigate media terrain that's appreciably less hospitable.

One of the political right's key advantages is the mass-media echo chamber. Many a spun story and loopy canard bounces around the walls among outlets like the *Washington Times*, Rush Limbaugh's radio show, the *Wall Street Journal* editorial page, the *Weekly Standard,* and Fox News. Frequently, from there, the dubious stories and simple-minded polemics flood into mainstream talk shows, daily papers, slick magazines, broadcast news outlets, and cable TV networks.

Progressives have nothing comparable in terms of nationwide echo chambers. And the disparity often makes a pivotal difference. It's not nearly enough to put out a powerful exposé or release a cogent analysis in a few print outlets or on some Web sites or on a few dozen radio stations—or to briefly surface in a large national media venue. Such achievements, while important, are insufficient. They need to draw strength from each other—utilizing the best material available across the progressive board—while simultaneously finding ways to reach broader audiences, including via mass media, where cracks in the corporate walls beckon.

During the last few years, progressive advocates and independent journalists have learned a lot about how to realize "multiplier effects" among a wide array of media. When astute strategizing and cooperation flourish, we're finding ways to reach many people—sometimes millions or tens of millions—with information and analysis that otherwise would be confined to a relative few. The potential for further developing such productive media synergy is enormous.

In the process, we need to strengthen the many progressive media organizations that have been developing the skills, infrastructures, and cooperative spirit to grasp what is clearly possible: mutually supportive modes of operations that crosspollinate across extensive media terrain and propagate resistance to the status quo's deadening and often deadly corporate priorities.

While developing ways to regularly affect the content of major media outlets, the progressive media movement needs counterinstitutions that can inspire and sustain many people for the challenges ahead. No one media project is a potential solution by itself. No silver bullets need apply. At the same time, progressive funders ought to provide long-term support for an array of media work. By now, there are enough track records out there to supply empirical evidence of impressive results.

We urgently need to boost the resources and improve the coordination of progressive media work. Sure, by definition, corporate media and their allies inevitably have big bucks that dwarf the outlays of anticorporate crusaders. Extreme imbalances in funding come with the media territory. But in his fabled confrontation with Goliath, even David needed a slingshot. Long-term progressive media projects of all descriptions need at least minimal resources along with savvy strategies to put up a strong fight and make appreciable headway.

Meanwhile, our guiding ethos should be notably different than the right wing's preferred mode of top-down centralism. It should be possible for progressives to attain the creative advantages of sharp analysis, institutional growth, coordinated planning and agile cooperation while encouraging a decentralized, democratic, grassroots approach to social action.

Along the way, we should resist temptations to rely on a few left heroes on the mass-media battlefields. In the mid-1990s, while working on the launch of the Institute for Public Accuracy as a national consortium to get progressive voices into media, I received some advice to concentrate on grooming a few "superstars" to become regulars on national television. But the institute opted for a different approach: to develop a roster of many hundreds of policy analysts—including researchers, authors, and other experts from academia, public-interest groups, and grassroots organizations—representing a deep reservoir of knowledge and insights that routinely go untapped in the mass media.

This approach doesn't just move forward a few individuals and organizations; it widens the bounds of media discussion on a regular basis, not merely on occasion. Media outreach that successfully reflects the breadth and depth of progressive constituencies is more effective at being persuasive—and more capable of withstanding the right wing's demonization of a few individuals or accusations of elitism. Clearly, a lot more can be accomplished to move progressive advocates into mainstream media on a regular basis.

Overall, what's needed in our society—and what a progressive media movement should strive for—is a kind of media ecology that recognizes and promotes authentic diversity. This diversity holds great promise: not because of any mechanistic or "PC" concepts, but because tremendous human capacities and insights, routinely excluded from major media, are always present in the United States and the rest of the world.

Right now the cracks in the media walls are much too thin and much too scarce. The long haul of our struggle involves bringing down the institutional barriers that, in effect, soundproof much of the media world and muffle the First Amendment in the process. We can chip away at those walls and replace them with vibrant democratic discourse.

Norman Solomon is founder and executive director of the Institute for Public Accuracy. His latest book, *War Made Easy*, is scheduled for publication by Wiley in early 2005.

Pacific News Service

BY ALYCIA CAHILL

Pacific News Service (PNS) is a news service that provides ethnic news stories to newspapers across California. They send news to the public through smaller alternative newspapers and larger, mainstream media such as the *San Francisco Chronicle*, *The Sacramento Bee*, and the *Los Angeles Times*.

Pacific News Service has a long, well-established history. In 1970, Orrville Schell and Franz Schurman created the news service to provide independent coverage of the U.S. role in Indonesia during the Vietnam War. After the war, the news service shifted its focus to California and started to specialize in "anthropological journalism." They started to cover issues such as immigration, race relations, and a new generation of alienated youth. Pacific News Service strengthened their credibility with mainstream news in the late 1970s through syndication with the *Des Moines Register* and *Tribune Syndicate*. In 1991, PNS released *YO!: Youth Outlook*, a monthly youth magazine. In addition to print media, they also work with Berkeley-based *Youth Radio* and co-produced an Academy Award-winning film about Mark O'Brian, a poet who spent his life in an iron lung. Today, PNS continues to give a voice to the unheard.

PNS is constantly trying to diversify their outlets. In 1996, they launched *The Beat Within*, a weekly writing program for incarcerated youth, and New California Media (NCM), which contains 700 ethnic news organizations working together in order to promote inter-ethnic understanding. According to NCM's Web site, the goal of the organization is to raise the visibility of ethnic media reaching California's population of 17 million ethnic residents, to promote interethnic exchange, and to increase ethnic media's access to advertisers. The Web site also states that NCM is the "most comprehensive multicultural, multimedia coalition to reach beyond mainstream media." New California Media takes pride in giving the underrepresented a voice as well as using ethnic media to tap into underserved markets. New California Media enhances the scope of ethnic media and connects otherwise fragmented groups with each other.

Sandy Close, executive director of PNS, says that PNS is part of a wide network working with NCM as a hub. With Web sites, daily news, stories, film, and radio, PNS is trying to achieve their goal of bringing people together and promoting civic engagement by covering a wide range of California issues. PNS concentrates on news analysis, investigative reporting, and feature length commentary. On weekdays, they run up to four articles on their

Web site. Subscribers get the stories by email or on the Associated Press Data Feature Wire, which goes to small community newspapers and mainstream news media. When asked how this system was working for PNS, Close stated, "In a global society such as California where 40 percent of residents speak languages other than English at home [and] one out of four residents is an immigrant, no one ethnic/racial group is in the majority. Communication requires a horizontal axis that runs along the spine of society, not just a vertical axis that transmits information and news between the public sphere and the private sphere."

PNS and New California Media hold an annual EXPO & Awards show in order to increase advertisers' access to small ethnic publications. The EXPO & Awards raise over $35 million for all the organizations featured in their publications. More than just a fundraiser, the event is dubbed the "Ethnic Pulitzers." The EXPO is designed for all 700 of the ethnic news organizations to meet and exchange information. It is not only the largest gathering of ethnic media, but also the nation's first awards banquet for ethnic media, serving as a meeting place for not only those in media and advertising, but for the broader community as well.

There are newspapers around that have been giving minorities a voice for years. The *San Francisco Bay View* was started in 1972 as a primarily African-American publication based in Hunter's Point, San Francisco. The paper only circulates about 20,000 copies a week, but the Internet helps the paper reach a wider audience; online, the paper receives over a half a million hits. The web has also allowed the paper to acquire content from the Internet and e-mails. The paper covers a wide range of issues relevant to the African-American community. Mary Ratcliff, one of the editors in chief and co-owner of the *San Francisco Bay View*, states that the Internet is helping to develop "new ways of strengthening ourselves and our movements."

When asked about her feelings concerning mainstream media's tendency to ignore minorities, Ratcliff replied, "That's why we put out our paper!" She went on to emphasize the view that there is a strong effort in our society to marginalize those who aren't a part of the status quo out of fear of competition. The easiest way to keep from having to compete with these people is to keep them as poor and restrained as possible. The owners of corporate media are those who do meet the status quo, and that is why those who don't are ignored. By ignoring people, they become convinced that they aren't worth attention. She says that if people are convinced they aren't worth anything, they won't fight. "If we're going to bring any kind of equality, we have to do it together."

Media Alliance

BY LAUREN KETTNER

Media Alliance in San Francisco serves as a training center for media workers, community organizations, and political activists. With over 2,000 members stemming from the general public and group affiliates, Media Alliance offers services and support through their numerous programs. The group is membership driven, but Media Alliance has a wide scope "reaching a broader community that makes up the Media Alliance circle," states Jeff Perlstein, who has headed the group for the past two years. "We are comprised of people who are concerned."

Perlstein explains that a group of professionals concerned about the decreasing interest in in-depth reporting founded the group in the '70s. The use of freelance writers was on the rise, which threatened permanent journalism staff members and created a more hostile working environment. In order to combat these trends, Media Alliance started as a group committed to fostering investigative reporting. For 20 years, Media Alliance focused on media accountability and social justice. In 1976, one of their earliest displays of pro-union activity revolved around the *San Francisco Bay Guardian*'s refusal to provide job security for staff writers. Although the *Guardian* is still a non-union paper, Media Alliance's actions established itself as a political entity. In the past eight years, the organization has shifted its view to the needs of local communities.

Media Alliance publishes *MediaFile*; the *Bay Area's Review*, and the *People Behind the News*, which serve as guides for media professionals and as outlets for journalists. *MediaFile* debuted in 1980 as an eight-page, monthly media review. At the same time, the first edition of *People Behind the News* was published, providing a reference on 500 Bay Area journalists for those in the media business. *JobFile* grew during this time as well and is currently the job-referral service for people in the media profession. Training in computer skills, media advocacy, and writing techniques helps individuals hone their skills and become more successful in their fields. Perlstein explains, "Training for non-profit organizations is key to working with media and using multiple outlets for exposure." Perlstein adds that advancements in technology and media access have also allowed Media Alliance to grow. New ideas formed by the group revolve around the possibilities provided by Internet and television, especially since the introduction of the broadband digital spectrum.

Membership fees and donations support Media Alliance. With a $540,000 budget, their growth reflects the number of people being reached. Contributions allow for increases in production and distribution, as well as for expansion of existing programs. The association also depends greatly upon volunteers to help with everything from copying to graphic design. Members in the media profession can acquire health and dental benefits from Media Alliance along with other financial support in case of strikes or legal fees. Perlstein notes that Media Alliance is the only association that provides health insurance for members.

As strong advocates of media democracy, Media Alliance is often at the forefront of national organizing efforts, such as the fight against Clear Channel and media consolidation and the support of Pacifica Radio/KPFA. Through close ties with other distinguished groups such as Prometheus, the Media Justice Project, and Free Press, Media Alliance has been able to report on media concerns in the realms of broadcast radio, television, and print journalism. Attacking all forms of restriction of the media, recent stories include AT&T and Comcast merging to dominate the Internet, the plight of independent Internet radio, and the Bush Administration's intervention in San Francisco union negotiations.

Media Alliance continues to closely follow FCC decisions. Past issues of *MediaFile* have focused on the West coast FCC hearings, the war in Iraq and the lack of truthful media coverage, as well as on more local issues like San Francisco KMEL's refusal to air local artists and youth leaders. These stories and others from their archives have continued to attract people who demand accountability, responsibility, and change. Throughout the decades membership has continued to rise along with activist involvement.

Aside from defending individuals working in media and aiding unions in their battles, Media Alliance forms panels and plans major events to discuss progress and issues within the industry. Through scholarships and awards that celebrate the accomplishments of journalists and activists, Media Alliance strives to educate and motivate people to share in goals toward social change. Constantly looking for new voices and supporting disenfranchised sections of the population, Media Alliance created "Raising Our Voices," a program designed to give media access to homeless and low-income people. Participants are trained in creative writing, investigative journalism, and electronic publishing. The intent is to empower people to break through stereotypes while injecting their own voices into the public discourse. Working in collaboration with Galeria de la Raza and Arts Online, Media Alliance also features creative works by artists from South America, the Caribbean, Mexico, and the United States. The online art collection addresses racism in the media and displays works by both established and emerging artists who use different mediums to express their ideas regarding globalization, multiculturalism, and the social constructions of race.

From defending the rights of freelancers to walking picket lines, Media Alliance strives toward a more socially responsible community and promoting fair media practices. Perlstein says, "Media Alliance is focused on media accountability and works to improve outlets." Their first media justice summit will held in the summer of 2004 to discuss issues, develop a set of core principles, and invite others to participate and widen the circle of those interested in media justice. This forum will provide information on the abuse of the media, the negative stereotypes that are produced through mainstream outlets, and vision of a free open space that provides fair access to all cultures. "FCC Moves to Privatize Airwaves," published in *MediaFile*, was voted *Censored* #1 in 2002. Media Alliance has covered several Censored stories over the years that demonstrate its dedication to media accountability.

Grassroots Media

BY MELODY LINDSEY

The lack of substance in corporate media news has initiated the formation of grassroots media groups that cover news on a range of social issues ignored by corporate media. A few of these groups are We Interrupt This Message, the Youth Media Council, and Whispered Media.

We Interrupt This Message is a national non-profit organization based in San Francisco that focuses on issues of race and youth in the media. Their mission is to give people of color a voice and a place of respect in the media. We Interrupt This Message currently offers four publications that focus on empowering youth to challenge corporate media: *Speaking for Ourselves: A Youth Assessment of Local News Coverage; Soundbites and Cellblocks: Analysis of the Juvenile Justice Media Debate & A Case Study of California Proposition 21; Talking the Walk: A Communications Guide for Racial Justice;* and *In Between the Lines: How* The New York Times *Frames Youth.*

Two of the site's main goals are to teach others how to sift through corporate media reporting and how to assemble activist organizations. They offer help in start-up organizations, including workshops on developing campaigns and tools to challenge incorrect media coverage.

We Interrupt This Message's sister group, Youth Media Council, is a youth activist alliance made up of representatives from 11 Bay Area youth organizations. Lead by Malkia Cyril, who is also part of the activist listeners' group

Community Coalition for Media Accountability, Youth Media Council focuses on youth participation in community and economic development, juvenile justice, and public education. A main goal is to strategize media coordination between Bay Area youth and news media. They organize youth-run campaigns to keep the media accountable on public issues.

Since Clear Channel took over the Bay Area radio stations KMEL and KYLD from AMFM Inc. for $24 billion in 1999, there has been little or no access to the airwaves for social justice organizations. Youth Media Council advocates the mobilization of youth activism to get community voices heard and to fight for socially relevant programming.

The Youth Media Council is in the forefront of youth media activism. They held their second annual Youth-Journalist roundtable on April 24, 2004, at the NBC 7 studios in San Francisco. This forum allowed youth and journalists to address the fact that, while youth under 18 make up 27 percent of the Bay Area population, many issues that affect them most go uncovered by the media.

On April 25, 2004, eight members of the Youth Media Council appeared on the Nickelodeon's news program *Nick News* to share their opinions on U.S. foreign policy and national issues. Segments of the show will be played leading up to the presidential election in November. Two members of the Council also went to New York to discuss Latino stereotypes in the media with *Nick News*. That show is scheduled to air in September of 2004. The group also recently wrapped up a campaign addressing the effects of deportation on families since 9/11, which was covered by the *San Francisco Chronicle* and Univision Channel 14.

The Youth Media Council operates continuing projects aimed at connecting minority youth with local media, forming the necessary tools to critique and analyze popular media, and building relationships between Youth Media Council members and local journalists. These projects are The Public Eye, which focuses on media training skills; The ECHO Project, which focuses on 2004 youth and elections strategies; and The Media Accountability and Organizing Project, which focuses on Clear Channel Media accountability, media policy research, and cultural work. Their publications for media activism and accountability include *The Bay Area Media Map: A Youth Organizer's Guide to the Media Turf in the Bay Area and Beyond*; *Is KMEL the People's Station?: A Community Assessment*; and *Speaking for Ourselves*.

Video-based activist groups like Whispered Media, which is also part of the Video Activist Network (VAN), focus on social issues such as corporate globalization and worldwide efforts to stop corporations' growing influence and abuse of Third World countries. Whispered Media is an Internet-based organization whose Web site features worldwide independent video coverage of protests. They have many informative and unique documentary videos for sale, such as *Showdown in Seattle: Five Days that Shook the WTO* and *Breaking the Bank*—a documentary on the protests against the IMF and World Bank in Washington, DC. Their Web site also has an extensive list of related grassroots organizations and posts updates on upcoming independent media film festivals and related events.

With the dedication and perseverance of media activist groups like We Interrupt This Message, The Youth Media Council, and Whispered Media, there is hope of creating new, more responsive media and of salvaging existing media by holding large media corporations accountable.

SOURCES:
Video Activist Network (VAN)
P.O. Box 40130
San Francisco, CA 94140
Tel: (415) 789-8484
Web site: <www.videoactivism.org>

We Interrupt This Message
1215 York Street
San Francisco, CA 94116
E-mail: <we@interrupt.org>
Web site: <www.interrupt.org>

Whispered Media
P.O. Box 40130
San Francisco, CA 94140
Tel: (415) 789-8484
E-mail: <info@whisperedmedia.org>
Web site: <www.whisperedmedia.org>

Youth Media Council
1611 Telegraph Avenue, Suite 510
Oakland, CA 94612
Tel: (510) 444-0640, ext. 312
Fax: (510) 251-9810
E-mail: <malkia@youthmediacouncil.org>
Web site: <youthmediacouncil.org>

Danny Schechter and MediaChannel.org

BY AMBROSIA PARDUE

"As the media watch the world, we watch the media."

<MediaChannel.org> is a non-profit, public interest Web site based in New York that is dedicated to global media issues. It offers news, reports, and commentary from an international network of media organizations and publications, as well as original features from contributors and staff. It is concerned with the political, cultural and social impacts of media, large and small. The organization looks at the structure and trends in media from an issue-based perspective rather than focusing on personalities and shifts in corporate personnel. According to MediaChannel personnel, "It is about substance, not gossip."

The Web site gets its information from hundreds of national and international affiliated sites. These include media-watch groups, university journalism departments, professional organizations, anticensorship monitors, trade publications, and many others. According to many, the Web site contains the deepest, highest quality database of media-related news and information online.

<MediaChannel.org> got its start in 2000 as the brainchild of Danny Schechter, a former producer for ABC and 20/20. A Niemans Fellow in journalism at Harvard University, Schechter's work has received a number of awards and other recognitions. He produces a column about current issues and events that appears on the MediaChannel Web site regularly.

Like many in the industry, Schechter was initially drawn to media journalism because of his desire to shine a spotlight on the problems of the world. He quickly found, to his dismay, that the media system itself was one of the biggest problems and one that his editors were not particularly interested in having him cover. Building a successful career within the news industry involves a lot of self-censorship. For Schechter, it was a constant battle to get shows that covered issues related to public advocacy, abuses of power, or corporate malfeasance aired. The climate at the networks was increasingly hostile to such reporting.

Schechter was committed to the idea that all issues should be covered equitably. Stories should not be censored due to controversial content, nor should the coverage reflect only a few ideologies. He believed that there needed to be a media watchdog on a national and international scale. Thus emerged the concept behind <MediaChannel.org>.

The explosion of the Internet age allowed the organization to distribute news information cheaply and daily. MediaChannel started with a prototype that included 20 member organizations. The idea was to get the world involved—because media is a "global thing." Schechter realized that power and media tend not to be viewed this way. People have been lulled into believing that news is one-sided and of one mind. It is something pre-arranged that they receive, not something they participate in. Schechter wanted a pool of information and a broad spectrum of viewpoints, "creating a network for democratic media." He felt that it was important to build a bridge between people and their sources of information, developing a more democratic model of news media.

Since 2000, Schechter's strategy for creating that bridge—<MediaChannel.org>—has greatly expanded. Today, with 1,177 member organizations that contribute news and information, MediaChannel has become the world's largest online media network. It is known for asking hard questions and demanding the whole story from a global perspective. The organization reports what's not being reported...and talks about the way censorship operates. It's often not blatant or explicit. MediaChannel's approach is to highlight issues and to educate the audience by linking to other organizations so that the number of voices can be enhanced. "People like a diversity of sources," says one staffer. MediaChannel allows all views, but excludes hate-speech.

According to Schechter, "you can't just talk to yourself—there must be an open door to all others." One of his greatest motivations is to "mobilize people to reach out to the media to get fair coverage." He recommends that individuals "challenge media personally." He feels that if people come together with a unified voice, they can pressure the large media corporations for broader and more truthful news coverage. Schechter believes that a partnership between media insiders and independent media organizations would have the greatest influence on the media.

Schechter understands that the United States media has a "horrific concentration of power and service to the state." But he feels that the constant "outrage" he sees expressed is largely counterproductive. Even though there may be an unbalanced amount of power in our government, he feels that individuals should not "just focus on what's bad with the government because the media is sometimes more powerful." People in this society must "understand how media has changed. Digital media is changing the landscape"—as is evidenced by the number of people that daily flock to <MediaChannel.org>. "Political activists," he stresses, "often don't see media activism as part [of the means to a goal]." Therefore, when goals are achieved, or if progress is made, it is not seen as adequate. A person has to "understand how the media is changing if [they] want to change it."

In addition to giving a daily look at the news, the Web site offers many resources. MediaChannel has over 90 international advisors: journalists, academics, media professional, media critics, and activists. Advisors serve as MediaChannel's eyes and ears around the globe—keeping them informed about important issues and events, contributing commentaries and columns, and helping reach out to media organizations around the world.

Walter Cronkite has become MediaChannel's leading advisor, lending credibility and strength to its goals. In a taped message (posted on the Web site), Cronkite praises MediaChannel saying it will "undoubtedly be worth watching and taking part in." He is "deeply concerned about the merger mania that has swept our industry, diluting standards, dumbing down the news, and making the bottom line sometimes seem like the only line. Journalists shouldn't have to check their consciences at the door when they go to work for a media company…we must speak out because journalism *itself* is at risk." Cronkite believes that "MediaChannel opens an immediately available resource for media whistleblowers."

Indymedia

BY ANNA MIRANDA

In November 1999, the Independent Media Center (IMC) was created by activists to provide accurate and comprehensive coverage of the WTO protests in Seattle. Acting as a nerve center for the dissemination of information, Indymedia was able to counteract corporate media's biased coverage by recording, reporting and distributing up-to-the minute reports, photos, and audio and video footage of the events as they unfolded. Indymedia's coverage of the WTO protests became the catalyst for the development of other Indymedia chapters throughout the United States and around the world.

Today, there are over 130 decentralized, autonomous local Indymedia chapters spanning the globe. Indymedia is a non-hierarchical collective of journalists, activists, organizers and readers that is absented from corporate and government funding or sponsorship, political affiliation, and advertising. Freedom from these restraints allows Indymedia to invite users to produce and publish their own print, audio, and video media without fear of being censored: "Indymedia endeavors to empower people to become the media by presenting honest, accurate, powerful independent reports." The site offers an open publishing newswire that allows users to add stories in real time. However, readers must be cautioned that stories that appear on the newswire are not edited and filtered; therefore, they may possibly contain inaccurate, offensive, or degrading content.

Indymedia also faces challenges to its nonhierarchical organization when disagreements cause conflict and tension between members. Because of Indymedia's transparent nature, observers are able to follow disputes that happen within the group. For example, the San Francisco Indymedia Center experienced a rift between members that ultimately ended with the group splitting into two factions. Readers were able to follow the arguments that lead to the existence of two San Francisco Indymedia Centers now functioning independently and exclusively of one another as <www.sf.indymedia.org> and <indybay.org>.

Although Indymedia faces challenges, its overwhelming success as an autonomous, nonhierarchical grassroots independent media organization outshines its weaknesses. Unique in and of itself, one would have difficulty finding an organization that encourages its users to contribute and be a part of the media. With no financial backing from corporations, the government, or advertisers, it is quite an incredible feat that this organization is still up and running. More phenomenal is its explosive growth from one independent collective started in Seattle in 1999 to over 130 organizations worldwide within the last five years. See <www.sf.indymedia.org> for links to all sites.

News Without Borders

BY EMILIO LICEA

In our current world in which most news is a cloth of half-truths tailored to fit the corporate agenda, it is of some comfort that organizations exist to protect, report, and reveal the truth that exists in this world. In Berkeley, California, one such sentinel of truth is the Web-based organization <www.newswithoutborders.org>. News Without Borders believes that news should not have borders and that truth should always be reported.

The Web site was established in March 2003, at the same time the U.S. invaded Iraq. The founders were Joshua Bloom and Christopher Cook. The Web site reports on the "global perspectives on American empire." News Without Borders is dedicated to revealing what the international community is saying about the U.S. The Web site is updated on a weekly basis and is strictly an online news service. Joshua Bloom says of the Web site: "While the mainstream domestic media often omits key news coverage and fails to explain why events are really happening, there is a wealth of coverage available from international sources."

Currently, News Without Borders is updated on a weekly basis and is delivered to e-mail inboxes every Friday morning. The organization hopes to expand to daily updates. Bloom reports that, "Each week we scour the international press for the most illuminating coverage on expressions of the American empire and responses to it." The organization is composed of mostly undergraduate students at University of California–Berkeley. The reporters most often work in groups: "Each reporter has a support network of organizational and academic experts who they draw on for feed back on their selections." Bloom and Cook's team consist in part of about 10 reporters who work an average of about eight hours per week." The reporters cover all the developments relating to a specific themes, such as civil liberties, class war, education, gender and sexuality, globalization, immigrant rights, Iraq, labor, Middle East, and the war on terror. After researching the abundance of global information the information is, according to Bloom, "boiled down to six key stories that cover the material both most empirically salient and, from an analytical viewpoint, that is most illuminating in terms of the political dynamics of imperial advance and resistance to it."

The Web site is organized into three major areas: "Direct Intervention," "International Politics," and "The Homefront." Bloom explains that the organization focuses on four criteria for choosing each story: "1) Key Development—which news events are most empirically important in terms of their impact on the dynamics of extension of empire and resistance to it; 2) Analytic Frame—which stories provide a compelling analysis and clear frame that place this empirical development in its political context in the most illuminating way; 3) Uniqueness—which stories are least covered in the mainstream domestic media; and 4) Global Sources—wherever possible, we favor international or alternative domestic sources that our readers are unlikely to access otherwise." The group then takes this abundance of information, creates an online news e-mail, and sends it to all of its readers.

The work invested into this project is motivated, not by a drive toward economic prosperity, but rather by a drive to "expose the politics underlying the Bush Administration's invasion of Iraq," says Bloom. Bloom and Cook recognized that "many of us were spending countless hours online trying to understand what was happening by reading the global news. We realized that we could do this much more effectively and benefit others as well by coordinating our efforts."

CHAPTER 6

Challenging the New American Censorship

BY PETER PHILLIPS

Censorship in the United States today is more a factor of how the media is organized than a deliberate obstruction of news stories. We have known for a long time that the corporate media tends to not cover stories that might offend their major advertisers. And we have understood how organizational cultures emerge within news organizations that discourage coverage of certain news stories of concern to the board of directors and managers. However, we have not fully explained how the ongoing consolidation of corporate media is building a dependency on equally consolidated sources of news and how this dependency is creating a new American censorship.

On Sunday, February 29, 2004, Richard Boucher from the U.S. Department of State released a press report claiming that Jean-Bertrand Aristide had resigned as president of Haiti and that the United States facilitated his safe departure. Within hours the major broadcast news stations in the United States including CNN, Fox, ABC, NBC, CBS, and NPR were reporting that Aristide had fled Haiti. An Associated Press release that evening said "Aristide Resigns, Flees into Exile." The next day, headlines in the major newspapers across the country, including the *Washington Post, USA Today, The New York Times,* and *Atlanta Journal-Constitution,* all announced "Aristide Flees Haiti." *The Baltimore Sun* reported, "Haiti's first democratically-elected president was forced to flee his country yesterday like despots before him."

However on Sunday afternoon of February 29, Dennis Bernstein with Pacifica News Network was interviewing reporters live in Port-au-Prince, Haiti, who were claiming that Aristide was forced to resign by the U.S. and taken out of the presidential palace by armed U.S. Marines. On Monday morning, March 1, Amy Goodman with *Democracy Now!* interviewed Congresswoman Maxine Waters (D–CA). Waters said she had received a phone call from Aristide at 9:00 AM EST March 1, in which Aristide emphatically denied that he had resigned and said that he had been kidnapped by U.S. and French forces. Aristide made calls to others, including TransAfrica founder Randall Robinson, who verified Congresswoman Waters' report.

With this situation, mainstream corporate media was faced with a dilemma. Confirmed contradictions to headlines reports were being openly revealed to hundreds of thousands of Pacifica listeners nationwide. By Monday afternoon on March 1, mainstream corporate media began to respond to charges. Tom Brokaw on *NBC Nightly News* voiced, "Haiti in crisis. Armed rebels sweep into the capital as Aristide claims U.S. troops kidnapped him; forced him out. The U.S. calls that nonsense." Brit Hume with Fox News Network reported Colin Powell's comments: "He was not kidnapped. We did not force him onto the airplane. He went on to the airplane willingly, and that's the truth. Mort Kondracke, executive editor of *Roll Call* added, "Aristide, . . . was a thug and a leader of thugs and ran his country into the ground." *The New York Times,* in a story buried on page 10, reported that "President Jean-Bertrand Aristide asserted Monday that he had been driven from power in Haiti by the United States in 'a coup,' an allegation dismissed by the White House as 'complete nonsense.'"

THIS MODERN WORLD
by TOM TOMORROW

Still, mainstream/corporate media had a credibility problem. Their original story was openly contradicted. The kidnapping story could be ignored or back-paged as was done by many newspapers in the U.S. Or it could be framed within the context of a U.S. denial and dismissed. Unfortunately, the corporate media seemed not at all interested in conducting an investigation into the charges, seeking witnesses, or verifying contradictions. Nor was the mainstream media asking or answering the question of why they fully accepted the State Department's version of the coup in the first place. Corporate media certainly had enough pre-warning to determine that Aristide was not going to leave the country willingly. Aristide had been saying exactly that for the previous month during the armed attacks in the north of Haiti. When Aristide was interviewed on CNN on February 26, he explained that the terrorists and criminal drug dealers were former members of the Front for the Advancement and Progress of Haiti (FRAPH), which had led the coup in 1991, killing 5,000 people. Aristide believed they would kill even more people if a coup was allowed to happen. It was also well-known in media circles that the U.S. Undersecretary of State for Latin America, Roger Noriega, had been senior aide to former Senator Jesse Helms (R–NC) who, as chairman of the Senate Foreign Affairs committee, was a longtime backer of Haitian dictator Jean-Claude Duvalier and an opponent of Aristide. These facts alone should have been a red flag regarding the State Department's version of Aristide's departure. Weeks later, most news stories on Haiti published in the U.S. still claimed that Aristide "fled" Haiti while reporting the ongoing civil unrest in the country.

The corporate media's recent coverage of Haiti embodies how the new American censorship works. If other news stories contradict the official

sources of news, they tend to be downplayed or ignored. Corporate/mainstream media have become dependent upon the press releases and inside sources from government and major corporations for their 24-hour news content and are increasingly unwilling to broadcast or publish news that would threaten ongoing relationships with these official sources.

This means that freedom of information and citizen access to objective news is fading in the United States. In its place is a complex entertainment-oriented news system, which protects its own bottom line by servicing the most powerful military-industrial complex in the world. Corporate media today is interlocked and dependent on government sources for news content. Gone are the days of deep investigative reporting teams challenging the powerful. Media consolidation has downsized newsrooms to the point where reporters serve more as stenographers than researchers (Barsamian 1992).

The 24-hour news shows on MSNBC, Fox, and CNN are closely interconnected with various governmental and corporate sources of news. Maintenance of continuous news shows requires a constant feed and an ever-entertaining supply of stimulating events and breaking news bites. Advertisement for mass consumption drives the system and pre-packaged sources of news are vital within this global news process. Ratings demand continued cooperation from multiple sources for ongoing weather reports, war stories, sports scores, business news, and regional headlines. Print, radio, and TV news also engage in this constant interchange with news sources.

The preparation for and following of ongoing wars and terrorism fits well into the visual kaleidoscope of pre-planned news. Government public relations specialists and media experts from private commercial interests provide ongoing newsfeeds to the national media distribution systems. The result is an emerging macrosymbiotic relationship between news dispensers and news suppliers. Perfect examples of this relationship are the Iraq War press pools organized by the Pentagon both in the Middle East and in Washington, DC, which give pre-scheduled reports on the war to selected groups of news collectors (journalists) for distribution through their respective corporate media organizations. The Pentagon's management of the news has become increasingly sophisticated with restrictions and controls being added cumulatively to each new military action or invasion in which the U.S. is involved (Andersen 2003).

During the Iraq War, embedded reporters (news collectors) working directly with military units in the field were required to maintain cooperative working relationships with unit commanders as they fed breaking news back to the U.S. public. Cooperative reporting was vital to continued access to government news sources. In addition, rows of news story reviewers back at corporate media headquarters were used to rewrite, soften, or spike news stories from the field that threaten the symbiotics of global news management or might be perceived by the Pentagon as too critical.

Journalists working outside of this approved mass media system faced ever-increasing dangers from "accidents" of war and corporate media dismissal of their news reports. Massive civilian casualties caused by U.S. troops, extensive damage to private homes and businesses, and reports that contradicted the official public relations line were downplayed, deleted, or ignored by corporate media, while content was analyzed by experts (retired generals and other approved collaborators) from within the symbiotic global news structure.

Symbiotic global news distribution is a conscious and deliberate attempt by the powerful to control news and information in society. It is the overt manifestation of censorship in our society. The Homeland Security Act Title II Section 201(d)(5) specifically asks the directorate to "develop a comprehensive plan for securing the key resources and critical infrastructure of the United States including… information technology and telecommunications systems (including satellites)… emergency preparedness communications systems." Corporate media's cooperation with these directives ensures an ongoing transition to inevitably tighter controls over news content in the United States. From a Homeland Security agency perspective, total information control would be the ideal state of maximized security for the media systems in the U.S.

Corporate media today is perhaps too vast to enforce complete control over all content 24 hours a day. However, the goal of government and of many multinational corporations is for the eventual operationalization of a highly controlled news system in the U.S. The degree to which corporate media is hastening moves in this direction is directly related to the high level embeddedness of the media elite within the corporate power structure in the United States.

This new American censorship is facilitated by the continuing consolidation of the corporate media. Since the passage of the Telecommunications Act of 1996, a gold rush of media mergers and takeovers has been occurring in the U.S. Over half of all radio stations have been sold in the past eight years, and the repeatedly merged AOL Time Warner (CNN) is the largest media organization in the world. Only a handful of major media corporations now dominate the U.S. news and information systems. Clear Channel owns over 1,200 radio stations. Ninety-eight percent of all cities have only one daily newspaper and huge chains like Gannett and Knight Ridder increasingly own these (Bagdikian 2004).

Media corporations have been undergoing a massive merging and buyout process that is realigning the sources of information in America. Conglomeration changes traditional media corporate cultures. Values such as freedom of information and belief in the responsibility of keeping the public informed are adjusted to reflect policies created by bottom-line-oriented CEOs. These structural arrangements facilitate the new censorship in America today. It is not yet deliberate killing of stories by official censors, but a rather subtle system of information suppression in the name of corporate profit and self-interest.

The big corporations that now dominate media in America are principally in the entertainment business. The corporate media is narrowing its content with news reports that often look very much the same. Between media consolidation, the primacy of bottom line considerations, and the ignoring of important but complex political issues, it is now believed that Americans are the best entertained, least informed people in the world (Postman 1986).

Media owners and managers are economically motivated to please advertisers and upper-middle-class readers and viewers. Journalists and editors are not immune to management influence. Journalists want to see their stories approved for print or broadcast, and editors come to know the limits of their freedom to diverge from the bottom line view of owners and managers. The results are an expansion of entertainment news, infomercials, and synergistic news all aimed at increased profit taking.

Corporate media are multinational corporations in their own right, with all the vested interests in free-market capitalism and top-down control of society. In 1997, the 11 largest or most influential media corporations in the United States were General Electric Company (NBC), Viacom Inc. (cable), The Walt Disney Company (ABC), Time Warner Inc. (CNN), Westinghouse Electric Corporation (CBS), The News Corporation Ltd. (Fox), Gannett Co. Inc., Knight Ridder Inc., New York Times Co., Washington Post Co., and the Times Mirror Co. Collectively, these 11 major media corporations had 155 directors in 1996. These 155 directors also held 144 directorships on the boards of *Fortune* 1,000 corporations in the United States. These 11 media organizations have interlocking directorships with each other through 36 other Fortune 1,000 corporations creating a solid network of overlapping interests and affiliations. All 11 media corporations have direct links with at least two of the other top media organizations. General Electric, owner of NBC, has the highest rate of shared affiliations with 17 direct corporate links to 9 of the 10 other media corporations (Phillips 1998).

These directors are the media elite of the world. While they may not agree on abortion and other domestic issues, they do represent the collective vested interests of a significant portion of corporate America and share a common commitment to free-market capitalism, economic growth, internationally protected copyrights, and a government dedicated to protecting their interests.

Given this interlocked media network, it is more than safe to say that major media in the United States effectively represents the interests of corporate America, and that the media elite are the watchdogs of acceptable ideological messages, parameters of news content, and general use of media resources.

Corporate media promote free-market capitalism as the unquestioned American ideological truth. The decline of communism opened the door for unrestrained free marketers to boldly espouse market competition as the final solution for global harmony. Accordingly, corporate media have become the mouthpiece of free-market ideology by uncritically supporting the underlying assumption that the marketplace will solve all evils, and that we will enjoy economic expansion, individual freedom, and unlimited bliss by fully deregulating and privatizing society's socioeconomic institutions.

The corporate media have been fully supportive of the U.S. policy of undermining socialist or nationalist leaning governments and pressuring them into ideological compliance. The full force of U.S. dominated global institution—World Trade Organization (WTO), World Bank, International Monetary Fund (IMF), and the North American Free Trade Agreement (NAFTA)—focus on maximizing free-market circumstances and corporate access to every region of the world. Economic safety nets, environmental regulations, labor unions, and human rights take second place to the free flow of capital and investments. The corporate media elites are in the forefront of this global capital movement with an unrelenting propaganda agenda that gives lip service to democracy while refusing to address the contradictions and hypocrisies of U.S. global policies.

A closer examination of this American media supported ideology reveals that "free market" essentially means constant international U.S. government intervention on behalf of American corporations. This public–private partnership utilizes U.S. embassies, the CIA, FBI, NSA, U.S. military, Department of Commerce, USAID, and every other U.S government institution to protect, sustain, and directly support our vital interest: U.S. business.

This ideological mantra affects the U.S. population as well. We are still riding on the betterments from the first three-quarters of the twentieth century and have not faced the full impacts of the economic bifurcation that has occurred in the past 30 years. Poverty levels are rising, the numbers of working poor is expanding, and homelessness is one paycheck away for many. In the last quarter-century, economic conditions have declined for the bottom 60 million Americans, and most of the next 100 million have barely held their own while the corporate and media elites have socked away fortunes (Sklar 2002).

In the past few years, corporate media outlets, under pressure from powerful corporate/government officials, have fired or disciplined journalists for writing critical stories about the powerful in the United States. These terminations have sent a chilling message to journalists throughout the U.S.: If you attack the sacred cows of powerful corporate/governmental institutions, your career is on the line. Journalists who fail to recognize their role as cooperative news collectors are disciplined in the field or barred from reporting, as in the Iraq War II celebrity cases of Geraldo Rivera and Peter Arnett.

In a well-known case of pressure by powerful institutions, Fox TV news reporters Steve Wilson and Jane Akre were fired by WTVT in Tampa for refusing to change their story on the dangers of Monsanto's bovine growth hormone (rBGH) in the Florida milk supply. Scientific research has shown that when injected into cows to expand milk production, rBGH results in the increase of insulin-like growth factor IGF-I in milk. IGF-I has been linked to breast and prostate cancer. Monsanto claims that the milk is safe, but new scientific evidence suggests otherwise. Monsanto put pressure on Fox Television in New York, WTVT's parent company, threatening dire consequences if the story ran. When Wilson and Akre refused to say the milk was unchanged, they were fired by the Fox station general manager, who was quoted as saying, "We paid $3 billion for these stations: We'll decide what the news is. The news is what we tell you it is" (Wilson and Akre 2000).

Perhaps the most infamous case of media willingly succumbing to external pressures by the government is the retraction by CNN of the story about U.S. military's use of sarin gas in 1970 in Laos during the Vietnam War. After an eight-month investigation, CNN producers April Oliver and Jack Smith, reported on June 7, 1998 on CNN, and later in *Time* magazine, that sarin gas was used in Operation Tailwind in Laos and that American defectors were targeted. The story was based on eyewitness accounts and high military command collaboration.

After the airing of the Tailwind story in June of 1998, CNN came under a firestorm of pressure from the Pentagon, Henry Kissinger, Colin Powell, Richard Helms, veteran groups, and other media to retract the story. CNN president Rick Kaplan told Oliver and Smith that CNN did not want to end up in congressional hearings across from Colin Powell and that the story had become a "public relations problem." A CNN investigation into Oliver and

Smith's story by attorney Floyd Abrams and CNN's vice president David Kohler resulted in a recommendation for retraction claiming that the evidence did not support the use of sarin gas. On July 10, 1998, Ted Turner made a public apology for airing the Tailwind story before the Television Critics Association. CNN and *Time* retracted the story saying that "the allegations about the use of nerve gas and the killing of defectors are not supported by the evidence"; CNN then fired Oliver and Smith. Columnists and pundits across the nation attacked Oliver and Smith for their alleged unprofessional journalism. *Newsweek* even wrote on July 20, 1998, that the allegations were "proven wrong."

Oliver and Smith have steadfastly stood by their original story as accurate and substantiated. As Oliver states in *Censored 1999* (Oliver 1999), "We stand by the story. We are not novices at newsgathering... The Tailwind story was carefully researched and reported over eight months, with our bosses' [CNN] approval of each interview request and each line of the story's script. It was based on multiple sources [six eyewitnesses], from senior military officials to first-hand participants...in addition to half a dozen on-camera sources, more than a dozen pilots told us of the availability or use of a special 'last resort' gas...gb (the military name for sarin), or cbu-15 (a sarin cluster bomb)."

What is troubling about this issue is the speed with which CNN/*Time* withdrew their support for Oliver and Smith, after having fully approved the release of the story only weeks before.

Operation Tailwind can perhaps best be understood better in the context of the new Vietnam War revelations published in *The Blade* (Toledo) in October 2003 and also widely ignored by the corporate media. *The Blade* story discloses the unrestricted savaging of hundreds of civilians in the Central Highlands by an elite American Tiger Force during several months in 1967. This free-fire force was given authority to massacre at will anyone found in the region. Newly available government documents disclose how an army war crimes investigation in 1971 encouraged solders to keep quiet and how the case was closed in 1975.

The eight-month investigation by Michael Sallah, Joe Mahr, and Mitch Weiss for *The Blade* is eerily similar to the investigation of the Operation Tailwind story by CNN reporters April Oliver and Jack Smith in 1997–1998. Both stories reveal deadly illegal war crimes by U.S. forces in Southeast Asia, both stories were covered up by higher authorities in the Pentagon, and both stories challenge the fictionalized storyline of average GIs caught up in a lousy misunderstood war, who, in isolated incidents, made low-level field decisions that resulted in Mai Lai–type mistakes. The Operation Tailwind and Tiger

Force stories reveal higher level policies of a vicious win-at-any-cost war officiated by Pentagon and high-level government officials. It is the revelation of these policies that the Pentagon seems strongly motivated to suppress.

Anyone who actually reads CNN's investigative report can see the overwhelming evidence that supports the original version of the story (CNN 1998). However, the CNN report uses a new standard of absolute proof by saying that the ability to stand up in a court of law is the criteria for airing stories. Such a standard, if enforced, would essentially eliminate investigative journalism; stories like Watergate, for example, would never have been published. It is the responsibility of media to stand firm on solid evidence and tell the truth about important social issues, but it is not journalistically feasible to research each story as if it were to be presented in a court of law. The fact that CNN failed to uphold a commitment to the First Amendment speaks more about the symbiotic relationship between corporate media and sources of news than it does about erroneous reporting.

Oliver eventually won a large settlement from her lawsuit for wrongful termination. Numerous media critics including Fairness and Accuracy in Reporting, Alexander Cockburn, Project Censored, *Democracy Now!*, and MediaChannel reported her side of the story, including how CNN caved in to pressure from the Pentagon. CNN officials clearly understood that they might not be invited to the next war unless a retraction occurred. CNN faced more than a public relations problem, they faced a bottom line profitability problem if they were refused access to military cooperation on future broadcasts. Kohler and Turner knew full well the necessity of cooperation with official sources.

Corporate media has also ignored many important questions related to 9/11, which would offend their sources of news in the government. Corporate news star Dan Rather in a interview with Matthew Engel for *The Guardian* (London) admitted that the surge of patriotism after 9/11 resulted in journalists failing to ask the tough questions. Rather stated, "It starts with a feeling of patriotism within oneself. I know the right question, but you know what? This is not exactly the right time to ask it" (Engel 2002).

When was the right time to question the levels and intensity of civilian deaths during and after the bombings of Afghanistan? According to CNN Chairman Walter Isaacson, there was never a good time. In a memo to his CNN correspondents overseas, Isaacson wrote, "We're entering a period in which there's a lot more reporting and video from Taliban-controlled Afghanistan. You must make sure people [Americans] understand that when they see civilian suffering there, it's in the context of a terrorist attack that caused enormous suffering in the United States." Isaacson later told the *Washington Post*, "…it seems perverse to focus too much on the causalities of hardship in Afghanistan." This is the same Walter Isaacson, who, when assuming the chairmanship of CNN in August 2001, claimed that news needed to be redefined. "There would be a greater focus on entertainment, technology, health and fitness," he said. "The goal should be to make the news smart, but also fun and fascinating" (Engel 2002).

Marc Herold, an economics professor at the University of New Hampshire compiled a summation of the death toll in Afghanistan—concluding that over 4,000 civilians died from U.S. bombs—more than the number of people who died at the World Trade Center. Nevertheless, only a handful of newspapers covered his story. *Time* magazine reviewed Herold's report but dismissed it stating, "In compiling the figures, Herold drew mostly on world press reports of questionable reliability." *Time* went on to cite the Pentagon's unsubstantiated claim that civilian casualties in Afghanistan were the lowest in the history of war (Herold 2002).

At times the corporate media starts in on a story and realizes that it may lead into areas of concern to their sources of news. Numerous papers in the country including the *San Francisco Chronicle* on September 29, 2001, reported how millions of dollars were made buying pre-9/11 put options on United Airlines and American Airlines stocks. Yet by mid-October, nothing else was ever printed on the subject. The director of the Chicago Office of the FBI, Tom Kneir, admitted on August 17, 2002, at the American Sociological Association's meetings in Chicago, that the FBI conducted an investigation into the pre-9/11 stock options, but he refused to disclose who bought the stock, and the corporate media has never asked.

At times, the hypocrisy of corporate media news coverage is overwhelming. During the first week of December, 2003, U.S. corporate media reported that American forensic teams were working to document some 41 mass graves in Iraq to support future war crime tribunals in that country. Broadly covered in the media as well was the conviction of General Stanislav Galic by a U.N. tribunal for war crimes committed by Bosnian Serb troops under his command during the siege of Sarajevo in 1992–1994.

These stories show how corporate media likes to give the impression that the U.S. government is working diligently to root out evildoers around the world and to build democracy and freedom. This theme is part of a core ideological message in support of our recent wars on Panama, Serbia, Afghanistan, and Iraq. Governmental spin transmitted by a willing U.S. media establishes simplistic mythologies of good versus evil, often leaving out historical context, special transnational corporate interests, and prior strategic relationships with the dreaded evil ones (Solomon 2003).

The hypocrisy of U.S. policy and corporate media complicity is evident in the coverage of Donald Rumsfeld's stopover in Mazar-e-Sharif, Afghanistan, on December 4, 2003, to meet with regional warlord and mass killer General Abdul Rashid Dostum and his rival General Ustad Atta Mohammed. Rumsfeld was there to finalize a deal with the warlords to begin the decommissioning of their military forces in exchange for millions of dollars in international aid and increased power in the central Afghan government.

Few people in the U.S. know that General Abdul Rashid Dostum fought alongside the Russians in the 1980s, commanding a 20,000-man army. He switched sides in 1992 and joined the mujahideen when they took power in Kabul. For over a decade, Dostum was a regional warlord in charge of six northern provinces, which he ran like a private fiefdom, making millions by collecting taxes on regional trade and international drug sales. Forced into exile in Turkey by the Taliban in 1998, he came back into power as a military proxy of the U.S. during the invasion of Afghanistan.

Charged with mass murder of prisoners of war in the mid-'90s by the U.N., Dostum is known to use torture and assassinations to retain power. Described by the *Chicago Sun-Times* (October 21, 2001) as a "cruel and cunning warlord," he is reported to use tanks to rip apart political opponents or crush them to death. Dostum, a seventh grade dropout, likes to put up huge pictures of himself in the regions he controls, drinks Johnnie Walker Blue Label, and rides in an armor-plated Cadillac.

A documentary entitled *Massacre at Mazar* released in 2002 by Scottish film producer, Jamie Doran, exposes how Dostum, in cooperation with U.S. special forces, was responsible for the torturing and deaths of approximately 3,000 Taliban prisoners of war in November of 2001. In Doran's documentary, two witnesses report on camera how they were forced to drive into the desert with hundreds of Taliban prisoners held in sealed cargo containers. Most of the prisoners suffocated to death in the vans and Dostum's soldiers shot the few prisoners left alive. One witness told *The Guardian* (London) that a U.S. Special Forces vehicle was parked at the scene as bulldozers buried the dead. A soldier told Doran that U.S. troops masterminded a coverup. He said the Americans ordered Dostum's people to get rid of the bodies before satellite pictures could be taken.

Dostum admits that a few hundred prisoners died, but asserts that it was a mistake or that they died from previous wounds. He has kept thousands of

Taliban as prisoners of war since 2001 and continues to ransom them to their families for $10,000 to $20,000 each.

Doran's documentary was shown widely in Europe, prompting an attempt by the U.N. to investigate, but Dostum has prevented any inspection by saying that he could not guarantee safety for forensic teams in the area.

During the recent meeting with Dostum, Donald Rumsfeld was quoted as saying, "I spent many weeks in the Pentagon following closely your activities, I should say your successful activities" (*Washington Post,* December 5, 2003). The *Post* reported that General Dostum was instrumental in routing Taliban forces from northern Afghanistan in the early weeks of the war two years ago, but said nothing about General Dostum's brutal past. U.S. broadcast media still has not aired Doran's documentary.

A number of other questions remain unasked and unresolved regarding events surrounding 9/11 attacks. Both the BBC and the *Times of India* published reports several months before 9/11 that the U.S. was then planning an invasion of Afghanistan. The Unocal oil pipeline from the Caspian Sea region was to be built through Afghanistan and the U.S. needed a cooperative government in power. Agence France-Presse in March 2002 reported that the U.S.-installed interim leader of Afghanistan, Hamid Karzai, had worked with the CIA since the 1980s and was once a paid consultant for Unocal.

A report from France, still unacknowledged by the U.S. press, informs how the Bush administration, shortly after assuming office, slowed down FBI investigations of Al Qaeda and terrorist networks in Afghanistan in order to deal with the Taliban on oil. The ordered slowdown resulted in the resignation of FBI deputy director John O'Neill, an expert in the Al Qaeda network who was also in charge of the investigation. O'Neill later took a job as chief of security at the World Trade Center where he died "helping with rescue efforts" (Brisard 2002).

An October 31, 2002, report in the French daily *Le Figaro* disclosed that Osama bin Laden had met with a top CIA official while in the American Hospital in the United Arab Emirates to receive treatment for a kidney infection earlier that summer. *CBS News* reported one time on January 28, 2002, that Osama bin Laden was in a Pakistani military hospital on September 10, 2001.

On 9/11, four planes were hijacked and deviated from their flight plans, all the while on FAA radar. The planes were all hijacked between 7:45 and 8:10 AM Eastern Standard Time. It was a full hour before the first plane hit the World Trade Center. But it was an hour and 20 minutes later—after the second plane hit—that the president, who was visiting a Florida school, became officially informed. Then, he gave no orders. He continued to listen to a student talk about her pet goat. It was another 25 minutes until he made a statement (Griffin 2004).

Because of corporate media's failure to investigate questions around 9/11 conspiracy theories abound in America. Corporate media chooses to offer mindless entertainment in place of deeper investigations into important national questions. The result is that the general public knows more about Winona Ryder's shoplifting trial and the Peterson murder case then they do about the history of U.S. involvement in Afghanistan and Iraq.

The First Amendment provides for freedom of the press and was established to protect our democratic process by guaranteeing an informed electorate. Yet we hold national elections in which millions of voters refused to participate. We denigrate and blame nonvoters for being uncaring citizens, yet the corporate media has failed to address core issues affecting most people in this country. Voter participation levels are directly related to issues that the citizenry feels are important. Many people no longer trust the corporate media to provide the full truth. This opens people's susceptibility to believing in conspiracies and plots to explain unanswered questions. Cynicism has deterred many from voting.

How can we free ourselves from this dilemma? We can advocate strongly for corporate media to invest in democracy by supporting deep investigative reporting on key national issues. We can advocate for full and clear reporting on the policies and plans emerging from the public and private policy circles of the American corporate and governmental elites. Full analysis and disclosure of the published plans of the Trilateral Commission, The Council on Foreign Relations, The Hoover Institute, The Heritage Foundation, The Cato Institute, the World Bank, and the Project for the New American Century would go a long way in showing the road maps that the policy elites are building for the world. We don't need macroconspiracy theories to understand that powerful people sit in rooms and plan global change with private advantage in mind.

If open debate on sociopolitical policies were offered nationwide, it would certainly draw wider voter participation. Imagine a Silicon Valley computer programmer thinking about social policies that would prevent the outsourcing of his job to foreign firms. Imagine his enthusiasm voting for representatives who would work to protect his livelihood.

Recognition of corporate media compliance with sources of news is an important step in understanding our new American censorship. A full media reform movement that challenges continued corporate media consolidation is underway in the U.S., and tens of thousands of people are involved (McChesney 2004).

Knowing the importance of the role of media in the continuation of democracy, we have a huge task before us. We must mobilize our resources to redevelop our own news and information systems from the bottom up, while at the same time attempting reform at the top. We can expand distribution of news via small independent newspapers, local magazines, independent radio, and cable-access TV. By using the Internet, we can interconnect with like-minded grassroots news organizations to share important stories globally.

Emerging in the corporate media news vacuum are hundreds of independent news sources. Independent newspapers, magazines, Web sites, radio, and TV are becoming more widely available. Independent media centers (see <www.indymedia.org>) have sprung up in over 200 cities in the past five years. Thousands of alternative news organizations already exist and are listed in *The Project Censored Guide to Alternative Media and Activism* (Phillips 2003).

There is a compelling need to encourage activists and concerned citizens to avoid the propaganda of corporate news and to focus instead on news from independent sources. The more corporate news you watch, the less you really know (Schechter 1997).

Imagine "real news" as media information that contributes to the lives and sociopolitical understandings of working people. Such real news informs, balances, and awakens the less powerful in society. Real news speaks truth to power and challenges the hegemonic top-down corporate entertainment news systems. Real news empowers and keeps key segments of working people in America tuned in, informed, and active. Real news cannot be measured with Arbitron ratings. It is not there for the selling of materialism or capitalist propaganda. It is not there for nationalistic grandiosity. Nor is it there to provide entertaining stimulation to the alienated suburbs. Real news can only be measured through its success in building democracy, stimulating grassroots activism, and motivating resistance to top-down institutions.

Real news builds movements for social change. It keeps the 5 percent radical vanguard aware of our power and our collective ability to influence positive change. Real news is about stimulating social activism in our daily lives and making each act deliberate and heart centered. Real news reports to the center of self and helps us find the collective for shared action. Real news organizes movement towards betterment, shapes policy for equality, and stands in the faces of the robber-baron corporate power brokers.

Peter Phillips is department chair and professor of sociology at Sonoma State University and director of Project Censored..

BIBLIOGRAPHY

Andersen, Robin. "The Made-for-TV 'Reality' War on Iraq." In *Censored 2004*, edited by Peter Phillips and Project Censored. New York: Seven Stories Press, 2003.

Bagdikian, Ben H. *The New Media Monopoly*. Boston: Beacon Press, 2004.

Barsamian, David. *Stenographers to Power: Media and Propaganda*. Monroe, ME: Common Courage Press, 1992.

Brisard, Jean-Charles, and Guillaume Dasquie. *Forbidden Truth: U.S. Taliban and Secret Oil Diplomacy and the Failed Search for bin Laden*. New York: Nation Books, 2002.

CNN, "Tailwind Report," July 1998. <www.cnn.com/US/9807/02/tailwind.findings/index.html>.

Engel, Matthew. "War on Afghanistan: American Media Cowed by Patriotic Fever, Says Network News Veteran." *The Guardian*, May 17, 2002, 4.

Engel, Matthew. "Media: Has Anything Changed?" *The Guardian*, September 2, 2002, 2.

Griffin, David Ray. *The New Pearl Harbor: Disturbing Questions about the Bush Administration and 9/11*. New York: Olive Branch Press, 2004.

Herold, Marc. "Truth About Afghan Civilian Casualties." In *Censored 2003*, edited by Peter Phillips and Project Censored. New York: Seven Stories Press, 2002.

McChesney, Robert. *The Problem of the Media*. New York: Monthly Review Press, 2004.

McLaughlin, Martin. "The Evidence of U.S. Nerve Gas Use in Operation Tailwind," July 1998, *World Socialist* Web Site, <www.wsws.org/news/1998/july1998/cnn2-j24>.

Oliver, April. "The Censored Side of the CNN Firings Over Tailwind." In *Censored 1999*, edited by Peter Phillips and Project Censored. New York: Seven Stories Press, 1999.

Pauwels, Jacques. *The Myth of the Good War*. Halifax, NS, Canada: Lorimer & Company, 2002.

Phillips, Peter. "Self-Censorship and the Homogeneity of the Media Elite." In *Censored 1998*, edited by Peter Phillips and Project Censored. New York: Seven Stories Press, 1998.

Phillips, Peter, ed. *Project Censored Guide to Alternative Media and Activism*. New York: Seven Stories Press, 2003. See also <www.projectcensored.org>.

Postman, Neil. *Amusing Ourselves to Death: Public Discourse in the Age of Show Business*. New York: Penguin, 1986.

The Blade (Toledo), "Elite Unit Savaged Civilians in Vietnam," October 2, 2003, <www.toledoblade.com/apps/phcs.dll/article?AID=/20031002/SRTIGERFORCE/>.

Schechter, Danny. *The More You Watch, the Less You Know*. New York: Seven Stories Press, 1997.

Sklar, Holly, and L. Mykyta and S. Wefald, *Raise the Floor: Wages and Policies that Work for All of Us*. Cambridge, MA: South End Press, 2002.

Solomon, Norman. "Media Fog of War." In *Censored 2004*, edited by Peter Phillips and Project Censored. New York: Seven Stories Press, 2003.

Solomon, Norman and Reese Erlich. *Target Iraq*. New York: Context Books, 2003.

Wilson, Steve and Jane Akre. <www.foxbghsuit.com>, 2000.

CHAPTER 7

The Best of PR Watch: Spins of the Year

BY LAURA MILLER

1. WHITE HOUSE INFORMATION WARRIORS, PART I: IRAQ

When it comes to the top 10 PR stories of 2003, an itemization of all the stunts and deceptions that went into the selling the invasion and subsequent occupation of Iraq by the White House and Pentagon could easily fill all 10 spots and more. Some of the stunts, like George W. Bush's Thanksgiving visit to troops in Baghdad, could instantly be recognized as image enhancing photo-ops, while other White House and Pentagon PR plays, like "embedding" journalists with troops, were subtler.

The PR campaign to convince Americans and the world that it was necessary for the United States to invade Iraq, remove Saddam Hussein from power, and set up an occupation was complex, involving a confluence of political, ideological, and corporate interests. The funding and actors came from both the public and private sectors. Months of pro-war rhetoric saturated the airways. Corporate media uniformly marginalized dissenting opinions.

The Center for Media and Democracy tracked many of these manipulations and distortions as they happened. Our book *Weapons of Mass Deception*—authored by the center's Sheldon Rampton and John Stauber—examined the propaganda that led to the invasion of Iraq. As we were wrapping up the book, a triumphant Bush landed on the USS Lincoln. In a made-for-TV moment, he proudly declared victory to Americans and the world, the "mission accomplished" banner hanging in the background. But like so many other White House moments, there was little truth in the image.

As the weeks and months unfolded, the Bush Administration faced an increasingly difficult struggle to keep a happy face painted on the situation in Iraq. Referring to the occupation in August 2003, a vacationing Bush said, "We've made a lot of progress." The pronouncement was timed with the release of a 24-page report called "Results in Iraq: 100 Days Towards Security and Freedom." *The New York Times'* Maureen Dowd called it "yet another spun-up government document on Iraq" that "burbled with gimcrackery about the '10 signs of better infrastructure'—days before an oil pipeline and then a water pipeline were blown up—and about soccer balls and science textbooks." In September, *PR Week's* Douglas Quenqua wrote, "Determined to change the tone of the national debate over Iraq, the White House and Republicans in Congress launched a tightly coordinated effort last week to begin providing the media with stories of American progress in the still-turbulent country."

As the Bush Administration had less and less good news to spin, it reined in the communications flow even more. Crisis management PR emphasizes the strict control of information, and top administration spokesmen strained to keep word of the unfolding military and human rights disasters from reaching Americans. "Impartial information is increasingly hard to come by in Iraq," Reuter's Fiona O'Brien reported in the spring of 2004. "As fighting has intensified on the ground, U.S. authorities have stepped up a separate battle for public opinion, tightly controlling the flow of information to journalists whose ability to move freely in Iraq has been limited by increasing danger."

U.S. military officials refused to discuss mounting Iraqi civilian casualties and in some cases entirely denied them. "There's a big controversy now with the Arab press, Al Jazeera in particular, reporting U.S. atrocities and war crimes in Fallujah, and the U.S. press tamely reporting Brigadier General Mark Kim's claims [that] no such thing is happening. I can tell you from what I have seen with my own eyes that Al Jazeera is much closer to the truth," U.S. journalist Rahul Mahajan wrote in April 2004. U.S. officials also leaned heavily on the Arab press to tell a more "balanced" story. Secretary of State Colin Powell visited Qatar to express U.S. concern about the reporting of the Qatari-based Al Jazeera network. "The friendship between our two nations is such that we can also talk about difficult issues that intrude into that relationship, such as the issue of the coverage of Al Jazeera," Powell told his Qatari counterpart.

The violent pandemonium in Iraq, however, is proving to be too large for U.S. image-makers to control. The Pentagon's ban on images of returning dead U.S. soldiers was openly challenged in April 2004. The Sunday edition of the *Seattle Times* published a front-page photo of the flag-draped coffins of soldiers killed in Iraq. Other newspapers followed suit. Then, at the end of the month, Americans and the rest of the world were shocked by pictures—first aired by CBS—of Iraqi prisoners in the Abu Ghraib prison who had been abused and tortured by the U.S. military. These photos struck the final blow to the U.S. campaign for the "hearts and minds" of Arabs and Muslims. World opinion of the U.S. plummeted even further. And maybe for the first time, images in the U.S. media challenged the belief held by many Americans of a successful Iraq war.

2. IRAQI INTELLIGENCE: MANUFACTURED IN THE USA

The U.S. justification for its invasion of Iraq was based on claims that Saddam Hussein was an imminent threat who had connections with Osama bin Laden and weapons of mass destruction. Beginning in the summer of 2003, the major U.S. media began to raise serious questions about the intelligence upon which these claims were based and its sources. And while there were hints that defectors and intelligence provided by the controversial Ahmed Chalabi and his group, the Iraqi National Congress (INC), were suspect, Chalabi and the INC weren't fully exposed as U.S.-funded propagandists until 2004. Nonetheless, a large percentage of the U.S. public still believe the claims, based on INC fabrications, that sold the war.

The INC and Chalabi are no strangers to Washington. Funded first by the Central Intelligence Agency (CIA) in the post-Operation Desert Storm era, then by the State Department, and most recently by the Pentagon, the INC has received tens of millions of taxpayer dollars. The CIA and State Department came to distrust the organization. But top Defense Department officials—including Donald Rumsfeld, Paul Wolfowitz, and Douglas Feith—became strong supporters of Chalabi and INC information. "The Pentagon's critics are appalled that intelligence provided by the INC might shape U.S. decisions about going to war against Baghdad," *The American Prospect*'s Robert Dreyfuss wrote in December 2002. "At the CIA and at the State Department, Ahmed Chalabi, the INC's leader, is viewed as the ineffectual head of a self-inflated and corrupt organization skilled at lobbying and public relations, but not much else."

The INC *should* know all about PR. It was created in 1991 by the Rendon Group, a secretive Washington PR firm, as a covert CIA operation to foment the overthrow of Saddam Hussein. The Pentagon later hired the Rendon Group in the aftermath of 9/11 on a no-bid, $397,000 four-month contract, which was later optioned by the Joint Chiefs of Staff. The group has worked in places like Panama, the Balkans, and Haiti, and currently is working on government contracts in Afghanistan and Colombia. (For more on the Rendon Group, see *PR Watch*, 4th Quarter 2001, on <www.PRWatch.org> and "Rendon Group" on <www.Disinfopedia.org>).

"The [INC's] intelligence isn't reliable at all," said Vincent Cannistraro, a former senior CIA official and counterterrorism expert, quoted by Dreyfuss. "Much of it is propaganda. Much of it is telling the Defense Department what they want to hear. And much of it is used to support Chalabi's own presidential ambitions. They make no distinction between intelligence and propaganda, using alleged informants and defectors who say what Chalabi wants them to say, [creating] cooked information that goes right into presidential and vice presidential speeches." A classified study prepared by the National Intelligence Council in early 2003 found that only one of Chalabi's defectors could be considered credible, *The New Republic* reported in December 2003. A more recent investigation undertaken by the DIA found that practically all the intelligence provided by the INC was worthless.

Yet throughout 2003, the INC maintained its favor with the Pentagon and the White House. In late March, Chalabi and other INC members were flown by the military into Iraq and presented as an opposition group. Chalabi was chosen to be a member of the Iraqi Governing Council. Back in the U.S., the INC was receiving PR support from Burson-Marsteller (B-M, who had been working for the group since 1999 under a State Department contract. According to the PR trade publication *The Holmes Report*, B-M worked to "enhance the credibility" of the INC as it sought to "establish itself as a legitimate force in post invasion Iraq." B-M told reporters it was "helping the INC get out statements and videos that made clear that the exiled opposition was consolidating and moving."

Perhaps most stunning was the relationship Chalabi had with *The New York Times* reporter Judith Miller, who used sources and information provided by Chalabi in her stories on several occasions both in the lead up to war and during the occupation. In June 2003, the *Washington Post*'s Howard Kurtz wrote that Miller "played a highly unusual role in an army unit assigned to search for dangerous Iraqi weapons, according to U.S. military officials, prompting criticism that the unit was turned into what one official called a 'rogue operation.' More than a half-dozen military officers said that Miller acted as a middleman between the army unit with which she was embedded and Iraqi

National Congress leader Ahmed Chalabi, on one occasion accompanying army officers to Chalabi's headquarters, where they took custody of Saddam Hussein's son-in-law." Miller herself had known ties to the ideological neoconservatives who were close to Bush and with whom Chalabi was a favorite. According to William E. Jackson Jr., writing in *Editor & Publisher*, the *Times* editors knew that Miller thoroughly identified with the neocons and that she "had called for the overthrow of Saddam's regime in non-*Times* publications and had also spoken out before the war in public speeches for which she was paid." Despite this, Miller wrote front-page stories on Iraq and weapons of mass destruction and the *Times* editors have yet to acknowledge the conflict of interest.

In March 2004, Knight Ridder reported that the false INC intelligence fed to the U.S. intelligence agencies was also distributed to news outlets in the United States, Britain, and Australia. "A June 26, 2002, letter from the Iraqi National Congress to the Senate Appropriations Committee listed 108 articles based on information provided by the Iraqi National Congress's Information Collection Program, a U.S.-funded effort to collect intelligence in Iraq....The assertions in the articles reinforced President Bush's claims that Saddam Hussein should be ousted because he was in league with Osama bin Laden, was developing nuclear weapons and was hiding biological and chemical weapons," Knight Ridder reported.

The revelation of the INC letter to the Appropriations Committee prompted calls for a Congressional General Accounting Office probe into the INC's use of State Department money between 2001 and 2002. The issue under scrutiny is whether the INC violated its agreement with the State Department not to use U.S. funds for activities "associated with, or that could appear to be associated with, attempting to influence the policies of the United States government or Congress or propagandizing the American people."

3. THE PR BATTLE OF THE BULGE

As the expanding American waistline becomes a public health crisis, the food industry has turned to PR campaigns and lobbying to protect its interests. In July 2002, PR giant Golin/Harris (G/H), sensing a burgeoning PR need, distributed a news release about its new "Global Obesity Task Force." The task force didn't seek to fight childhood obesity; rather it offered to protect the interests and image of the multibillion-dollar food and entertainment industries. "The increase in childhood obesity has special interest and government groups seeking to hold someone responsible. And corporate America is the likely target," the release stated. G/H, whose clients include McDonald's and

Tyson Foods, offered its services to a wide ranges of "vulnerable" interests—including the "quick service restaurant companies, snack makers, beverage producers, [and] the television and video game industries"—that "need to act to protect their brands, businesses, and reputations."

The world's largest soft-drink manufacturer, Coca-Cola, was one of the first to jump into the obesity PR game. Under fire for paying school districts for exclusive vending machine contracts, Coke launched its "Step With It!" campaign, which promoted walking to middle school students by giving them pedometers and encouraging them to walk 10,000 steps a day. Coca-Cola also partnered with the American Academy of Pediatric Dentistry (AAPD). According to CorpWatch, the $1-million deal involves a research grant to the academy to "support important clinical, basic, and behavioral research" and "create public and professional educational programs, based on science, that promote improved dental health for children." The AAPD denied Coke would have any influence on the research. But the non-profit group Center for Science in the Public Interest wrote, "Regardless of what the money is used for, the grant will make the AAPD a captive of Coca-Cola, making it extremely unlikely that the AAPD will take positions antagonistic to the company, like opposing soft-drink machines in schools, or supporting labeling of the added-sugar content of foods."

Campaigns in 2003 by Kraft and McDonald's signaled a "new phase" in how the food industry was responding to the obesity crisis, *PR Week* commented. The industry initially tried to deflect the blame for America's growing waistlines by promoting physical activity. But seeking further protection from "lawsuits that would rival or surpass those brought against the tobacco industry," food companies started reworking products and marketing.

"Kraft Foods grabbed the PR high ground in the public debate about obesity and America's unhealthy eating habits by announcing a series of planned changes in how it will make and market its products," *PR Week* reported in July 2003. In September, McDonald's introduced its new "Go Active" meal, which included a salad, water, or soda, a pedometer, and an information booklet by Oprah Winfrey's personal trainer Bob Greene. McDonald's said the new meals were part of an "effort to exert leadership in another area of social responsibility. We feel it's our obligation to go out there and help change the discussion." The fast-food chain said the new salad line had been a hit with mothers of young children and expected the Oprah connection to continue to draw that group. McDonald's and Kraft's "healthier" products are more than lawsuit protection. They also allow companies to keep selling their products to the consumers who actually have decided to modify their eating habits.

While publicly attempting to appear responsible, the food industry is quietly and vigorously lobbying "against tax measures and labeling that would discourage consumption of high-fat foods," the *Wall Street Journal* reported. The industry has also effectively stopped the government from making recommendations about changing dietary guidelines. In June 2002, the Centers for Disease Control and Prevention (CDC) announced a $125 million advertising and PR campaign to encourage children to be more physically active. The VERB campaign, which was aimed at 9-to-13-year-olds, hired Publicis Group's Saatchi & Saatchi—which had also done marketing for several General Mills brands like Fruit Roll Ups and Go-Gurt—to create TV ads. CDC also sponsored TV shows on Nickelodeon and MTV to promote its "positive lifestyle" campaign. While getting kids to exercise is definitely important, *Advertising Age* reported that CDC specifically decided *not* to address another factor that contributes to childhood obesity: diet.

4. HOW NOW, MAD COW?

In May 2003, a Canadian cow tested positive for mad cow disease. In the years leading up to the discovery, public health activists had warned that mad cow disease was likely to emerge in North America if the U.S. and Canada continued to allow the feeding of slaughterhouse waste to livestock. England and other European nations had already banned the practice, but U.S. and Canadian regulators seemed unconcerned. Presented with proof of mad cow disease in North America, the U.S. Department of Agriculture (USDA) still refused to place any new regulations on the livestock industry. Instead, they reassured American consumers that U.S. beef was safe. The claim proved hollow, however, when a U.S. cow tested positive for mad cow disease in December 2003.

PR Week reported that PR staffers at the American Meat Institute (AMI) and the National Cattlemen's Beef Association (NCBA), working with PR giant Burson-Marsteller, handled a flood of media calls about mad cow disease over the Christmas holiday. The USDA held daily press briefings, which were followed by "technical briefings" for the press held by NCBA. "Key message points the industry was stressing revolved around the safety of the U.S. beef supply and the extent of efforts underway to track down how the disease reached U.S. shores," *PR Week* wrote.

But Paul Holmes, a longtime PR trade journalist, blasted the arrogance and stupidity of the U.S. beef industry and its protectors at USDA, over the emergence of mad cow disease in the U.S. Holmes wrote that "more than a decade has passed since an epidemic of bovine spongiform encephalopathy, better known as mad cow disease, ravaged British beef and dairy herds, so it's fair to say American cattlemen have had every opportunity to study that outbreak and learn from it. Yet to say the industry failed to learn would be an understatement. It's almost as if American cattlemen looked at the catastrophic events in the U.K. and decided to ignore every lesson while duplicating—and if possible exacerbating—every mistake."

Through the spring of 2004, government officials did little to assess the actual safety of U.S. beef by increasing testing of cattle for the disease. Instead, they continued to focus on the public's perception of beef safety. When Creekstone Farms, a specialty beef producer, attempted to get approval to test ever cow it processed at its Kansas slaughterhouse for the disease, the USDA opposed the action because of concern that Creekstone's testing would imply that other U.S. beef might not be safe. Creekstone wanted 100 percent testing in order to resume sales to Japan, South Korea and other countries banning U.S. beef; the inability to export was costing the company at least $40,000 a day and had forced it to lay off 50 employees, the *Christian Science Monitor* reported. Industry associations, including the AMI and NCBA, applauded the USDA, saying 100 percent testing is "not based on sound science."

5. THE SOUND OF PRO-INDUSTRY SCIENCE

"When George W. Bush and members of his administration talk about environmental policy, the phrase 'sound science' rarely goes unuttered," Chris Mooney wrote in the *Washington Post*. "On issues ranging from climate change to the storage of nuclear waste in Nevada's Yucca Mountain, our president has assured us that he's backing up his decisions with careful attention to the best available research....It all sounds noble enough, but the phrases 'sound science' and 'peer review' don't necessarily mean what you might think. Instead, they're part of a lexicon used to put a pro-science veneer on policies that most of the scientific community itself tends to be up in arms about."

The problem with the phrase "sound science" is that there is no meaningful definition of the concept. Tracking its use by industry and government agencies, one discovers "sound science" invariably refers to scientific data that supports industry's interests and government inaction. The popularity of the phrase points to a larger issues: the widespread manipulation of scientific research by industry to protect itself from regulations and culpability and industry-heavy influence on the political system. *The Observer* (U.K.) reported in January 2004 that the Bush administration criticized the World

Health Organization's strategy for fighting obesity, which includes limiting sugar consumption, for its lack of "sound science." The British paper wrote Bush and Republican senators have received hundreds of thousands of dollars in funding from "big sugar" and other food industry interests.

A leaked e-mail sent to the press secretaries of all Republican congressmen said, "From the heated debate on global warming to the hot air on forests, from the muddled talk on our nation's waters to the convolution on air pollution, we are fighting a battle of fact against fiction on the environment." According to *The Observer*, the e-mail—sent on February 4, 2004—based its assertions that "global warming is not a fact" and that other kinds of environmental degradation aren't really happening on claims by industry-supported scientists and organizations, including the Pacific Research Institute (a think tank that has received $130,000 from ExxonMobil since 1998), the discredited Danish statistician Bjorn Lomborg, and Richard Lindzen, a climate-skeptic scientist who has consistently taken money from the fossil fuel industry. "We wanted to show how the environment has been improving," Republican House Conference director Greg Cist, who sent the memo, told *The Observer*. "We wanted to provide the other side of the story."

6. WHITE HOUSE INFORMATION WARRIORS, PART II: THE WAR AT HOME

The White House's secrecy and manipulation of information is not limited to the Iraq War. During Bush's tenure, the administration's obsession with controlling information forced journalists to seek official information elsewhere. "Americans seeking to know what President Bush said in his phone conversation with Russian President Vladimir Putin . . . went to the obvious place: the Kremlin," the *Washington Post*'s Dana Milbank wrote. "It may come as a surprise to some that the Kremlin, symbol of secrecy and repression, has become more transparent that the White House, symbol of freedom and democracy." Milbank noted that the White House has also refused to confirm meetings with foreign dignitaries, domestic trips, overseas diplomatic appointments, and T-ball games announced by others.

In the area of scientific research, the White House systematically distorted scientific data and reports in order to support their corporate-friendly policies. In June 2003, *The New York Times* reported that the White House had altered a draft report by the Environmental Protection Agency (EPA) on the state of the environment. "The editing eliminated references to many studies concluding that warming is at least partly caused by rising concentrations of smokestack and tail-pipe emissions and could threaten health and ecosystems," the *Times* wrote. "Among the deletions were conclusions about the likely human contribution to warming from a 2001 report on climate by the National Research Council that the White House had commissioned and that President Bush had endorsed in speeches that year. White House officials also deleted a reference to a 1999 study showing that global temperatures had risen sharply in the previous decade compared with the last 1,000 years. In its place, administration officials added a reference to a new study, partly financed by the [industry-funded] American Petroleum Institute, questioning that conclusion."

In February 2004, more than 60 influential scientists, including 20 Nobel laureates, joined with the Union of Concerned Scientists, accusing the administration of "repeatedly censoring and suppressing reports by its own scientists, stacking advisory committees with unqualified political appointees, disbanding government panels that provide unwanted advice and refusing to seek any independent scientific expertise in some cases," *The New York Times* wrote.

7. SHH . . . WE'RE OFFSHORING

2003 was not a great year to look for work in the United States. "U.S. corporations are picking up the pace in shifting well-paid technology jobs to India, China and other low-cost centers, but they are keeping quiet for fear of a backlash," Reuters reported in December 2003. "Analysts predict as many as 2 million U.S. white-collar jobs such as programmers, software engineers and applications designers will shift to low cost centers by 2014." The continuing trend of moving jobs overseas, where labor costs are cheaper, is euphemistically called "offshoring." But the companies laying off or passing over U.S. workers—including Microsoft, IBM, AT&T, Walt Disney, CNN, and Fox News—aren't talking about it publicly. One analysis said, "Nobody has come up with a way to spin it in a positive way."

Sternly disapproving of the media's coverage of U.S. jobs loss, *PR Week* wrote, "The fact that offshoring is a complex matter doesn't mean the media has treated it with a sober approach. The body of accurate reporting on the often intricate economic motivations for moving jobs abroad is dwarfed by the more emotional, even sensational, reporting on the effects of offshoring on American workers."

Industry-funded front groups, however, have sprouted up to "defend the outsourcing of jobs." The *Wall Street Journal* reported in March 2004 that the U.S. Chamber of Commerce, the National Association of Manufacturers, and the Information Technology Association of America have formed the Coalition for Economic Growth and American Jobs. Contrary to its name, the coalition "is quietly mounting an offensive against state and federal efforts to keep jobs at home and otherwise restrain globalization." An election year focus on jobs and the recent outsourcing of white-collar positions have led to some 80 anti-outsourcing bills being introduced in 30 states.

Meanwhile in Congress, Republicans tout "insourcing," or foreign companies hiring U.S. citizens. "You can't get upset about outsourcing without considering the benefits of insourcing," said the director of the Organization for International Investment, the trade group that coined the term "insourcing" and that represents the U.S. subsidiaries of large international companies like Toyota, Nestle, and Siemens.

8. NUKES ARE ON THE RISE

Nuclear energy is back, billing itself as a way to decrease U.S. dependency on foreign oil *and* as a source of energy that does not generate greenhouse gases. The American Nuclear Society, European Nuclear Society and industry front group the Nuclear Energy Institute commemorated the fiftieth anniversary of Dwight Eisenhower's "Atoms for Peace" speech at their 2003 joint meeting and held a special session on "Atoms for Prosperity: Updating Eisenhower's Global Vision for Nuclear Energy." PR trade newsletter *The Holmes Report* credited good public relations as part of the industry's comeback, noting that ongoing campaigns in Washington, DC, have been very successful in winning the support of opinion leaders. In fact, the nuclear industry feels so much support that two consortiums applied for licenses to build the first new commercial nuclear power plants in decades. The applications are an integral part of the Bush Administration's "Nuclear Power 2010" program, a public/private partnership to "deploy" new plants "in the 2010 timeframe."

On the state and local level, grassroots groups with little money find themselves in a "David-and-Goliath-style public relations war" with the nuclear industry. In February 2003, the *Brattleboro Reformer* reported that Nuclear Free Vermont, a small group of volunteers wanting to shut down a nuclear power plant near Brattleboro, had about $2,000 to spend on distributing anti-nuclear power 'Vote Yes' yard signs, mailing literature, and airing a handful of radio ads. But the industry-funded Coalition Against Shutting Down Vermont's Electricity Options engaged in "a $200,000 public relations blitz that includes mass mailings, newspaper ads, and 'Vote No' radio ads featuring the voice of a former Vermont governor," the *Reformer* reported.

In April 2004, University of Texas professor Sheldon Landsberger has admitted that a pro-nuclear column he submitted under his own name to the *Austin American-Statesman* was actually written by the Potomac Communications Group, a Washington PR firm that works for the nuclear power industry. "For at least 25 years," the *Austin Chronicle* reported, an employee of Oak Ridge National Laboratory in Tennessee named Theodore M. Besmann has moonlighted for Potomac Communications, penning "nuclear love songs in newspapers across the country, under his own or others' names."

9. THE REGULATORY REVOLVING DOOR

Government agencies became increasingly ineffective, as the revolving door in Washington between regulatory agencies and the industries they regulate spun even more rapidly and brazenly. "Two top Environmental Protection Agency officials who were deeply involved in easing an air pollution rule for old power plants just took private-sector jobs with firms that benefit from the changes," Knight Ridder's Seth Boronstein reported in September 2003. "Days after the changes in the power-plant pollution rule were announced last week, John Pemberton, the chief of staff in the EPA's air and radiation office, told colleagues he would be joining Southern Co., an Atlanta-based utility that's the nation's No. 2 power-plant polluter and was a driving force in lobbying for the rule changes. Southern Co., which gave more than $3.4 million in political contributions over the past four years while it sought the changes, hired Pemberton as director of federal affairs." Ed Krenik, associate administrator for congressional affairs, left EPA to joined Bracewell & Patterson, a top Houston-based law firm that coordinated lobbying for several utilities on easing the power-plant pollution rule and houses the Electric Reliability Coordinating Council, which advocated for rule changes the EPA just enacted.

The door, of course, revolves both ways. A current EPA air and radiation administrator, Jeffrey Holmstead, previously worked as a lawyer and lobbyist for chemical companies and industry groups seeking looser pollution standards. And the man in charge of the White House's Council on Environmental Quality, James Connaughton, prior to his June 2001 appointment, earned his living as a lawyer defending asbestos companies and other industrial polluters. Connaughton and his staff were responsible for the EPA's failure to properly inform New Yorkers of the dangers of the fallout from the collapse of the World Trade Center towers according to a report by the EPA's inspector general released in August 2003.

10. ALL ROADS LEAD TO PHRMA

"When the House voted [in July 2003] to let Americans import less expensive medicines from Canada and Europe, 53 Senators signed a letter opposing the legislation, a letter that the industry trade group, which vigorously opposed the measure, hailed as proof of its argument that the bill would jeopardize patient safety," *The New York Times* reported. "What the trade group, the Pharmaceutical Research and Manufacturers Association [PhRMA], did not say, at the time, was that it helped coordinate the signature campaign… The trade group's involvement in gathering signatures, detailed in a document obtained by the *Times*, is not a surprise. It offers a glimpse into the aggressive efforts by the pharmaceutical manufacturers to defeat the import provision." PhRMA's lobbying activities have begun to anger many lawmakers, according to the *Times*. "This is a multiarmed octopus we're dealing with," said Representative Gil Gutknecht, the Minnesota Republican who is the chief sponsor of the measure. "All roads lead to PhRMA."

PhRMA is one of the largest and most influential organizations in Washington, lobbying on Medicare and other drug company-related issues. Representing 48 pharmaceutical companies, PhRMA funded several pro-industry Astroturf organizations to promote its interests, including the United Seniors Association and Citizens for Better Medicare. The trade group has also spent over $1 million dollars to change the Canadian health-care system and eliminate subsidized prescription drug prices in Canada.

The millions of dollars spent by PhRMA and other trade associations to win legislative battles—as well as the campaign to sell the Iraq war and the reassurances that U.S. beef is safe to eat and nuclear power is clean—serve the agendas and interests of the few, while exposing the public to greater risk. Instead of advancing a government by, for and of the people, these kinds of propagandistic campaigns are corroding our democracy.

Laura Miller is managing editor of *PR Watch*, a publication of the Center for Media and Democracy. For 10 years, *PR Watch* has investigated and exposed manipulative and deceptive PR and propaganda campaigns. For more information, go to <www.prwatch.org>.

THIS MODERN WORLD

by TOM TOMORROW

GOSH--I **WANT** TO SUSTAIN MY UNQUESTIONING SUPPORT FOR THE WAR--

--BUT THE NEWS FROM IRAQ IS **SO** DEPRESSING!

DON'T **DESPAIR**, CITIZENS!

WHY, IT'S SPARKY--THE **REPUBLICAN PENGUIN!** SPARKY--HOW CAN WE STAY **UPBEAT** WHEN THINGS ARE GOING SO **BADLY?**

EASY! BLAME EVERYTHING ON THE PEOPLE WHO **TELL** YOU THAT THINGS ARE GOING BADLY!

FOR INSTANCE--WHOSE FAULT DO **YOU** THINK IT IS THAT THE ABU GHRAIB TORTURE PHOTOS HAVE INFLAMED ANTI-AMERICAN SENTIMENT WORLDWIDE?

UH--THE **TORTURERS?**

THEIR **COMMANDERS?**

WRONG!! IT'S THE **NEWS MEDIA'S** FAULT--FOR **PUBLISHING** THOSE PHOTOS!

I **SEE!** SO WE SHOULDN'T BLAME THE CHAOS IN IRAQ ON THE **ADMINISTRATION**--BUT RATHER, ON THE MEDIA WHICH **REPORT** THE CHAOS!

EXACTLY! IF THEY DIDN'T **TELL** US-- WE'D NEVER **KNOW!**

AND A FEW YEARS FROM NOW, WHEN WE'RE TRYING TO FIGURE OUT WHO'S RESPONSIBLE FOR OUR HUMILIATING **DEFEAT**--RATHER THAN POINTING THE FINGER AT DONALD **RUMSFELD**, OR CONDI **RICE**, OR PAUL **WOLFOWITZ**--?

OH--**I** KNOW--

--WE'LL BLAME IT ALL ON **MICHAEL MOORE!!**

AND THE **ANTI-WAR PROTESTERS!!**

MY WORK HERE IS DONE.

TOM TOMORROW©2004... www.thismodernworld.com

CHAPTER 8

FAIR's Fourth Annual "Fear & Favor" Report—2003

MORE EXAMPLES OF MEDIA'S VULNERABILITY TO POWER
BY PETER HART AND JULIE HOLLAR

It's no secret that advertisers, media owners, and powerful political figures pressure journalists to ignore critical stories or sing the praises of a corporate pet project. With diminished journalistic resources available due to corporate cost cutting in the media industry, news outlets often put commercial or political priorities ahead of journalistic ones.

Each year, Fairness and Accuracy in Reporting (FAIR) puts together a collection of specific incidents of interference, in order to provide real-world illustration of the pressures on working journalists and to encourage the exposure of such efforts to muzzle journalists and shape media coverage. This report is nowhere near an exhaustive recounting of all such abuses in the past year, but it does illuminate some of the critical threats facing independent journalism.

IN ADVERTISERS WE TRUST

In commercial media, advertisers have enormous influence over what appears in print or over the airwaves. Advertisers pay the bills—that's a lesson publishers and other media decision makers know all too well.

When war with Iraq began to seem imminent, media companies fretted over how to "serve" their advertisers, who worried that news about death and battle wouldn't put their consumers in a shopping mood. *U.S. News & World Report's* solution, as reported by *MediaWeek* (February 24, 2003): If the U.S. went to war, the magazine would "create a new war-free zone in which buyers can be assured their ads are next to less traumatic fare, including stories on health, science, business, and culture." The section, called "Second Front," soon appeared, giving the magazine a safe place to sell products amidst commercially friendly content.

That urge to please advertisers with news content is pervasive in commercial media. But several cases in 2003 went beyond suppressing or even altering stories at an advertiser's behest: At some outlets, the news itself was simply put up for sale.

➤ "Synergy was on display on *CNN Headline News* last night, big time," wrote Frank Barnako of CBS's <MarketWatch.com> (May 9, 2003). Barnako watched a segment about last minute Mother's Day gifts reported by someone with a peculiar on-screen identification: "Regina Lewis, AOL." As Barnako put it, "instead of reporting, Lewis shilled for AOL advertisers on the company's news outlet." The gift ideas all came, coincidentally, courtesy of prominent AOL advertisers like 1-800-Flowers and <Diamond.com>. Corporations looking to advertise with AOL must value the free exposure: paid ads on the AOL Internet service *and* free plugs on the cable channel it owns.

➤ When AOL purchased $15 million in advertising from Viacom's Infinity Radio, it received quite a bit more. According to internal memos obtained by Detroit's *Metro Times* (June 11, 2003), the deal required newscasters at Infinity stations to promote AOL's broadband Internet service on the air. The casual mentions were not supposed to sound like ads; as a memo to the staff of Infinity's WWJ put it, "You are being asked to use AOL for broadband every day while you are on the air and make reference to the interesting content you find there."

According to *Metro Times*, the station's on-air hosts were expected to log six AOL mentions every day. A follow-up in *Advertising Age* (June 16, 2003) found that other Infinity stations in St. Louis and Chicago were also part of the promotional arrangement.

The WWJ memo included this bizarre guidance: "While AOL would LOVE us to be 'evangelists' for their product, do stay close to your comfort zone when it comes to promoting material. Don't do anything that makes you feel queasy from an ethical standpoint." (There was no word on what radio hosts should do if the whole idea of disguising advertising as news content made them queasy.) Another memo cited by *Metro Times*, from WWJ operations manager Georgeann Herbert, had a quite different tone: "Don't forget those AOL-for-Broadband mentions! And no . . . saying something is 'sponsored by AOL-for-Broadband' doesn't satisfy the requirement."

Once the *Metro Times* (June 11, 2003) began investigating the story, the station indicated that its news division was not going to play along and plug the Internet service. Other Infinity stations seemed to agree: "We'll protect the integrity of WBZ," said one station official in Boston (*Boston Globe*, June 16, 2003), where the spots would run apart from the news programming.

➤ The Pioneer Press, a division of Hollinger International, publishes dozens of papers in the suburbs of Chicago. But the newspaper company made news outside the area in August when veteran arts and entertainment editor Virginia Gerst abruptly resigned from the company.

The trouble started on May 8, when Gerst's section ran a critical review of a restaurant that happened to be an advertiser. Her superiors weren't happy; in Gerst's words, she was reminded that the Press was "not in the business of bashing business" (*Chicago Reader*, September 5, 2003). Weeks later, Gerst was handed a new review of the same restaurant; this one was decidedly more upbeat, written not by a normal news staffer but by someone in the Pioneer Press marketing division.

➤ The NBC-TV affiliate WLBT in Jackson, Mississippi, announced the sale of two-and-a-half-minute news segments for a "weekly investment of $500." WLBT station manager Dan Modisett told the *Washington Post* (November 3, 2003) that the station was abandoning the program—not because it was unethical, but because "it was too much effort for really not enough financial gain." A month earlier (October 16, 2003), the *Post* reported that another NBC affiliate—WFLA in Tampa, Florida—was charging for segments on its morning show, which is technically not part of the news division.

Such distinctions are often obscure to news audiences. As *Editor & Publisher* noted (November 19, 2003), "custom publishing" allows newspapers to print special sections that cater to certain advertisers. According to an editor at the Gannett-owned *Des Moines Register*, "the sections sell advertising to local businesses and create stories by their own staff writers, often primarily using advertisers as prime sources, with some stories running next to the source's ad." An unusual arrangement that can also be a deceptive one, since *Editor & Publisher* found that "a number of the *Register*'s special sections, however, have had nothing that explicitly identified them as an advertising product. A line at the top of the front page simply reads: 'A *Des Moines Register* Custom Publication.'"

➤ A Florida company called WJMK exploits the blurring of news and commerce by producing "news breaks" that appear on public television stations (*The New York Times*, May 7, 2003). The segments have been hosted by prominent journalists like CNN anchor Aaron Brown and former CBS anchor Walter Cronkite—who failed to tell viewers that WJMK is producing these "news" spots on behalf of healthcare companies.

According to the *Times*, the hosts "provide a general introduction to segments that profile health care companies or their products. According to WJMK documents, the companies pay WJMK about $15,000 in connection with the segments and other services and are allowed to edit and approve the videos, which are two to five minutes long."

Some of the segments are presented under the title "The American Medical Review," and a WJMK official told the *Times* that 30 million households see each one, thanks to public TV. While some stations were careful to steer clear of the promotional tapes, others told the *Times* that they were content to air the segments because they were free. The *Times* also noted that "the videos do not mention that the companies paid WJMK to produce them—which may violate federal communications law."

After this arrangement garnered some media attention, some of the journalists involved suddenly had second thoughts. Cronkite and Brown ended their relationships with WJMK in May (*The New York Times*, May 9, 2003).

➤ The "public affairs programming" heard by millions of passengers on airlines like American, United, Delta, and Northwest is produced by a company called Sky Radio. The programming appears just after a block of straight news from NPR and other outlets. But the nature of Sky Radio's programming was revealed (*The New York Times*, October 27, 2003) when producers called up Joanne Doroshow, executive director of the Center for Justice and Democracy, and asked if she would discuss tort reform on a "talk show." When she said yes, she was told it would cost her $5,900.

Paying a fee to be interviewed should be no big deal, explained Sky Radio producers: Announcers disclose every now and again that guests "may have paid a fee," and besides, they charge *everyone*—whether they represent British Petroleum or McDonald's. In order to be interviewed without paying, said Sky founder Marc Holland, "You have to be a president. You have to be a secretary of state. You'd have to be huge. Or you'd have to have influence with us. It's a gift." So next time you're listening to what sounds like a news interview on airline radio—just think, for several thousand dollars, that could be you.

THE BOSS'S BUSINESS

Some reporters at the *New York Post* are said to refer to page 2 of the paper as the "Pravda page"—"reserved for news of owner Rupert Murdoch's business and political interests" (*Washington Report on Middle East Affairs,* June 2003). While Murdoch may be a particularly "hands-on" media mogul, he's far from the only owner who has discovered how useful a media outlet can be in promoting one's own personal interests.

➤ The 2003 deregulation by the Federal Communications Commission (FCC)—which offered big media companies even bigger shares of the public airwaves and invited newspaper and television companies to merge—was one of the biggest industry-related stories of the year. But reporting a story with their own industry as its subject created some tension in corporate media.

Newspapers owned by companies looking to cash in on the FCC decision—like the *Los Angeles Times* (May 16, 2003) and the *Chicago Tribune* (March 9, 2003), both owned by Tribune Co.—editorialized in favor of relaxing the restrictions on their owner. Perhaps it's too much to ask that a news outlet's editorial positions be independent of owner interests, but what about the influence of those interests on what those outlets consider to be news?

The Arizona Republic is owned by Gannett, which also owns a TV station in Phoenix that it will have to sell if the FCC doesn't change the rules about TV/newspaper cross-ownership. When FCC Commissioner Michael Copps came to Arizona to host a public forum about these changes, *The Republic* didn't find the event worth mentioning to its readers. As the rival *East Valley Tribune* (April 10, 2003) put it, "Supporters of the rule change say that the integrity of news coverage would not be harmed by the rule change. Some even suggest the combined resources of a broadcast station and a newspaper would lead to better coverage. What does the absence of forum coverage in *The Arizona Republic* tell you?"

➤ As the lines between news and advertising grow increasingly blurry, so crumbles the wall between media companies' entertainment and news divisions. Last year saw a number of instances where news outlets were able to offer significant "extras" to pop stars in order to secure exclusive interviews.

Pop singer Britney Spears, for example, was set to do an interview with NBC, until ABC came along and reportedly promised a prime-time special, in addition to coverage on the network's news programs (*New York Post,* August 18, 2003).

This conforms to what one report suggested was a new push by ABC to secure more high-profile interviews by dangling extra promotional goodies. According to *New York* magazine (July 28, 2003), "the news division has teamed with *Entertainment Tonight* [ET] to offer celebrities *ET* coverage if they agree to do exclusive sit-downs on *Good Morning America, 20/20,* or *Primetime."*

➤ *The New York Times* reported (January 21, 2004) that last year the network offered representatives of singer Michael Jackson a remarkable deal: The network would pre-empt a one-hour *Dateline* program critical of the pop star that was set to air in February if Jackson would sit down for an interview and allow NBC access to some of his video tapes.

In an e-mail published in the *Times*, NBC executive Marc Graboff offered $5 million for "exclusive rights to the footage and the interview," and assured the Jackson camp that the deal would "have the added benefit of pre-empting NBC's planned broadcast of the one-hour *Dateline* scheduled for February 17." The only detail that is in doubt is whether NBC was agreeing to permanently cancel the show or simply postpone it for airing at a later date. NBC says it was only agreeing to postpone the show, but Jackson reps say the network was promising to kill the show altogether. When the $5 million deal fell through and Fox got the exclusive, *Dateline*, as if in retaliation, aired an extended, two-hour show critical of Jackson, labeled "Michael Jackson Unmasked."

➤ Florida's *St. Petersburg Times* took a keen interest in an important civic debate: a referendum on whether a local airport would be kept intact or turned into a waterfront park development. According to the area's alternative paper, the *Weekly Planet* (October 30, 2003), the *Times* editorially backed the development project without mentioning that the *Times'* corporate parent, the Poynter Institute, would likely benefit from the project. As the *Planet* pointed out, the Poynter Institute owns much of the land near the proposed development—land that would presumably increase in value if the waterfront project was approved by voters. Journalistic notions of disclosure would seem to require the paper to reveal its interest. But Poynter president Karen Brown Dunlap doesn't seem to think so, telling the *Planet:* "We own the *Times* and they have an obligation to report about us. Is this a story in itself? I don't think so. Is there a specific story about how [the airport issue] affects Poynter? Maybe a little one."

According to a survey by *Planet* reporter Jim Harper, the paper's news coverage was skewed in the same direction as its editorial position. Harper notes that between April and September 2003, "the *Times* published seven news stories about the petition drive to close the airport and turn half of it into a public park. Admiring in tone, the stories emphasized the underdog nature of the campaign, often focusing on the idealistic young people who were gathering the signatures." And the other side? "During the same period," writes Harper, "the *Times* published just two stories about residents who want to see the airport appreciated for what it is: a unique asset in a city already blessed with abundant waterfront parks."

➤ It's not unusual for newspapers to ignore or downplay citizen protests. But what about when the protest reaches the newsroom—literally? That's what happened on November 6, when a labor rally ended up inside the newsroom of *The Providence Journal.* The rally was intended to pressure the paper's management to resume negotiations with the Newspaper Guild, after a contract offer was rejected in June. The demonstrators, many from the Communications Workers of America, started outside *The Journal's* building, according to an account in *The Providence Phoenix* (November 14, 2003), before some demonstrators made their way into *The Journal's* newsroom, to the astonishment of many of the paper's staffers.

The Phoenix also pointed out that there was one place you weren't able to read about the protest: *The Providence Journal,* which failed to include any mention of the labor action. *Phoenix* reporter Ian Donnis wasn't surprised: "In the almost four years that members of the Providence Newspaper Guild, which represents more than 400 workers at *The Journal,* have been working without a contract, the *ProJo* has barely covered the ongoing union-management fight." That's not to say the paper is reticent about reporting on its corporate parent, the Dallas-based Belo Corporation; Donnis told *The Phoenix* that the paper occasionally "puts a corporate-friendly spin on the news—using a photo of Belo CEO Robert Decherd, for example, to illustrate an October 30 business-front story on a rebound in media advertising."

POWERFUL PLAYERS AND PR

While advertisers and media owners have direct means of influencing coverage, they're certainly not the only ones. Powerful institutions can find ways to shape coverage to suit corporate or other agendas—sometimes thanks to the willing participation of journalists who should know to avoid such conflicts of interest.

➤ The *San Francisco Chronicle* (February 23, 2003) reported that local KTVU news anchor Ross McGowan had more than time invested in then–city supervisor Gavin Newsom, whom he interviewed 84 times over five years on the Fox affiliate's *Mornings on Two* show. McGowan also had $25,000 in a business partnership with Newsom, who owns several restaurants, bars, and wine shops in the Bay Area. McGowan maintained that the business relationship didn't affect his coverage of Newsom, who chatted on the air with McGowan about a wide range of both political and personal fare, including his controversial "Care Not Cash" homeless reform program and his mayoral campaign, which he eventually won in a close runoff election. "If Gavin was doing something that needed the tough questions, I like to think I'd ask him," McGowan said. Under pressure from his editor, McGowan sold his stake in the partnership days after the story broke (*American Journalism Review*, June/July 2003).

➤ Joe Scarborough, host of MSNBC's *Scarborough Country*, brought attorney Mike Papantonio on his August 29 show to expose the "Rat of the Week"—a company called Osmose whose arsenic-treated wood was used in playground equipment. Papantonio, a frequent guest on *Scarborough Country*, accused Osmose of having "figured out how to poison our children and make a profit in the meantime." Scarborough encouraged viewers to contact the EPA and demand an immediate recall of the wood in question, which the agency had scheduled to be phased out of production by January 2004.

What Scarborough neglected to mention was not only that Papantonio was his law partner, but that their firm had filed a lawsuit against Osmose. Ostensibly to balance things out, Scarborough invited Osmose representative Jim Hale on the show (September 9, 2003) to give his side of the story. When Hale pointed out Scarborough's connection to both Papantonio and the Osmose lawsuit, Scarborough responded, "It may be shocking to you that Papantonio is my friend and law partner, but our audience has heard that a thousand times"—and immediately changed the subject away from the Osmose suit. On a later show (September 12, 2003), he admitted that he was a shareholder in the firm and received a fixed stipend, which he eventually agreed to give up. Scarborough told viewers, "GE and NBC bend over backwards to preach and enforce integrity of their employees and our actions."

➤ *U.S. News & World Report's* May 12 cover featured a picture of a military jet pilot performing a "Top Gun"–style stunt. The photo illustrated "A Day in the Life of the Military"—which was not so much a cover story as an eight-page photo spread taken from the book *A Day in the Life of the United States Armed Forces*. If readers thought it looked like a commercial for the Pentagon, they were close—at the very bottom of the second page of the spread, in white-on-gray lettering in the tiniest type imaginable, one could find, buried between the publisher and the copyright information, the phrase "The project underwriter is the Boeing Co." That's right: *U.S. News* published eight pages on the military that was sponsored by the nation's second-largest military contractor—a company that makes, among other things, Navy jets like the one the pilot is flying on the cover of the magazine. Apparently a nearly invisible explanation is what passes for disclosure at *U.S. News*.

➤ The New York *Daily News* reported (December 18, 2003) that "Toy Guy" Christopher Byrne, who for years has been interviewed about toy recommendations by news outlets around the country, is more than just a "toy expert" and the editor of a toy industry trade publication. As a paid representative of Litsky Public Relations, Byrne commands $5,000 to $15,000 per product mention in a broadcast interview. "I have credibility," said Byrne. "I won't take a toy on TV that I haven't played with, with kids." You'd also be hard pressed to find Byrne on TV with a toy he hasn't been paid to plug. Byrne acknowledged that in most of his interviews, he only mentions toys made by companies that pay him.

➤ On Sacramento's KXTV, popular news anchor Cristina Mendonsa could frequently be seen narrating a recurring spot that highlighted the off-court achievements of Sacramento's WNBA team, the Monarchs. Only the news anchor wasn't filing a standard news report: The segment was a promotional piece that ended by urging the audience to "come be a part of the 2003 Monarchs season" and displaying a phone number to call.

The *Sacramento Bee* reported (February 27, 2003) that KXTV's marketing staff wrote the promo, which the ABC affiliate says the Monarchs didn't pay for. KXTV had recently signed a three-year deal with Maloof Sports, owner of both the Monarchs and the Sacramento Kings. "We want to be a good partner," KXTV news director Ron Comings explains. "If it appears we're getting a little too close to the commercial side, we're probably okay with that."

GOVERNMENT AND OTHER "OFFICIAL" PRESSURE

Reporters are normally wary of the appearance of government interference in the news—such influence is probably what most people think of when they hear the term "censorship." But that's not to say that journalists always steer clear of such conflicts.

➤ The *Denver Post* (January 13, 2003) seemed to think that disclosing its special interview deal with an outgoing sheriff preempted any ethical questions. In an article on Jefferson County Sheriff John Stone just before he left office, *Post* reporter Kieran Nicholson noted that Stone "consented to be interviewed for this story only if his critics were not contacted." Stone certainly has critics, as the article itself pointed out: The Columbine shootings happened in Jefferson County on his watch, and he has been accused of withholding information related to the incident. But, said *Post* editor Greg Moore (*Westword*, January 23, 2003), "We wanted to close the book on his tenure from his perspective." No doubt that's what Stone wanted as well.

➤ The *Eastside Journal* in Bellevue, Washington took cutting deals with the sheriff's office a step further and actually ran a false story at the office's request. On March 23, 2002, the paper (now the *King County Journal*) ran a seven-sentence report about a "suspicious" house fire that had taken place the day before. The article pleased King County inmate Steven Sherer, who officials say had offered a former cellmate $17,000 to burn down the house while its occupants were at home. Sherer mailed his accomplice directions to the location of his reward—evidence that was used to bring charges against Sherer.

The problem with the arson story, as the paper revealed a year later (April 17, 2003), is that it never happened. Tipped off about Sherer's plan, investigators staged the arson in order to produce the evidence they needed for their case. The paper, notified in advance by officials that Sherer wanted a newspaper clipping as proof that the arson had been carried out, agreed to cooperate by publishing the phony story. "Journalistically, we'll probably take some heat for it, but we have a responsibility to the community and that weighed heavily in our decision," said *Journal* editor Tom Wolfe (*Seattle Times*, April 18, 2003). As the newspaper took on the responsibility of protecting the community from criminals, it was left to the prosecutor's office to take on the responsibility of championing journalistic integrity: "We would not have authorized it if we'd known," said chief of staff Dan Satterberg (*Seattle Post-Intelligencer*, April 25, 2003). "It was not sensitive to the institutional role of the press. It just wasn't appropriate. We don't want the public to think we've changed the rules in our office."

➤ When the Hawaii Visitors and Convention Bureau sent Governor Linda Lingle to Japan to drum up tourism, they wanted news coverage back home. A trip to Japan can be expensive, but ABC affiliate KITV was happy to comply—because the government picked up the tab. The governor's press secretary, Russell Pang, said the idea came from the station: "KITV called us originally," Pang said. Speculation arose that the trip was KITV's reward for airing a 17-minute speech by the governor the previous week, a speech three other local TV news stations rejected, "judging it political rather than public service in nature" *(Honolulu Advertiser,* July 10, 2003).

KITV agreed to pay its own way after Democratic lawmakers pointed out that accepting taxpayer money for television coverage of the governor raised ethical questions for both the station and the government. "We don't think there's a conflict of interest, but the perception of a conflict of interest is something we can't live with," station manager Mike Rosenberg said. At the same time, Rosenberg acknowledged, "Had we considered going on this trip originally, knowing the cost involved, I'm not sure [we would have gone]" (Associated Press, July 10, 2003).

Apparently, KITV was not the first station to cozy up to the Hawaiian government: The *Advertiser* (October 26, 2003) reported that the Maui Visitor's Bureau had paid KGMB-TV to fly to New York to cover Maui's float in the Macy's Thanksgiving Day Parade. The former director of the MVB who oversaw the deal now serves as Governor Lingle's tourism czar.

➤ Reporting for a paper while serving as an elected official is generally considered to be inappropriate. But *Bar Harbor Times* staff writer Carrie Ciciotte's position as city council member for the town of Ellsworth didn't trouble the owners of the paper. In fact, Courier Publications decided that her "close ties to Ellsworth"—a small town near Bar Harbor, Maine—made her the ideal candidate to take over as associate editor of Courier's *Ellsworth Weekly,* and she was offered that position with over a year remaining in her three-year council term (*Bangor Daily News,* July 26, 2003). Fortunately, two weeks after accepting the *Ellsworth Weekly* job, Ciciotte announced her resignation from the council to "avoid an appearance of a conflict of interest." "I was concerned about a perception of bias," Ciciotte said. "I couldn't rationalize being both."

OP-ED'S ODD ETHICS

Readers expect opinion columnists to express a strong point of view. But what if those views are colored by a financial benefit or other personal interests? At a few major U.S. papers, readers were left to find out such information long after the fact.

➤ On May 28, *USA Today* ran a column in which former Republican Senator Alan Simpson argued that the major airlines and their Web site Orbitz are trying to "tilt the playing field" and squeeze out competitors in the online airline reservation market. Simpson called on the White House and the Senate to "stand up for independent businesses and consumers." What the column failed to note was that Simpson got paid by one of those independent businesses to put his name on the piece.

Roll Call (June 5, 2003) reported that Simpson was negotiating a lobbying contract with one of Orbitz's leading competitors, Galileo International, which paid Simpson to sign his name to the ghostwritten column. When *USA Today* asked its usual question about financial ties, Ernest Baynard, the lobbyist responsible for placing the op-ed, told them twice that Simpson had no financial stake in the issue.

Simpson, who said he's been paid for signing ghost-written op-eds numerous times, claimed he'd never spoken to either Baynard or anyone at *USA Today* and that his freelance contract didn't ask about financial interests. "I didn't know a goddamn thing about *USA Today*," he said. "I got paid for doing the op-ed piece. I did not know where it was going to go. I received the money and went back to bed." Baynard has been relieved of his post; *USA Today* has changed its freelance contract to ask op-ed writers directly about financial interests (*Roll Call*, June 12, 2003).

➤ The *Wall Street Journal* published an op-ed on August 14 co-authored by Richard Perle, a member (and former chair) of the Pentagon's Defense Policy Board, supporting a hotly contested $18 billion Pentagon plan to lease 100 tanker aircraft from Boeing. "It takes a special government green-eye-shade mentality to miss the urgency of the tanker requirement," the op-ed writers declared, identified below the piece as "resident fellows at the American Enterprise Institute."

Four months later, the *Financial Times* (December 4, 2003) reported that Boeing had committed to invest $20 million in Perle's venture capital firm, Trireme, in April 2002. Though Perle denied receiving compensation from Boeing for the op-ed, readers might have been interested in the fact that the company was putting millions into his business.

➤ On November 4, *The New York Times* published an op-ed by Mark Medish headlined "Make Baghdad Pay." The author argued that Iraq's tens of billions of dollars of debt should not be cancelled. Calls for relief are "misguided," according to Medish, who wrote that Iraq "should be expected to be able to pay its obligations."

That idea isn't exactly remarkable, but it's worth knowing more about the author pushing it. Medish, according to the bio at the bottom of the piece, "was deputy assistant secretary of the treasury from 1997 to 2000." But when he wrote a similar op-ed for the *Washington Post* on October 19, they added this helpful background: Medish "represents international corporate creditors of Iraq"—in other words, the banks and corporations that want Iraq to pay up. Days later, the *Times* (November 6, 2003) published a note regarding the omission. But that wasn't all; as *Slate*'s Eric Umansky wrote (November 5, 2003), "Medish wrote an op-ed last year for the *Financial Times* arguing that Russia's old debt should be…yes, forgiven."

DISSENT UNWELCOME IN WARTIME

The major story of 2003 was the U.S.-led invasion and occupation of Iraq. The independence of journalism in times of war is almost always compromised by government pressure in one form or another; during the early stages of the invasion, the Pentagon's embedding process served to restrict and color mainstream reporting of the conflict.

But overt government pressure is not the only force acting on the media. Some outlets were prone to acts of self-censorship and the stifling of dissent— decisions made by owners or those with some degree of editorial authority. The February 2003 cancellation of Phil Donahue's MSNBC talk show had more to do with his views on the war than with anything else. According to an internal NBC memo (leaked to the All Your TV Web site, February 25, 2003), the network worried that Donahue would be a "difficult public face for NBC in a time of war….He seems to delight in presenting guests who are antiwar, anti-Bush, and skeptical of the administration's motives." The report warned that the Donahue show could be "a home for the liberal antiwar agenda at the same time that our competitors are waving the flag at every opportunity."

Sometimes those hired to give opinions were encouraged to keep quiet if they had reservations about the war. Brent Flynn, a reporter for Texas' *Lewisville Leader*, was told he could no longer write a column for the paper in which he had expressed antiwar views. "I was told that because I had attended an antiwar rally, I had violated the newspaper's ethics policy that prohibits members of the editorial staff from participating in any political activity other than voting," Flynn wrote in a note on his personal Web site. "I am convinced that if my column was supportive of the war and it was a pro-war rally that I attended, they would not have dared to cancel my column….The fact that the column was cancelled just days before the start of the U.S. invasion of Iraq raises serious questions about the motives for the cancellation."

Although Flynn was ostensibly sanctioned for compromising the paper's "objectivity," he continues to serve as a news reporter for the paper, losing only the part of his job where he was expected to express opinions.

Some reporters were sanctioned for antiwar activism that had nothing to do with their reporting. Henry Norr, a technology writer for the *San Francisco Chronicle*, was suspended without pay by his paper for using a sick day to get arrested at an antiwar protest. According to Norr (*Berkeley Daily Planet*, April 1, 2003), his supervisors knew in advance he would be doing civil disobedience that day. Defending the punishment, *Chronicle* readers' representative Dick Rogers (April 3, 2003) noted that subsequent to Norr's suspension, the paper had "strengthened its policy to prohibit public political activity related to the war." Rogers argued that the *Chronicle* ought to have a sign at its entrance reading, "Check your activism at the door."

CHAPTER 9

Index on Censorship: Annual Report

BY SIGRUN ROTTMANN

2003 was yet another terrible year for press freedom. Media organizations and advocates of freedom of expression like *Index on Censorship* were once again forced to register too many attacks against journalists around the world: Media workers (reporters, cameramen, soundmen, photographers, and support staff) were censored, harassed, put behind bars, viciously assaulted, and killed for their work. At the end of 2003, the Committee to Protect Journalists (CPJ) counted at least 136 journalists in prison worldwide, 39 in China alone. As this book goes to print, China continues to jail more journalists than any other country, heading the list of countries that CPJ reckons are the world's worst places in which to be a journalist. It shares this list with Iraq, Cuba, Zimbabwe, Turkmenistan, Bangladesh, Eritrea, Haiti, Russia, and the West Bank and Gaza.

Especially troubling is the increase of physical attacks on media personnel. While around 19 journalists were killed in 2002, last year at least 36 lost their lives in the course of work. The war in Iraq took a heavy toll. Thirteen journalists were killed, and two disappeared during the war, by far the most important international news story of the year—and the most dangerous place to be.

While 2003 has proved to be a dangerous year for Iraqi journalists as well, most of the 13 above were foreign correspondents. With the war being televised around the globe, the deaths of Australian, German, Spanish, Ukrainian, Palestinian, Iranian, Jordanian, and U.S. journalists provoked outrage far beyond their countries of origin. One year on, questions are still being asked as to how they could have ended up in the line of fire, a fact that is even more puzzling given that at least four of them were killed by U.S. troops. Jordanian Al Jazeera correspondent Tarek Ayoub died on April 8 when a U.S. missile struck the network's bureau in Baghdad. It was the second attack by U.S. forces on Al Jazeera after its Kabul offices were bombed in 2001. The fact that the television network had notified the Pentagon of the position of its offices both in Kabul and in Baghdad has raised serious doubts about the army's claim that Al Jazeera was hit accidentally.

On the same day, cameramen Taras Protsyuk from Ukraine and José Couso from Spain died when a U.S. tank fired a shell at the Palestine Hotel in Baghdad. Despairing at a rushed and rapidly terminated inquiry by the U.S. Army, Reporters Without Borders (RSF) conducted its own investigation into the shelling and concluded that the army's claim that the attack was an act of self-defense in response to shooting from the hotel was a lie. Whereas the Pentagon and television viewers around the world were aware that the hotel had been turned into an improvised media center, nobody had bothered to tell the U.S. soldiers on the ground. It remains unclear whether this information was withheld "deliberately, because of misunderstanding, or by criminal negligence," the RSF report states.

This uncertainty might well never be cleared up. Media organizations and journalists' associations have, so far in vain, called for the inquiry into the shelling of the Palestine Hotel to be reopened. They have also asked for full investigations into the deaths of all journalists killed by U.S. forces and for supposedly classified reports to be released. This includes information about the death of Reuter's cameraman Mazen Dana, who was shot dead by

THIS MODERN WORLD — by TOM TOMORROW

machine gun fire from a U.S. tank while filming near Abu Ghraib prison near Baghdad in August.

It bodes ill for the future of war reporting that the Pentagon refuses to look into the killings committed by the U.S. Army. Independent investigations would give the U.S. government a chance to demonstrate its support for media staff and to devise strategies that would prevent such tragedies in the future. Instead, it seems determined to stick to the position articulated by spokespersons during the war, who warned that only embedded journalists could count on the protection of the U.S. forces. "We know only those journalists who are working with us," Pentagon spokesman General Vincent Brooks said. Such remarks set the scene for the ensuing tragedies: journalists who chose to cover the war unilaterally not only had to look after themselves, but even ran the risk of being ignored.

As a result of the high number of journalists killed during the conflict and the increasing dangers for Westerners in occupied Iraq and other countries, the safety of media personnel on high-risk assignments became a top priority in 2003. The debate has taken on a more sinister note since the '90s, when war reporters in Bosnia argued about the virtue of moving around in armored vehicles and bulletproof vests. Major news media have employed supposedly unarmed security advisers to escort correspondents in Iraq. Some have considered hiring armed bodyguards, and there have been reports of journalists carrying guns themselves. Others have warned that civilians do not trust journalists who are accompanied by armed escorts. Doesn't such conduct, they ask, endanger a journalist's position as a noncombatant and neutral observer? New dangers loom: the consequences of journalists or their bodyguards becoming involved in armed exchanges would be extremely serious.

Western media organizations can afford to provide armored vehicles and guards when staff and equipment are sent on special assignments. Elsewhere in the world, unprotected journalists work in hostile environments every day. Of the media workers killed in 2003, most lost their lives in their own countries where armed conflict, lawlessness, or totalitarian governments reign. They ploughed on with their work despite real threats to their freedom or even their lives. Among them was reporter Guillermo Bravo Verga in Colombia, who had received death threats for denouncing corrupt public officials on his radio show and was killed by an unknown gunman. Another of the many tragedies behind the statistics is that of APTN-cameraman Nazih Darwazeh, shot dead by Israeli forces while filming clashes between Palestinian youths and Israeli troops on the West Bank.

The International News Safety Institute (INSI) was set up last year to provide safety programs and information for media workers and their employers. INSI has already trained Iraqi and Colombian journalists and is setting up a training program in risk-reduction for local journalists worldwide.

The INSI program is an important step forward in increasing safety for media workers. However, at a time when the global war on terrorism is used in many parts of the world as an excuse for repression, it is also imperative to step up campaigns against the impunity enjoyed by many who attack journalists. For instance, Israeli soldiers who target Palestinian and foreign media staff must be held accountable. Government officials, drug dealers, and members of armed groups in Colombia, Russia, or the Philippines who ruthlessly assassinate journalists in reprisal for criticism have to be brought to trial. Independent investigations into the killings of journalists at the hands of U.S. forces must become the rule.

On May 3, 2003, World Press Freedom Day, UNESCO Director-General Koïchiro Matsuura reminded media audiences that in crisis situations and violent conflicts, the public relies even more on journalists, who put their lives on the line to bring us accurate and independent information. "The debt we collectively incur when journalists suffer on our behalf must be repaid in practical ways," Matsuura said. "At the very least, we must declare war on impunity."

INDEX INDEX

Index Index is a regularly updated chronicle of free expression violations worldwide, logged by *Index on Censorship* and published online and in the magazine. Here are selections from just some of the entries for the more than 90 countries we tracked in 2003.

AFGHANISTAN: On May 2, the Committee to Protect Journalists (CPJ) placed Afghanistan fourth in its list of the world's top 10 worst places to be a journalist, citing the unchecked threat of physical intimidation and assaults carried out on the order of politicians and military commanders.

ALGERIA: Foreign correspondents covering the July 2 release of Islamic Salvation Front (FIS) figureheads Abassi Madani and Ali Belhadj were ordered by Algerian officials not to report the event. Visiting reporters were confined to their hotels and several were expelled.

ARGENTINA: On October 5, Clara Britos, owner and editor of the newspaper *La Tapa* in Guernica, Buenos Aires, province, was seized by a group of men in a passing car and threatened in connection with her reports on alleged local government corruption in Guernica. She had reported a similar attack in February and received death threats throughout the year.

AZERBAIJAN: Journalist Rauf Mirqadirov of the newspaper *Zerkalo* was fined 82,500 Manats (US$18) on July 7 after angering Baku Mayor Hacibala Abutalibov with questions about problems with the city's roadworks. When Mirqadirov asked who was in charge of road repair, the mayor replied: "I am in charge of everything here, and you had better mind your own business." Policemen seized Mirqadirov and assaulted him and charged with him "hooliganism."

BANGLADESH: Hiramon Mondol, local correspondent for the daily *Dainik Prabartan*, was attacked on August 8 by members of a police special unit and ended up seriously injured in Khulna prison hospital, charged with theft. Mondol had accused the unit of stealing fish from a market.

BOLIVIA: In October, journalists were the targets of systematic intimidation as they covered Bolivia's social and political crisis. Among the threatened were staff at Radio Fideles, Canal 2 and Canal 39 Television, and staff at Pachamama, Celestial, and Erbol radio. Journalist Juan Yupanqui of the daily *El Diario* was beaten up by police as he followed demonstrators. On October 15, all issues of the daily *El Diario* and the weekly *Pulso* were seized by security forces, and a bomb destroyed the transmitters of the Catholic radio station Radio Pio XII and Televisión Universitaria television.

BRAZIL: Over the summer, at least four journalists were murdered. On June 3, Melyssa Martins Correia of the daily *Oeste Noticias* in São Paulo state was shot in the head. Her assassination was probably prompted by the paper's coverage of criminal investigations. Edgar Ribeiro Pereira de Oliveira, co-owner of the weekly *Boca do Povo*, was killed on June 9 in Campo Grande.

His paper was known for its reporting on public corruption. On June30, Nicanor Linhares Batista, owner of Radio Vale do Jaguaribe in Limoeiro do Norte, was assassinated in the studio by unknown gunmen. Basta's hard-hitting commentaries had angered local politicians and public officials. Freelance photographer Luiz Antonio Costa was shot dead on July 23 when he was preparing a report on a land occupation for the weekly *Apoca*.

BURMA: In November, the military government released five top opposition National League of Democracy (NLD) figures from house arrest, but left NLD leader Aung San Suu Kyi in detention. The five—Than Tun, Nyunt Wei, Soe Myint, Hla Pe, and Lun Tin, all in their 70s and 80s—were freed two weeks after U.N. human rights envoy Paulo Sergio Pinheiro visited Burma and called for the release of the detainees.

CAMEROON: Remy Ngono, host of satirical program *Konde Chaud* on Radio Television Siantou, was fined US$360 and jailed for six months for criminal defamation after he mocked embezzlement allegations mad against a local businessman.

CANADA: *Fat Girl*, a film banned in 2002 by the Ontario Film Review Board because of a lengthy sex scene between a 15-year-old girl and an adult man, was approved for release in a decision that the censors presented as signalling its newly progressive policies.

CHAD: Publisher Nadjikimo Bénoudjita and deputy editor Mbainaye Bétoubam of the weekly *Notre Temps* were jailed for six months on February 6. The paper had quoted court documents alleging that the president's mother-in-law, Hadjé Billy Douga, ordered the torture of men suspected of stealing her jewelery.

CHILE: TV commentator Eduardo Yáñez was given a two-month suspended jail sentence and fined US $460 for showing "disrespect" for the Chilean judiciary under Pinochet-era laws. In 2001, Yáñez called Chilean judges "immoral, cowardly, and corrupt" for not compensating an unjustly jailed woman.

CHINA: Authorities continued to put Internet writers behind bars. On March 27, a 17-year-old girl was arrested for posting "harmful information" in a central Chinese Internet chatroom at an Internet café in Xinmi city. On May 28, the Bejing Intermediate Court sentenced Internet journalists Xu Wei, Jin Haike, Yang Zili and Zhang Honghai on subversion charges to up to ten years in prison. Internet essayist Du Daobin was arrested on October 28. His wife was told by police in Hubei Province: "We have spoken to Du Daobin several times, but he did not listen." They also warned her to not inform the foreign media about her husband's arrest.

COLOMBIA: On August 18, camera operator Jorge Real Castilla of RCN TV in Valledupar, northern Colombia, was assaulted by members of the Colombian Army's La Popa battalion. Castilla was reporting on the deaths of alleged members of the National Liberation Army (ELN) guerrilla group and the seizure of military equipment.

CUBA: The government launched a massive crackdown on dissidents and arrested around 46 political opponents and 29 independent journalists. They were sentenced to prison terms ranging between 14 and 27 years. Many were moved to prisons far from their homes, where they denounced humiliating prison conditions and poor medical attention.

EUROPE: A report *Eastern Empires: Foreign Ownership in Central and Eastern European Media* by the European Federation of Journalists (EFJ) warned that foreign takeovers of the national media have devastating consequences for local independent groups. The report also shows that since the fall of the communist regimes in Central and Eastern Europe, the encroachment of Western media conglomerates into these countries has prevented the growth of independent nationally based media groups.

THE GAMBIA: The government inaugurated the controversial National Media Commission, empowered to ban papers, jail journalists, and force them to reveal sources, in the face of strong objections from the Gambian Press Union, media rights groups and the Gambian Bar Association.

GUATEMALA: Jose Ruben Zamora, publisher of the daily *el Periódico*, was attacked at home on June 24 by a group of men who held him and his family for two hours. One attacker asked why Zamora had a problem with the "people at the top." Zamora had written articles exposing the military's continuing influence in Guatemalan politics.

HAITI: In an increasingly volatile political and social climate, journalists reported numerous threats and attacks. Radio Inter ceased broadcasting because of the increasing number of threats to its journalists and technical staff. News director Michèle Montas, whose husband and colleague Jean Dominique was murdered in April 2000, announced on air: "Three of our people have already been killed, and we don't want to lose anyone else."

INDIA: The government announced that in 2002, censors cut 12,121 metres of film from more than 900 Indian movies and 1,367 metres from 290 foreign films. Continuing this trend, the documentary *Aakrosh* based on interviews with survivors of the Gujarat religious riots was refused a certificate allowing its showing in India or abroad in March. The film board said the documentary could incite religious tensions.

INDONESIA: In May, Major General Endang Suwarya warned journalists that they should neither report on statements issued by the separatist Free Aceh Movement (GAM) nor carry news supporting the separatist cause. Military officials issued warnings to the regional daily *Serambi Indonesia* and the broadcaster Metro TV for carrying reports considered to be in favour of GAM.

IRAN: On June 23, Canadian freelance photographer Zahra Kazemi was arrested after photographing outside of notorious Evin Prison, which holds most of Iran's reformist prisoners. She died on July 12 after falling into a coma due to head wounds suffered during her interrogation.

IRAQ: The country became a high-risk zone during the war and the subsequent occupation. Threats to journalists came also from U.S. forces, who killed, arrested, and attacked local and foreign journalists. Among those detained by U.S. troops was Al Jazeera cameraman Nawaf al-Shahwani, who was arrested on July 27 after filming an attack on U.S. soldiers in the northern city of Mosul. Kazatuka Sato from the *Japan Press Weekly* was assaulted and briefly detained by U.S. troops on July 28 when he tried to film a raid on a house in a search for ousted President Saddam Hussein.

ISRAEL: A documentary about the Israeli army's invasion of the Jenin refugee camp in the West Bank can be shown in Israel, the Supreme Court ruled on November 11. Israel's film board had banned *Jenin, Jenin* on the grounds that it presented a distorted version of events, but the court rejected this argument. "The fact that the film includes lies is not enough to justify a ban," said Justice Dalia Dorner in her verdict.

ITALY: Journalists and press workers called a strike in June to protest against increasing government influence over the national media following the resignation of Ferrucio de Bortoli, editor of the daily *Il Corriere della Sera*, a critic of media magnate and Prime Minister Silvio Berlusconi's government.

KYRGYZSTAN: In June, the opposition Russian-language newspaper *Moya Stolitsa* was forced to close under the weight of punitive fines for libel suits brought by state employees.

MALAWI: In June, national broadcasting chief General Evans Namanja banned community radio stations from transmitting news bulletins, limiting news programming to the official Malawi Broadcasting Corporation and Television Malawi.

MEXICO: On September 10, Communication Ministry Officials (SCT) officials trying to forcibly close down *La Voladora* community radio stations were deterred by a human barricade of station staff. This incident broke a government promise to negotiate an end to a long-running licensing row with Mexico's community radio stations.

MOZAMBIQUE: On January 31, five men accused of killing journalist Carlos Cadoso were convicted and jailed for 23 years each. Hitsquad leader Anibal dos Santos was sentenced to 28 years' imprisonment.

NEPAL: Journalist and teacher Gyanendra Khadka was dragged from a village school, tied to a post, and had his throat cut by Maoist rebels on September 7. Khadka worked for the government news agency Rastriya Samachar Samiti (RSS).

NIGERIA: During the second day of a July national strike over a government hike in fuel prices, riot police stormed a workers rally and beat journalists and union workers with whips and rifle butts. At least three journalists, including Associated Press photographer George Osodi, were injured in the attack.

PALESTINE: Amongst those killed by Israeli troops was British cameraman and film producer James Miller who was shot dead in the Gaza Strip by Israeli tank fire on May 3. He was filming a documentary for the American cable network HBO.

PHILIPPINES: In October, Article 19 and the Manila-based Center for Media Freedom and Responsibility made a submission to the U.N. Human Rights Committee on freedom of expression in the Philippines. It cited issues such as laws threatening freedom of expression, the high rate of murdered journalists, and the lack of a freedom of information law.

RUSSIA: Russia's constitutional court ruled on October 30 that amendments to election laws forbidding "political agitation" in the media were unconstitutional and that the term "campaigning" had been defined too broadly to allow a clampdown on journalists. The clause had effectively barred coverage of candidates' backgrounds, speculation of the results and analysis of politics.

SAUDI ARABIA: Editor Jamal Kashoggi of *al-Watan* was dismissed on May 27 on orders of the Saudi Information Ministry after prominent cleric Abdullah bin abd al-Jebrein issued a fatwa against the relatively liberal paper, urging Saudis to boycott it.

SOUTH AFRICA: On November 11, the Bloemfontein high court upheld a lower court ruling requiring journalist Ranjeni Munusamy to testify before a special investigations commission despite threats to her life if she does. Munusamy had worked on the story at the heart of the commission's investigation that National Director of Prosecutions Bulelani Nguka was an informer for the apartheid-era secret services.

TURKEY: Sisters Nurcihan and Nurulhak Saatçioglu were jailed again for four years after serving seven months for protesting against the prohibition on headscarves in 1999. They were charged with "attempting to change the constitutional order by force." The court decided a stricter sentence was needed under the Meetings and Demonstration Law and the sisters were arrested on October 3. Their mother and another sister are also in jail.

UNITED KINGDOM: The deputy director of BBC News, Mark Damazer, warned that the BBC's credibility is on the line with overseas audiences because it shies away from showing shocking war images on its international news channel. He said this had led to *BBC World* showing one version of the recent war in Iraq, while other news networks like Al Jazeera were broadcasting something completely different. Damazer said that for too long the BBC and other U.K. news broadcasters had sanitized their coverage from war zones.

UNITED STATES: The media monitoring organization Fairness and Accuracy in Reporting (FAIR) claimed that in the weeks after the invasion of Iraq, U.S. television networks gave more airtime to political commentators who supported the war that to those who opposed it. Sixty-four percent were pro-war, while only 10 percent were antiwar.

ZIMBABWE: On May 16, *Guardian* correspondent Andrew Meldrum was deported, despite three court orders prohibiting his expulsion. One of the last foreign journalists in the country, he had been fighting expulsion for a year. His lawyer, Beatrice Mtetwa, was arrested and beaten in October, suffering bruises and cuts. She later tried to press charges, without result.

SOURCES: Agence France-Presse, <Allafrica.com>, World Association of Community Broadcasters (AMARC), Article 19, BBC, Committee to Protect Journalists (CPJ), European Federation of Journalists (EFJ), Fairness and

Accuracy in Reporting (FAIR), Freedom House, Freedom of Expression Institute (FXI), Fundación para la Libertad de Prensa (FLIP), *Globe & Mail, Guardian,* Indo-Asian News Service (IANS), Inter-American Press Association (IAPA), International Federation of Journalists (IFJ), *Kurdistan Observer,* Media Institute of Southern Africa (MISA), *Miami Herald, Periodistas Frente a la Corrupción (PFC),* and Reporters Without Borders (RSF).

Sigrun Rottmann is a freelance journalist and works as a researcher for *Index on Censorship.*

THIS MODERN WORLD

by TOM TOMORROW

FLUFFY BUNNY and HAPPY MOUSE discuss the WAR IN IRAQ!

CHAPTER 10

Haiti: The Untold Story

BY LYN DUFF AND DENNIS BERNSTEIN

It's the 200-year anniversary of independence for the first black nation in the world and Haitians find themselves again under the oppressive thumb of foreign domination.

On February 29, 2004, the United States government completed its coup d'etat against Haiti's democratically elected government of Jean-Bertrand Aristide. Since Aristide's reelection to the Haitian presidency in 2000, the Bush Administration had led an effort to destabilize Haiti by initiating an economic aid embargo, providing massive funding and political support for both paramilitary forces and opposition groups led by Haitian elites, as well as spearheading a propaganda offensive against Aristide.

U.S. efforts to destabilize Haiti culminated in January as millions of Haitians celebrated the bicentennial. Right-wing opposition groups who reportedly received millions of dollars from both the European Union and the U.S.'s International Republican Institute, rallied for Aristide's removal. In the forefront of opposition protests was Andre Apaid, a well-connected Haitian-American businessman and Chalabi-like political operative who created the "Group of 184," which was organized specifically to call for an end to the democratic government in Haiti. Apaid, a U.S. citizen who owns numerous sweatshops in Haiti, led the unsuccessful fight to prevent Aristide from doubling the minimum wage and was known as a prominent supporter of the 1991 coup against Aristide.

While Apaid received a great deal of media play internationally, the Haitian poor, who marched to defend the government with the motto "we will not go into hiding again," were largely ignored. On February 7, 1 million people—

over half of the population of the capital city—took to the streets vowing never to give in to anti-democracy violence. The march, which included an eighth of the population of the entire country, was described by *The New York Times* as a "small crowd."

Tragically, later that month, hundreds of former Haitian military and paramilitary forces—trained by U.S. military in the Dominican Republic and armed with U.S.-made M-16s and M-60s—came across the Dominican border and launched attacks throughout Northern Haiti. Targeting loyal police forces and the pro-democracy poor, they burned down homes, police stations, and government offices, murdering and terrorizing the population.

On February 28, echoing France's call three days earlier for Aristide to resign, President Bush publicly pushed for a regime change in Haiti. That night U.S. military forces took over key sites in Port-au-Prince including the National Palace and the airport. U.S. military forces entered Aristide's home and, in what he says was akin to a "kidnapping," took him against his will to the airport where he was put on a U.S.-chartered plane and flown to the Central African Republic.

Within hours the rebel forces were in Port-au-Prince hunting down Aristide supporters. Bodies of civilians, many with their hands still tied behind their backs, were dumped throughout the city. The head of the Port-au-Prince morgue acknowledged to a National Lawyers Guild delegation that he oversaw the disposal of more than 1,000 bodies between March 7 and March 24.

According to international human rights organizations, the former military and reconstituted death squads have murdered hundreds and possibly thousands of people. In February, more than 2,000 U.S. Marines joined French, Chilean, and Canadian troops in an international invasion of Haiti. These troops have at best stood by and allowed the violence to continue and at worst openly collaborated with a witch hunt targeting the pro-democracy populace.

While the mainstream media focuses on atrocities in Iraq, most are silent about the hundreds of Haitians being brutalized each day under the eye of military forces. Some Haitians, however, have taken a stand against the foreign occupation of their country. These are their stories.

"The Marines have sophisticated weapons. They shoot [flash and smoke grenades] in the air to blind people," alleged Confederation of Haitian Workers human rights activist Damas Glomere, "and then shoot people with silencers. Seventy-eight people have died...this has taken place especially in Bel Air." Glomere says he's interviewed dozens of individuals who say marines have shot unarmed civilians who were not resisting arrest.

Camille Chalmers, secretary general of the Haitian Platform to Advocate for an Alternative Development (PAPDA) and a vocal opponent of Aristide, described reports that 60 people died in one day in Bel Air, adding, "The multinational forces cannot provide security. They increase insecurity with their tanks and their missiles."

Even those who have come to power through the U.S. invasion have been affected by indiscriminate violence on the part of American marines. One leader of the Civil Society Initiative told this reporter, "I have a friend whose car took 45 bullets when he drove through a U.S. checkpoint. The American military are more violent than the other [troops]." Troops from five nations have been deployed to Haiti, but only American troops have been accused of human rights violations.

It was after midnight on May 10, 2004, when American marines stormed the home of 69-year-old well-known artist Annette Auguste. They blew up the entryway with grenades, decapitated the family's puppy and burst into the home with heavy artillery including high-tech rifles and explosives. Although Conrad Tribble, an American embassy official, told reporters that marines do not arrest or detain Haitians—he said they only accompany Haitian National Police (HNP) officers who do the actual detention or arrest—no HNP officers were present at any time.

Marines stormed Auguste's home, arresting her without warrant or charge, handcuffing and blindfolding 11 people including Shashou, Auguste's six-year-old grandson. Three other children, ages 10, 12, and 14 were also arrested, shackled, and had black hoods placed over their heads by marines.

Although Marine spokesperson Col. Dave Lapan acknowledged to the press that no weapons were found in the Auguste home, he says such force was necessary because marines need to show those whose homes they are raiding that "we mean business." Auguste, who is recovering from recent surgery, was remanded to the Petionville prison by marines who claim that she advocated the killing of American troops.

Tribble says, "Our troops are partnering with the Haitian national police to conduct an intelligence-driven process of home raids [for illegal weapons.]" So far these raids have been unsuccessful and less than 200 weapons were seized in the first four months of the American presence in Haiti. "There is one successful raid for every six house searches in Iraq; it is even less successful here." Lapan stated to the press that intelligence reports indicated Auguste was harboring arms.

Auguste denies the charge and states that the raid was designed to prevent her from participating in the leadership of a large anti-occupation rally for Haitian Flag Day, May 18. The arrest of Auguste was unlawful, said a Haitian police official who asked not to be named, because marines have no power to arrest citizens, did not have a warrant, and had no evidence of wrong-doing on Auguste's part. "The American Marines are operating on their own system with their own idea of justice," he said. "They are not known to respect our constitution."

The Flag Day demonstration did take place. It constituted the largest protest against the coup and the foreign occupation to date. On the morning of the May 18, tens of thousands of people gathered from the neighborhood of Bel Air calling for the return of President Aristide and an end to the occupation. Under heavy police presence and watched over by both helicopters and hundreds of foreign troops, demonstrators marched towards the National Palace. It was there that Haitian police opened fire on the crowd. Witnesses say that nine people, an unverified number, were killed. One man, however, was shot while an American filmmaker stood by and captured the event on videotape that clearly shows unarmed civilians peacefully demonstrating. Neither the protest nor its violent suppression received international press coverage.

In February, marines took over half of the national penitentiary in Port-au-Prince, where they held Haitian citizens for interrogation, some of whom have been there for months without being allowed to see an attorney or being charged with a crime. Among those being held without charge is Jocelme Privert, Aristide's minister of interior.

On the night of March 12, 16-year-old Evans Dubuisson was sent by his mother to buy groceries in the Port-au-Prince neighborhood of Bel Air. Densely populated, Bel Air is known as a hotspot of anti-occupation sentiment and has frequently been targeted by American troops for late-night raids. But it was only just after 8 PM when Dubuisson stepped out of his home and headed up the hill where merchants gathered with their baskets of bread, fruit, packaged spaghetti, and canned milk.

"I was hanging out. I said hi to a few friends and to the market women. There was a light rain, so the area was not as busy as it usually was," the lanky teen recalls. "And then the shooting started. It was loud, and I felt pain, and then I felt nothing at all."

During the few minutes it took Dubuisson to walk to the corner market, a large contingent of American marines had invaded Bel Air. "There were at least 50 marines in trucks and Humvees," says community organizer Paul Lafortune who witnessed the attack from his home nearby. "The marines were standing all over the street, even on the piles of garbage. They had their guns out and they were aggressive, pointing them at children and shouting in English."

The street quickly emptied as residents ran for cover. "We'd heard about the marines killing and shooting people, like they shot that man who was out after curfew getting asthma medication for his child," explained 15-year -old Ulrick Pierre, referring to a late-night checkpoint incident last March in which two were shot by marines in Port-au-Prince. "No one wanted to be near the white military. We weren't taking any chances."

No dispersal order was given to the small crowd of shoppers patronizing the street vendors, say the more than two dozen witnesses who spoke with this reporter. No civilians in the area had weapons, they say, and no one threatened or attacked the marines.

But something happened—some theorize that the marines were spooked by a flash of metal they thought was a gun—and in a three-minute barrage of gunfire, dozens were shot and at least 12 killed, say witnesses.

Dubuisson saw the guns and turned to run into a store when he was shot in the back. Daniel Cassamajor, 23, was shot in the neck. Although he survived, Cassamajor has extensive damage to his face; doctors report that his jaw will never function normally again, limiting his ability to eat and speak properly. His five-year-old child cries when she sees him, Cassamajor says, his face so swollen that she is unable to recognize her own father.

Worse than his own wounds, says Cassamajor, are the nightmares of what he saw take place that night.

"There was a woman passing through the neighborhood, and she was hysterical because she didn't know where to go to escape the bullets," he recalls. "I grabbed her and held her to me, pulling her down to the ground. I tried to shield her, but when I looked at her a moment later, I realized she was already dying."

"I can't figure out why they started shooting," says Pierre Esperance, a 30-year-old welder who watched events unfold from a friend's window. "They just marched right into the street. They were everywhere. One minute they were standing on the street, the next minute they were shooting....Dozens of people were shot. There were too many bodies to count."

In the growing darkness, American marines marked the bodies with green glow sticks and called for an ambulance parked a few blocks away to fetch the dead. The wounded, however, were denied medical treatment. Witnesses say they begged marines to take Cassamajor to a hospital, but their pleas were met with abuse as marines hit them with the butts of their rifles and threatened to arrest those who gathered near the wounded.

At least a dozen bodies, including the woman Cassamajor tried to help, were loaded into black zippered body bags and thrown into the ambulance and a military truck, say witnesses. While no one got a complete count of those killed, estimates ranged from one to two dozen. There were so many killed that marines ran out of body bags, says Claude (last name withheld), who watched from a nearby hiding place. "When the Americans went back to get more bags, we quickly ran into the street and dragged back two bodies which we hid from the marines."

After returning to find the bodies missing, the marines reportedly became enraged and searched the neighborhood for over an hour, at times shooting into people's homes, say numerous witnesses.

Marie Antoine, 73, says marines attacked her house while they were searching for the two missing bodies, shooting out every window in the house and riddling the walls with so many bullets that chucks of plaster and concrete fell out of the walls. Showing some of the bullets to a reporter, she is angry: "What problem do they have with an old woman like me? Do I look like I have guns? I am old, and I want to live in peace. The Americans should go back to their own country."

The two bodies were those of Frantzy Louis and Rony Hyppolite, also known as "Ti Paste." Hyppolite was a former street child who was raised by Jean-Bertrand Aristide when Aristide was a parish priest running Lafanmi Selavi home for street children prior to being elected president of Haiti. The two were close and Aristide regarded him as a son, say family members. Hyppolite, 25 at the time of his death, was the father of three.

"He was a peaceful man," says Marjorie Paul, who heard the shots that killed her husband from their home a block away. "He hated the foreign occupation [of Haiti]. But he fought with his words, not his fists. I miss him so much. Every moment I remember him. Now my children and I are alone."

While soldiers searched for the missing two bodies, Dubuisson's mother approached the very marines who shot her son to ask them to bring a doctor, but as the high school student lay with a bullet lodged next to his spine, she says marines refused to provide medical attention and threatened her with their guns. Eventually, neighbors took Dubuisson to a clinic where he underwent emergency surgery.

"They could have easily killed that boy," reports one of Dubuisson's doctors who spoke on the condition of anonymity. "The bullet penetrated the child's lower back close to the spine. He could have been paralyzed for life." Dubuisson is now confined to bed in the two-room house he shares with his mother and four siblings. "I'm in a lot of pain. My friends come here to visit, but I just want to return to school. It hurts a lot all the time, and I cannot sleep," he says.

A military spokesperson refused to comment on the incident, but confirmed that U.S. forces have changed their rules of engagement, empowering marines to shoot "if they feel threatened," unlike their previous orders to shoot only if shot at. A U.S. embassy official stated that no investigation into the incident would be ordered.

Like thousands of Haitians, Frantz Elie Legros, 23, was sick of being in hiding. After two months of staying inside, the student leader who attended the Faculty of Law at the State University of Haiti in Port-au-Prince decided to return to class. Late on a Thursday afternoon he walked onto campus, showed his ID card to the guard and sat down in class. Within moments a crowd of jeering opposition students had surrounded him, calling for his arrest.

The students harassing Legros were part of Federation des Etudiants Universitaire Haitienne (FEUH), a student organization formed, trained, and funded by the United States through the International Republican Institute. According to Pamela Callen, deputy director of USAID in Haiti, leaders of FEUH attended a "democracy enhancement" training in the Dominican Republic last fall, funded entirely by the U.S. government. The students returned to create an "anti-Aristide" organization on their campus that advocated the violent overthrew of the democratically elected government and called for the establishment of a government run by the mulatto elite.

Herve Saintilus, a leader of the FEUH, worked for the Haitian parliament prior to the establishment of democracy in Haiti, under the leadership of the Haitian elite who now comprise the Democratic Convergence (an opposition group supported by the United States that has been integrated into the new government).

"He registered as a university student simply to create a student opposition movement," said one human rights worker who asked not to be identified. "Saintilus traveled to the Dominican Republic with the Convergence people to participate in IRI [International Republican Institute] trainings last year."

Legros was targeted by FEUH because he was an outspoken student leader who advocated for the rights of Haiti's poor majority.

According to Callen, $2.4 million in U.S. aid was distributed to political opposition groups and human rights organizations in Haiti through "democracy enhancement programs" in the past year. The two human rights organizations funded by USAID are the National Coalition for Haitian Rights (NCHR) and the Carli hotline.

NCHR has been widely criticized for its partisan stance. The new government announced in April 2004 that they would rely on NCHR to "investigate and identify human rights violators. Anyone named as a criminal by NCHR will be arrested and prosecuted," explained Minister of National Security Harard Abraham. International human rights observers decry this decision, saying that it prevents victims of government or military human rights violations from feeling safe seeking help. While NCHR claims it will assist those victimized by the new regime, the organization's leaders have made numerous statements to the Haitian and foreign press that there are no systematic human rights abuses being carried out by the new government or the American military.

Perhaps NCHR has that stance because they have not attempted to speak to the hundreds of victims anxiously trying to tell their stories, say critics. Fito Esperance of NCHR stated that the group does not intend to investigate human rights crimes in Bel Air, Maritssant, Bois Neuf, La Saline, and Cite Soleil because "those neighborhoods are too dangerous for us....The people there are supporters of Aristide." Inhabitants of these neighborhoods make up approximately 80 percent of the population of the Port-au-Prince metropolitan area.

"People are dying, and there are bodies everywhere....These systematic human rights violations have been happening since February 29, and human rights organizations haven't said anything. We know these human rights organizations' funding comes through USAID and the IRI," said one victim.

Another added, "I have no human rights organization to turn to because they are all bought off by the bourgeoisie."

Each day at 4 PM a list, provided by the U.S.-funded Carli hotline, of people who have been "blacklisted," is read over the radio. Names are also read throughout the day, and calls are made to arrest or sometimes, to kill, those whose names are announced.

"Haiti is in total chaos and a very scary one. Names are being listed on the radio, and the political climate is one of a terror campaign," explains Patrick Elie, who served as minister of security under the previous government.

Father Edner DeValcin, a member of Lafanmi Lavalas (the political party that Aristide belongs to) also talked about the use of radio to advocate political repression: "There should be no arrests without a warrant, but when the radio says your name, you are arrested."

Legros was one of those whose name was read over the radio after being put on the Carli list, which was why he initially went into hiding. Two months later, after returning to class, he was held hostage for hours at the Faculty of Law while Radio Caraibes announced where Legros was being held and repeated opposition students' demands that police arrest him.

"Essentially, this hotline is a key part of the terror campaign," says Melinda Miles, co-director of the Maryland based Quixote Center's Haiti Reborn project, who investigated Legros' case. "The media is being used to disseminate terror, to advocate for the abuse of human rights."

Like Legros, Jeremy Dupin, 18, has been in hiding since February. A quiet and intelligent high school student, at age 11, Dupin became a youth reporter for *Radyo Timoun* ("Children's Radio"), a radio station based in Port-au-Prince and staffed primarily by street children from the Lafanmi Selavi home. A former street child himself, Dupin had been living for several years with his aunt in a run-down section of the capital. After the February 29 forced removal of President Aristide, Dupin decided to go into hiding.

"Everyone associated with the radio station is identified with Aristide. They knew that he had supported the radio station and that we were the children of Lafanmi Selavi who started the radio station. Many, many children from the radio station were killed by the macoutes [death squads], in the past two months," Dupin spoke haltingly from his hiding place in April.

"The new regime has it out for us. The police cooperate with the new FRAPH [death squads] and the new government is filled with the former military, criminals and drug traffickers. They have the support of the foreigners and are using their power to kill and destroy anyone who stands for the rights of the poor.

"You live in hiding and you fear for your life. You know that you are the walking dead and when they come to your house for you, your time is up."

When the death squads showed up at Dupin's door, the teen was not home, having fled into hiding weeks before. After searching the house and not finding Dupin, a group of heavily armed men shot his aunt. She died on the way to the hospital, but not before naming her attackers. For fear of his own safety, Dupin did not attend the funeral of his last remaining family member.

"The new government should recognize that we children are not to be harmed. I do not have guns that I use against the government or the foreign military. I am a student, and I am a radio journalist. All I have are my books and my voice," said Dupin.

Dupin fled the country this month and is still in hiding, now abroad. "I want to return to my country, but there is no freedom in Haiti today for those who oppose the occupation and the new regime. If you are not a friend of the wealthy, you are not welcome to speak."

The newly reformed death squads, like the ones who killed Dupin's aunt, are led by individuals such as Jean Pierre Baptiste (also known as Jean

Tatoune), who organized the FRAPH (Front for the Advancement and Progress of Haiti), paramilitary death squads responsible for the murders of thousands during the 1991–1994 coup against the first Aristide Administration. Tatoune was convicted of numerous human rights violations and murder for his leadership in the infamous April 22, 1994, Raboteau massacre. In July 2003, Tatoune escaped from a Gonaives prison and emerged as one of the leaders of the Cannibal Army that violently took control of Gonaives on February 5, starting the armed revolt against Aristide.

Tatoune is joined by others who escaped from the National Penitentiary on February 29, 2004, during a massive prison break, such as Carl Dorelien, who received a life sentence for his role in the Raboteau massacre after being deported by U.S. immigration authorities in January 2003.

Other leaders of the "rebel army" include Louis-Jodel Chamblain, a convicted assassin and former leader of FRAPH. Guy Phillipe, a major drug trafficker, fled Haiti in 2000 after being implicated in an abortive coup attempt. Trained by the U.S. special forces in Ecuador, Phillipe is a former police chief and member of the Haitian military cited by the U.N. International Civilian Mission for summary execution of suspects.

Tatoune and other death squad leaders were praised by new U.S. appointed prime minister Gerald Latortue as "freedom fighters" in a speech March 20 attended by Organization of American States (OAS) ambassador David Lee in Gonaives.

Tribble says that the United States embassy has no intention of encouraging the re-arrest of convicted human rights violators now terrorizing people throughout the country: "We don't see them as a threat to our mission in Haiti, so advocating for their arrest is not our priority."

Rather than being prosecuted, members of the "rebel army" are being integrated into the police force at the direction of Latortue. Minister of National Security Harard Abraham has been spearheading this effort and also is working to have non-rebel members of the disbanded Haitian military recruited into the police force. He scoffs at criticism that soldiers of the disbanded army, notorious for its history of violent repression of the country's poor, shouldn't be in the police force, saying that these soldiers "have the discipline and, more importantly, weapons training" that will give the police force "the strength and character it needs to be respected."

Frances, 13, was targeted after death squads armed with brand new M-16 rifles—which reportedly came from a shipment of 20,000 guns from the U.S. Department of State to the Dominican Republic last year—raided her school and discovered a photograph of her handing flowers to President Aristide during a children's assembly.

Now in hiding, she writes eloquently about her experiences: "I know now that I am a dead person. I am a dead person getting up in the morning. A dead person eating rice. A dead person listening to the news on the radio.

"Should I bother getting out of bed? Should I bother dressing or eating or opening my Bible? It is just a question now of when I will physically die because my body is already marked for death. I have not yet begun to live, but I know that I will die, and today I no longer cry. I have courage. I know truth. I do not weep anymore.

"The truth is that I will die, but they can not kill every single person in the country. In the future the killing will have to stop, and I talk to you now so that before my life is finished, you know that there was a girl who lived in Cap Haitian who once gave flowers to President Aristide and who is now gone.

"That is the only thing I want, it is to be remembered. To be remembered is to be human. That is what it means to be respected and to have peace in your heart."

Lyn Duff first traveled to Haiti in 1995 to establish that country's first children's radio station. As a writer for Pacific News Service, she has been covering Haiti for the past nine years. Dennis Bernstein is the executive producer of Pacifica Radio's *Flashpoints* and has reported widely on Haiti since the 1980s.

THIS MODERN WORLD

by TOM TOMORROW

CHICKEN HAWK DOWN

WHILE OTHERS RISKED THEIR LIVES IN IRAQ AND AFGHANISTAN, *HE* FOUGHT BRAVELY ON THE BATTLE-FIELD OF THE *INTERNET!*

I'M WAGING WAR ON THE ISLAMO-FASCISTS--ON MY *BLOG!*

EACH DAY HE SURFED THE WEB WITH *STEADFAST RESOLVE!*

THIS WALL STREET JOURNAL EDITORIAL *PROVES* THAT CRITICS OF THE ADMIN-ISTRATION ARE OBJECTIVELY *PRO-TERROR!*

I SHALL LINK TO IT *IMMED-IATELY*--IN THE NAME OF *FREEDOM!*

HE MAY NOT HAVE BEEN DODGING BULLETS--BUT HE *DID* RECEIVE THE OCCASIONAL *NASTY EMAIL!*

Hey moron, if you think the war is such a good idea, why don't you enlist??

YIKES--*IN-COMING!*

BUT THEN ONE DAY, THIS COURAGEOUS ARMCHAIR WARRIOR WAS FELLED WITHOUT WARNING--BY *CARPAL TUNNEL SYNDROME!*

AAUUGH! MY WRIST!

MEDIC!!

SHAKEN BY THE LOSS, HIS COMRADES NONETHELESS SOLDIERED ON WITH-OUT HIM.

DAMMIT! WE LOST ANOTHER GOOD MAN!

WAR IS *HELL!!*

HEY MA--ARE WE OUTTA *CHEETOS?*

TOM TOMORROW©2003... www.thismodernworld.com

CHAPTER 11

U.S. Media Coverage of Israel and Palestine: Choosing Sides

BY ALISON WEIR, executive director, If Americans Knew

The most monumental coverup in media history may be the one I'm about to describe. In my entire experience with American journalism, I have never found anything as extreme, sustained, and omnipresent.

Three and a half years ago, when the current Palestinian uprising began, I started to look into Israel and Palestine. I had never paid much attention to this issue before and so—unlike many people—I *knew* I was completely uninformed about it. I had no idea that I was pulling a loose piece of thread that would steadily unravel, until nothing would ever be quite as it had been before.

When I listened to news reports on this issue, I noticed that I was hearing a great deal about Israelis and very little about Palestinians. I decided to go to the Internet to see what would turn up and discovered international reports about Palestinian children being killed daily, often shot in the head, hundreds being injured, eyes being shot out.[1] And yet little of all this was appearing in NPR reports, *The New York Times*, or the *San Francisco Chronicle*.

There was also little historic background and context in the stories, so this, too, I began to fill in for myself, reading what has turned into a multitude of books on the history and other aspects of the conflict.[2] I attended presentations and read international reports.

The more I looked into all this, the more it seemed that I had stumbled onto a coverup that quite possibly dwarfed anything I had seen before. My former husband had been one of the founders of the Center for Investigative

Reporting (CIR), an institution known for its powerful exposés. He and CIR have won numerous well-deserved awards from Project Censored from the very beginning of its creation. Nevertheless, the duration and violence of the injustice I was discovering and the extent of its omission and misrepresentation, even in Project Censored itself, seemed unparalleled.

In February and March of 2001, I went to the Palestinian territories as a freelance reporter, traveling alone throughout Gaza and the West Bank. I saw tragedy and devastation far beyond what was being reported in the American media; I saw communities destroyed, ancient orchards razed, croplands plowed under. I saw children who had been shot in the stomach, in the back, in the head. I still see them.

I saw people convulsing and writhing in pain from a mysterious poison gas that had been lobbed at them; they said it felt like there were knives in their stomach.[3] I talked to men who had been tortured.[4]

I watched as a mother wept for her small son, and I took pictures of his spilled blood. I watched a son grieve for his mother, killed on her way home from the market on a day that I was told was the Muslim equivalent of the day before Christmas, or Passover, and I thought of my own son, the same age.

I listened to old people who described the start of this holocaust—over 50 years ago, at the end of an earlier one. They described what it was like when three-quarters of your entire population is ethnically cleansed from their homes and land, children dying along the roadside while aircraft shell the fleeing families. They told of dozens of massacres of entire villages, and I've since read accounts by Israeli soldiers, published in Israeli publications, of how they raped the women and then killed them, of how they used sticks to crush the skulls of children.[5] I discovered the message sent by Menachem Begin, later elected Israeli Prime Minister, to troops following the massacre of over 100 Palestinian men, women, and children in one village, Deir Yassin:

"Accept my congratulations on this splendid act of conquest. Convey my regards to all the commanders and soldiers. We shake your hands. We are all proud of the excellent leadership and the fighting spirit in this great attack... Tell the soldiers: you have made history in Israel with your attack and your conquest. Continue this until victory. As in Deir Yassin, so everywhere, we will attack and smite the enemy. God, God, Thou has chosen us for conquest."[6]

CENSORSHIP AT WORK

And I saw the coverup. I saw how one of the most massive and brutal displacements of a people in modern times has largely been swept under the rug, and how the continuing and ruthless methods used by a theocratic, exclusionary state[7] to rid itself of people of the "wrong" religion/ethnicity are covered up. Let me describe how this censorship works.

A few days after the deaths of the little boy and of the mother I mentioned above, there was a suicide bombing in Israel. I went to a hotel in East Jerusalem and saw that *The New York Times* had published a front-page story about it.[8]

I wondered if the paper had run similar headlines about, or at least had mentioned, the Palestinian deaths in the days before, and I discovered that they had not. But I noticed that the story about the suicide bombing had at least contained some information about these preceding Palestinian deaths—one phrase each, in the second paragraph. Near the end of the story, full of extensive, graphic descriptions of the Israeli tragedies, I also saw that there were a few paragraphs about Israeli crowds beating random Palestinian Israelis to a pulp—one was almost killed—and chanting "Kill Arabs."

A few days later I was back in the San Francisco Bay Area, and went to the library to see how the *San Francisco Chronicle* had covered these events. (I had e-mailed them on-the-scene reports, incidentally, about both Palestinian deaths.) I noticed that this paper, also, had neglected these deaths at the time. It had, however, carried *The New York Times* report about the suicide bombing that had followed. When I looked at the *San Francisco Chronicle's* version of this report, however, I was astounded: someone had surgically excised the sentences near the top of the story telling of the Israeli killing of a nine-year-old Palestinian boy and a mother of three. The person had also deleted all information about the Israeli mob violence.

Since that time I've monitored the media closely and investigated numerous similar incidents in an attempt to discover the nuts and bolts of obfuscation on Israel.

Not long ago Admiral Thomas Moorer, former chairman of the Joint Chiefs of Staff, passed away. For many years Moorer, a four-star admiral and World War II hero, had strongly condemned Israel's 1967 attack on the USS Liberty[9], a virtually unarmed U.S. Navy intelligence ship. Israeli forces had killed 34 American servicemen and injured 172; stretcher-bearers were machine-gunned and lifeboats were shot out of the water. In addition, Moorer had been outraged at the U.S. government's abandonment of this crew. Following the attack, crew members, surrounded by blood and body parts, had been ordered by the government not to speak to anyone about what had just been done to them and were dispersed to new postings around the world. One critically injured crewman who had been evacuated to a hospital in Germany woke up to find military policemen on either side of him and an identity band on his wrist with someone else's name on it.[10]

Moorer had long called for an investigation of all this. Last fall, in fact, he had chaired an independent commission on this incident, reading a report on Capitol Hill that said, among other things: "Israel committed acts of murder against American servicemen and an act of war against the United States."[11] Another admiral—who had been the head of the Navy's legal branch—read a just-released affidavit by the officer who had been the chief attorney to the quickie Naval court of inquiry set up by Admiral John S. McCain, Jr. (Senator John McCain's father) to look into the attack. This affidavit revealed that there had been a cover-up at the presidential level—that President Lyndon Johnson and Secretary of Defense Robert McNamara had ordered the court to find, despite all evidence to the contrary, Israel innocent of culpability.[12]

The story of the commission's unprecedented findings died after one day of coverage. Despite an excellent Associated Press (AP) report on it, a search of 300 newspapers only turned up 10 that had printed it.

A few months later Moorer died. The first quick AP obituary that came out about him contained one sentence about the Israeli attack. It was minimal, but present. Within a few hours a longer obit came out, containing a great deal of additional information about Moorer. But the sentence on the Israeli attack had been taken out.

I have phoned AP many times, asking them why information on the USS Liberty was removed from the obituary and who removed it. Each time, the person I reached agreed that the Liberty information was important and told me they would get back to me. I'm still waiting.

I'll discuss just four more telling examples. While such groups as Amnesty International have condemned Israel for its routine torture of Palestinian prisoners for decades[13], coverage of such abuse virtually never appears in American media.

In October of 2002[14] I received e-mail reports of a Palestinian farmer who had been brutally tortured by Israeli settlers. I felt this was an important story and decided to check it out. I phoned the American on the scene who had sent out the report and asked for more information. He filled in the gruesome details, sent me photos, and gave me the name and address of the hospital where the victim was being treated. I then phoned the *San Francisco Chronicle* and gave the foreign desk all the information I had gathered. I suggested that they send one of their correspondents in the area to cover it, since although *Chronicle* reporters always reside in Israel, they do occasionally visit the Palestinian territories.

No word, however, ever appeared of this incident in the *Chronicle*.[15] In fact, a search of the *Chronicle* looking for the words "torture" and "Israel" in lead paragraphs turned up only one article in the past 10 years: an editorial in 1999 that opined: "Israel's Supreme Court was courageous, idealistic, and absolutely right to outlaw torture as an interrogation technique by the Shin Bet security force."[16] Unfortunately, Israeli torture did not end after this decision.[17]

Earlier this year, American media reported prominently on a prisoner swap in which an Israeli businessman imprisoned by Lebanon was traded for three Lebanese resistance leaders and a few hundred Palestinians (who had been scheduled for release within a few months anyway). Earlier news stories had reported that the Israeli had been tortured in Lebanon, but, happily, upon his release the man stated that he had been treated well by his captors.[18]

On the other hand, I learned through Al Jazeera that one of the Lebanese leaders just released had, two days before, testified for 10 hours in an Israeli court describing gruesome sexual abuse by Israeli prison guards, his claims validated by a member of the International Red Cross.[19] (Incidentally, I subsequently saw that accounts of this abuse had been reported in the foreign press for years).[20]

I was in Washington, DC, at the time, and noticed that there had been no mention of any of this in the *Washington Post*, despite extensive coverage of the swap. I then did a search of the *Post* Web site, typing in " Mustafa Dirani" and "torture," and was surprised to find a full, detailed report on it by Peter Enav of the Associated Press.[21] In other words, the *Washington Post* had the information on Dirani, the story was on their Web site, but they had not printed a word of it in the newspaper. (And you only found it on the Web site if you knew to look for it.)

I phoned the *Post* and was referred to the editor responsible for foreign news. I asked why the paper had not contained information about Dirani's testimony and corroborating statements by others. He replied that they were waiting to look into it further and would probably cover it sometime in the future. I pointed out that alleged torture of an Israeli—since proved to be false—had been printed, and asked, unsuccessfully, for an explanation of this double standard in news coverage. To date, this projected coverage has still not come.

In fact, index searches revealed that while many newspapers had covered the prisoner swap extensively, and a number of newspapers around the country had carried the report of Dirani's abuse buried on their Web sites somewhere, I could find only nine newspapers that had printed these serious allegations of Israeli torture of a major Lebanese figure—interestingly, most of them local papers.

Moreover, in my searches I also came across the fact that Dirani's young nephew Ghassan had been imprisoned by Israel for 10 years. Israel had never contended that Ghassan was even political, much less a member of any resistance groups; he was simply held as a bargaining chip. At some point he had apparently suffered a complete mental breakdown and was transferred to a psychiatric prison. Finally, he was released to his family in Lebanon, his mind reportedly gone. All of this, also, was unmentioned in American coverage of the prisoner swap.[22]

In June 2002, *Foreign Service Journal* published what should have been an explosive exposé on Israel's torture of American citizens.[23] Yet when I went to the journal's Web site, I could not find the article. In fact, there was no mention that the issue even contained such a piece. I phoned the editor, and discovered that they had decided it was too controversial to put on their Web site. Today, the Web site does mention the article (in an extremely expurgated fashion—minus the word torture, for example), but there is still no link to the actual report.[24] In addition, I have not been able to find a single American news source that even mentioned this thoroughly documented report.

Finally, in the midst of the unfolding scandal about torture and humiliation of Iraqi prisoners at Abu Ghraib, two international human rights organizations released findings that 374 Palestinian teenagers imprisoned by Israel were being treated with similar cruelty. There was a short AP story on the report. It was sent to Britain, Europe, Africa, India, and Asia. It was not, however, sent to American newspapers. Phone calls to AP asking why it was deemed newsworthy in the rest of the world but not in the United States went unanswered.

MEDIA STUDIES

Soon after my visit to the occupied territories I founded an organization called If Americans Knew[25] to monitor the media and to provide Americans with accurate information on this topic. Two years ago, prompted by such anecdotal evidence of massive omission, If Americans Knew began conducting statistical case studies on coverage of Israel and Palestine. We chose categories that would be universally acknowledged as significant and as immune as possible from subjective interpretation. We recorded the number of deaths of both Palestinians and Israelis mentioned in headlines, and then compared the percentages of overall deaths that were covered.[26]

Our findings are staggering.

We discovered, for example, that the *San Francisco Chronicle* had prominently covered 150 percent of Israeli children's deaths—i.e., many of the deaths were the subject of more than one headline in the paper—and 5 percent of Palestinian ones. In other words, Palestinian deaths were rarely accorded headline coverage even once.

In the first three-and-a-half months of the current Palestinian uprising against Israel's continuing confiscation of Palestinian land and suppression of human rights, Israeli forces killed 84 Palestinian children. The largest single cause of their deaths was gunfire to the head.[27] During this period, not one Israeli child was killed. Not one suicide bombing against Israelis occurred.[28]

Of these 84 Palestinian children, only one received headline coverage in the *Chronicle*—Mohammed al-Durra, the little boy whose murder while he was cowering with his father was recorded for all the world to see by a French TV crew.

Was the *Chronicle* alone in such unbalanced news coverage?

No. A study of National Public Radio that Seth Ackerman[29] conducted for Fairness and Accuracy in Reporting (FAIR) showed that NPR had reported on 89 percent of Israeli children's deaths and 20 percent of Palestinian ones. In other words, NPR, which has been accused of being "pro-Palestinian," reported Israeli deaths at a rate four and a half times greater than Palestinian deaths.

Two studies we conducted of the *San Jose Mercury News*—for a total of 12 months of data—also revealed enormous distortion in coverage. For example, we discovered that front-page headline coverage of all deaths (adults and children) had so emphasized Israeli deaths over Palestinian ones that the newspaper had, in effect, reversed reality—and then widened the gap. While 313 Israelis and 884 Palestinians had been killed during this period, *Mercury News* front-page headlines had reported on 225 Israeli deaths, and only 34 Palestinian ones—72 percent of Israeli deaths and 4 percent of Palestinian ones.[30]

What do these case studies tell us about American coverage in general? A great deal.

Let us imagine what would have happened if a newspaper's headlines had reported the World Series backwards—that the score had been reversed, the winning team declared the loser. The paper would have been the laughing-stock of the country; late-night comics around the nation would have had a field day.

Yet here was an equivalent error in a situation involving life and death, literally, and virtually no one noticed. Why? The logical conclusion is that the entire environment of news most people were accessing—television, radio, magazines—communicated similar inversion.

As a result, the public is staggeringly misinformed. During the current intifada, Palestinian children were being killed—often shot in the head—day after day, week after week, month after month, before a single Israeli child's death. Yet a survey taken later that year showed that 93 percent of the respondents either had no idea which children had died first or believed them to be Israeli.[31] And this despite ample coverage of the conflict in general: the *Chronicle*, for example, ran over 250 stories on Israel and Palestine during this period.

Also omitted was information on U.S. tax money to Israel: well over $10 million per day—more than to all of sub-Saharan Africa and the Caribbean put together.[32] Our study showed that in six months of extensive reporting on Israel, the *Chronicle* had never even once reported the total amount of U.S. money being sent to Israel.

And this is just the tip of the iceberg of omission on this issue.

Let us look at Project Censored, itself—a highly respected media-monitoring institution intent on bringing attention to critical information not covered by the corporate media. Each year it screens thousands of articles in hundreds of journals, drawing on the participation of a long list of experts. It has helped publicize profoundly valuable information on a wide variety of topics, with particular sensitivity to injustice, racism, and the plight of oppressed populations.

Yet it has largely missed one of the longest and most egregious cases of oppression of the twentieth (and now twenty-first) century.

Over 50 years ago, the massive dispossession of almost an entire indigenous population was carried out by a colonial population pursuing ethnic "purity"[33]—a purity Muslim and Christian Palestinians did not fit into. Israeli writer Yshar Snmilasky described this beginning: "We came, shot, burned, blew up, pushed, and exiled....will the walls not scream in the ears of those who will live in this village?" [34]

In 1967, this nation then overran the small remnants of land left to the indigenous population and placed the inhabitants under brutal military occupation. In 1982, this apartheid nation[35] invaded yet another country in its quest to prevent the original inhabitants of what was now Israel from returning to their land. Some 20,000 men, women, and children in Lebanon were killed, and hundreds of thousands injured—through the illegal use of American-made weapons. One American physician wrote at the time that she had never before seen "such hideous injuries." In one day, 1,000 mangled limbs were amputated.[36]

In 1986, there was more violence, when the virtually unarmed indigenous population in the occupied territories attempted to rise up against their occupiers and died at the rate of 10 per every one Israeli death. The Palestinian death rate would have been higher, but the occupation forces chose a less reported form of violence to subdue the rebels—soldiers held them down and broke their bones. In the first three days of this new strategy, 197 people were treated for fractures at one hospital in Gaza alone.[37] Yitzhak Rabin, the Israeli leader later known as a "peacemaker" before being assassinated by a Jewish extremist, implemented the policy. One episode was caught on film and can be viewed in various documentaries.[38] Israeli forces later killed the Israeli cameraman.[39]

Through this entire period there was an ongoing campaign to break the indigenous people's spirit. Tens of thousands were incarcerated without recourse to judge and jury. Tens of thousands were tortured, humiliated, maimed. Homes were destroyed by the thousands, and cropland plowed under and replaced with concrete colonies from which the ancestral owners of the land were to be eternally excluded. Families were ripped apart, sons deported, schools closed.[40]

And in its first 20 years, Project Censored made no mention of any of this—of this profoundly covered-up conflict, of these people, of this oppression. The longest-standing military occupation of modern times—unmentioned. The largest refugee population in today's world (an estimated 8 million), and the longest dispossessed—unmentioned.

Actually, Project Censored carried one story on Israel during this period—an exposé of its support of oppression in Central America. Then finally, in 2001, in Project Censored's twenty-fifth anniversary edition, there was notice of Israel's oppression of Palestinians—it was mentioned in the introduction and in a story about ethnically specific bioweapons.[41]

Astoundingly, the first time that a topic pertaining to Israel's treatment of Palestinians made it onto the Project Censored list was just last year. After including a story about U.S. tax money to Colombia in the previous volume—the #3 choice of that year—Project Censored decided to also cover U.S. tax money to Israel—a vastly larger amount, that has been dispensed far longer. This story was #24. Since many reports about Project Censored list only the top 10 stories, this low rating meant that this story went widely unmentioned.

Such long neglect of this issue is startling, particularly given the subject matter that Project Censored regularly addressed and the numerous powerful exposés on Israel related to these subjects that were ignored by the mainstream press—stories that seemed right up Project Censored's alley.

For example, Project Censored has done an excellent job of covering nuclear power and proliferation. Yet through all these years there was no mention—ever—of Israel's possession of hundreds of nuclear weapons; no mention of the young technician who blew the whistle on their nuclear weapons program and was then kidnapped by Israel, brought back for a kangaroo trial under grotesque conditions and held in solitary confinement in a cell two meters by three meters for over 12 of his 18 years of incarceration.[42]

Similarly, Project Censored promoted important articles about Iran-Contra and on the oil embargo that shot oil prices through the roof and threw thousands out of work. Yet there was no mention of the fundamental role played by Israel in both events.[43]

Projected Censored highlighted a moving and powerful report on the "Death of a Nation: The Tragedy of Transkei" in South Africa, yet there was no such article about the death of Palestine and the various strategies being implemented to expel its remaining inhabitants.[44]

While Project Censored contained valuable information on "The Most Powerful Secret Lobby in Washington" (the Business Roundtable), there was no mention of the pro-Israel lobby that has been at the forefront of influencing U.S. foreign policy in the Middle East for over half a century.[45]

If space permitted, this list would go on and on. Even last year, after Project Censored had begun to discover Palestine, the book's top *Censored* story of the year, which exposed the neoconservatives' role behind the attack on Iraq, astonishingly omitted any mention whatsoever of these neoconservatives' close, long-term ties to Israel and the documented record of their work on its behalf.[46] Similarly, there was no mention of what should have been an award-winning exposé on Israeli torture of American citizens that came out the same year.

Finally, this year, a story revealing that top U.S. governmental officials have been investigated by U.S. intelligence agencies for decades for spying for a foreign government—a story that should have produced reverberations throughout the country, resulting in Congressional inquiries and calls for special prosecutors[47]—was not only unmentioned by the mainstream media, it was missed by Project Censored and its array of experts as well. The foreign government was Israel.

In other words, while the corporate media was ignoring the slaughter, torture, and dispossession of Palestinians, while it was ignoring a presidential coverup that dwarfed Watergate in its significance, while it was ignoring the attempts of abandoned vets to get recourse from their government, while it was ignoring multitudes of stories of potentially world-shaking importance about Israel and its actions, Project Censored was, too.

I don't know why or how this has been happening, but I suspect that Project Censored's omission of this issue is largely a reflection of what has been going on throughout much of the progressive press—and community—for many years. A search of the Center for Investigative Reporting's (CIR) Web site, for example, reveals only two stories, 25 years apart, about Israel or Palestine—both by the same author.

When we approached CIR and Media Alliance, another organization known for its ethical actions against censorship, to join us in activities regarding our *Chronicle* and *Mercury News* studies, the reaction was disappointing. CIR, we were told, was in the midst of negotiating with the *Chronicle* on some future projects. (We also later noticed that David Yarnold, executive editor of the *Mercury News*, is on the CIR advisory board.) When we contacted Media Alliance about cosponsoring a forum on our studies, a project that we had thought would mesh well with the organization's progressive philosophy, our phone calls went unreturned.

When we asked Peace Action why their brochures about nuclear weapons omitted any mention of Israel's large arsenal of such weapons, we were told that discussing Israel would interfere with the group's ability to lobby Congressman Tom Lantos (one of Israel's most fervent Capitol Hill supporters and a major promoter of both Iraq wars).

These are not isolated incidents.

All of the above organizations—and many others with equally dubious records on Palestine—have produced profoundly important, often courageous, work. Why has there so often been a "blind spot" on Israel?

I suspect that the causes are complicated and multifactorial. I suspect that I and others like me—who remained ignorant and negligent on this issue for so long—bear much of the guilt. I suspect that others whose emotional ties to Israel served as blinders on this subject share in our culpability. I suspect that still others who knew the truth and refused to speak of it, or who participated in its coverup, bear a significant portion of this awful responsibility. I suspect that the career damage[48] and death threats[49] that often result when one begins to speak out on this issue played a part.

Whatever the cause, it is time that we all, finally and resoundingly, move forward. It is time that we bring to an end what we have all helped to perpetuate.

Perhaps one of the places we can start is by recognizing and disseminating the immense body of work created through the years by journalists diligently digging up the still mostly-buried facts on Israel and Palestine. Many of these people are nearing the end of their careers, and it is time we thanked them and joined in their efforts.

I propose a special Lifetime Most *Censored* Award and that among the first to receive it be the following writers whose extraordinary work has continually been censored out of American discourse on the Middle East: (in alphabetical order) Richard Curtiss, for his massive research into all aspects of Israel and Palestine, in particular on U.S. aid to Israel and Israeli PACs; James Ennes, for being the first to gather and expose the story of the USS Liberty and its coverup; Andrew Killgore, for his numerous writings and his historic role, with Richard Curtiss, in founding and keeping alive the *Washington Report on Middle East Affairs* and the American Educational Trust book publishing; Paul Findley, for ground-shaking research on the Israel lobby and the injustice being done to Palestinians and Muslims; Stephen Green, for his meticulous investigative reporting on Israeli spying and arms procurement; Alfred Lillienthal, for his early and principled exposes of Israel; and, especially, Donald Neff, for his brilliant and comprehensive books on all aspects of Israel, Palestine, and the core injustice at the center of the Middle East.

In memoriam awards should go to Edward Said, who broke through this censorship, and to Grace Halsell and Elmer Berger, who sadly did not. I am at a loss to describe the tribute that should go to 23-year-old Rachel Corrie, whose life and death, as well as whose words have been largely erased or distorted in media discourse on Israel and Palestine—including by some publications once considered progressive, such as *Mother Jones*.[50]

Next, I hope future editions of Project Censored will include work by some of the other superb writers and reporters on this topic today: Ali Abunimah, Naseer Aruri, Dennis Bernstein, Jerri Bird, Jeff Blankfort, Lenni Brenner, Andrew Cockburn, Kathleen Christison, Norman Finkelstein, Delinda Hanley, Rashid Khalidi, Janet McMahon, Rachelle Marshall, Nur Masalha, Nigel Perry, Jason Vest, Ahmed Yousef, Mazen Qumsieh, Charlie Reese, and the many others deserving of recognition. I apologize for those I'm forgetting to mention, and I hope others will add to this list. (I have not included here foreign journalists of note because it is my understanding that Project Censored concentrates on censorship inside the U.S.)

Finally, we must help to end the censorship of the ongoing reports by Palestinian and international journalists, including Israeli ones, who report at great risk from inside the Palestinian territories (in the past four years, 12 journalists have been killed there and 295 wounded[51]), as well as by writers from such organizations as Christian Peacemaker Teams and the International Solidarity Movement and especially from among the Palestinian population itself, who are daily sending out searing first-hand accounts from the very center of the violence. May they all survive.

UN-CENSORING:
SOME RECOMMENDED READING ON ISRAEL-PALESTINE:

The Passionate Attachment by George W. Ball and Douglas Ball
The New Intifada edited by Roane Carey
The Fateful Triangle by Noam Chomsky
Perceptions of Palestine by Kathleen Christison
Assault on the Liberty by James Ennes (first-hand account of Israel's attack on U.S. Navy ship)
Deliberate Deceptions by Paul Findley
They Dare to Speak Out by Paul Findley
Zealots for Zion: Inside Israel's West Bank Settlement Movement by Robert Friedman
Journey to Jerusalem by Grace Halsel
Expulsion of the Palestinians by Nur Masalha
Fallen Pillars: U.S. Policy towards Palestine and Israel since 1945 by Donald Neff
Fifty Years of Israel by Donald Neff
Sharing the Land of Canaan by Mazin B. Qumsiyeh
Jewish Fundamentalism in Israel by Israel Shahak and Norton Mezvinsky
Sameed by Raja Shehadeh
The Lobby by Edward Tivnan

NOTES:

1. A few of the best online sources include Al Jazeera, <english.aljazeera.net/HomePage>; reports by Robert Fisk and Phil Reeves in *The Independent* (London), <www.independent.co.uk>; *The Guardian* (U.K.), <www.guardian.co.uk>; *The Washington Report on Middle East Affairs*, <www.wrmea.com>; The Palestinian Red Crescent Society, <www.palestinercs.org>; and B'Tselem, <www.btselem.org>. Regarding eye injuries, an example is: "By May 2001, there were already 200 people treated for eye wounds at St. John Eye Hospital in Jerusalem alone."—Tanya Reinhart, *Israel/Palestine* (New York: Seven Stories Press, 2002), 115.

2. Some of the best books I have read are listed at the end of the article and online at <www.ifamericansknew.org/about_us/materials.html#books>.

3. For more information about the nerve gas being used, see: James Brooks, "The Israeli Poison Gas Attacks: A Preliminary Investigation," *Media Monitors Network*, January 8, 2003, <www.mediamonitors.net/jamesbrooks2.html>.

4. There are numerous human rights reports on Israeli torture, see, for example, "Israel Increases Its Use of Torture Practices Among Palestinian Prisoners," a report issued by the Palestinian Prisoner Society, June 21, 2002, <www.ppsmo.org/e-website/Reports/Israeli%20Tourture%20July%202002.htm>.

5. *Davar*, June 9, 1979 (testimony of an Israeli soldier who participated in the massacre at al Duwayma Village on October 29, 1948): "[they] killed between 80 to 100 Arabs, women and children. To kill the children, they fractured their heads with sticks. There was not one house without corpses. The men and women of the villages were pushed into houses without food or water. Then the saboteurs came to dynamite the houses. One commander

ordered a soldier to bring two women into a house he was about to blow up…Another soldier prided himself upon having raped an Arab woman before shooting her to death. Another Arab woman with her newborn baby was made to clean the place for a couple of days, and then they shot her and the baby. Educated and well-mannered commanders who were considered "good guys"…became base murderers, and this not in the storm of battle, but as a method of expulsion and extermination. The fewer the Arabs who remained, the better." For additional information on Israel's beginnings, see: Nur Masalha, *Expulsion of the Palestinians: The Concept of "Transfer" in Zionist Political Thought, 1882-1948* (Washington, DC: The Institute for Palestine Studies, 1992).

6. George W. Ball and Douglas B. Ball, *The Passionate Attachment: America's Involvement with Israel, 1947 to the Present* (New York: W. W. Norton & Company, 1992), 29.

7. See, for example, Amir S. Cheshin, Bill Hutman, and Avi Melamed, *Separate and Unequal: The Inside Story of Israeli Rule in East Jerusalem* (Cambridge, MA: Harvard University Press, 1999), and David McDowall, *Palestine and Israel* (University of California Press, 1989), 123-145.

8. Deborah Sontag, "Suicide Bomber Kills 3 Israelis," *The New York Times*, March 5, 2001. It's interesting to see how this situation was reported elsewhere; for example, the *Houston Chronicle* carried Sontag's story under the headline: "Palestinian Suicide Bomber Kills 3 Israelis: Attack Gladdens West Bank Mourners as Conflict Grows."

9. For more information about the attack on the Liberty, visit <www.ifamericansknew.org/us_ints/ussliberty.html>.

10. *Assault on the Liberty* (Random House, 1980; Ballantine, 1986; Reintree Press, 2002), <www.ussliberty.org>.

11. <www.ifamericansknew.org/us_ints/ul-commfindings.html>.

12. <www.ifamericansknew.org/us_ints/ul-boston.html> and <www.freewebs.com/gidusko/boston>.

13. Neve Gordon and Ruchama Marton, *Torture: Human Rights, Medical Ethics and the Case of Israel* (London: Zed Books). See, for example, Amnesty International Report, "Israel and the Occupied Territories: Mass Detention in Cruel, Inhuman, and Degrading Conditions," May 23, 2002, <web.amnesty.org/library/index/engmde150742002>.

14. <www.flashpoints.net/index-2002-10-30.html>.

15. For first-hand reports, visit <www.palsolidarity.org>; <www.hearpalestine.org>; or <www.cpt.org/hebron/hebron.php>.

16. *San Francisco Chronicle*, September 10, 1999: A20.

17. See, for example, Amnesty International Report, "Israel and the Occupied Territories: Mass Detention in Cruel, Inhuman, and Degrading Conditions," May 23, 2002, <web.amnesty.org/library/index/engmde150742002>.

18. <www.cnn.com/2004/WORLD/meast/01/29/prisoner.exchange>.

19. "Hizb Allah Leader Says Israel Tortured Him," Al Jazeera, January 27, 2004, <english.aljazeera.net/NR/exeres/EC01FA53-F114-44AF-89F9-75903CB8008F.htm>; Matthew Gutman and Tovah Lazaroff, "Dirani to Testify on Rape Charges," *Jerusalem Post*, January 27, 2004.

20. For example, "Facility 1391: Israel's Secret Prison," *The Guardian* (U.K.), November 14, 2003, <www.guardian.co.uk/israel/Story/0,2763,1084796,00.html> and "Lebanese Group Calls on ICRC to Prevent Israeli Torture in Jails," Deutsche Presse-Agentur, March 13, 2000.

21. Peter Enav, "Militant Says He Was Abused by Israel," Associated Press, January 27, 2004.

22. "Israel Surrenders A Bargaining Chip," *Washington Post*, April 6, 2000: 1.

23. Jerri Bird, "Arab-Americans in Israel: What 'Special Relationship'?", June 2002, <www.partnersforpeace.org/inmedia/db200206010/>.

24. <www.afsa.org/fsj/2002.cfm>

25. If Americans Knew is dedicated to providing full and accurate information to the American public on topics of importance that are underreported or misreported in the American media. Our primary area of focus at this time is Israel/Palestine. For more information, visit us online at <www.ifamericansknew.org>.

26. All four of our studies completed so far can be found online at <www.ifamericansknew.org/media/report_cards.html>.

27. Information about Israeli and Palestinian children killed in the conflict is available online at <www.rememberthesechildren.org >.

28. <www.btselem.org>.

29. Seth Ackerman, "The Illusion of Balance: NPR's Coverage of Mideast Deaths Doesn't Match Reality," *Extra!*, November/December 2001, <www.fair.org/extra/0111/npr-mideast.html>.

30. The second study is online at <www.ifamericansknew.org/media/merc2/report.html>.

31. Retro Poll of September/October 2002 is online at <www.retropoll.org/results_poll_01.htm>.

32. Richard Curtiss, "The Cost of Israel to U.S. Taxpayers," *Washington Report on Middle East Affairs*, December 1997: 43-45, <www.wrmea.com/backissues/1297/9712043.html>.

33. There are numerous excellent histories that cover this period; two are Mazin B. Qumsiyeh, *Sharing the Land of Canaan* (Pluto Press), and Nur Masalha, *Expulsion of the Palestinians: The Concept of "Transfer" in Zionist Political Thought, 1882-1948* (Washington, DC: The Institute for Palestine Studies, 1992). A book list can be found at <www.ifamericansknew.org/about_us/materials.html#books>.

34. <www.wrmea.com/backissues/0794/9407072.htm>.

35. Desmond Tutu and Ian Urbina, "Against Israeli Apartheid," *International Herald Tribune*, July 2002.

36. Sally V. Mallison and W. Thomas, *Armed Conflict in Lebanon 1982: Humanitarian Law in a Real World Setting* (American Educational Trust).

37. David McDowall, *Palestine and Israel: The Uprising and Beyond* (University of California Press, 1989): "Defense Minister Yitzhak Rabin, shifted away from firearms, telling his soldiers to use 'might, power, and beatings'… Soldiers armed with cudgels beat up those they could lay their hands on regardless of whether they were demonstrators or not, breaking into homes by day and night, dragging men and women, young and old, from their beds to beat them. At Gaza's Shifa Hospital 200 people were treated during the first five days of the new policy, most of them suffering from broken elbows and knees. Three had fractured skulls…A government official explained: 'A detainee sent to prison will be freed in 18 days… but if soldiers break his hand, he won't be able to throw stones for a month and a half."

38. For example, *People and the Land*, directed by Tom Hayes, and *Palestine is Still the Issue*, directed by John Pilger.

39. Personal conversation with filmmaker Tom Hayes, director of *People and the Land*.

40. <www.hrw.org/un/chr59/israelot.htm>, <www.dci-pal.org/reports/dcireports.html> , and <www.amnestyusa.org/countries/israel_and_occupied_territories/reports.do>.

41. "Human Genome Project Opens the Door to Ethnically Specific Bioweapons," #16.

42. Mordechai Vanunu; see Mark Gaffney, *Dimona, The Third Temple?: The Story Behind the Vanunu Revelation* (Brattleboro, VT: Amana Books, 1989).

43. Stephen Green, *Living by the Sword*: 193-218; <www.wrmea.com/backissues/0591/9105011.htm>; Donald Neff, *Fifty Years of Israel*: 279-287; <http://www.wrmea.com/backissues/1097/9710070.html> ; Donald Neff, "Nixon Administration Ignores Saudi Warnings, Bringing On Oil Boycott," *Washington Report on Middle East Affairs*, October/November 1997: 70-72.

44. <www.wrmea.com/backissues/032486/860324012.html> and <www.wrmea.com/backissues/0689/8906021.htm>.

45. <www.ifamericansknew.org/us_ints/pg-blankfort.html>; <www.wrmea.com/aipac>; and <www.wrmea.com/backissues/0198/9801065.htm>.

46. Numerous excellent articles can be found at <www.ifamericansknew.org/us_ints/neocons.html>. Israeli media, by the way, have covered this aspect openly. For example, in *Ha'aretz*, April 4, 2003: "The war in Iraq was conceived by 25 neoconservative intellectuals, most of them Jewish, who are pushing President Bush to change the course of history…"

47. Stephen Green, "Serving Two Flags," *CounterPunch*, February 28-29, 2004, <www.counterpunch.org/green02282004.html>.

48. Paul Findley, *They Dare to Speak Out* (Chicago: Lawrence Hill Books, 1989): 295-314; "San Francisco Chronicle Fires Reporter for Attending Peace Protest," *Democracy Now!*, April 24, 2003; and <www.veteransforpeace.org/sf_chronicle_fires_042403.htm>.

49. <www.ifamericansknew.org/about_us/death_threat.html>.

50. Phan Nguyen, "Mother Jones Smears Rachel Corrie: Specious Journalism in Defense of Killers," *CounterPunch*, September 20, 2003, <www.counterpunch.org/nguyen09202003.html>. In contrast, *Harper's* magazine ran a number of Corrie's letters. These can be read in full at <www.ifamericansknew.org>

51. *Palestine Monitor,* "Palestinian Intifada Fact Sheet," <www.palestinemonitor.org/factsheet/Palestinian_intifada_fact_sheet.htm>.

CHAPTER 12

Death of a Nation: Conservative Talk Radio's Immigration & Race "Curriculum"

BY JOSÉ A. PADIN, Portland State University,
AND SHELLEY SMITH, Portland, Oregon

Conservative political talk radio took the U.S. airwaves by storm in the 1990s. Today a handful of conservative talk radio (CTR) hosts are household names across the country, multimedia megastars plying their trade in cable television and routinely topping bestseller charts. CTR celebrities pose as populist "intellectuals" and command loyal mass audiences that are as highly mobilized politically as they are profitable. These are true "freelancers" wielding their spear without allegiance to any standard of integrity. Yet owing to its fabulous economic success, CTR has forced traditional news organizations into a "race to the bottom" that eviscerates professional journalism.

The CTR industry, and the fear mongering on which it thrives, deserves careful critical scrutiny for at least three reasons: (1) CTR packages and markets an essential public good, political information, but operates free from any standard of quality (Alterman 2003). (2) CTR presents itself as the face of angry populism, but is part and parcel of the momentum towards the corporate debasement of the media (McChesney 2004). (3) Far from being an automatic market response to consumer demand, CTR is the product of a deliberate three-decade conservative strategy, and a massive investment in information infrastructure, to define, capture, and colonize political "common sense" in the United States (Brock 2004).

This chapter presents the result of systematic analysis of CTR content on immigration and immigrants, issues that inevitably come up in any body of rhetoric that self-consciously sets out to articulate views of a *nation under siege*. Although there are currently studies of immigrant and immigration images in television and newspapers, to date there is no systematic study of them in talk radio. Before discussing the "immigration curriculum" championed by leading talk radio hosts, we would like to briefly review some recent literature that offers a perspective on the significance of conservative talk radio.

THE GROWTH AND REACH OF CTR

The reach of talk radio in general and CTR in particular is remarkable and has increased over the last decade. A 2003 Gallup survey found 31 percent of respondents receiving their news every day or several times a week from talk radio. This figure was up from 17 percent in 1995. The Pew organization found that 37 percent of respondents to a 2002 poll listened to talk radio regularly or sometimes, while a core of 17 percent used talk radio regularly as a source of news (Brock 2004, 279). In 1983, there were 59 talk show stations in the United States, but after the 1990s boom, the number of talk radio stations surpasses 1,200. The largest personality-centered shows are all conservative: Rush Limbaugh has 14.5 million regular listeners, followed by Sean Hannity (11.8 million), and Michael Savage (7 million) (De la Vina

THIS MODERN WORLD   by TOM TOMORROW

2004). These conservative talk radio hosts also dominate the cable and book market talk radio spin-offs (Brock 2004). By the mid-1990s, regular talk radio listeners constituted around 20 percent of U.S. voting adults (Barker and Knight 2000).

PROFILE OF THE CTR AUDIENCE

The portrait of the talk radio audience is somewhat surprising. Talk radio listeners are slightly better off than nonlisteners (Hoyt 1992; Hofstetter et al. 1994). Although there is a difference in distribution of listeners and nonlisteners into income classes, educational differences are more marked. A 1993 *Times Mirror* survey found that 60 percent of non-listeners had a high school degree or less, compared to 46 percent of listeners; only 17 percent of non-listeners had college degrees, compared to 28 percent of listeners (Owen 1996).

Exit polls in the 1990s showed politically active CTR listeners were predominantly and disproportionately white and disproportionately male (Bolce and De Maio 1996). A clear gender gap exists in the world of CTR: the top rated hosts in the *political* talk circuit are men, and most of the callers are also men (Kohut and Parker 1997).

Talk radio listeners are predominantly conservative. While in the general electorate conservatives outnumber liberals two-to-one, among talk radio listeners the margin is much wider (Bolce and De Maio 1996). (It was four-to-one in the 1994 midterm elections.) Talk radio listeners are more likely to identify with a political party, and Republican Party affiliation is associated with more listening and calling (Owen 1996).

CTR audiences may be discontented, but they are not alienated or isolated. Starting with Hofstetter et al. (1994), most studies have found that, compared with nonlisteners, CTR listeners are more active in politics, and they tend to believe they are more effective in their political action. This is true along most dimensions of political engagement. CTR listeners are more active in voting, registering to vote, letter writing, attending public meetings, and making contributions to political campaigns (Owen 1996). CTR listeners are more issue-oriented and informed than nonlisteners, and they are more avid users of every form of media (Bolce and De Maio 1996; Owen 1996). A majority of listeners report turning to talk radio primarily for political information (Hofstetter et al. 1994; Owen 1996).

FEATURES OF THE TALK RADIO FORMAT
THAT MAKE CTR EFFECTIVE

Research on talk radio in general, and CTR in particular, has tended to study its influence on attitudes, opinion, and political behavior. We review some key findings shortly. But *what* specifically about the CTR format accounts for its influence? Our knowledge here relies more on theory and speculative reflection because it is more difficult and costly to organize a controlled study of different radio formats. Nonetheless, it is useful to review key arguments.

A substantial percentage of U.S. adults turn to talk radio for news, which is odd because talk radio is not news. Facts are secondary in this format, and professional standards for the validation of "facts" are nonexistent. As the most influential Republican pollster, focus group guru, and slogansmith of the last decade puts it: "A compelling story, even if factually inaccurate, can be more emotionally compelling than a dry recitation of the truth" (Brock 2004, 252). Sober expert analysis is not only secondary, but even a liability. Contributions are entertaining, or they are nixed, and a basic rule is that the host always wins (Gimpel 1996). Baffling as it may seem, this is all part of a procedure that gives information obtained from talk radio its *credibility*.

Talk radio is not influential because it builds on expertise or relies on professional integrity to produce "facts." It is influential because the message is clear, consistent, and repetitive (Barker, "Rush to Action," 1998). Talk radio hosts also accrue credibility by putting on display their (staged) ability to crush opposition viewpoints, even those of experts. An important measure of credibility also derives from callers reinforcement and validation (also orchestrated). Rush Limbaugh, one of the masters of the format, confided in a moment of candor: "The fact is I am merely enunciating opinions and analysis that support what they already know...Finally, they say, somebody in the media is saying out loud what they have believed all along (Brock 2004, 265).

Talk radio is probably also influential because it belongs to a class of media that elicits participation and engagement (Hofstetter 1998), or at least the appearance of these. Add the brash demeanor of hosts, their seeming independence, a format that appears to flaunt the rigid script of conventional news, and the total package gives the real impression of participatory, popular, contestation. Arguably, it is the very dearth of these experiences in a flawed democracy that allows talk radio occupy the vacuum: CTR provides a forum, or a rhetorical space, where people can articulate an active and attractive citizen identity and offers the semblance of a civil society where citizens can exercise some power to put a check on those in power (Kane 1998).

THE INFLUENCE OF POLITICAL TALK RADIO

CTR has been credited with considerable influence at critical political junctures over the last decade. To understand the effects of CTR it is useful to outline some salient lines of influence.

The Echo-Chamber Effect

Recent studies of the conservative media establishment (Brock 2004; Alterman 2003) identify an "echo-chamber" effect. A leading talk radio host breaks some news, and actual news organizations are forced to follow the story in their tracks. Talk show hosts are not professional journalists and do not have a staff of professional investigators, so these "scoops" might be provided by a think tank, a congressional staffer, by Republican party operatives, and in some cases, boldly harvested from the Internet rumor mill. Systematic data analysis finds convincing evidence of this echo-chamber effect, on presidential nominations (Page and Tannenbaum 1996), and in the scuttling of the Clinton health plan (Barker, "Rush to Action," 1998).

Issue Articulation

Public opinion on a variety of issues is not fully formed, is contradictory, or is more nuanced than most suspect. Political action and mobilization seems to involve rhetorical projects that firm up convictions, reduce ambiguities, and capitalize on poorly articulated grievances—and they do so in a selective way. Kane (1998) cites data showing that Americans understand quite generally that governments and market economies are abundantly imperfect. Concentration and abuse of power can be political, economic, or a tangled mix of both. Yet CTR articulates apprehensions about concentrated power to selectively mount a critique of government, but not of corporate power. This selectivity begs the question, why?

Insider Booster/Outsider Neutralization Effect

Listening to CTR is a form of participation in virtual community networks. Barker ("The Talk Radio Community," 1998) finds, after controlling statistically for a long list of factors, that participation in the community of Limbaugh listeners is clearly associated with *increases* in the sense of political efficacy and political participation among conservatives and moderates. Although the evidence is more inconclusive, Barker also argues it is possible that CTR has a demoralizing effect on listeners who are not conservatives or moderates. There is also a related *saturation effect* at play: the more frequently Rush Limbaugh entertains a particular argument, the stronger is the influence on listener's opinion (Barker and Wright 2000).

Propaganda: Misinformation and "Killing the Messenger" Effects

Misinformation. Carefully crafted studies of the political knowledge of listeners and nonlisteners show that: (1) CTR listeners are less informed about basic, non-ideological, facts about the U.S. political system, and (2) CTR listeners believe a greater amount of ideological information that is factually wrong. These are avid seekers of information who, ironically, are more misinformed. Exposure to moderate talk radio does have the same effect (Hofstetter 1999).

"Killing the Messenger." CTR hosts influence listeners, whether they focus on issues or address individuals or groups. The "Limbaugh effect" is, however, much stronger when an individual or group is the target of slanderous invective (Barker and Wright 2000). CTR's influence, therefore, seems strongest when it operates through character assassination—discrediting and killing the messenger rather than engaging the message. Although there is no reason this is unique to conservative propaganda, it so happens that the airwaves are dominated by CTR.

OUR STUDY

Our study examines the rhetoric on immigration and immigrants in leading CTR shows. We selected Oregon for this study because it is a "defended" state: Oregon is still predominantly white, but has experienced one of the highest rates of Latino population growth over the last decade, and is bordered by California, a state where high immigration has been a charged political issue for some years.

Five shows are the focus of the analysis: three national CTR shows (Rush Limbaugh, Bill O'Reilly, and Michael Savage) and two local shows (Mark and Dave, and Lars Larson). These programs were selected because they had the highest audience ratings, respectively, of national and local shows in the Portland, Oregon, metropolitan market in the fall of 2002. The findings in this article are based on a systematic content analysis of a random sample five two-hour segments from each of the shows—a segment per week—over the course of five weeks in the fall of 2002. The entire sample consists of 50 hours of talk radio, encompassing 200 quarter-hour segments.

KEY FINDINGS

Who Participates and Who Gets Talked About

If CTR is a virtual town meeting of sorts, it is very curious to see who is in charge, who is in attendance, and who is the topic of conversation. All the hosts in our sample of top rated shows are white men. Among the callers we were able to identify, 74 percent were men, and 62 percent were white men. This is consistent with the gender patterns noted by other studies of talk radio content (Kohut and Parker 1997) and with suggestions that CTR listeners are disproportionately white (e.g., Hoyt 1992). Yet most striking was how frequently those "not at the meeting" were the subject of conversation. Ethnic or racial outsiders were a topic of conversation in 57 percent of our talk show segments (114 of 200). Predictably perhaps, African Americans were the most frequently discussed racial outsiders, but immigrants are the subject of discussion in 39 percent of all segments where the discussion revolves around problematic "racial" or ethnic populations.

The Word on Immigrants

One image casts a long shadow over all the CTR discussion of immigrants— the illegal alien. Segments where immigration was a topic of conversation were compulsively drawn to the problem of "illegal aliens." About 93 percent of all references to immigrants are in connection to this "problem." When we tallied the most common idea associations in segments discussing immigrants or immigration, the following distinctions stood out:

➤ Illegal = not welcome
➤ "Illegals" are not real or welcome immigrants

➤ Immigrants = old stock immigrants, European immigrants
➤ Illegals = crime, dirt, of color, Third World refuse

Immigrant and immigration discussions were consistent and overtly stereo-typical. Immigrants were presented as a group that should be controlled by the government (39 percent of immigration segments), terrorists (32 percent), a cultural threat (27 percent), receiving special rights (20 percent), an eco-nomic drain (18 percent), and a crime threat (16 percent) by hosts. During show segments when immigration is a topic of discussion, hosts raise the immigrant-as-threat theme an average of 1.6 times per segment; callers on average chime in on the immigrant-as-threat theme just over once per call. Further, hosts argue in 45 percent of show segments that borders should be more strictly controlled or that immigrants should be tracked or denied ser-vices such as health care and public education. Thirty percent of callers make these same suggestions. Although 61 percent of immigration discourses do not identify a particular immigrant group, immigration is most often associ-ated with racial and ethnic minority populations.

Latinos/Mexicans were the single pan-ethnic or ethnic population most commonly mentioned. This is not surprising given the composition of recent immigration to Oregon, the size of the Hispanic population in neighboring California, and nativist, anti-Hispanic, fears stroked by talk radio celebrities (Savage 2003) and even higher brow public intellectuals (Huntington 2004). When Hispanics were the subject of discussion, they were most commonly reduced to the "illegal immigration problem," and to a "Hispanic vote" and a "radical Hispanic lobby" that abets this scourge. These examples of His-panic political activity could well be construed as examples of a very Amer-ican tradition of civic engagement, but instead they were construed as sinister forces encouraging illegal activity.

Patterns of Racialization

White immigrants were never a part of the immigration problem in the CTR segments we analyzed. Controversy always revolved around "Third World" immigrants, Hispanics, Haitians, Arabs, in sum, non-white immigrants. Although African Americans were also overwhelmingly the subject of discus-sion (by non-blacks) harping on a plethora of imagined black pathologies, the pattern of "racialization" was different in discussions of blacks and immigrants.

Blacks were given a concrete and familiar public face in many of the dis-cussions delving into "what is wrong with blacks": Rev. Al Sharpton or Jessie Jackson, standing in for the unscrupulous, sleazy, exploitative, civil rights establishment; Michael Jackson, representing pathological fatherhood and freakish and doomed attempts to conform; various NBA basketball players representing the entire gamut of deviance, from crime to dysfunctional families. Latino immigrants, in contrast, remained an anonymous mass of lawbreakers and social leaches. Not a single Latino public figure surfaced in our sample. In a town meeting where participants were firming up their sense of who belongs to the nation, blacks were the familiar internal threat, while Latinos were inscrutable outsiders.

Explicit discussions of the problem of racism focused on blacks overwhelmingly, but only to blame blacks for unfairly playing the race card, and in effect, defining them as the major source of contemporary racism. Other groups, including Latinos (who in these discussions were equated with immigrants), rarely received mention in discussions of racism, except for the occasional Michael Savage broadsides castigating the ACLU for teaching pliant immigrants that "America is racist." Whites participating in these discussions were defining their post-civil rights racial identity in relation to the issue of racism, and primarily in reference to imagined power of black racism.

When the conversation turned from racism to the subject of "special rights," however, immigrants and African Americans shared equal burden. "Special rights" is an umbrella term used to dismiss offhand a variety of social policies and to discredit the character of groups that advocate for them. According to the CTR curriculum, "the nation" has two primary "special rights" problems: affirmative action, associated with blacks, and social services associated with the "radical Hispanic lobby" and politicians who cave into pressures from the "Hispanic vote"—bilingual education, immigrant worker protections, legalization proposals, etc. The subtext of these conversations is not all that subtle: blacks—who have only themselves to blame for their disadvantages and are today the major racists—and immigrants (of color)—who flaunt the law, and are quick with their own demands for "special rights"—are circling in on whites, the core of the nation under siege. "Liberals" is given the same rhetorical function assigned to "communists" and "Bolsheviks" in decades past—these are anti-American race-traitors. While the color coding of this drama seems straightforward enough, the racial definition of the American nation is not always explicit. Limbaugh, for instance, tiptoed around the issue in one of the segments:

> Liberals like to say Columbus brought…racism, sexism, homophobia, destruction of the environment…that he conquered *a bunch* of free independent, indigenous peoples and made them slaves…they think

the problem in the world is America, that we are the oppressors...
(our italics)

Recognition of racism is un-American; concern with the environment, sexism, and homophobia is also un-American; and *we*, the nation, does not seem to include the *bunches* of not-really-free Indians nor the slaves and their descendants. Limbaugh's fumbling effort represents the milder end of the spectrum. Michael Savage, in contrast, left little to the imagination in an all-too-typical tirade:

> I mean that we have to decide which countries we want the immigrant to come from. That goes to the demographics of the nation. How do we want America to look in 20 years? Do we want it to be more white? Do we want it to be more Asian, less Asian? Do we want it to be more Hispanic?[...] No nation on Earth has ever had its demographic base changed as rapidly...that had not been invaded and defeated in war and then the women raped by the invaders.

CONCLUSION

Our study analyzed the content and rhetoric on immigrants and immigration in a 50-hour sample of conservative talk radio. The findings were barely ambiguous. Immigration and immigrants are part of a political analysis bent on conceptualizing power, prosperity, and threats to the good life in terms of a Manichean battle between nation-members and nation-enemies. Immigrants in general, and Hispanics in particular, figure in this analysis as an ominous threat to the livelihood and civilization of (white) Americans. Problem immigrants were clearly color coded.

The "immigration curriculum" in conservative talk radio would be a smaller concern if the audience were miniscule and politically disengaged, or if the information spigot were widely regarded as propaganda. But this is not the case. CTR audiences are large, politically active, and media-hungry. Research shows that the information they obtain through CTR influences their attitudes and political choices. The political learning taking place through this medium bodes poorly for the climate of new immigrant reception in the U.S. The implicit curriculum on immigration and race we found in our sample of CTR is also a sobering reminder of the wide currency of racialized definitions of nation, belonging, and human worth as we enter the fifth decade of the post-civil rights era.

The CTR immigration and race curriculum is as troubling for its silences and omissions as it is for its racialized rhetoric. Burning and challenging issues of corporate power, tax equity, forces undermining labor standards, global economic relations, imperial war, are made entirely invisible and are thus beyond the pale of discussion. Some urgent tasks in the challenging battle to democratize the U.S. media are the unmasking of the conservative talk radio fiasco, a demand for quality control before profit in the airwaves, and the creation of engaging interactive radio formats that *develop* and *refine* citizen's understandings of the real and complex forces that threaten the livelihood of people the world over.

REFERENCES

Alterman, Eric. *What Liberal Media? The Truth About Bias and the News*. New York: Basic Books, 2003.

Barker, David C. "Rush to Action: Political Talk Radio and Health (un) Reform." *Political Communication* 15(1) (1998): 83-97.

————— "The Talk Radio Community: Non-Traditional Social Networks and Political Participation." *Social Science Quarterly* 79(2) (1998): 261-272.

Barker, David C., and Kathleen Wright. "Political Talk Radio and Public Opinion." *Political Opinion Quarterly* 64 (2000): 149-170.

Bolce, Louis, and Gerald De Maio. "Dial-In Democracy: Talk Radio and the 1994 Election." *Political Science Quarterly* 111(3) (1996): 457-481.

Brock, David. *The Republican Noise Machine: Right Wing Media and How it Corrupts Democracy*. New York: Crown Publishers, 2004.

De la Vina, Mike. "Air Partisan." *Air Demographics* (February 2004): 20-22.

Gimpel, James G. "A Political Scientist Rides the Radio Talk Circuit." *Political Science and Politics* (December 1996): 717-719.

Hofstetter, C. Richard, Mark C. Donovan, Melville R. Klauber, Alexandra Cole, Carolyn J. Huie, and Toshiyuki Yuasa. "Political Talk Radio: A Stereotype Reconsidered." *Political Research Quarterly* 47(2) (1994): 467-80.

Hofstetter, C. Richard. "Political Talk Radio, Situational Involvement, and Political Mobilization." *Social Science Quarterly* 79(2) (1998): 273-286.

Hofstetter, C. Richard, David Barker, James T. Smith, Gina M. Zari, and Thomas Ingrasia. "Information, Misinformation, and Political Talk Radio." *Political Research Quarterly* 52(2) (1999): 353-369.

Hoyt, Mike. "Talk Radio Turning Up the Volume." *Columbia Journalism Review* 31(3) (November/December 1992): 44-50.

Huntington, Samuel P. "The Hispanic Challenge." *Foreign Policy* 141 (March/April 2004): <www.foreignpolicy.com>.

Kane, Thomas. "Public Argument, Civil Society, and What Talk Radio Teaches About Rhetoric." *Argumentation and Advocacy* 34(3) (1998): 154-161.

Kohut, Andrew, and Kimberly Parker. "Talk Radio and Gender Politics." In Pippa Norris (Ed.) *Women, Media, and Politics.* New York: Oxford University Press, 1997: 221-234.

McChesney, Robert W. *The Problem with the Media: U.S. Communication Politics in the Twenty-First Century.* New York: Monthly Review, 2004.

Owen, Diana. "Who's Talking? Who's Listening? The New Politics of Radio Talk Shows." In Stephen C. Craig (Ed.), *Broken Contract: Changing Relationships Between Americans and Their Government.* Boulder, CO: Westview Press, 1996: 127-146.

Page, Benjamin I., and Jason Tannenbaum. "Populistic Deliberation and Talk Radio." *Journal of Communication* 46(2) (1996): 33-54.

Savage, Michael. *Savage Nation: Saving America from the Liberal Assault on Our Borders, Language and Culture.* Nashville, TN: Thomas Nelson, 2003.

CHAPTER 13

A PROJECT CENSORED INVESTIGATIVE REPORT

Newspaper Fraud Victims are Diverse

BY GEOFF DAVIDIAN

Research Assistance from Brittny Roeland, Pat Carlson, and Matt Hagan

"One of the fundamental corner posts of our government is a free and independent press.

The exhibits attached to this document raise questions of whether the press is serving its function when the issue concerns whether one of its members is betraying their privileged position by leveraging politicians into allowing illegal monopolies; that one of their members is bartering favorable treatment in editorial and news pages in exchange for help in fighting off the federal agencies whose responsibility it is to ensure a free, independent, diverse and competitive press.

Why have the large media conglomerates ignored rather than investigated conduct set out in the exhibits? Why haven't the other members of the press asked Hearst to explain the facts as set out in the attached exhibits? Are there more important news stories than the possibility that a giant in the free press is corrupting a major corner post of our government?"—Federal Antitrust Complaint in *Norris et al. v. The Hearst Corporation, et al.*, United States District Court, Southern District of Texas, at Houston.

Two unrelated circulation fraud cases alleging strikingly similar facts are in federal district courts in Texas and New York. Discovery in the cases coupled with an investigation by the House Judiciary Committee could lead to a roll back of the consolidation of newspaper ownership—or demonopolization.

A seven-month Project Censored investigation has revealed a pattern of newspaper takeovers and closures by the Hearst Corporation, allegedly funded in part by money obtained by defrauding advertisers.

According to documents obtained by Project Censored, management at Hearst's Houston *Chronicle* directed circulation managers to get auditors drunk at "titty bars" the night before they were to review *Chronicle* records for the Audit Bureau of Circulations (ABC). Plaintiffs in *Norris v. Hearst* say management hoped auditors would be hung over the following day and not properly monitor how the paper reported its numbers. The ABC is the official industry source for how many copies of a newspaper are purchased, and it is on the basis of those figures that advertisers decide where to spend their money. By falsely inflating the circulation figures, a publisher can appear to justify raising advertising rates and at the same time deny the competition revenue by making the competition seem irrelevant in the market by comparison. It was during this period of alleged fraud that the *Chronicle*'s competitor the Houston *Post* went out of business.

In subsequent years, distributors claim they were forced to "buy" more papers than there was demand and were paid to destroy them or take them to a dump, fabricate subscribers, and claim street sales were higher than they were.

Ed Rossi, a plaintiff in the Houston case, came to Texas from post-Fascist Sicily as an eight-year-old immigrant in 1947. Three years later, he still didn't speak English, but he was a capitalist.

When he was 11, Rossi started selling newspapers on a north Houston street corner. On his first day, he recalled, he bought five papers for a dime each and sold each for 15 cents. He worked that corner all the way through

THIS MODERN WORLD   by TOM TOMORROW

CONSERVATIVES REMAIN *VERY SUSPICIOUS* OF THE NEW YORK TIMES' PRE-WAR COVERAGE OF IRAQ...

I THINK THEY DELIBERATELY *UNDERSTATED* THE THREAT POSED BY SADDAM--TO MAKE THE PRESIDENT LOOK *FOOLISH* FOR TAKING US TO *WAR!*

WHAT *ELSE* COULD EXPLAIN SUCH ONE-SIDED REPORTING?

DAMN THE DEVIOUS LIBERAL MEDIA!

IN REALITY, OF COURSE, THE NEW YORK TIMES HELPED TO *BOLSTER* THE CASE FOR WAR...RUNNING NUMEROUS FRONT-PAGE STORIES ABOUT IRAQI WMD'S BY REPORTER JUDITH MILLER--WHOSE PRIMARY SOURCE WAS THE BUSH ADMINISTRATION'S THEN-FAVORITE IRAQI EXILE, *AHMED CHALABI*...

JUDY--YOU *MUST* BELIEVE ME! SADDAM'S GENETICISTS HAVE CREATED A SECRET ARMY OF *GIANT MUTATED LIZARDS* THAT, UM, SHOOT *LASER BEAMS!* OUT OF THEIR *EYEBALLS!*

SOUNDS LIKE AN ABOVE-THE-FOLD *SCOOP* TO ME!

school, delivering to residences by foot in his spare time. Later, he bought a bike for $30, put a basket on it, and started a route. He did so well he won a motor bike in a *Chronicle* paperboy contest. By age 15, he was delivering 200 papers a day. It was honest work, and his hustle paid off.

"I loved it," Rossi said. "We used to tie the papers with twine. I used to be able to roll and tie 50 papers in three-and-a-half minutes." By 1961, Rossi was grossing $1,500 a month and had built his single copy sales to 450 a day. By 1995, Rossi was distributing 3,500 papers a day and grossing $80,000 a year. Rossi knew that newspapers had a special place in American society; even though he couldn't read, he recalled that people hungered for the Korean War stories his papers carried.

Rossi, now 65 years old, is one of the six plaintiffs in the Houston case.

Rossi says after Hearst purchased the company, he was told to falsely inflate the number of newspapers he distributed as a condition of employment. "I felt betrayed," Rossi said. "I gave them my life and they did this to me?"

While allegedly tweaking the circulation figures and hiking ad rates, the Hearst Corporation went on a newspaper buying binge, closing down the competition and creating news monopolies.

The chairman of the House Judiciary Committee, Representative F. James Sensenbrenner (R–WI), has demanded that the U.S. Department of Justice (DOJ) explain why it continues to authorize Hearst takeovers of competing papers when Hearst immediately closes them.

Sensenbrenner also asked the DOJ's antitrust division in a February 10, 2004, letter whether the "use of illicit means to falsely inflate circulation fig-

ures in a one newspaper town might violate the antitrust laws," especially if those funds were used to buy other newspapers and close them, leaving presses still, workers idle, and dissenting voices quiet from coast to coast.

This pattern is not just the dark side of corporate culture, says Houston attorney Jerry S. Payne, who represents the six former distributors suing Hearst. The pattern is intentional monopolizing, which is a felony. But much worse, he said, is the impact on society.

"Newspapers didn't just offer an opportunity to make money for any kid who understands rubber bands or has a bike," says Payne, who himself had a *Chronicle* route as a child. "They are watchdogs of government. They are a pillar of our democracy."

So important are newspapers to a democratic society that in 1970 Congress passed the Newspaper Preservation Act, which exempted newspaper joint operating agreements (JOAs) from antitrust laws if one of the newspapers was failing.

The Newspaper Preservation Act, known officially as Title 15, Chapter 43– Newspaper Preservation, begins: "In the public interest of maintaining a newspaper press editorially and reportorially independent and competitive in all parts of the United States, it is hereby declared to be the public policy of the United States to preserve the publication of newspapers in any city, community, or metropolitan area where a joint operating arrangement has been heretofore entered into because of economic distress or is hereafter effected in accordance with the provisions of this chapter."

A media monopoly is 10 times more dangerous than other monopolies because of their ability to affect voting, Payne said. "This is a national emergency. And as they get more monopolies, every step up gets harder because they control politicians."

San Francisco attorney Joseph Alioto agrees. In an interview with Project Censored's Brittny Roeland, Alioto, who represented Clint Reilly in an antitrust suit that failed to stop the Hearst takeover of the *Chronicle*, says Hearst bartered editorial content favorable to politicians for support of Hearst's efforts to obtain a monopoly in San Francisco.

ALIOTO: We favor competition in the media; it is the rule of trade unlike anywhere else in the world. Media competition is necessary in sustaining the First Amendment. There should not be monopolies. We need opinions and diversity in editorials. In the late '60s Citizen Publishing Company decided that they did not want to compete. They wanted to run the newspapers under the joint operating agreement so they could have the same prices for advertising. Ads are the lifeblood of the newspapers; without the ads you have no newspaper. The DOJ sued Citizens Publishing Co., and the Supreme Court said they could not run under the JOA because it was in violation of the antitrust laws.

All the big newspapers at the time did not like this, so they went to their friends in Congress and asked them to pass a special exemption for them within the antitrust laws. The newspapers did not want competition. The newspapers were so powerful that Congress passed this. Congress was very concerned about what the newspapers would write about them. Probably because the newspapers come out every day. President Nixon reviewed the law (Newspaper Preservation Act, or NPA). The Newspapers said they would not support him if he did not approve of the NPA. He approved the law, and needless to say, it allowed two newspapers to get together and do whatever they wanted, except they were to maintain a diverse editorial voice in each of the papers. The special exemption within the JOA is if the other newspaper is going broke, then the stronger paper might as well save it. With the Reilly case, the DOJ said it was okay for [Hearst] to sell the *Examiner*—the failing paper. Yet the Hearst-owned *Examiner* was not going out of business. They wanted to keep the dying paper in business. This was so they could close down the "failing" paper (after three years of lost money—special exemption) and have their monopoly in San Francisco.

PROJECT CENSORED: Do you believe that Hearst traded favorable editorial treatment to Willy Brown for his approval of the Hearst takeover of the *Examiner*?

ALIOTO: Yes, [former *Examiner* publisher Timothy] White said yes. He said this nonchalantly.

PROJECT CENSORED: Do you think that Tim White was forced to retire, retired on his own will, or was he fired?

ALIOTO: Tim White was fired, and he actually sued Hearst and was paid $5 million. Other Hearst employees were proven to be liars. The judge pronounced the chief executive officers of Hearst are not credible.

PROJECT CENSORED: Are there any prominent facts that the DOJ had to ignore in order to approve the Hearst purchase of the *Chronicle*?

ALIOTO: The company buying the newspaper was the same company that owned the competing paper (*Examiner*). Instead of investing their money, they killed the paper. The DOJ ignored that the *Chronicle* would become a monopoly in San Francisco.

PROJECT CENSORED: Why would they ignore this?

ALIOTO: The Antitrust Department have consistently failed in their obligations to preserve competition in the U.S. by prosecuting antitrust laws. (DOJ sides with monopolies and files against citizens standing up to Hearst) The DOJ has failed with stopping monopolies in many areas—oil companies, computer companies, television companies, newspaper companies. These mergers increase prices, people lose their jobs, and there is less innovation and more destruction to citizen freedoms.

PROJECT CENSORED: Who is controlling this?

ALIOTO: It's politics. Politics, all of it is controlling this. Big money is power. Private parties like yourself and Reilly are the only people who can stop them.

PROJECT CENSORED: What are your ideas about the Hearst purchase scenario? What did the various parties get in return?

ALIOTO: Hearst got their monopoly.

PROJECT CENSORED: Did the DOJ know the truth about Hearst dealings? Did they keep any of this from the judge or Congress? Why? Were there any documents pertaining to this issue that were not allowed into the trial?

ALIOTO: Either the DOJ did not know what to do with the evidence, or they did not want to do anything with it, it is one or the other. The judge invited the DOJ to appear in court, and they decided not to.

PROJECT CENSORED: Why not?

ALIOTO: Probably because they didn't want me to ask them any questions.

PROJECT CENSORED: What would you have asked them?

ALIOTO: The same questions I asked the Hearst executives. How can you allow the weaker paper to buy the other? How can you support a monopoly? This is an extraordinary organization, the fourth estate, editorials are for sale. The media should reveal the economic interest inside our government's dealings, but it is not required to. We definitely should require this of our fourth estate.

In response to Representative Sensenbrenner's letter, Assistant Attorney General William B. Moschella answered on May 19, 2004, acknowledging the DOJ had conducted three antitrust investigations of Hearst between 1993 and 2000:

➤ In 2000, Hearst gave away its *San Francisco Examiner* and $66 million for operational expenses to Ted Fang and his family, who published a free tabloid in order to get DOJ's Antitrust Division's approval of Hearst's bid to acquire the competing *San Francisco Chronicle.* Although Hearst said the deal would preserve all jobs, within two years of the change in ownership the *Examiner* was being published by just eight people. Under Fang's ownership, the *Examiner* became a free tabloid, and by the time it was sold again in February 2004 for $20 million, the circulation had dropped from 95,800 in 2000 to 69,000.

➤ In 1995, the Antitrust Division investigated the acquisition by Hearst, which operated *The Houston Chronicle,* of its major daily newspaper competitor, *The Houston Post.* The division did not challenge the acquisition, after determining that the *Post* was a "failing firm" under established case law. Specifically, the division gathered evidence and determined that the *Post,* (a) was unable to meet its financial obligations in the immediate future, (b) was unable to reorganize successfully under Chapter 11 of the Bankruptcy Act, and (c) had completed good faith efforts to elicit reasonable alternative offers of acquisition that would keep its assets in the market. The *Post* subsequently ceased publication. The DOJ did not mention the alleged circulation fraud that may have driven the *Post* under.

➤ In 1993, the division investigated Hearst's acquisition of the *San Antonio Express-News.* Hearst owned the *San Antonio Light,* the other daily newspaper in San Antonio, Texas. Again, the DOJ's Antitrust Division did not challenge Hearst's acquisition, after determining that the *San Antonio Light* met the requirements of the "failing firm" defense. The *San Antonio Light* subsequently ceased publication.

Moschella noted that the DOJ currently is "conducting a thorough investigation of a newspaper joint operating agreement between Hearst and the Seattle Times Company."

"This investigation is intended to determine whether any conduct associated with the operation of that agreement raises significant competition concerns under the federal antitrust laws. Based on the division's findings, the department will take whatever steps are necessary to preserve competition in the relevant market."

To recap:

- In Houston, Hearst bought the *Post's* assets and has a monopoly with the *Chronicle.*

- In San Francisco, Hearst had the weaker *Examiner* and managed to acquire the stronger—and viable—*Chronicle,* resulting in a *de facto* monopoly.

- In San Antonio, Hearst had the weaker *San Antonio Light,* but bought *San Antonio Express-News* and closed its own paper, resulting in a monopoly.

In Seattle, Hearst says its *Post-Intelligencer,* with a daily circulation of 157,558, is a "failing newspaper," while its partner in the JOA, the *Seattle Times,* reports daily sales of 224,140 and has lost money for the past three years. Under the terms of the JOA, the *Times,* owned by the Blethen family, can pull out of the agreement after three unprofitable years, but Hearst is suing to force the *Times* to honor the agreement despite the escape clause. The *Times* says the *Post-Intelligencer* is trying to bleed it until it goes broke.

In a letter to readers, Frank, Bob and Will Blethen complained that in their battle with Hearst, media are not giving it the coverage it deserved. They said Hearst's attempt to muscle out the *Times* was being reported as "a relatively low profile dispute."

"Many of you may not be aware of what is at stake for this community and, from a larger perspective, what this dispute means in the battle to preserve independent ownership of media rather than having it consolidated into the hands of three or four powerful corporations in America. You have a right to know."

"Hearst has a history of squeezing out the competition and becoming the absentee owner of the only daily newspaper. It did it in San Francisco, San Antonio, and Houston, and now that's what it's trying to do in Seattle," the Blethens write.

"The Blethen family could have sold the *Times* years ago to a media giant like Hearst for more money than we could spend in several lifetimes. But for us, this is not about money. It is about our responsibility to the First Amendment and the traditions of a free press responsive to the communities in which we reside.

"We will do all we can to make sure Hearst will not end independent journalism in Seattle. We are unified in our resolve. We are selling real estate to provide cash to minimize additional cutbacks at the *Times,* especially in our news staff and content. If Hearst wins, it will surely do as it has done elsewhere and drain this community by slashing the news staff, increasing advertising rates and siphoning off profits to its New York headquarters."

Hearst has billions of dollars, 12 daily newspapers (including the nation's tenth and eleventh biggest), 17 magazines and 27 television stations (Hearst-Argyle reported net revenues for the quarter ended March 31, 2004 of $166.9 million, up 11.8 percent, from $149.3 million in the first quarter of 2003).

How do newspapers continue to increase ad revenue at a time when newspaper readership has bottomed with the Internet growing as a source of information, and while in cities like Seattle, Hearst calls its *Post-Intelligencer* a "failing newspaper" and one of the city's two daily papers will not likely see the end of the decade?

Whether they paid by American Express or food stamps, Americans last year had $40.50 added to the cost of their purchases after the price of national newspaper advertising was passed on to consumers as higher prices.

From baby formula and bread to automobiles and houses, U.S. consumers in 2003 took an $11.8 billion hit for national newspaper ads—7.7 percent of the $153 billion national advertisers spent on all media. This 8 percent increase over newspaper ad revenue in 2002 is in addition to the markup on local products and services advertised locally, like car dealerships and grocery stores, whose costs are not included in the national figures reported by the Newspaper Association of America. For the $27 billion spent on local retail and general local advertising, deduct another $92 from your wallet.

These increases in advertising revenue occurred at a time when newsprint consumption decreased 1.6 percent in 2002 and production declined about 10 percent, from 5.7 to 5.2 million metric tons.

This reverse correlation between newspaper production and advertising revenue to date defies logical explanation.

Among the issues investigated during the project was whether Hearst paid the price of obtaining the monopolies through a pattern of racketeering and criminal fraud, illegally crippling its competition, then using fabricated circulation figures to generate advertising revenue necessary to buy the failing competitor—and whether the Department of Justice turned its back on the whole deal.

In Houston, plaintiffs' attorney Payne accused Hearst of using the money generated by the fraud to obtain and shutdown the competition, but also asserted, "However, the money is not traceable. If they need $100 million, they can just pull it out of a different subsidiary."

Meanwhile, in New York, a federal class action lawsuit on behalf of advertisers names *Newsday* and its parent Tribune Publishing Company in charges of racketeering.

Attorney Joseph Giaimo also names as defendants The Tribune Company's Spanish language newspaper, *Hoy*, four distributors and eight individuals. The advertisers who brought the suit are four Queens businesses who claim *Newsday* stole from them through the fraud for about 10 years.

Giaimo says there are thousands of potential class members whose ads ran in the papers.

The suit alleges that *Newsday* participated in "an enterprise designed to defraud, steal, and embezzle from the plaintiffs by means of false and fraudulent pretenses and representations as to the circulation volume of the newspapers."

The suit claims that the defendants "executed such schemes through use of the United States mail, telephone communication, telephone facsimiles, and the Internet in interstate and foreign commerce."

"Defendants secretly and fraudulently padded and inflated the circulation volume through various means such as dumping unsold *Newsday* newspapers; creating false circulation reports and affidavits submitted to the circulation auditing agency, Audit Bureau of Circulations; compelling their newspaper distributors under threat of *Newsday*'s termination of the distributorship to inflate reported circulation volume by falsely decreasing the number of *Newsday* newspapers returned to the distributors by retailers and falsely increasing *Newsday* sales volume; creating false street sale ("hawker") programs; paying retailers to purchase *Newsday* newspapers with the knowledge that the newspapers would be unsold and dumped by the retailer; and other nefarious devices."

While the Audit Bureau of Circulations (ABC) is responsible for checking up on publishers' statements of how many copies are sold, the not-for-profit industry organization has not interviewed one witness or plaintiff in either the Houston or New York fraud cases. While stating that it has revisited the documents audited and found them truthful, ABC lawyers have not interviewed the plaintiffs.

The costs are not just at the checkout counter. Attorney Payne says if the public had as much information about the newspaper monopolies as they do about Enron or Halliburton, they would be up in arms.

But our research shows that only newspapers in the same markets wanting to humiliate the Houston *Chronicle* and *Newsday* have reported on the lawsuits.

"Hearst has a toe hold on the politicians," Payne said. "You need some event that shows the media they have to report it. If a jury finds Hearst intentionally monopolized, it is a felony, and Hearst would be a felon. Then we'd see the politicians demand change. There would be a domino effect."

Geoff Davidian is a veteran reporter and editor who has worked for Hearst in Houston, as well as at the *Roswell Daily Record* (New Mexico), the *Arizona Republic*, the *Oregonian*, the *Milwaukee Journal, Maine Sunday Telegram*, and the *Lowell Sun* (Massachusetts). He has lectured at Sonoma State University and at Marquette University and taught investigative reporting at the Krishnamurti school in Varanasi, India.

A special thanks to Washington, DC, researcher and Freedom of Information Act (FOIA) expert Michael Ravnitzky for his guidance.

CHAPTER 14

Corporate Media Neglects Anti-globalization Movements

BY DEEPA FERNANDES

Zapatista leader Subcomandante Marcos has called corporate globalization "a war against humanity" while back in 1999, Ralph Nader worried that people world over would suffer enormously due to what he called "globalization's tactic" of eliminating democracy in individual nations, rendering irrelevant local laws and accountability structures, and instead imposing a corporate "coup d'etat."

Nader, along with many others, predicted that for people in poor countries who would have globalization forced on them, the results would be catastrophic: widespread hunger, malnutrition, deadly diseases, irreversible ecological devastation, natural resource shortages, growing unemployment, and political chaos.

For us in the world's few rich countries, while we would also live the growing unemployment, ecological devastation, depletion of natural resources, and even the deadly diseases, our lives would be materially richer. Globalization's tactic with us, the generation who, at best, protest globalization while sipping on a Starbuck's latte, is to blind us to the consequences of this easy living. Because if the majority knew that people were living and dying in misery around the world in the name of our new Gap tank top or our upgraded SONY laptop, would we allow it to happen? Yet the victims of corporate globalization are also prolific in U.S. and other rich countries, and they are mostly people of color and poor whites.

In the years 2003 and 2004, as corporate globalization tactics reached unprecedented lows, the people-struggles against them also ratcheted up accordingly. There are so many examples. In Bolivia, a group of U.S. and British corporations attempted to have the government of that small Andean nation sign over the country's vast natural gas resources, which it planned to run through a port off the coast of Chile and then ship to California. No fair price would be paid and no public accountability offered, in a country where 8 out of 10 Indigenous people live in dire poverty and the majority do not have 24-hour electricity nor access to constant running water. Bolivians got wind of the secret deal and gave their government an emphatic, "No way!" And when the government, backed by the multinational corporations, ignored the people and went ahead with the plans, tens of thousands took to the streets, days upon days upon days, until President Gonzalo Sanchez de Lozado was forced from office. And the corporations, along with their elaborate gas-heist scheme, were sent packing.

One also remembers certain African nations that refused to accept GMO crops as aid that the U.S. was forcing on them and the Central American banana farmers who finally got a day in a U.S. court against their pesticide wielding bosses (Dow, Dole, and Shell among them) alleging that being forced to work with DCBP, a chemical that is banned in the US, made them sterile.

2003 and 2004 also saw people-of-color movements in the U.S. tell corporate giants that their communities were akin to a Third World within a First World. In Immokalee, Florida, the poor Central American tomato farmers who are kept virtually enslaved for the sake of Taco Bell products, organized, risking their jobs and their status in the U.S. to demand basic rights. And in California, poor black and brown residents of Englewood, California, told Wal-Mart that its new superstore was not worth a few minimum wage jobs at the expense of local businesses and sweatshop-labor products flooding their communities.

But if two particular stories of 2003 and 2004 can best illustrate the state of globalization for those struggling against it: stunning victories for some and tragic defeat for others, they are the case of Coca-Cola in India and the lot of Third-World rice farmers as they are squished into oblivion by international agriculture policies that are stealing their livelihoods.

A recent immigrant to India, Coca-Cola had a particularly bad 2003 in the sub-continent. Activists argue that the spoils of globalization merely came back to punish the multinational cola giant, while Coke worked overtime to convince the Indian authorities and cola-drinking public that its product was not toxic. Coke began 2003 fending off accusations from poor villagers in the southern Indian state of Kerala that it had depleted precious water supplies of nearby local communities. It ended the year facing the possibility of being expelled from the world's second most populous country.

If you visit Coke's India Web site, it boasts that "after a 16-years absence, Coca-Cola returned to India in 1993." While the Web site goes on to tout all that the corporation has done for the Indian people, there is scant mention of the gifts of globalization that Coke has benefited from. Yet people-led struggles across India one decade later forced some of those freebies into much public scrutiny, though if one were to follow the U.S. establishment press, you wouldn't know it.

Perhaps two of the biggest globalization gifts that Coke has been enjoying in India were exposed this past year by affected communities and independent scientists. Coke exploited the land to extract vast amounts of the most critical ingredient in making its product: water. Coke has also been allowed to benefit from extremely lax Indian standards on water quality. But both these things almost came to an end for the cola giant in 2003, due in no uncertain terms to widespread community organizing backed by scientific evidence, that try as they might, Coca-Cola has not been able to refute or successfully counter.

In India, 60 percent of the population lacks access to safe drinking water and tens of thousands of people die each year from water-borne diseases. Coke's 2003 India woes started when poor villagers in Kerala, mostly Dalits and Adivasis, began to complain that their water supplies were drying up. They blamed the nearby Coca-Cola plant for sucking up huge quantities of ground water. Coke was accused of drawing nearly 1.5 million liters of groundwater for every 85 truckloads of product that left the factory premises. In 2002 there were also accusations that Coke, running out of water to fill its many bottles, took water from wells in neighboring villages. A government inquiry, conducted in January 2003 by the Kerala State Groundwater Department, found depleted water levels and deterioration in the quality of the ground water. While the government attributed this to the lack of rainfall, it also called for the immediate preservation of all ground water sources.

Coke immediately denied all water depletion accusations and used the government's excuse of drought to explain the lack of water. Villagers and workers of the Kerala Coke plant have accused the company of having 600 wells inside its compound, a charge Coke disputes. Coke says its average water consumption per day is 0.5 million liters. Environmentalists in Kerala have calculated that the amount of ground water extracted by Coca-Cola's Kerala plant is enough to satisfy the total domestic needs of close to 20,000 people.

The establishment Indian press began 2003 firmly on the side of Coca-Cola. Early on it trumpeted Coke's lack-of-rainfall argument, and those who were challenging Coca-Cola, including affected villagers and youth organizations of the area, were reduced by the media to "agitators" and "anti Coca-Cola protestors." The national media in India also portrayed the community organizing as a case of Left parties co-opting illiterate villagers for political gain. That was until an independent Delhi based NGO, the Center for Science and Environment (CSE), released explosive results of a study they had conducted that showed the cola giants (Coca-Cola and Pepsi) were guilty of having too-high levels of pesticides in their product. In fact, CSE called Coca-Cola and its other soft-drink products a "deadly cocktail of pesticide residues."

Further tests by different organizations, the Central Food Technological Research Institute, Mysore, and the Central Food Laboratory, Kolkata, also discovered that samples of Coke contained levels of pesticides that were higher than permissible European Union (EU) norms. The test found that the pesticide DDT was 12 times higher than EU norms in 58 percent of the samples. Lindane was found to be higher than EU norms in 33 percent of the samples while Chlorpyrifos exceeded EU norms in 75 percent of samples.[1]

The CSE report also harshly criticized the government for having weak regulations over the soft-drink industry. CSE tested Indian Coke using pesticide levels permissible in Europe because the Indian levels were way too low. Furthermore, CSE's report pointed out that there are no standards at all to define "clean" or "potable" water in India, a fact that many argue makes a country like India such a gift for a corporate giant like Coca-Cola.

Coke launched a massive offensive campaign. A toxic product, even if it happens to be in a poor, brown, country had the potential to harm global sales. First, Coca-Cola India used its multimillion-dollar power to state that the toxic allegations were simply not true. Coke then attempted to discredit CSE's methodology by conducting its own tests. Unsurprisingly, Coke's analysis of its drinks came up clean. The courts of India, however, chose to rely on randomly tested product conducted by government and independent research labs. It also threatened the government and Coke workers with severe job losses. Sanjiv Gupta, president of Coca-Cola India stated that the findings had "scared consumers unnecessarily and jeopardized thousands of jobs throughout the country." [2]

After multiple court decisions found against Coca-Cola India, the company embarked on a media campaign. Coke hired Indian public relations firm Perfect Relations to get itself back into consumer good-books. A series of television commercials were produced that outraged many. In one, a group of women are walking in hot weather, obviously thirsty, to a village well. They look disappointed as a stranger starts to pull up a bucket of water. The stranger turns out to be a famous Bollywood star and, low and behold, the bucket turns out to be full of bottles of Coca-Cola.

The PR firm also embarked on some "social responsibility" projects—corporate style. In December 2003, Coca-Cola India announced that it had decided to establish a so-called India Environment Council chaired by a former chief justice of India—a "community-based initiative" according to Coke.[3] Another, almost more sinister tactic of the Coke PR machine, was to target Indian children. The campaign, "Fun Time for Coke Drinkers," cut to the chase; children didn't care about pesticide poisoning or drying up water wells, at least they wouldn't if Coca-Cola was cheap and came in appealing packaging. According to Gupta, the company would get to children by a "nationwide poster campaign at retail outlets, meet-your-favorite-star program bringing our young consumers and our popular brand ambassadors together, plant visits for school children, special offers, attractive packaging, and various contests."[4]

Yet with the pesticide findings, the issue of water depletion did not disappear for Coke. In December 2003, Kerala's High Court found in favor of villagers, telling Coca-Cola India that while it may own the land where its plant is situated, it does not own the water below the ground. It gave Coke one month to find alternative water sources saying the water belonged to tribal villagers as "property held in trust." The court order was explicit in its condemnation of the multinational's globalization gift saying that the government had no right to allow a private company to extract large amounts of water from the ground because this would result in the drying up of ground water resources. The court's decision came as over 1,000 of India's most marginalized people, Dalit and Adivasis villagers, completed day 605 of protest.[5] A real victory for David over Goliath if there ever was one.

After the pesticide findings were revealed, Indian media coverage shifted substantially against the U.S. corporation. On August 27, the Indian publication *The Financial Express* reported favorably that elected officials in the Health and Family Welfare Ministry were pushing through an ordinance that would categorize water as a food item thereby bringing some enforceable safety standards for drinking water under India's Prevention of Food Adulteration Act. The October 1 edition of *Business Line* magazine reported that Coke and Pepsi had started a misinformation campaign saying it would be impossible to apply EU standards to the Indian beverage industry because most would fail to meet the standards. The cola company also claimed that if

India were to adopt these standards, it would be unprecedented and counter to international norms. Other media driven investigations of the cola giants also began. On September 30, *The Indian Express* and the *New Indian Express* reported that many shops in the southern Indian city of Chennai were selling very old Coca-Cola, bottles that were well passed the best-before date, by offering huge discounts.

With the widespread coverage of toxic coke in the Indian media, people were becoming hesitant to buy it. And as the year progressed, public protests against Coca- Cola also grew. With the protests came allegations that force was being used to suppress demonstrators. In Kerala, on August 30, some 13 activists were arrested during a peaceful demonstration and a leader of the movement was severely beaten by the police. In September, in the state of Uttar Pradesh, a peaceful demonstration of over a thousand community members was violently attacked by armed security forces. There were reports of serious injuries. However, while direct links between uniformed attackers and Coca-Cola are yet to be proven, activists argue that state-controlled police and military forces functioning on the side of the multinationals in poor countries is another gift of globalization.[6]

It seemed that the pesticide scandal in India was beginning to affect Coke globally. Wall Street had its say as Coke's stock dropped from $55-$50 on the New York Stock Exchange (NYSE) in the six sessions following the August 5 pesticide disclosure.[7] However, on October 17, Coca-Cola reported to the Securities and Exchange Commission (SEC) that all the charges against it in India were false.[8]

The U.S. press barely found the Coke scandal newsworthy. Reuters reported it once and *The New York Times* also saw fit to cover this huge story only once in 2003. The August 23 article by Amy Walden begins with Coke's line, poking but the faintest of holes in its spin and proceeds to report categorically that Coke had been vindicated after a government study tested various samples and found them to be nontoxic. The "accusation" of a toxic product, reports Walden, has been definitively "rebuffed by the health ministry." What Walden did not tell readers was that the government tests used India's 1950s levels for pesticides which are way below the European permissible levels, under whose standards even the government tests give Coke a failing grade. Walden went on to absolve Coke further by blaming the government "the problem was not with multinationals, but with the government that failed to regulate them."

The government of India has said it welcomes Coke's industrial development in India. But in January 2004, the Parliament building in New Delhi stopped selling Coca-Cola and other Coke products in its cafeteria because the company had not been able to disprove the findings of high pesticide levels. And in February, members of Parliament voted to uphold CSE's findings, a significant victory against the multinational corporation. Yet this government indictment against Coca Cola was only big enough news for a few in the British press, *The Financial Times* and *The Guardian*. The U.S. press? Not a single word.

2003 was also the year the World Trade Organization (WTO) held its fifth Ministerial meetings in Mexico's computer-created tourist hub, Cancun. The WTO was birthed in 1995 by multinational corporate leaders in collaboration with a group of mostly unelected representatives of rich countries to regulate and enhance world trade. During its inception, the WTO creators promised that the body would not interfere in an individual country's democratic policy making nor would it pose a threat to any single country's sovereignty. Yet for millions of poor farmers around the world, the WTO has single handedly sanctioned their loss of livelihood by aggressively working with and for agribusiness in the U.S. and EU.

During the 2003 Cancun ministerial meetings, agriculture issues dominated. Negotiators from 146 countries met inside the plush hotels on the sealed-off boomerang shaped peninsula that connects to mainland Cancun. Both inside the highly protected meetings and on the streets of mainland Cancun where all the demonstrators were contained, there were many voices protesting agriculture subsidies. For the first time in WTO history, a group of four of the poorest African countries, Benin, Burkina Faso, Chad, and Mali, asked the U.S. to end its $3.2 billion subsidies to its 25,000 cotton farmers, which have destroyed the livelihoods of 10 million African farmers. Negotiators from another 21 developing countries also demanded that both the U.S. and the EU cancel all agricultural subsidies.

Meanwhile, outside the official talks, thousands were in the streets protesting all range of WTO abuses. One of the largest delegations came from Korea, rice farmers who had a united message: the WTO kills farmers. On day one of the official ministerials, in a devastating action to highlight just how desperate times are for rice farmers in Korea, one farmer, Lee Kyung Hae stabbed himself in the heart atop the gate that separated protestors from the hotels where the meetings were occurring.

Free Speech Radio News (FSRN) producer Kata Mester and reporter Renee Feltz were the last journalists to speak with the rice farmer before he died. Lee explained that protective subsidies for U.S. and EU farmers meant that he, and many like him, were literally out of work. Though his English was minimal, Lee used printed articles to explain that poor countries, whose people had subsisted on the staple of rice, were now forced to import the grain from rich countries and charge a much higher price because their own rice farms had been devalued by at least 50 percent, in many cases much more. Lee Kyung Hae was the former president of the Korean Farmers Association and a former elected lawmaker in Korea.

While Lee's suicide was roundly reported as a dramatic stunt amid a moment of violent protest, enacted to overshadow the proceedings inside the ministerial meetings, very few in the press found it worthy to mention that Lee's protests had begun a long while back, nor did Lee's simple message warrant any deep coverage of the plight of third world farmers under WTO sanctioned subsidies.

In February and March of 2003, when the agriculture proposals were first being drafted, Lee went to the WTO headquarters in Geneva where he staged a hunger strike. His message was simple and desperate: poor Korean farmers are dying because of U.S. and EU subsidies to agribusiness. In Geneva, Lee was completely ignored.

The U.S. and international press followed suit and also completely ignored Lee's hunger strike, his message, and the plight of Korean farmers. A thorough search of both U.S. and international press during that time period rendered only one Associated Press article, which only briefly mentioned the hunger strike.

In April, Lee did make international headlines, only in poor countries, that is, when he issued statements decrying the dramatic drop in rice prices that pushed many Korean farmers into life-threatening poverty, urban slums, and bankruptcy. Lee told the world of one farmer who could not continue to scratch out an existence under the burden of massive debts and so drank a toxic chemical to end his life. "I could do nothing but hear the howling of his wife," said Lee, "If you were me, how would you feel?."9

During his brief interview with *Free Speech Radio News*, Lee raised the key question that anti-WTO protestors have long asked as he cited a statement of his in the April 2003 issue of *Korea Agra-Food*, "I am crying out my words that have boiled for so long in my body: For whom do you negotiate now?"

Poor people's movements, especially those ravaged by WTO policies, have long asked the question that is all but ignored in the establishment media: on whose behalf are trade negotiations occurring? It is in forums like the WTO that agreements are drawn up, rich with gifts for multinational corporations, gifts that come directly on the backs of poor people and their local environments across the world. It was unprecedented that the protests from so many of the negotiators from poorer countries actually rendered the Cancun meetings fruitless for the big guns. Yet, as many protestors noted, the decisions would just get kicked back to Geneva where the deed would be completed with little fanfare or scrutiny from the press, leaving one to wonder if Lee's death meant anything.

Meanwhile, from the streets of Cancun, there was no substantial media coverage of Lee's death in the U.S. press. *FSRN*'s Kata Mester points out that had there been other reporters in the streets actually talking to protestors about their grievances with the WTO, they too might have heard Lee's articulate critique. What we got instead was a slew of sensational and superficial articles about both Lee's suicide and the anti-WTO protestors.

One of the National Public Radio (NPR) correspondents in Cancun, Gerry Hadden, who was staying in the same hotel as *FSRN*, described himself to us as the man sent to "cover the streets." Hadden wanted to use the sound of Lee's voice from *FSRN* in his evening report, as obviously it was the biggest news "from the streets." It was disappointing, though not surprising, when we learned that Hadden's report, more a postcard from Cancun than a news report, was thin in content, and in using the sound of Lee's last words spoken to *FSRN*, Hadden did not even do Lee the minimum of stating his name. But neither did the *Washington Post* or other establishment media outlets, and those that did print Lee's name could barely get the spelling correct. Only one article in the slew actually identified Lee as a former elected official in South Korea.

Protestors at the WTO meetings immediately reacted to the negative media coverage and the slogan "todos somos Lee" ("We are All Lee") came to summarize the plight of not only the protestors in Cancun, but also the millions they collectively represented in their home countries. What was most commonly reported, however, was not that the majority of the protestors wanted Lee's message to be taken seriously by the negotiators inside, but that host president Vicente Fox's reaction to Lee's suicide was to call him a "globophobe," the word that the Mexican government used in the lead up to the September meetings to describe those gathering to protest the WTO and globalization.

While *The New York Times* did distinguish itself from the rest in the days following Lee's suicide by publishing an extensive profile from Lee's home in South Korea, in a post-Cancun November article, *The New York Times* actually blamed the protestors for the lack of serious follow up after Lee's death, reporting that the protestors' turnout in Cancun was too low to "take much of a political charge from Lee's death."[10]

According to corporate leaders, international elected officials, and especially the media, Lee was a simple farmer who didn't give globalization a chance to let it improve his life; instead he chose to fight it, and in the process, only harmed himself and other Korean farmers. However, to many of the world's poor, who heard relayed messages of Lee's suicide and flooded his funeral back in South Korea with words of thanks and solidarity, Lee was a martyr who had made the ultimate sacrifice in their name by standing up to the rich and powerful.

But Lee is not alone in the phenomenon of death-by-globalization. Each year thousands, perhaps tens of thousands perish worldwide due to the policies of corporate elites. On farms and sweatshops or simply due to the misfortune of living in the path of a corporation bent on exploiting the local environment, too many poor people world over have been pushed over the edge.

Deepa Fernandes is a journalist and media trainer. She is an award-winning radio features producer for the BBC, ABC, and Pacifica Radio. Deepa anchors nationally syndicated daily news show *Free Speech Radio News* and is a 2003 OSI NYC Community Fellow for her work as founder of Radio Rootz, Youth Media Collaborative. LexisNexis and Factiva research for this article was conducted by Lauren Kettner (Project Censored Intern) with help from Peter Hart (FAIR).

NOTES:
1. *Hindustan Times*, August 28, 2003.
2. <www.retailyatra.com/Smartbuild.asp?WCI=Robot&WCE=PageId=2282>.
3. *PR Weekly*.
4. <www.retailyatra.com/SmartBuild.asp?WCI=Robot&WCE=PageId=2507>.
5. <www.atimes.com/atimes/South_Asia/EL19Df06.html>.
6. <www.guerrillanews.com/globalization/doc3764.html>.
7. *Business Line*, New Delhi, October 3, 2003: 9.
8. *Business Standard*, New Delhi, October 17, 2003, Page 9.
9. Tom Hayden, "Cancun Files: Remembering Lee Kyung Hae," *AlterNet*, September 12, 2003, <www.alternet.com>.
10. "Them Against the World, Part 2," *The New York Times*, November 16, 2003, late ed., Sec. 6, Col. 1: 58.

CHAPTER 15
The Media Reform Movement and Global Media Concentration

BY CHRISTOPHER ROBIN COX

This is a dangerous time in America. Rampant self-censorship by journalists whipped by the corporate lash is combined with a level of class separation that is simply epidemic in its effect upon the independence of the press. The rampant consolidation of corporate ownership and control of media and communications into the hands of the enfranchised few represents the hijacking of American democracy. In the words of Bill Moyers, "What we're talking about is nothing less than rescuing a democracy that is so polarized it is in danger of being paralyzed and pulverized" (Moyers 2003). The rescuers Moyers is referring to are the courageous media activists who are working their brains to mush in a mad attempt to bring back the kind of journalism that promotes democracy by creating outlets for public policy examination and participatory politics.

The "media reform movement," as it is commonly referred to, is arguably the most important social movement in the past century and quickly becoming the most important one ever. The movement has grown, out of sheer necessity, from a disaggregated statement against media monopoly into a full-blown war against the neoliberal ideologies that are force-fed to the demos by the power elite. We have become what Noam Chomsky says is, "a state capitalist society with very close ties between state and corporate power, a very obedient intellectual class, and a narrow political spectrum primarily reflecting the interests of power and privilege." The media reform movement aims to reclaim the very democratic and progressive ideals America was founded upon.

There is yet a bigger problem: the neoliberal agenda has gone global. Corporate monopolies have already gobbled up most of the American media supply, which includes the vast majority of news, information, and entertainment sources, and are already moving on like locusts on the hunt for a new harvest. The ex-CEO of Intel, Andy Grove, said it best: "The goal of the new capitalism is to shoot the wounded."

Writing about neoliberalism going global, Robert W. McChesney and Dan Schiller state, "The United States is important in this context because it is the U.S. model of communication provision (including both media and communications) that is being exported across the planet." Neoliberalism is the order of the decade, and it has been executed masterfully. As McChesney and Schiller state, "Few industries, indeed, have been as changed by capitalist globalization as communications." Furthermore, conventional wisdom tells us that control of media and communications is control of the very information citizens use as the criteria by which to vote for their leaders and form opinions of public policy decisions made in their name. Therefore, corporate capitalist globalization ideology, or neoliberalism, is the most evil enemy of a free and independent press. To understand the global implications of media ownership and policy making, we must first look at the history of media conflict in the United States.

The U.S. has a very long history of threats to the independence of the press, beginning literally with the very first independent newspaper. It was a little three-pager out of Boston called *Publick Occurrences Both Foreign and Domestick*, published in 1690. As Bill Moyers notes, "The government shut it down after one issue—just one issue!—for the official reason that printer Ben Harris hadn't applied for the required government license to publish." The key word there is "official." The unofficial reason for shutting it down was most likely Harris's reason for starting the paper, which was "to cure the spirit of lying much among us." Sadly, we can say that the government, due to the politically unpopular opinion a publisher had toward it, shut down the very first paper in this country.

That was 1690, the start of the newspaper business and the first sign of what Robert W. McChesney calls "the problem of the media." The problem is found in the relationship between the private good and the collective good. Corporate globalization, no matter how it is sold, is an ideology that is concerned primarily with pure, unfettered capitalism. Furthermore, capitalism without government regulation is a proponent of the private good, totally at the expense of the collective good. McChesney writes, "Just as capitalism is not the 'natural' social system for humanity, so commercial media are not nature's creation either. Our social system and our media system both require aggressive and explicit government activity to exist."

The battle between those who seek the private good and those who seek the collective good can never be more clearly witnessed than in the constant battle over media ownership policy and corporate globalization. The term regulation is always subject to interpretation. McChesney writes, "The real struggle is over whose interests the regulation will represent." One could say that the first case of government regulation of the media industry is found in the First Amendment of the Bill of Rights, which explicitly states that "Congress shall make no law respecting an establishment of religion, or prohibiting the free exercise thereof; or abridging the freedom of speech, or of the press; or the right of the people peaceably to assemble, and to petition the government for a redress of grievances." The term deregulation is also a bit deceiving, depending upon how one thinks of it. Essentially, one could say that deregulation is simply another form of regulation, in that deregulation basically furthers the interests of the most powerful corporate players in the media industries. For more on the specific regulations and deregulations within the U.S., see Josh Sisco's report, "Media Reform, the FCC and the Rising Opposition to More Consolidation" at the end of this chapter.

The first real social battle over regulatory policy in the United States media was fought early in the late eighteenth century, upon the introduction of the Post Office Act of 1792. At that time, and for a long time to come, the Post Office of the United States was the primary form of mass communication— no telephones, no televisions, no cars, no planes, and a huge expanse of land between the East and the West. McChesney reports, "In 1794, newspapers made up 70 percent of post office traffic; by 1832, the figure had risen to well over 90 percent." The source of the first real battles over regulation and policy making in the media was the question of how much newspaper publishers should be charged to send them through the mail. That debate still goes on today. Many political figures of the nineteenth century, primarily progressives of course, thought there should be no charge at all for newspapers to be sent through the mail. Madison fought harder than anybody else, declaring that any charge at all was a "tax" on newspapers that was "an insidious forerunner of something worse." After all, in those days, the post office was profiting well enough from regular use by virtually all citizens. Other alternative forms of long distance communication simply did not exist for the average American.

As can be seen from the above example, the history of media regulation in America begins with a debate over free-market capitalism and the collective good. It was a long fight, but in 1851, Congress did approve free postal access to weekly newspapers, which at the time gave 20 percent of newspapers free postage. This was a giant victory, one that was seen not only as a victory for the collective, but as a "subsidy for democracy," as McChesney puts it. Timothy Cook concluded, "Public policy from the outset by the American republic focused explicitly on getting the news to a wide readership and chose to support news outlets by taking on costs of delivery and, through printers' exchanges, of production."

A media reform movement has been brewing boldly since the passage of the Telecommunications Act of 1996. It comes at a time that is much more desperate than ever before in U.S. history. Less than 10 massive media conglomerates own and operate every imaginable outlet for news and entertainment in the U.S. According to *Common Cause*, "since 1995, the number of companies owning commercial TV stations has declined by 40 percent." Americans are resisting media consolidation in huge numbers. FCC commissioner Jonathan Adelstein estimates that by the end of the summer of 2003, over 2.3 million people will have contacted the FCC or Congress to voice their opposition to further media concentration.

Public interest in media ownership policy in the United States is at a fevered pitch and congressional reform combined with citizen action is ongoing. In addition, the amount of independent and progressive news sources around the world, both in print and on the Web, is increasing by the minute as a direct response to media concentration. The movement is indeed alive and becoming stronger. Unfortunately, so is the well-funded global neoliberal front. As stated earlier, the U.S. form of communication provision is being exported, expertly, across the entire planet. In Italy, Prime Minister Silvio Berlusconi is, as Bill Moyers puts it, "Italy's richest citizen. He is also its first media mogul." There are numerous examples of this kind of infiltration of free-market concentration all over the world. Many would say it all reeks of conspiracy by the corporate elites of the world. But it is well-known in conspiratorial circles that "a good conspiracy cannot be proven." Corporate global domination is aided by the control of the media. According to Moyers, "Conspiracy is unnecessary when ideology hungers for power, and its many adherents swarm of their own accord to the same pot of honey." This is the battle that the media reform movement is courageously taking on; we must now step forward proudly and join forces in solidarity with the rest of the world.

With the rise of neoliberalism in the 1980s, under then president Ronald Reagan, came total transformation of the international corporate model. "Unions, tariffs, taxes, public investment, and regulations—anything that got in the way of corporate accumulation strategies—were the evil demons on the world stage." (McChesney and Schiller 2003) This kind of focus upon corporate privilege and exception has become commonplace in America, and the rest of the world has begun to catch up nicely. McChesney and Schiller go on to say, "The United States government in particular aggressively and persistently acted as if only a profit-driven media system as in the United States, with U.S.-style professional journalism, could be considered acceptable for a free society." The rest is history. Massive media mergers are already a cold reality in most of Europe and the rest of the world. In Europe, for example, five companies run all of terrestrial television. In New Zealand, Rupert Murdock (Australian-American) controls all pay television and Irishman Tony O'Riley controls most of commercial radio broadcasting and magazine publishing. McChesney and Schiller aptly state, "The rulers of New Zealand's media system could squeeze into a closet."

Reporting on media and communications concentration in the world has been largely ignored by the commercial media. However, neoliberal infiltrations have not gone unanswered. Many countries around the world have gone to extensive lengths to protect their domestic media and cultural industries from the American hard sell of global media systems. McChesney and Schiller add, "Norway, Denmark, and Spain to Mexico, South Africa, and the Republic of Korea keep their small domestic film production industries alive with government subsidies." In the summer of 1998, in response to growing concern over global media ownership, culture ministers from 20 countries met in Ottawa to discuss ways in which they could set some ground rules to protect against what they call the "Hollywood juggernaut." That is, what McChesney and Schiller cite as "the specter of U.S. cultural imperialism." They go on to say, about the meetings in Ottawa, that "their main recommendation was to keep culture out of the control of the WTO."

The WTO is certainly, above anything else, in the service of multinational corporations. Therefore, it is safe to say that the WTO is far from an advocate of responsible, pro-cultural, localized media systems. The Hollywood juggernaut, as absurd as it may sound, is real, and it is as much a part of the ethos of the WTO as tax breaks. Even in France, which is widely known to be a "cultural nationalist" country, 9 of the 10 highest grossing films in that country were produced by giant Hollywood production houses. Just as is the case here in America, the intellectuals and academics of France certainly decry most American films, but the bulk of the population buys into them at a consistently rising rate. New and challenging battles are building up fast around the world. Debates over how to maintain a stance against the infiltration of U.S.-based media giants and developing competitive media markets within the EU are now commonplace. On the other hand, as McChesney and Schiller point out, "The wave of commercialization of European media has put the EU in the position of condemning some of the traditional subsidies to public service broadcasters as 'noncompetitive.'" Sadly, the once-great example of social democracy in Europe, public service broadcasting, has already begun to be reduced to "locating a semi-commercial niche in the global system" (McChesney and Schiller 2003).

Corporate control of news and culture is in full swing here in the United States, and it is becoming our number-one export. Media and communications concentration is the love child of free-market capitalism and social Darwinism: "The global media system is better understood as one that advances corporate and commercial interests and values and denigrates or ignores that which cannot be incorporated into its mission" (McChesney and Schiller 2003).

The disenfranchised peoples of America and beyond have begun to awaken to the corporate capitalist burglars threatening to steal from us our only method of questioning government authority. The media reform movement, especially in America, has risen and continues to grow stronger every day. Project Censored has developed a resource guide to over 1,000 independent progressive media sources in North America <www.Projectcensored.org>. While we must not underplay the incredible advances made by media activism in recent years, we must also not spend too much time patting each other on the back. Bill Moyers reminds us, "The greatest moments in the history of the press came not when journalists made common cause with the state, but when they stood fearlessly independent of it." Fierce independence is what must be exercised nationally and globally. Monopoly capital should not be tolerated, for it is the enemy of free people everywhere, and it is the friend of those who venture out to manufacture consent.

"The history of all hitherto existing society is the history of class struggles" (Marx and Engels 1848). That statement could have been made today, commanding the same relevance. But it was not. Karl Marx and Friedrich Engels stated it in 1848 in the very first paragraph of *The Communist Manifesto*. One does not have to be a communist in America to accept that if the same statement, no matter how relevant, were to be written on the pages of any mainstream newspaper or read aloud on corporate television news, the government would have much to say about it.

Our fight is enormous. It requires the entire human race to stand up and fight against the corporate information machine that spreads the seeds of social inequality by centralizing the control of communications. Our reform movement has brought to light the importance of policy making as it relates to ownership and control. There is an old saying: "If you're not at the table, you're not part of the deal." McChesney says it best: "Our job, as scholars, as citizens, as democrats, is to knock down the door and draw some more chairs up to the table." The media reform movement is truly a sign that we, as the disenfranchised masses, are done politely knocking on the doors that close us out of the meetings and policy decisions of the enfranchised few. We are hammering through them with enraged eyes of red and hearts full of resolve. This fight has only just begun and the whole human race is encouraged to participate.

SOURCES:

Chomsky, Noam. Interview with M. Junaid Alam, February 6, 2004, <www.dissentvoice.org>.

Marx, Karl, and Friedrich Engels. *The Communist Manifesto.* New York: Simon and Schuster, Inc., 1964 (originally published in London, 1848).

McChesney, Robert W. *The Problem of the Media: U.S. Communication Politics in the Twenty-First Century.* New York: Monthly Review Press, 2004.

McChesney, Robert W., and Dan Schiller. *The Political Economy of International Communications: Foundations for the Emerging Global Debate about Media Ownership and Regulation.* United Nations Research Institute for Social Development. New York, 2003.

Moyers, Bill. Address, National Conference on Media Reform. The Schumann Center for Media and Democracy, Madison, Wisconsin, November 8, 2003.

Media Reform, the FCC and the Rising Opposition to More Consolidation

BY JOSH SISCO

"Mr. Programmer, I got my hammer
And I'm gonna smash my, smash my radio!
We Want the Airwaves!"
—The Ramones.

THE PROBLEM AND THE ROLE OF REGULATIONS

The 1927 Radio Act was designed to stop the chaos on the radio airwaves by requiring federal licensing for programmers who, up until that point, were continually trying to drown out each other's frequencies. The 1934 Communications Act that followed was supposed to be a compromise between BBC-style federal broadcasting and total private enterprise. The 1934 act created the Federal Communications Commission (FCC) to ensure, in part, that broadcasters provide noncommercial, public interest programming. Renewal of their licenses was contingent upon such programming (McChesney 1999, 215–218).

The problem with the current media structure is that the decisions regarding media regulations are made largely without input from the public. In the debate leading up to the passage of the 1934 act, "A primary barrier [to media reform] was its inability to get press coverage. Most Americans were unaware that it was even within their province, or that of Congress, to determine what type of broadcasting system the United States should have," writes media studies professor Robert McChesney (1999, 214).

THE DEBATE

President Bush has made it clear on several occasions that he desires an expedited process for the repeal of ownership regulations. FCC Chairman Michael Powell's speeches to the broadcast industry and private meetings with industry leaders reveal his disinclination to equate the public interest mandate of the FCC with the need for accuracy and diversity within our media outlets. Michael Powell—son of Colin Powell—stated before the Federal Communications Bar Association in June 2001, "Serving the public interest means crafting the conditions and the environment that will allow innovation to bring new and improved products and services to all Americans at reasonable prices." According to Powell, serving the public interest means increasing our ability to consume, rather than to be informed (Prometheus Radio Project Web site).

Attempts at further media industry deregulation were anticipated when the FCC announced its biennial review in September 2002. What was not anticipated was the widespread opposition toward further control of our information by a few unaccountable and uninterested corporate powers. What was even less anticipated was that the opposition would also come from within the FCC. The two Democratic commissioners, Michael Copps and Jonathan Adelstein, were convinced that the rules governing a public resource should be debated by the public. They put constant pressure on Powell and the two other commissioners, Kathleen Abernathy, a former lobbyist for the broadcast industry, and Kevin Martin, a lawyer representing corporate communications clients, to open the debate to the public (McChesney 2004, 260).

The call for public debate was split along partisan lines. Public hearings on media consolidation were held nationwide during 2002–2003, mostly due to the initiative of Copps and Adelstein. Powell finally agreed to attend one official hearing in Richmond, Virginia, on February 27, 2003. Twelve more hearings were held around the country in the months preceding the June 2 vote on the new FCC rules on media ownership. All the hearings were attended by Copps and most by Adelstein. The other FCC commissioners did not attend a single one (McChesney 2004, 265). At these hearings, thousands of people expressed their concerns about further media consolidation. Many of the hearings were attended by local congresspersons who also expressed their dismay.

These hearings produced unprecedented public scrutiny and pressure on a government agency. "I don't recall ever seeing before the level of open and very public dispute among the commissioners on these issues," stated a Clear Channel lobbyist (McChesney 2004, 265). Powell, however, not only snubbed the public, but his two opposing commissioners as well. The changes that were to be voted on were not made available to Copps and Adelstein until the minimum of three weeks prior to the vote. When they requested a delay of the vote, Powell rejected the request, citing advice from Abernathy and Martin. Such a request had never before been denied (McChesney 2004, 285).

During the period of public comment, between September of 2002 and January of 2003, hundreds of thousands of people wrote the FCC to express their discontent with the current state of the media and their opposition to the FCC's planned changes. By the end of the summer of 2003, Adelstein estimated that approximately 2.3 million people had contacted the FCC and Congress through letters, e-mails, and phone calls with overwhelming opposition to the new relaxation of rules (McChesney 2004, 289).

Powell wanted the process to proceed as quickly as possible. He rejected a request for the extension of the public comment period and maintained that it was unnecessary to hear from the American public. "In the digital age, you don't need a nineteenth century whistle-stop tour to hear from America," Powell said (McChesney 2004, 264). He claimed that consumer patterns supported further media consolidation. He stated that Internet and cable would provide sufficient media diversity and that the elimination of regulations was necessary to prevent the broadcast industry from failing financially —despite unprecedented increases in revenues reported by the companies.

Powell also cited a 2002 Washington, DC, District Appeals Court ruling that shifted the burden of proof onto those who favored the FCC regulations. In cases involving News Corp/Fox and Viacom/CBS, the DC Court ruled that unless overwhelming evidence is presented to the contrary, the regulations governing media ownership should be eliminated. Speaking before the Media Institute, a non-profit media policy research foundation, on March 27, 2003, Powell stated, "The court roundly rejected the FCC's view of Congress's intent, holding that Congress clearly expressed a preference for deregulation and placed the burden on the Commission to prove a restriction's worth" (McChesney 2004, 259, 266). The regulations are thus guilty until proven innocent.

On June 2, 2003, the FCC announced the results of its biennial review process. They had severely reduced the six remaining regulations that limited the types and amounts of media a single company can own. They increased from 35 percent to 45 percent the number of TV-owning households that can be reached by a single media company. The FCC furthermore removed rules against one company owning assortments of radio stations, TV stations, and newspapers in a single market. If there were more than nine media outlets in a particular market, media cross-ownership bans were eliminated.

These changes represent a radical shift in policy. Up to now, media policies had been reviewed and altered piecemeal. Even the 1996 Telecommunications Act focused primarily on ownership limits for radio only. Legislators deliberated on television and print media as well, but could not agree on a solution. Instead they mandated that the FCC review the remaining ownership regulations every two years.

The United States media is at the center of an increasingly global mass communication network. Media corporations are powered by their ability to own public goods and services while not being held accountable in their uses and distribution of those goods and services. A new paradox has arisen. The media are here to hold human action accountable, but are owned and run by people who want no accountability. These people spend great sums of money to ensure that such accountability never becomes an issue.

THE FINAL STAND IN THE COURTS

In the fall of 2003, a host of lawsuits were filed against the FCC to repeal rule changes that allowed for greater consolidation. On September 3, judges effectively stayed all new FCC rules in order to allow for further deliberation. The court ruled that this delay of the new rules would cause no harm to the regulatory agency and the industry that it regulates, but could prevent irreparable harm to the petitioners (*Prometheus Radio Project v. Federal Communications Commission*).

One such case, filed by the Prometheus Radio Project, is being heard by the 3rd District Court of Appeals in Philadelphia. The Prometheus suit is being represented by Andrew J. Schwartzman of the Media Access Project in Washington, DC. Prometheus assists community groups in obtaining licenses and setting up low-power FM (100-watt) stations. During the FCC's public comment period in the final months of 2002, Prometheus spoke out extensively on the merits of diverse media ownership and opinions as well as adamantly opposing the premise on which the commission based its final decision: "...It is well recognized that a diversity of business sizes in all industries, mature and emerging, is in the interest of the public and well within the sphere of appropriate government action." A government that mandates a healthy and dynamic movement, allowing for constant changes within the marketplace, will hold media companies accountable to the people who use them. If the public is dissatisfied with the amount and or quality of information being provided by one source, they should be allowed to exercise their options by looking elsewhere. "It is of special concern when the media corporation owns, or is owned by, other corporations. Is it not fair under the circumstances to presume that there may in fact be some conflict of interest between the interests of the corporation and the media's duty to provide the public with full and complete information?" (Prometheus Radio Project Web site).

The Prometheus Radio Project goes on to state, "It is also important to remember that a media corporation is not just another corporation. It is, in fact, a very special and powerful kind of corporation because it controls access to and circulation of perhaps one of the most crucial ingredients of a working democracy—information" (Prometheus Radio Project Web site).

On February 11, 2004, oral arguments for both sides were heard in Philadelphia. Groups as diverse as the AFL-CIO, NRA, and the National Organization of Women (NOW), spoke in the public interest while industry spokespersons and the powerful media lobby, the National Association of Broadcasters (NAB) supported the new relaxing of FCC rules. A final ruling is expected this year.

Gene Kimmelman, director of public policy for the Consumers Union, one of the plaintiffs in the case, stated, "We believe the court recognizes the incredible importance of diversity and localism in our media, and we have demonstrated today that the FCC failed to uphold those important goals by creating rules that are the death knell to independent and local media" (Consumers Union 2004).

On May 25, 2004, a debate was held at the CATO Institute between Schwartzman and Adam Their, the director of telecommunication studies at the institute. Schwartzman appeared optimistic about the decision in Philadelphia. "The court took the case very seriously... The judges were incredibly well prepared, wanted to hear everything, and expressed a lot of skepticism." He went on to say that this represents a "fundamental change in the environment in which media ownership has been viewed over the last year" (CATO Institute, May 25, 2004).

FCC PRESENTS FAULTY EVIDENCE

In the fall of 2003, the FCC released 12 studies that comprised much of the research on which they based their final June 2 decision. Many groups, including Prometheus, blasted the overemphasis on economic factors, treating the public as passive consumers of media goods, instead of as participants of an everevolving democratic society. "By seeking out only the opinions and studies of economists, the FCC hasn't even attempted to connect the dots down to how mass media affects actual people...in tangible ways..." (Prometheus Radio Project Web site).

One such study concluded that programming diversity means different television formats: cop shows, comedies, dramas, etc. It ignored the lack of programming by and for different ethnic, religious, and cultural groups across the country. Another study on consumer usage of media conducted by Nielsen Media Research used only "pre-qualified TV viewers" (Prometheus Radio

Project Web site). For links to and criticism of the 12 studies, please see the Media Access Project at <www.mediaaccess.org>.

A narrow range of programming formats is easier and cheaper for the big media firms. Less difference in products that one company sells equals less money that they need to spend. A larger, faster profit is made when a company can sell one product to everyone instead of tailoring products to meet the needs of often drastically different groups. The problem with catering to one general global consumer model is the subjection of cultural, ethnic, and religious differences that have existed for centuries to one dominant corporate culture.

Big media wants a few cheap, general styles of programming and sources of information to be accepted by everyone. If they are able to sell the same thing to everyone, they make more money. If they control this information, they shed their accountability for this cultural destruction.

All parties involved will be waiting for and scrutinizing the Philadelphia Court's final decision. If they conclude that the FCC went ahead too hastily and ignored the public interest, Powell and company must go back to the beginning and follow the lead of Copps and Adelstein who supported public discourse throughout the entire messy process.

CONGRESSIONAL OPPOSITION AND THE DIRTY DEALS THAT RUN WASHINGTON

The public was not alone in its opposition to Powell. Media studies professor, critic, and historian Robert McChesney writes, "Literally scores of members of Congress wrote to Powell in 2003 making explicit their conviction that the appeals court interpretation of congressional intent was wrong" (McChesney 2004, 267). A January 2003 congressional hearing was convened to question FCC commissioners about telecommunication regulations. The topic quickly turned to media consolidation and the actions of the FCC. The DC court's ruling on the News Corp/Viacom case was based on the assumption that placing the burden of proof on those trying to maintain regulations was the will of Congress when they passed the 1996 Telecommunications Act.

On June 19, 2003, the Senate Commerce Committee headed by John McCain (R–AZ), voted to overturn significant parts of the deregulation. This included returning to the 35 percent cap and requiring hearings in at least five different geographic locations before future rules are repealed. The equivalent committee in the house led by Representative Billy Tauzin (R–LA) showed no signs of following suit, with Tauzin and spokesman Ken Johnson saying, "We have absolutely no intention of taking up the Senate bill." Johnson dismissed the issue as "...a political soap opera, and given the chance, Tauzin intends to cancel its run" (McConnell 2003).

In July, the Appropriations Committees in both branches of Congress voted for a return to 35 percent by restricting funding through a massive budget bill under deliberation.

In an unprecedented move, the Senate voted on September 16, to overturn the entirety of the rule changes. They used the Congressional Resolution of Disapproval, a seldom-used provision of the Congressional Review Act. But immediately after, House Majority leader Tom DeLay (R–TX) said a similar proposal in the House would be "dead on arrival." However, over 200 signatures were gathered on a letter to House Speaker Dennis Hastert (R–IL) on November 5, asking for a floor vote on the same resolution of disapproval (*NOW with Bill Moyers*, January 30, 2004).

In November 2003, during a committee conference meeting between both branches of Congress, Republicans and Democrats agreed to keep the broadcast audience limit at 35 percent. As is often the case though, last minute, off-the-record deals happen in Washington that can undermine the democratic process. When the official conference ended, Republican members secretly agreed to the White House position and supported a cap of 39 percent. The White House position, heavily lobbied by Viacom and Rupert Murdoch's News Corporation, allowed both companies to retain all media holdings that exceeded the 35 percent limit before the proposed rules changes in June 2003 (Moyers, January 30, 2004).

Senator Byron Dorgan (D–ND), who had attended the conference, was appalled by a change that occurred without the involvement of all the participants. In an interview with PBS's Bill Moyers, he said that he was never informed of the change and heard about it while listening to his car radio: "That which had been decided by Congress was later negotiated by a few members of Congress and the White House." The $1 trillion Omnibus Appropriations Act completed its path through Congress at the end of January with the 39 percent compromise in place (Moyers, January 30, 2004).

There are currently several bills in both houses scrutinizing more extensive consolidation of American media. These include the Media Ownership Reform Act of 2004, introduced in the House at the end of March. Included in the text of this bill is a return to pre-June 2003 regulations. Among the stated purposes are: "to inform the public of the scope of media rules and regulations that have been weakened and lost over the past two decades; to restore fairness in broadcasting; to reduce media concentration; to ensure that broadcasters meet their public interest requirements; and to promote diversity, localism, and competition in American media" (<www.the orator.com>).

TAKING IT TO THE STREETS

In the wake of the incredible public denunciation, congressional disapproval, and the initial rulings of the Philadelphia Court, reforming the current mass media situation has become and important national issue. With the 3rd Circuit's stay of the FCC's new rules, Michael Powell has finally succumbed to public pressure. In August 2003, he announced six hearings on localism in the media throughout the country. The hearings, which include commissioners, industry members, and public interest advocates, will gauge public opinion before any final decisions are made. Meetings were scheduled in 2003–2004 for Charlotte, North Carolina; San Antonio, Texas; Rapid City, South Dakota; Monterrey, California; Portland, Maine; and Washington, DC. Described by the FCC's Web site, the "Localism Task Force will play a critical role in gathering empirical data and grassroots information on broadcast localism and advising the commission on concrete steps it can take to promote localism in radio and television broadcasting" (<www.fcc.gov>).

POWELL FAILS TO SHOW

Although he was in the Rapid City, South Dakota, area at the time, Powell did not attend the meeting that he initiated. At the hearing, people expressed outrage at his absence. Rapid City area resident John Courage said, "It appears that what the commission is trying to do is put absolute power over media into the hands of very few" (Moyers, January 30, 2004).

Josh Silver at the nonpartisan media policy organization Free Press stated: "It is an outrage that the chairman of the FCC can find the time to meet with big media lobbyists and insiders, but won't even meet with the public at an event that he himself called for" (<www.freepress.net>). Since the biennial review was announced over two years ago, FCC officials held 71 "closed-door, off-the-record meetings with corporate media CEOs and their lobbyists, but only five such meetings with public interest groups" (McChesney 2004, 282).

In South Dakota, Native American groups voiced opinions on lack of accurate representation in the media. They were however upset, as were others, with the two-minute limits on public comments (*Aberdeen News*, May 26, 2004).

Also at the hearing was former U.S. Senator Larry Pressler from South Dakota (R–SD). Pressler was co-author of the 1996 Telecommunications Act. He said that the degree of consolidation was unforeseen. "We had anticipated that the antitrust laws and the Federal Trade Commission would be more active in those areas." He went on to say "I think we have to try to do everything we can to preserve that local reporter and local newscast. We have some property out in the Black Hills, and I always try to find a local radio news show, and it seems though they're harder and harder to find" (Associated Press, May 24, 2004).

CONCLUSION: MEDIA REFORM ISN'T JUST FOR LEFTIES

Perhaps the most striking aspect of this entire debacle is the widespread bipartisan support. At the CATO debate, Schwartzman recognized the wide range of groups speaking and acting out against media consolidation. He stated that the "ability of American citizens to participate in the democratic process is dramatically affected by the structure of media ownership in this country. That's the commonality, that's the shared interest" (CATO Institute, May 25, 2004).

Independent representative Bernie Sanders from Vermont (I–VT) held five town meetings in his state before the June 2 vote and was impressed with the broad range of support. Speaking with Moyers, Sanders stated, "The people are concerned. Not just progressives like myself, but conservatives, they have the same objections.... Let there be a vote, Mr. Speaker, and he has refused" (Moyers, January 30, 2004).

Former Senate majority leader Trent Lott (R–MI) has also supported the opposition. It is a rare issue that can bring the National Organization of Women (NOW) to the same opinion as Mr. Lott. Speaking to Senator Dorgan (D–ND), Moyers stated, "It was an anomaly to look upon the screen and see you and Trent Lott standing there side by side on the same side of an issue" (Moyers, January 30, 2004). Senator McCain (R–AZ) has called media reform "a classic populist issue."

SOURCES

McChesney, Robert W. *The Problem of the Media: U.S. Communication Politics in the 21st Century*. New York: Monthly Review Press, 2004.

McChesney, Robert W. *Rich Media, Poor Democracy: Communication Politics in Dubious Times*. New York: The New Press, 1999.

Bilotta-Dailey, Dharma, Pete Tridish, Alex Dodson, Anthony Mazza, Moira O' Con-
nell, Saadia Toor. "Prometheus Radio Project Comments on Media Ownership
Proceeding Before the Federal Communications Commission," <www.prometheus
radio.org/prometheus_comments_1.shtml>.

*Prometheus Radio Project, petitioner v. Federal Communications Commission; United
States of America, respondent.* No. 03-3388. U.S. Court of Appeals for the 3rd Circuit. September 3, 2003.

Consumers Union. "Consumer Advocates Anticipate Court Will Overturn FCC
Rules," February 11, 2004, <www.freepress.net/news/article.php?id=2525>.

Schwartzman, Andrew, and Adam Thierer. "The FCC's Media Ownership Decision
One Year Later." The CATO Institute, May 25, 2004.

McConnell, Bill. "Tauzin Says Rereg Is DOA." *Broadcasting and Cable*, June 23, 2003.

NOW with Bill Moyers, PBS, January 30, 2004.

108th Congress, 2nd Session, H.R. 4069. "Media Ownership Reform Act of 2004,"
March 30, 2004, </www.orator.com/bills108/hr4069.html>.

"FCC Chairman Powell Launches 'Localism in Broadcasting' Initiative," August 20,
2003, <www.fcc.gov/localism/documents.html>.

Lammers, Dirk. "FCC Opens Airwaves at Hearing," *Aberdeen News*, May 26, 2004.

Lammers, Dirk. "FCC Members to Hear About Local Radio at Rapid City Hearing,"
Associated Press, May 24, 2004.

The People Begin to Win—
The Latest Update

The grassroots media reform movement defeated big business and their efforts
to drown out our nation's diversity of voices in the name of profit. The 3rd
Circuit Federal Court of Appeals in Philadelphia ruled 2–1 in favor of the
Prometheus Radio Project in their case against the Federal Communications
Commission (*The New York Times*, June 25, 2004). The FCC now has to either
rework their ownership regulations or appeal to the Supreme Court. "The public, Congress, and the courts now speak in one voice against the agency's
efforts to loosen public interest media ownership limits," said Free Press
Managing Director Josh Silver (<www.freepress.net>).

The court struck down crossownership of print and broadcast media and
increased ownership concentration among local stations and broadcast affiliates all within a single market. In the largest metropolitan areas of the country,
those rules would have made it possible for a single company to own three TV
stations, eight radio stations and the major newspaper (<www.freepress.net>).

The reasoning behind the new rules was rejected. The diversity index that the FCC said proved the existence of a plethora of media voices was discredited for equating highly localized broadcast outlets with major network stations. Under the FCC's diversity index, New York's Dutchess County Community College TV station was given the same market share as the ABC Station (*The New York Times*, June 25, 2004). The burden of proof for deregulation was also placed back onto the need to dispose of the rules as opposed to proving why they should be kept (<www.freepress.net>).

The decision, however, is not an end, but only a small portion of the means towards one. Current assets of major media companies will not have to be divested (*The New York Times*, June 25, 2004). The cheaply negotiated 39 percent compromise is still in place and the need for review of current ownership regulations was affirmed. It must also be remembered that rules in place before June 2, 2003, were not much better and much work is yet to be done. Said Copps, "The commission has a second chance to do the right thing (<www.prometheusradio.org>)."

APPENDIX

Censored 2005 Resource Guide

SOURCES OF THE TOP 25 CENSORED STORIES

For the complete *Project Censored Guide* (with over 1,000 media sources) go to: <www.projectcensored.org>.

THE AMERICAN PROSPECT
200 L Street NW, Suite 717
Washington, DC 20036
Tel: (888) MUST-READ
or (617) 547-2950
Fax: (617) 547-3896
E-mail: <letters@prospect.org>
Web site: <www.prospect.org>

Founded in 1990 as an authoritative magazine of liberal ideas, committed to a just society, an enriched democracy, and effective liberal politics..

ASHEVILLE GLOBAL REPORT(AGR)
P.O. Box 1504
Asheville, NC 28802
Tel: (828) 236-3103
E-mail: <editors@agrnews.org>
Web site: <www.agrnews.org>

AGR covers news underreported by mainstream media, believing that a free exchange of information is necessary to organize for social change.

AWAKENED WOMAN
E-mail:
<editor@awakenedwoman.com>
Web site:
<www.awakenedwoman.com>

News and inspiration for women who want to change the world!

THE BALTIMORE SUN
501 N. Calvert Street
Baltimore, Maryland 21278
Tel: (410) 332-6000 or (800) 829-8000
E-mail: <publiceditor@baltsun.com>
Web site: <www.baltimoresun.com>

Maryland's leading news and information site.

BUZZFLASH
P.O. Box 618354
Chicago, IL 60661
E-mail: <buzzflash@buzzflash.com>
Web site: <www.buzzflash.com>
BuzzFlash provides headlines, news, and

commentary for a geographically diverse, politically savvy, pro-democracy, antihypocrisy Web audience, reaching 3.5 million visitors a month and growing.

CENSORSHIP NEWS
Newsletter of National Coalition Against Censorship (NCAC)
275 Seventh Avenue
New York, NY 10001
Tel: (212) 807-6222
Fax: (212) 807-6245
E-mail: <ncac@ncac.org>
Web site: <www.ncac.org>

The NCAC, founded in 1974, is an alliance of 50 national non-profit organizations, including literary, artistic, religious, educational, professional, labor, and civil-liberties groups. United by a conviction that freedom of thought, inquiry, and expression must be defended, we work to educate our own members and the public at large about the dangers of censorship and how to oppose them.

CENTER FOR INVESTIGATIVE REPORTING (CIR)
131 Steuart Street, Suite 600
San Francisco, CA 94105-1238
Tel: (415) 543.1200
Fax: (415) 543.8311
E-mail: <center@cironline.org>
Web site: <www.muckraker.org>

The Center for Investigative Reporting (CIR) is an independent news organization that strengthens democracy by exposing injustice and abuse of power. To achieve this, CIR investigates critical, underreported issues; produces compelling, in-depth stories for print, broadcast, and Internet news outlets;

and provides its reporting to citizens and decisionmakers so they can take informed action

CHICAGO MEDIA WATCH
P.O. Box 6496
Evanston, IL 60204
Tel: (773) 604-1910
E-mail: <cmw@mediawatch.org>
Web site: <www.mediawatch.org>

Aims to ensure that the region's media remains open, honest, and responsive to the people's needs.

CHRISTIAN SCIENCE MONITOR
1 Norway Street
Boston, MA 02115-3195
Tel: (617) 450-2000
E-mail: <orders@csmonitor.com>
Web site: <www.csmonitor.com>

An 87-year-old daily newspaper covering national and international news.

COMMON DREAMS
P.O. Box 443
Portland, ME 04112-0443
Tel: (207) 775-0488
Fax: (207) 775-0489
E-mail: <editor@commondreams.org>
Web site: <www.commondreams.org>

A national non-profit, grassroots organization whose mission is to organize an open, honest, and nonpartisan national discussion of current events.

COVERTACTION QUARTERLY
E-mail: <covertactionorg@aol.com>
Web site: <www.covertaction.org>

Believes that the overwhelmingly dominant corporate media have become merely the voice of an increasingly unilateral and controlled empire, devoted to the indoctrination of the public in the interests of corporate, industrial, military, and ruling powers. The Institute for Media Analysis, Inc., was established in 1986 with the primary purpose of providing to the public educational materials relating to the workings of government and of the media, and in particular the relations between the two.

DEMOCRACY NOW!
P.O. Box 693
New York, NY 10013
Tel: (212) 431-9090
Fax: (212) 431-8858
E-mail: <mail@democracynow.org>
Web site: <www.democracynow.org>

Democracy Now! is a national, daily, independent, award-winning news program airing on over 225 stations in North America. Pioneering the largest public media collaboration in the U.S., *Democracy Now!* is broadcast on Pacifica, community, and National Public Radio stations, public-access cable television stations, satellite television (on Free Speech TV, Channel 9415 of the DISH Network), shortwave radio, and the Internet.

DISSIDENT VOICE
E-mail: <editor@dissidentvoice.org>
Web site: <www.dissidentvoice.org>

Dissident Voice is an Internet newsletter dedicated to challenging the distortions and lies of the corporate press and the privileged classes it serves. The goal of *Dissident Voice* is to provide hard-hitting, thought-provoking, and even entertaining news and commentaries on politics and culture that can serve as ammunition in struggles for peace and social justice.

DOLLARS AND SENSE
740 Cambridge Street
Cambridge, MA 02141
E-mail: <dollars@dollarsandsense.org>
Web site: <www.dollarsandsense.org>

Dollars and Sense continues to meet the need for "left perspectives on current economic affairs," as our masthead proclaims. We print articles by journalists, activists, and scholars on a broad range of topics with an economic theme: the economy, housing, labor, government regulation, unemployment, the environment, urban conflict, and activism.

EARTH FIRST! JOURNAL
P.O. Box 3023
Tucson, AZ 85702-6900
Tel: (520) 620-6900
Fax: (413) 254-0057
E-mail: <collective@earthfirstjournal.org>
Web site: <www.earthfirstjournal.org>

Earth First! Journal reports on radical environmental movements. The journal publishes hard-to-find information about strategies to stop the destruction of the planet.

EAT THE STATE!
P.O. Box 85541
Seattle, WA 98145
Tel: (206) 903-9461
E-mail: <ets@scn.org>
Web site: <www.eatthestate.org>

EAT THE STATE! is a shamelessly biased political journal. We want an end to poverty, exploitation, imperialism, militarism, racism, sexism, heterosexism, environmental destruction, television, and large ugly buildings, and we want it fucking now. We are not affiliated with any political group or party.

GLOBAL INFORMATION NETWORK
146 West 29th Street, #7E
New York, NY 10001
Tel: (212) 244-3123
Fax: (212) 244-3522
E-mail: <webmaster@globalinfo.org>
Web site: <www.globalinfo.org>

Global Information Network, a not-for-profit news and world media operation, is the largest distributor of developing world news services, including the award-winning Inter Press Service, in the U.S.

GLOBAL OUTLOOK
Magazine of Centre for Research on Globalization
R.R. #2
Shanty Ray, ON L0L-2L0 Canada
Tel: (888) 713-8500
Fax: (888) 713-8883
E-mail: <editor@globaloutlook.ca>
Web site: <www.globaloutlook.ca>

Global Outlook, based in Montreal, publishes news articles, commentary, background research, and analysis on a broad range of issues, focussing on the interrelationship between social, economic, strategic, geopolitical, and environmental processes.

THE GUARDIAN (LONDON)
3-7 Ray Street
London EC IR 3DR U.K.
E-mail: <editor@guardianlimited.co.uk>
Web site: <www.guardian.co.uk>

HIGH COUNTRY NEWS.ORG
119 Grand Avenue
P.O. Box 1090
Paonia, CO 81428
Tel: (970) 527-4898
E-mail: <editor@hcn.org>
Web site: <www.hcn.org>

The High Country Foundation is a non-profit media organization whose mission is to inform and inspire people to act on behalf of the West's land, air, water, and inhabitants.

IN THESE TIMES
2040 North Milwaukee Avenue
Chicago, IL 60647
Tel: (773) 772-0100
Fax: (773) 772-4180
Web site: <www.inthesetimes.com>

In These Times is a national, biweekly magazine of news and opinion published in Chicago. For 27 years, *In These Times* has provided groundbreaking coverage of the labor movement, environment, feminism, grassroots politics, minority communities and the media. *In These Times* features award-winning investigative reporting about corporate malfeasance and government wrongdoing, insightful analysis of national and international affairs, and sharp cultural criticism about events and ideas that matter.

THE INDEPENDENT (LONDON)
Independent House

191 Marsh Wall
London E14 9RS U.K.
Tel: (020) 7005 2000
E-mail:
<customerservices@independent.co.uk>
Web site: <www.independent.co.uk>

An independent, daily London
newspaper.

INFORMATION CLEARING HOUSE
P.O. Box 365
Imperial Beach, CA 91933
E-mail:
<Tom@informationclearinghouse.info>
Web site:
<www.informationclearinghouse.info>

This Web site is a noncommercial,
independent media source of
unreported (or underreported) news
from around the globe.

INTERNATIONAL SOCIALIST
REVIEW (ISR)
P.O. Box 258082
Chicago, IL 60625
Tel: (773) 583-7884
Fax: (773) 583-6144
E-mail: <info@isreview.org>
Web site: <www.isreview.org>

The *ISR* is published bimonthly by the
Center for Economic Research and
Social Change.

INTER PRESS SERVICE (IPS)
Via Panisperna, 207
00184 Rome, Italy
Tel: +3906 485692
Fax: +3906 4817877

E-mail: <online@ips.org>
Web site: <www.ips.org>

Inter Press Service, the world's leading
provider of information on global issues,
is backed by a network of journalists in
more than 100 countries, with satellite
communication links to 1,200 outlets.
IPS focuses its news coverage on the
events and global processes affecting
the economic, social, and political
development of peoples and nations.

FLASHPOINTS WITH
DENNIS BERNSTEIN
KPFA Radio
1929 M. L. King Jr. Way
Berkeley, CA 94704
Tel: (510) 848-6767
Fax: (510) 848-3812
E-mail: <editorial@flashpoints.net>
Web site: <www.flashpoints.net>

Hard-hitting investigative reports on
the issues of our times.

LEFT TURN MAGAZINE
P.O. Box 445
New York, NY 10159-0445
E-mail: <leftturn@leftturn.org>
Web site: <www.leftturn.org>

Bi-monthly publication of the Left Turn
activist network features political
analysis, debates and interviews with
activists in the international movement
against capitalist globalization and war

THE MOSCOW TIMES
Ulitsa Vyborgskaya 16, Bldg. 4
125212 Moscow
Russia
Tel: (7-095) 937-3399
Fax: (7-095) 937-3393
E-mail: <moscowtimes@imedia.ru>
Web site: <ww.moscowtimes.ru>

The Moscow Times is an objective,

reliable source for English-language news on business, politics, and culture. It remains an unrivaled advertising medium for reaching local business people and decision makers.

MULTINATIONAL MONITOR
P.O. Box 19405
Washington, DC 20036
Tel: (202) 387-8030
Fax: (202) 234-5176
E-mail: <monitor@essential.org>
Web site: <www.multinationalmonitor.org>

Tracks corporate activity, especially in the Third World.

THE NATION
33 Irving Place
New York, NY 10003
Tel: (212) 209-5400
Fax: (212) 982-9000
E-mail: <info@thenation.com>
Web site: <www.thenation.com>

The Nation will not be the organ of any party, sect, or body. It will, on the contrary, make an earnest effort to bring to the discussion of political and social questions a really critical spirit, and to wage war upon the vices of violence, exaggeration, and misrepresentation by which so much of the political writing of the day is marred.

NEW INTERNATIONALIST
P.O. Box 1062
Niagara Falls, NY 14304
Tel: (906) 946-0407
Fax: (906) 946-0410
E-mail: <magazines@indas.on.ca>
Web site: <www.newint.org>

An international journal that exists to report on the issues of inequality and world poverty; to focus attention on the unjust relationship between the powerful and the powerless in both rich and poor countries; and to debate the campaign for the radical changes necessary.

NEW SCIENTIST
151 Wardour Street
London W1F 8WE U.K.
Tel: +44 (0)20 8652 3500
Fax: +44 (0)20 7331 2777
E-mail: <letters@newscientist.com>
Web site: <www.newscientist.com>

An English journal devoted to science and technology and their impact on the way we live.

THE NEW YORK DAILY NEWS
450 West 33 Street
New York, NY 10001
Tel: (212) 210-2100
E-mail: <news@edit.nydailynews.com>
Web site: <www.nydailynews.com>

A New York City daily newspaper.

NEWS FROM NIRS
1424 16th Street, NW, Suite 404
Washington, DC 20036
Tel: (202) 328-0002
Fax: (202) 462-2183
E-mail: <nirsnet@nirs.org>
Web site: <www.nirs.org>

NIRS/WISE is the information and networking center for citizens and environmental organizations concerned about nuclear power, radioactive waste, radiation, and sustainable energy issues.

NORTH BAY PROGRESSIVE
P.O. Box 14384
Santa Rosa, CA 95402
Tel: (707) 525-1422

Fax: (707) 578-5974
E-mail:
<commentary@northbayprogressive.org.>
Web site:
<www.northbayprogressive.org>

An independent weekly newspaper for the Northern Bay Area in California.

ONEWORLD.NET
River House
143-145 Farringdon Road, Second Floor
London EC 1R 3AB
United Kingdom
Tel: (020) 7239 1400
Fax: (020) 7833 3347
E-mail: <foundation@oneworld.net>
Web site: <www.oneworld.net>

OneWorld is the world's favorite and fastest-growing civil society network online, supporting people's media to help build a more just global society.

ORGANIC CONSUMERS
ASSOCIATION
6101 Cliff Estate Road
Little Marais, MN 55614
Tel: (218) 226-4164
Fax: (218) 353-7652
E-mail:
<campaigns@organicconsumers.org>
Web site:
<www.organicconsumers.org>

Organic Consumers Association is a grassroots non-profit organization concerned with food safety, organic farming, sustainable agricultural, fair trade, and genetic engineering (biotechnology and transgenic).

PEACE MAGAZINE
P.O. Box 248, Station P
Toronto, ON M5S 2S7

Canada
Tel: (416) 588-8748
E-mail: <office@peacemagazine.org>
Web site: <www.peacemagazine.org>

Journalists, educators, and activists keep up to date on the important work of peacemaking by reading this popular and respected magazine. Four times a year we publish articles, news stories, book and film reviews, letters, and a peace crossword. We discuss disarmament; conflict resolution; nonviolent sanctions; peace institutions (e.g., the United Nations and the World Court); conflicts and crises around the world; profiles of activists and researchers; and controversies about development, population, and environmental protection.

THE PHILADELPHIA
INQUIRER
P.O. Box 8263
Philadelphia, PA 19101
Phone: 215-854-2000
E-mail: <info@phillynews.com>
Web site: <www.philly.com>

Founded June 1, 1829, *The Philadelphia Inquirer* is America's third-oldest surviving daily newspaper.

THE PROGRESSIVE
409 East Main Street
Madison, WI 53703
Tel: (608) 257-4626
Fax: (608) 257-3373
E-mail: <editorial@progressive.org>
Web site: <www.progressive.org>

The mission of *The Progressive* is to be a journalistic voice for peace and social justice at home and abroad. We champion peace, social and economic justice, civil rights, civil liberties, human rights, a preserved environment, and a reinvigorated democracy.

THE PUBLIC EYE
Newsletter of: The Political Research Associates
1310 Broadway, Suite #201
Somerville, MA 02144
Tel: (617) 666-5300
Fax: (617) 666-6622
E-mail: <pra@igc.org>
Web site: <www.publiceye.org>

Political Research Associates is an independent, nonprofit research center that studies antidemocratic, authoritarian, and other oppressive movements, institutions, and trends. PRA is based on progressive values, and is committed to advancing an open, democratic, and pluralistic society. *The Public Eye* is a quarterly newsletter featuring an in-depth analysis and critique of issues pertaining to the U.S. political right wing.

SALON
22 4th Street, 16th Floor
San Francisco, CA 94103
Tel: (415) 645-9200
Fax: (415) 645-9204
Web site: <www.salon.com>

<Salon.com> is an Internet media company that produces 10 original content sites as well as two online communities—Table Talk and The WELL.

SCOOP.CO.NZ
Scoop Media Ltd.
P.O. Box 11 501
Wellington

New Zealand
E-mail: editor@scoop.co.nz
Web site: www.scoop.co.nz

Scoop is a "fiercely independent" press-release-driven Internet news agency accredited to the New Zealand Parliament Press Gallery and also fed by a multitude of business, non-government-organization, regional government, and public relations communication professionals.

SUNDAY HERALD (SCOTLAND)
200 Renfield Street
Glasgow G2 3QB
Scotland
Tel: (0141) 302 7800
Fax: (0141) 302 7815
E-mail: <editor@sundayherald.com>
Web site: <www.sundayherald.com>

THE TEXAS OBSERVER
307 West 7th Street
Austin, Texas 78701
Tel: (800) 939-6620 or (512) 477-0746
E-mail: <editors@texasobserver.org>
Web site: <www.texasobserver.org>

The Texas Observer writes about issues ignored or underreported in the mainstream press, in pursuit of a vision of Texas in which education, justice, and material progress are available to all. Our goal is to cover stories crucial to the public interest and to provoke dialogue that promotes democratic participation and open government.

URANIUM MEDICAL
RESEARCH CENTER
476 Parliament Street, Suite 302
Toronto, ON M4X 1P2
Canada
Tel: (416) 465-1341
Fax: (416) 465-5961
E-mail: <info@umrc.net>
Web site: <www.umrc.net>

VOICES FROM THE EARTH
Newsletter of Southwest Research
and Information Center (SRIC)
105 Stanford SE
P.O. Box 4524
Albuquerque, NM 87106
Tel: (505) 262-1862
Fax: (505) 262-1864
E-mail: <info@sric.org>
Web site: <www.sric.org>

Southwest Research and Information
Center (SRIC) exists to provide timely,
accurate information to the public on
matters that affect the environment,
human health, and communities in
order to protect natural resources,
promote citizen participation, and
ensure environmental and social
justice now and for future generations.

WAR TIMES
EBC/*War Times*
1230 Market Street, PMB 409
San Francisco, CA 94102
Tel: (510) 869-5156
E-mail: <info@war-times.org>
Web site: <www.war-times.org>

War Times is a free, mass produced,
biweekly, and nationally distributed
tabloid-sized newspaper.

WORLD PRESS REVIEW
Web site: <www.worldpress.org>

<Worldpress.org> was founded in 1997
and we are committed to offering our
readers a first-hand look at the issues
and debates that occupy the world's
newspapers and magazines. As the
space devoted to thoughtful, incisive
reporting of foreign news shrinks in the
U.S. media, many subjects and
perspectives of vital international
importance are increasingly obscured
or invisible to Americans.

WORLD SOCIALIST
E-mail: <editor@wsws.org>
Web site: <www.wsws.org>

The *World Socialist* Web Site
(WSWS) is the Internet center of the
International Committee of the Fourth
International (ICFI). It provides analysis
of major world events; comments on
political, cultural, historical, and
philosophical issues; and valuable
documents and studies from the heritage
of the socialist movement. The *WSWS*
aims to meet the need, felt widely today,
for an intelligent appraisal of the
problems of contemporary society. It
addresses itself to the masses of people
who are dissatisfied with the present
state of social life, as well as its cynical
and reactionary treatment by the
establishment media.

YALE DAILY NEWS
202 York Street
New Haven, CT 06511
Tel: (202) 432-2418
Fax: (202) 432-7425
E-mail:
<onlinepub@yaledailynews.com>
Web site: <www.yaledailynews.com>

Z MAGAZINE
18 Millfield Street
Woods Hole, MA 02543
Phone: (508) 548-9063
Fax: (508) 457-0626
E-mail: <zmag@zmag.org.>
Web site: <www.zmag.org>

Z is an independent monthly magazine
dedicated to resisting injustice,
defending against repression, and
creating liberty. It sees the racial,
gender, class, and political dimensions
of personal life as fundamental to
understanding and improving
contemporary circumstances, and it
aims to assist activist efforts for a
better future.

Index

Labor Notes, 118
Lancet, 103
land mines, 150
Latin America, 109-110, 217
Latinos, 111-112, 114, 308-309
Lay, Kenneth, 39, 64, 79-82
Le Figaro, 131, 227
Le Monde, 131
lead, 46, 52, 129
  lead industry, 46
Leavitt, Mike, 56, 159
Lebanon, 50, 289-290, 292, 299
Lee, Martin, 24
Left Turn, 91, 98, 108, 121-123, 149,
  151, 165, 357
leukemia, 147
Libby, I. Lewis, 133
liberals, 78, 303, 309
librarians; libraries, 9-13, 15-16, 140
Library Awareness Program, 11
Life (magazine), 51, 182
Limbaugh, Rush, 75, 180, 200, 302,
  304, 306-307
Lockheed Martin, 59-60, 138
Lopez, Jennifer, 172
Los Alamos, 118, 144
Los Angeles Times, 113, 148, 152, 160,
  203, 251
Lott, Trent, 133, 350
"Lula" da Silva, Luiz Inacio, 108-109
Lutz, William, 24
Lynch, Jessica, 173-174
Macedonia, 129
mad cow disease, 239-240
Madonna, 170-172
mainstream media, 38, 41, 44, 53, 57,
  69, 76, 81, 86, 90, 95, 97, 100, 104,
  107, 110, 112-113, 132, 148, 157,
  169, 172-173, 195, 200, 202-204,
  217-218, 274, 293-294, 353, 360
Malawi, 269
Malaysia, 163
Mali, 151, 331
malnutrition, 325
Malveaux, Julianne, 24
Marcos, Subcomandante, 325
Marines, 216, 274-279

Marx, Karl, 340-341
mass media, 24, 200-202, 219, 346,
  349
Mauritius, 151
Mays, Lowry, 161, 179
McCain, John, 288, 347
McCarthy era, 11
McChesney, Robert W., 24, 230, 312,
  336, 341-342, 347, 350
McDonald's, 115, 237-238, 250
MCI, 92
McKinley, William, 54
McKinney, Cynthia, 25
McNamara, Robert, 27, 195, 288
Media Access Project, 345, 347
media activism, 200, 208, 211, 340
Media Alliance, 16, 199, 205-207, 295
media criticism, 200
Media Ownership Reform Act of 2004,
  348, 351
media reform, 17, 178, 200, 228, 335-
  338, 340-342, 350-351
media watchdog groups, 107
MediaChannel, 15, 33, 199, 210-212,
  224
MediaFile, 160-161, 205-207
Medicare, 124, 245
Meese, Edwin, 61
mergers, 98-99, 219, 318, 339
Mexicans, 308
Mexico, 44-45, 71, 99, 109, 115-116,
  118, 120-121, 123, 144, 206, 269,
  323, 331, 339
Microsoft, 192, 242
Middle East, 91, 94, 112-113, 121,
  132-133, 147, 151, 162, 164, 174,
  214, 218, 251, 294, 296-297, 299-
  300
Miller, Laura, 7, 16, 20, 233, 245
Miller, Mark Crispin, 7, 20, 25, 177, 180
Milosevic, Slobodan, 131-132
minimum wage, 77, 79, 273, 326
miners; mining, 54-55, 71, 121, 159
miscarriage, 158
Missile Defense Agency, 145
missiles, 49, 120, 127, 142, 275
Mobil. *See also* Exxon Mobil.

About the Editor

Peter Phillips is a professor/department chair of sociology at Sonoma State University and Director of Project Censored. He teaches classes in media censorship, sociology of power, political sociology, and sociology of media. He has published eight editions of *Censored: Media Democracy in Action* from Seven Stories Press. Also from Seven Stories Press is the *Project Censored Guide to Independent Media and Activism 2003*.

Phillips writes op-ed pieces for independent media nationwide having published in dozens of publications newspapers and Web sites including *Z Magazine*, *CounterPunch*, *Common Dreams*, *Social Policy*, and *Briarpatch*. He frequently speaks on media censorship and various sociopolitical issues on radio and TV talks shows including *Talk of the Nation*, *Air America*, *Public Interest*, *Talk America*, *World Radio Network*, *Democracy Now!*, and the *Jim Hightower Show*.

Phillips is the national and international news editor of the *North Bay Progressive* newspaper in Santa Rosa, California. The *North Bay Progressive* is a monthly regional publication serving a five-county area north of San Francisco.

Phillips earned a B.A. degree in social science in 1970 from Santa Clara University and an M.A. degree in social science from California State University at Sacramento in 1974. He earned a second M.A. in sociology in 1991 and a Ph.D. in sociology in 1994. His doctoral dissertation was entitled *A Relative Advantage: Sociology of the San Francisco Bohemian Club*, <lib-web.sonoma.edu/regional/faculty/Phillips/bohemianindex.htm> .

Phillips is a fifth-generation Californian, who grew up on a family-owned farm west of the Central Valley town of Lodi. Phillips lives today in rural Sonoma County with his wife Mary Lia-Phillips.

How to Support Project Censored

NOMINATE A STORY

To nominate a *Censored* story, send us a copy of the article, and include the name of the source publication, the date that the article appeared, and the page number(s). For Internet published news stories of which we should be aware, please forward the URL to <censored@sonoma.edu>. The final deadline period for nominating a most *Censored* story of the year is March of each year.

CRITERIA FOR PROJECT CENSORED NEWS STORIES NOMINATIONS

1. A censored news story is one which contains information that the general United States population has a right and need to know, but to which it has had limited access.
2. The news story is timely, ongoing, and has implications for a significant number of residents in the United States.
3. The story has clearly defined concepts and is backed up with solid, verifiable documentation.
4. The news story has been publicly published, either electronically or in print, in a circulated newspaper, journal, magazine, newsletter, or similar publication from either a foreign or domestic source.
5. The news story has direct connections to and implications for people in the United States, which can include activities that U.S. citizens are engaged in abroad.

SUPPORT PROJECT CENSORED BY MAKING A FINANCIAL GIFT

Project Censored is a self-supported 5019(c)3 non-profit organization. We depend on tax-deductible donations and foundation grants to continue our work. To support our efforts for freedom of information send checks to the address below or call (707) 664-2500. Visa and MasterCard accepted. Review our Web site at <www.projectcensored.org>.

Project Censored
Sonoma State University
1801 East Cotati Avenue
Rohnert Park, CA 94928
E-mail: <censored@sonoma.edu>